Managing Online Risk

Managing Online Risk
Apps, Mobile, and Social Media Security

Deborah Gonzalez
Law2sm, LLC

AMSTERDAM • BOSTON • HEIDELBERG • LONDON
NEW YORK • OXFORD • PARIS • SAN DIEGO • SAN FRANCISCO
SINGAPORE • SYDNEY • TOKYO
Butterworth-Heinemann is an imprint of Elsevier

Acquiring Editor: Brian Romer
Editorial Project Manager: Keira Bunn
Project Manager: Poulouse Joseph
Designer: Alan Studholme

Butterworth-Heinemann is an imprint of Elsevier
The Boulevard, Langford Lane, Kidlington, Oxford, OX5 1GB, UK
225 Wyman Street, Waltham, MA 02451, USA

Library of Congress Cataloging-in-Publication Data
Gonzalez, Deborah.
  Managing online risk : apps, mobile, and social media security / Deborah Gonzalez.
    pages cm
  ISBN 978-0-12-420055-5 (paperback)
  1. Computer networks–Security measures. 2. Internet–Security measures. I. Title.
  TK5105.59.G67 2015
  005.8–dc23
                              2014031130

British Library Cataloguing in Publication Data
A catalogue record for this book is available from the British Library

ISBN: 978-0-12-420055-5

For information on all Butterworth-Heinemann publications
visit our web site at http://store.elsevier.com

This book has been manufactured using Print on Demand technology. Each copy is produced to order and is
limited to black ink. The online version of this book will show color figures where appropriate.

Contents

About the Author...vii

Online Resources ix

Introduction..xi

CHAPTER 1   **Risk Management Digital Style** 1

CHAPTER 2   **Internal and External Risks** 25

CHAPTER 3   **Reputation and Identity** 53

CHAPTER 4   **The New Workforce** 79

CHAPTER 5   **Big Data**.. 101

CHAPTER 6   **Approaches to Content**... 127

CHAPTER 7   **Compliance**.. 153

CHAPTER 8   **Currency and Campaigns** 185

CHAPTER 9   **Digital Succession**... 213

CHAPTER 10 **The Future of Online Security** 237

Index 259

About the Author

Deborah Gonzalez, Esq. is the founder of Law2sm, LLC, a legal consulting firm focusing on helping its clients navigate the security and legal issues relating to the new digital and social media world. Deborah is the co-developer of the Socially Legal Audit® tool that assists a company to ensure that their online activity is in line with state laws, federal laws, and regulatory compliance.

Deborah graduated from New York Law School and is licensed to practice law in New York and Georgia.

Deborah began her career in the corporate arena working in various positions in the information technology area—from network administrator to manager of the IS department for a top-6 CPA firm in New York City. During her tenure she managed day-to-day IT operations; designed and implemented IT-related training for employees, managers, and IT staff; developed policies and protocols for IT-corporate use; and monitored emerging trends for IT business strategies and management including IT security concerns. Deborah used this foundation as a starting point with her legal practice, which is now transporting her beyond the Internet to the social space where the physical and digital dimensions of her clients co-exist and where she can leverage her legal expertise to their benefit.

Deborah is a sought after speaker, content contributor, and news commentator on online security issues and social media legalities. Past audiences include Fortune 500 companies, non-profit organizations, professional associations (ISSA WIS, TAG), college communities (students, faculty, and administration), legal professionals (lawyers and judges), both domestically in the US and abroad. Specific industries include: banking and financial, healthcare and medical, higher education, international trade, governments and politicians, marketing and public relations, and more.

Online Resources

Thank you for selecting Butterworth-Heinemann's *Managing Online Risk*. To complement the learning experience, the author has provided a number of online tools to accompany this edition. They can be found at http://managingonlinerisk.com. The tools available include

- Live links to chapter-specific resources and updates to case studies in the book, domestic and international.
- Downloadable handouts and checklists that you can use for your company.
- Useful infographics with additional statistics relating to online risk and security.
- Shareable risk and security funnies and humorous videos that can be used for training or just a quick break to put things in perspective.
- *The Managing Online Risk* (MORe) monthly blog with discussions on the latest risk management and security issues.
- An event calendar with upcoming risk and security conferences as well as the latest information regarding author tour dates and venues.
- A direct contact link to the author for questions and inquiries.
- Access to the Elsevier eCommerce store for purchases.
- And more.

Introduction

Engagement in online activity (including, but not limited to, social media) is quickly becoming nonnegotiable for many businesses and organizations as consumers continue to expect to be able to connect and interact with them in as many convenient ways as possible. There are many benefits to companies using digital and online technology, but there are many risks as well, the acknowledgment of which has led many an executive to question whether they should be in the space and how far they should go. News reports of companies getting into trouble because of compliance violations, loss of revenue because of reputational loss, and loss of customer trust because of confidentiality breaches bring concern to executives who are trying to balance the benefits of online activity and the potential loss of revenue due to negative public relations, litigation, and so forth.

In this new digital environment, executives need to put into place best practices and measures of security and risk management that address concerns such as data collection, storage, and security; human resource recruitment and employee communications; compliance violations of federal and state laws, as well as professional trade oversight organizations; security of technology devices (mobile, apps, cloud computing, etc.); and more.

This book strives to be a definitive resource by providing an overview of the risk mitigation strategies, solutions, and best practices to address risk, liability, and security concerns arising from corporate online and digital activity. It is a resource that executives and security professionals can turn to more frequently as issues related to risk management and security concerns arise from their corporate online and digital activity.

In addition, in a first-of-its-kind, digital integration, this book has a companion Web site (www.managingonlinerisk.com) that was developed in parallel with the book, offering the latest updates and resources for the issues we discuss. You can imagine with the speed of change in the technology and security areas some of what I wrote in the first chapters were outdated by the time I got to the final chapter. Between when this book is published and when you read it, who knows where that technology will be. So, as online and digital security and risk management continuously evolve, you will find this Web site to be an invaluable tool to ensure that skills and knowledge are kept up-to-date with the latest environmental and technology changes. This book gives the foundations and the Web site provides the nuances based on what is happening now. Use both to reap optimal benefits of the information.

Another interesting structure of this book is that it is based on content aggregation, seeking out the most recent information on the topics and integrating the best of them within the book itself. I took a "curation of content" approach to find the most up-to-date, interesting, and credible sources on the issues I discuss in the book. Again, because of the speed of change in the online technology and security area, some of these sources may end up contradicting themselves as technology and events evolve. For example, when I originally wrote about Bitcoin in Chapter 8, it was considered a currency. By the time I finished writing Chapter 10, we had a U.S. regulatory decision that Bitcoin and other virtual currencies are "property," not currency. More on that in Chapter 8. To ensure everyone receives the credit they deserve for their work, Creative Commons Licenses, the Fair Use Doctrine and traditional copyright permissions are relied on to allow the reader to have the most up-to-date analysis of the trends occurring in online and digital security and risk management.

This book presents readers with tools and resources to better understand the security and reputational risks of online and digital activity, as well as tools and resources to mitigate those risks and minimize potential loss for their companies. These tools and resources include case studies; industry and expert profiles; lessons learned; overview of relevant laws, regulations, and professional guidelines by industry; sample policies, disclaimers, and online community guidelines; and more.

This book contains 10 chapters focusing on particular areas of security and risk management concern in the digital and online environment. Since technology is all about connectivity, you will see that many of the issues discussed overlap and do not just fit in their designated chapters. However, each chapter was written to stand alone and still be comprehensive enough to offer strategic insight for that particular concern, so you as the reader can read the book sequentially or by chapter-topic interest. Except for Chapter 1, that is, which offers an overview of risk management and security concepts—a great place to start if you are new to the field or need a refresher recap—as well as Chapter 10, which focuses on what your company's future may or may not look like, and relies on previous concepts outlined throughout the book.

With Chapter 2, we begin to explore specific internal and external risks associated with digital and online activity. The internal explores corporate security perception, priority and budget setting, traditional and shadow information technology (IT), mobile and the Bring Your Own Device trend, and people, including employees, vendors, and third parties that can lead to cyber-risks such as computer security, computer viruses, computer fraud, and so forth. The external looks at issues with a lesser element of control for the corporation such as technology advances and new devices, cloud computing, hacking, regulation, and natural disasters and squirrels.

Chapter 3 focuses on different aspects of digital identity in relation to a corporation's reputation, including executive identity (specific individuals in the corporation) and brand identity (including virtual presence) of the corporation. The chapter defines these two identities and how they differ, explores why they are important in the digital space, and describes how they can be tarnished or lost because of digital activity. In addition, online activism (and hacktivism), social scoring, digital influence, and online credentials are discussed. The chapter offers various lessons learned and best practices to protect the identity and the corporate's reputation.

Chapter 4 explores the use of digital and online activity as it relates to employee–employer relationships and constructs. The chapter progresses based on the employment cycle: recruitment, hiring, employment, and termination. Specific discussions on social media policies and strategies, the mobile workforce, millennials and other worker generations, monitoring of employee online activity, employee privacy concerns, and so forth.

Chapter 5 focuses on an extremely important area related to online and digital activity—the collection, use, and storage of data—especially as relating to client or potential client information. The debate between enhanced, targeted marketing to meet customer needs and personal privacy concerns will be discussed and will include big data, the social graph, personally identifiable information, recent attempts to control this area (legislation), and best practices.

Chapter 6 looks specifically at data that are created for the digital space, the intellectual property rights and value they provide for a corporation, the risks of theft of intellectual property, the risks the content may create for the corporation (such as defamation, anticompetitive acts, etc.), and best practices to reduce those risks, as well as strategies on what to do if theft occurs.

Chapter 7 focuses on regulated industries (such as banking, health care, transportation, etc.) and the different risks associated with violation of compliance standards for online and digital activity. Discussions will focus on topics such as disclosure, disclaimers, professional trade oversight organizations and guidelines, federal and state legislation, and current best practices. For some, it may read like an alphabet soup—FDA, FTC, HIPAA, PCI DSS, OSHA, COPPA, and so forth.

Chapter 8 looks at the risks associated with financial in the digital and online space by corporations including digital payment systems, digital and cryptocurrency (Bitcoin and others), crowdfunding, online microfinancing, online investments, and so forth. The second part of this chapter focuses on one specific purpose of corporate spending through advocacy and digital campaigns (lobbying, charitable fund-raising, etc.).

Chapter 9 focuses on the emerging concerns of risks related to succession planning and management in the corporate environment. Topics such as succession planning, the IT security shortage, women in security, protection of digital assets, security of assets, continuation of digital activity and content management, digital expiration, and so forth will be discussed, as well as digital legacy, digital immortality, and digital resurrection.

Finally, Chapter 10 takes a look into the future to explore the future of information security and risk management. Four possible future scenarios are presented: growth, transformation, constraint, and collapse. Then particular future concerns regarding specific technologies will be discussed including the Internet of Things, drones, health and medical sensors, big data analysis systems for security intelligence, and privacy evolution.

Lastly, fear not: Although this book is written by an attorney, it is not written in legalese. Its perspective is from a practical standpoint—business, strategy, and management—and its purpose is to be referred to and used again and again. I acknowledge that legal aspects will always be part of security and risk management, especially within the context of compliance, but this book is a not a legal treatise. You will learn enough to understand why the risks exist and why certain solutions and best practices are proposed—and enough to know when to pass it on to the attorney. If you are an attorney reading this book, this book can serve as a starting point for some legal principles and how they apply in the overall business setting, but do not stop here.

So we begin with defining risk management and security in the context of the digital environment. Are they different because of this new context or have they just been expanded?

RISK MANAGEMENT DIGITAL STYLE

1

Which risks are relevant? Those that impact business goals.
Which risks impact business goals? They all do.

Did you hear the one about the IT security officer who "resigned" after it was discovered that a data breach at its retail operations headquarters that affected millions of customers could have been avoided if only one of over 60,000 alerts had been heeded?[1] Or the one about a security consultant who leaked information about a government surveillance program, bringing world leaders to the defense, who ended up exiled in Russia but had a great turnout at South by Southwest?[2] Or how about the one of

---

[1] Target Data Breach, 2013.
[2] Edward Snowden, NSA leak, 2013.

computer engineers who lost their life savings and their jobs in the misplacement of digital currency?[3] Or the one about the employee who left a company laptop connected to public Wi-Fi at the coffee shop that led to insider trading violations and criminal penalties?[4] Or the one…

I think you get the point. There have been a lot of "ones" in the news and even more not in the spotlight. In 2011, Verizon reported "855 incidents and 174 million compromised records."[5] To update that, the Online Trust Alliance (OTA) released their report in January 2014, which indicated that of over 500 data breaches in the first half of 2013 "31 percent of incidents were due to insider threats or mistakes; 21 percent resulted from the loss of computers, hard drives, and paper documents; 76 percent were due to weak or stolen account logins and passwords; and 29 percent of compromises resulted from social engineering."[6] What do these have in common? They all dealt with information technology in the online digital environment.

As we begin our exploration of online risk and security, it is useful to make sure we are on the same page. Defining the lexicon of the landscape allows us to define risk management and security in the context of the digital environment and determine whether they are different because of this new context or because they have they just been expanded. Therefore, we begin with standard definitions of risk management, risk, security, and threat. You may have your own favorite you use, but we will stick with these as we head out.

Risk management

The identification, analysis, assessment, control, and avoidance, minimization, or elimination of unacceptable risks.[7]

Risk

A probability or threat of damage, injury, liability, loss, or any other negative occurrence that is caused by external or internal vulnerabilities, and that may be avoided through preemptive action.[8]

Security

The prevention of and protection against assault, damage, fire, fraud, invasion of privacy, theft, unlawful entry, and other such occurrences caused by deliberate action; the extent to which a computer system is protected from data corruption, destruction, interception, loss, or unauthorized access.[9]

---

[3] Mt. Gox and their misplacement of Bitcoin, 2014.

[4] Raj Rajaratnam of the Galleon Group, 2014.

[5] Verizon, 2012 Data Breach Investigations Report, http://www.verizonenterprise.com/resources/reports/rp_data-breach-investigations-report-2012-ebk_en_xg.pdf.

[6] Pangburn, DJ, "2013 Was the Worst Year for Data Breaches," Motherboard Blog, http://motherboard.vice.com/blog/2013-was-the-worst-year-for-data-breaches, January 23, 2014.

[7] "What is Risk Management? Definition and Meaning," http://www.businessdictionary.com/definition/risk-management.html#ixzz2ZsV0ylRk (accessed 2/8/2014).

[8] "What is Risk? Definition and Meaning," http://www.businessdictionary.com/definition/risk.html#ixzz2ZsV8eFjd (accessed 2/8/2014).

[9] "What is Security? Definition and Meaning," http://www.businessdictionary.com/definition/security.html#ixzz2ZsVYEske (accessed 2/8/2014).

Threat

Indication of an approaching or imminent menace; negative event that can cause a risk to become a loss, expressed as an aggregate of risk, consequences of risk, and the likelihood of the occurrence of the event. A threat may be a natural phenomenon such as an earthquake, flood, or storm, or a man-made incident such as fire, power failure, sabotage, etc.; action or potential occurrence (whether or not malicious) to breach the security of the system by exploiting its known or unknown vulnerabilities.[10]

Most of those definitions should seem familiar to you. However, there are some key words within them that bear special consideration as we look at online security and risk management. First, risk management brings up the issue that there are acceptable and unacceptable risks—what would be an acceptable risk has long been debated by security professionals. One school of thought is that any risk is unacceptable. The other believes it is a return-on-investment (ROI) question—how much does it cost to mitigate the risk versus how much will the risk impact cost if left alone?

Second, notice that the definitions of risk and threat are symbiotic with two main differences: a threat is indicated as something that can be foreseen and is imminent; a risk is just a probability. But both indicate that they can be avoided to a certain extent—excluding natural disasters.

Third, security is presented to offer a safety net around property—whether tangible or intangible, such as online data. And last, risk management is about looking at risk and threats and setting up procedures to answer some specific questions to give a sense of security:

1. What are the real, material risks and threats?
2. What are we doing about them?
3. Is what we are doing actually working?

RISK MANAGEMENT MODELS

Companies cannot eliminate all risks for two reasons. First the internal and external threats that cause risk are very dynamic. Second, control investments eventually result in diminishing returns.[11]

There are quite a few risk management models out there. Just Google "risk management" and you will have, as I did in July 2013, over 388,000,000 results come up. But most of the models concur on a series of steps that make the process viable and effective.

STEP 1: RISK IDENTIFICATION

Identifying what risks may actually exist in a company's online infrastructure and digital activity is where it all begins. There are a number of tools to assist the internal risk management professional to complete this on their own, as well as a number of third-party companies that offer auditing and risk assessment services for a price.

---

[10] "What is Threat? Definition and Meaning," http://www.businessdictionary.com/definition/threat.html#ixzz2ZsZuuGxr (accessed 2/8/2014).
[11] Nige, The Security Guy Blog, "Security Program Best Practices," https://nigesecurityguy.wordpress.com/tag/security-life cycle-methodology/, June 14, 2013.

The gathering and compilation of this information should go beyond a report. It should be looked at as a dynamic and changing set of factors that need to be understood and dealt with in a strategic way, meaning in the best interests of the company (legally of course).

Many companies use a series of security and risk management questions to help guide their collection of the needed data. One good resource is a paperback called *The Ultimate Security Survey* by James L. Schaub and Ken D. Biery. It is in its second edition and a bit on the expensive side ranging from $625 to over $1000 on Amazon.com.[12] But it is very comprehensive.

At a minimum, an audit to gather risk information relating to online and digital activity security should include:

- The mission and demographics of the company
- Inventory of the current online footprint of the company (social media platforms, Web sites, intra and internets, blogs, etc.)
- Inventory of digital and mobile devices accessing company data (laptops, tablets, smartphones, etc.)
- Inventory of access points into and out of company data systems
- Review of current online and digital activity security and risk management strategies and plans
- Review of online/digital employee roles, responsibilities, and liabilities (social media managers, mobile directors, app developers, etc.)
- Review of current IT-related policies and procedures (including social media, IT, privacy, passwords, e-mail, etc.)
- Review of online digital disclaimers and disclosures
- Review of online digital assets (including copyrights, trademarks, trade secrets, content contracts, development contracts, etc.)
- Review of company terms of use and service agreements with third-party vendors
- Review of online and digital content/document retention policies and procedures (including cloud-related legal concerns)
- Review of data collection, data security, authentication, and access
- Review of online crisis and reputation management
- Review of federal and state laws, and industry regulations and compliances that the company is subject to regarding online and digital activity
- Review of human resources' use of online data for the employment cycle (including recruitment, interviewing, performance evaluation, and termination)
- Review of marketing's use of online and digital resources to ensure compliance with specific regulations (such as contest and promotion rules, gaming laws, truth-in-advertising requirements, etc.)
- Review of cyber-risk insurance and coverage

For an example of an audit specifically focused on social media risk and liability, see the Socially Legal Audit sidebar.

---

[12] Accessed April 1, 2014, http://www.amazon.com/Ultimate-Security-Survey-Second-Edition/dp/0750670916.

SOCIALLY LEGAL AUDIT®

http://sociallylegalaudit.com

The Socially Legal Audit™ (SLA) tool is an instrument developed by Law2sm, LLC (www.law2sm.com) and Avax Consulting (www.avaxusa.com) to assist a company to ensure that their social media presence and activity is in line with state and federal laws, as well as regulatory compliance.

The audit includes taking an inventory of the organization's social media/digital footprint, interviews with key staff members about social media usage in the firm, comprehensive assessment of legal risks associated with that footprint, and recommended strategies for protection of digital assets and reduction of liability. Components of the audit include:

- Inventory of social media footprint
- Comprehensive report of legal risks/liabilities
- Recommended legal strategies

Audits function as invaluable strategic tool for a company to ensure an ROI in regard to online and digital activity security and risk management. An Ernst & Young commissioned Forbes Insights Global Survey (2012) found that 75% of the respondents indicated that their internal audit function has a positive impact on their overall risk management efforts.[13] In an earlier 2010 survey, 96% of respondents indicate that their internal audit function has an important role to play in their overall risk management efforts.[14]

By asking the right questions, the SLA leads a company to:

- Strategic business insights
- Increased subject matter expertise (specialized knowledge)
- Compliance with laws and regulations
- Decreased liability and risk, including reduction in litigation expenses
- Improved employee–employer relations
- Enhanced customer and brand advocacy relations

Audits are conducted by SLA-certified auditors[15] and reviewed by SLA-trained attorneys who prepare recommendation reports for clients. Training and certification are provided various times throughout the year in various locations around the world.

[13]"The Future of Internal Audit is Now," Insights on Risk, July, 2012.
[14]"Unlocking the Strategic Value of Internal Audit," 2010.
[15]"Certified Auditors—Socially Legal Audit," http://sociallylegalaudit.com/certified-auditors/ (accessed 2/8/2014).

Some information gathering techniques include:

- Brainstorming—a process whereby an individual or a group thinks about a topic or issue and comes up with ideas to solve the problem without filtering them first. The key to this technique is spontaneity. Ideas are reviewed for feasibility later.
- Delphi Technique—a group of experts respond to a questionnaire, their answers are reported back to them anonymously, and they are encouraged to revise their previous answers based on the group's answers. This can be repeated a number of "rounds" or until a consensus is achieved, thereby producing the most "correct" answer.
- Interviewing—a process of asking a specific individual specific questions regarding a specific issue or matter. In the case of online risk management and security, the interviews are usually conducted on key personnel related to the area such as the security director, IT director, as well as some regular staff to understand the breadth of online activity and mobile use throughout the company. In addition, some security and risk management professionals from outside the company may be interviewed to get some insight into the trends and best practices of the industry.

- Root Cause Analysis—a process of evaluating what caused a specific breach or security incident to occur. This takes place after the event but can be used to prevent the event from repeating in the future.
- Checklist Analysis—a tool that lists specific risks that may occur for a specific project or are known to have occurred in other security/risk management systems. The lists can be developed from historical information (prior incidents) and/or knowledge and expertise of current staff.
- Assumption Analysis—a process in which the individual or team documents all the presumptions that they have regarding the issue at hand. These "assumptions" can include things the team believes to be true, which may or may not be true.
- Diagramming Techniques—different processes to visualize data and its relationships by showing them in a sketch, drawing, and/or outline.
- SWOT Analysis—the process of evaluating the strengths, weaknesses, opportunities, and threats of a company's particular security and/or risk management system.
- Expert Judgment—the seeking and use of a decision made by an individual with wide-ranging and authoritative knowledge and/or skill in a particular area after he or she has reviewed and evaluated certain evidence and/or data.

We will be discussing specific risks throughout the rest of the book; however, most online and digital activity risks fall within the following categories:

- IP/Sensitive Data Loss—disclosure or leakage of data that the company defines as proprietary information or confidential information that relates to clients, company strategies, competitive intelligence, etc.
- Compliance Violations—disclosure of information or inappropriate communication of information that violates regulations set forth by federal and state laws and/or regulatory agencies.
- Reputational Loss—one key to successful online activity with clients and the public is transparency of who is communicating and the assurance to the public that it is the company speaking through official company channels. Misperceptions, damaging perceptions, and misinformed assumptions can generate a loss of good will and tarnish a company's name in a matter of characters or minutes due to the prolific and exponential nature of content sharing in the online environment.
- Financial Loss—security and risk incidents can be expensive between the breach itself, the investigation, and remediation strategies put into place, and notification requirements specifically related to leaked data, etc. There have been circumstances where stock prices went down because of a Twitter Tweet. All of the losses on this list can have a monetary consequence.
- Safety Loss—online and digital activity not only leave footprints of where an individual has been but also can provide information as to where an individual can be, whether that is a person or a corporation. This can lead to a physical safety concern for traveling executives and key members of a company's management team, including the board of directors.
- Personal Reputation Loss—online postings may take on a personal nature, indicating specific traits of an individual or describing specific behavior of that individual that may be judged as negative by a company's client base. Concerns here can lead to claims of defamation or damage to a person's character leading to a loss of their livelihood.

STEP 2: RISK ANALYSIS/ASSESSMENT

> *When asked to name the top three challenges (in regards to risk management) the largest proportion of executives (47 percent) cite difficulty of understanding the entire risk exposure on a global enterprise basis, and nearly as many (44 percent) see the same problem at the business unit level.[16]*

A phrase I like to share with clients is "data that is formatted is information; information that is processed is knowledge; knowledge that is applied is wisdom; and wisdom that is shared leads to success."

A company's list of identified risks must then be put into a risk analysis process to help evaluate the risks in terms of the company's risk aptitude. Greg Chevalier from BlueWave Computing (see Blue-Wave Computing) calls it a "company's risk appetite." The overall susceptible risk environment is the elephant in the room for many companies, and their key question is "how does one eat an elephant?" According to Chevalier, "one bite at a time." This then leads to the second question, "how much of the elephant does the company want to eat?"

BLUEWAVE COMPUTING

http://www.bluewave-computing.com/

BlueWave Computing (BWC) was established in 1997 by Steven Vicinanza to provide comprehensive information technology services to small-to-mid-sized companies. Its mission statement reads:

> *BlueWave Computing is the IT management partner of choice for small and mid-size organizations that require the highest reliability and performance from their computing systems but for whom IT is not the core business. We deliver a comprehensive set of IT services that enables them to better achieve their objectives. We do this through highly educated, disciplined, and skilled employees, who aspire to be recognized as the best, and who are passionate about both the technology and the welfare of our clients.*

BWC's business strategy is to have laser-focused solution disciplines within the company to ensure that they can attract the right kind of expertise and build integrity in the market place. One of those focused areas is information security and management, and in 2009 it started the BlueWave Computing Information Security Group. By doing so, BWC expanded its offerings to include information security risk and vulnerability assessments, penetration testing and vulnerability scanning, $7 \times 24 \times 365$ managed security and monitoring that includes intrusion detection and prevention, information security education and training, and implementation of information security technologies. It is also set up to become a leader in information security education with a state-of-the-art training facility and Certified Information Systems Security Professional (CISSP)-compliant curriculum that will allow students to qualify for continuing education (CE) credits.

BWC is a nationally recognized managed service provider (MSP) that has won hundreds of awards and recognition by its peers and security industry associations. They currently have 140 employees, of whom 80% are engineers. They run both on-site and off-site operations for clients and in the security arena offer a "Chief Information Security Officer (CISO) In A Box" that provides the client a comprehensive turnkey solution—risk/compliance, security analysis, network security monitoring—and various complex analytical tools.

This is BWC's competitive edge—offering a one-stop shop for clients from audit to monitoring to compliance. This edge allows the BlueWave client to look at information security in business terms and not just technical terms.

---

[16] Economist Intelligence Unit (EIU) Global Risk Management Survey, sponsored by KPMG International. https://www.kpmg.com/Global/en/IssuesAndInsights/ArticlesPublications/risk-management-outpacing-capabilities/Documents/expectations-risk-management-survey.pdf, December 2012.

INDUSTRY EXPERT: GREG CHEVALIER

President, BlueWave Computing Information Security Group

http://www.bluewave-computing.com/BlueWaveServices.aspx?id=security

Greg Chevalier is currently the president of BlueWave Computing's Information Security Group.

Greg has more than 25 years of experience in the technology field including: 10 years within the IBM Company running a $250 million business unit; 7 years providing executive leadership in growth-stage companies in the $5 million to $100 million revenue range; and 9 years in biometric identification and information security markets including authentication technologies, encryption technologies, and network and wireless access technologies delivered throughout the world.

During an interview, Greg outlined some specific trends he saw in the future regarding information security:

1. Information security risk/advantage must become a front and center strategic decision for companies.
2. Information security and risk management is no longer a percentage of the IT budget but now its own budget with a number of line items, emphasizing its increased importance to the company.[17]
3. Cyber-security insurance is now an option weighed against potential data breaches to offset risk, but will become a standard offering to companies.
4. Within the next decade or so, self-policing of data will regulate privacy concerns as consumers will dictate to companies what data access they find acceptable and companies will adapt to these consumer demands.
5. Wall Street and Financial Analysts will increase their scrutiny of a company's IT security to determine the value of the company's stock and overall value of the company itself.
6. Advanced persistent threats (APTs) will become more evasive and more frequent requiring constant monitoring to detect and remediate these benign but sophisticated data breach attack methods and risks.
7. Mobile makes everything more complex and less controllable as it provides new entry points into a company's data environment. Standards, policies, and controls, and enhanced training will be developed to address mobile risks.
8. Education: it is my belief that information security awareness and education training, along with high-level information security degrees will grow into a national curriculum being pushed down to all levels of our education system—from elementary school to graduate programs.

[17]However, a 2013 Oracle Report found that "for 35% of organizations, their security spend was influenced by sensational informational sources rather than real organizational risks." Brian Pennington, "IT Security Still Not Protecting the Right Assets Despite Increased Spending," http://brianpennington.co.uk/2013/07/17/it-security-still-not-protecting-the-right-assets-despite-increased-spending-2/ (accessed 2/11/2014).

For many companies the answer depends on the risk analysis and the assessment of each risk in terms of:

1. What is the actual risk?
2. What is the probability of the risk occurring?
3. What is the likely impact the risk would have on the company should the risk occur?
4. What will it cost to minimize the risk?
5. What will it cost to remediate the risk should the risk occur?
6. What will it cost to do nothing at all?

Risk Analysis can be done from a qualitative or quantitative perspective and often encompasses both types for a more comprehensive overview of the actual impacts and costs of the risks. Qualitative Risk Analysis looks at the distinctive characteristics of the risk, while Quantitative Risk Assessment is about measuring *the extent, size, or sum of countable or measurable discrete events, objects, or phenomenon*, (of the risk) *expressed as a numerical value*.[18]

---

[18] "What is Quantity? Definition and Meaning," http://www.businessdictionary.com/definition/quantity.html (accessed 2/8/2014).

Some examples of Qualitative Risk Analysis Tools and Techniques include:

- Risk Probability and Impact Assessment—the process of evaluating the likelihood that a risk may occur and the impact it would have (financially, operationally, etc.) if it does.
- Probability and Impact Matrix—the organization of data divided by columns of categories to highlight potential risks in an easily readable format.
- Risk Categorization—the process of identifying risks by classification and grouping them by those classes to better understand them in relation to the security and/or risk management system.
- Risk Urgency Assessment—the process of identifying and ranking risks by the time range the risk may occur; near-future medium risks may become prioritized over significant risks that may not occur for a year or more.

Some examples of quantitative risk analysis tools and techniques include:

- Sensitivity Analysis—the process of evaluating how a change in a certain factor or system variable can affect the entire security/risk management system. This process allows for a "what-if?" analysis of different results.
- Expected Monetary Value Analysis (EMV)—this process allows you to put a dollar amount on the risk by looking at the likelihood of the risk and the financial impact the risk would have on the company. Each risk can be assigned an EMV, and decisions on priority and handling of certain risks can be made based on the EMV score.
- Cost Risk Analysis—this process focuses on evaluating the risk that certain costs may exceed their initial budgeted amount and, if they do, what the impact would likely be to the system being put into place.
- Schedule Risk Analysis—the process of evaluating certain task durations (in terms of time ranges) and their impact on the system should they not be completed in the time allotted.

The measurements here focus on time and money, two significant assets for a company, as each can be in limited supply.

Matrixes are common in qualitative and quantitative risk analysis. This way of organizing data gives a comforting sense that everything has a place and is accounted for.

The key to the matrix is the column structure; each column should identify the kind of information being collected and analyzed. Following are two examples of a social media risk assessment matrix structure.

Example one

The matrix example in Figure 1.1 has a simple 6 column structure: Risk/Threat, Control, Mitigation, Likelihood, Impact, and Risk Rating. Likelihood of Occurrence Scales generally flow in an escalating fashion. For example, one scale used in some of these types of matrixes include: *Negligible, Very Low, Low, Moderate, High, Very High, Extreme*; defining these as to whether they may occur between 5 years and multiple times a day. A different matrix may use: *Rare, Unlikely, Possible, Likely, Almost Certain*; and defines these as whether they may or may not occur within the next 12–24 months. Some of these matrixes also give each Likelihood level a numeric score, for example, *Rare* is 1–2 and *Almost Certain* is 9–10, that will then be used to give an overall risk rating for the particular risk, threat, or vulnerability. This is a format that can be followed for Impact Severity levels as well. The table below provides an example (Table 1.1).

Facebook Risk Assesment 2010

It should be noted that the bank's Facebook page is not used for marketing purposes AT ALL. There is no mention of any rates, products, promotions, etc. It is purely used to display the bank's activities within the community.

Risk/Threat	Control	Mitigation	Likelihood	Impact	Risk Rating
	Technical				
Virus Social media sites tend to be the target for virus attacks.	Facebook is blocked on the bank's network prohibiting it's access within the bank.	Facebook is blocked on the bank's network prohibiting it's access within the bank.	Medium	Medium	Medium
Cross-site Scripting Cross-site scripting (XSS) is a type of computer security vulnerability typically found in web applications that enables malicious attackers to inject client-side script into web pages viewed by other users.	Facebook is blocked on the bank's network prohibiting it's access within the bank.	Facebook is blocked on the bank's network prohibiting it's access within the bank.	High	Medium	Medium
Employee Productivity The use of Facebook on user's computers tends to distract employees from business priorities. If the bank's employees spend too much time on Facebook, it might affect his/her performance at work.	Facebook is blocked on the bank's network prohibiting it's access within the bank.	Facebook is blocked on the bank's network prohibiting it's access within the bank.	Low	Medium	Medium

FIGURE 1.1 Facebook Risk Assessment Matrix.

Table 1.1 Impact Severity Level Examples

	Example One		Example Two
Insignificant	Almost no impact if the threat is realized and vulnerability is exploited.	Insignificant (1–2)	The risk may have almost no impact to financial, operations, compliance, etc. (Enterprise Risk Management - ERM - categories).
Minor	Minor effect on the organization that will require minimal effort to repair or reconfigure.	Minor (3–4)	The risk may have a minimal impact to at least one ERM risk category.
Significant	Some negligible yet tangible harm that will require some expenditure of resources to repair.	Moderate (5–6)	The risk may have a significant impact to at least one ERM category.
Damaging	Damage to the reputation of the organization, and/or notable loss of confidence in the organization's resources or services. Will require expenditure of significant resources to repair.	Major (7–8)	The risk may have a substantial impact to at least one ERM risk category that will likely require a multi-year recovery.
Serious	Considerable system outage and/or loss of customer/business partner confidence. May result in the compromise of services or a large amount of customer/organization information.	Extreme (9–10)	The risk may jeopardize the company's primary mission and/or solvency.
Critical	Extended system outage or permanent closure. May result in complete compromise of services or confidential information.		

To calculate a final risk rating, some matrixes will add up the individual numbers of Likelihood and Severity. Example one combines the two factors into a Risk Level Matrix.[19]

Risk Levels						
Likelihood of Occurrence	**Impact Severity**					
	Insignificant	**Minor**	**Significant**	**Damaging**	**Serious**	**Critical**
Negligible	Low	Low	Low	Low	Low	Low
Very low	Low	Low	Low	Low	Moderate	Moderate
Low	Low	Low	Moderate	Moderate	High	High
Moderate	Low	Low	Moderate	High	High	High
High	Low	Moderate	High	High	High	High
Very high	Low	Moderate	High	High	High	High
Extreme	Low	Moderate	High	High	High	High

---

[19] Jesse Torres, "Sample Social Media Risk Assessment Matrix," http://www.JesseTorres.com/doc/socialmediaassessment.doc (accessed 02/11/2014).

Example two

This matrix example (Figure 1.2) offers a seven-column structure that takes into account what controls already exist in contrast to what recommended controls need to be implemented. It also allows for specific comments in the matrix itself, such as who is accountable for mitigating the risk, specific details, due dates, etc.

STEP 3: REMEDIATE

After the initial risk assessment, decisions can be made as to what to do regarding each risk based on their particular circumstances, including their current and projected financial situation. A remediation plan will be developed and put into place outlining the strategies to be implemented to remedy the risk, threat, and/or vulnerability as well as a timetable and budget to ensure that sufficient and appropriate resources are committed to complete the process.

One core set of remediation tools includes the development of a policy and control framework, as well as the drafting and implementation of the policies and controls themselves. Keep in mind that the controls have to make good business sense and align with the company's goals and culture. So the key question is, are the controls being deployed operationally effective?

We can surmise that online and digitally related risks can fall into one of four specific categories:

1. Process and procedure
2. Compliance/regulations
3. Policies and controls
4. Technical risks (data, application systems, mobile, networking, etc.)

If these are the categories, the controls and remediation solutions need to align with them. Some of the controls include key information assurance services such as:

- SSAE 16—Statement on Standards for Attestation Engagements (SSAE) No. 16, Reporting on Controls at a Service Organization, finalized by the Auditing Standards Board of the American Institute of Certified Public Accountants (AICPA) in January 2010.
- SOC 2—Service Organization Control (SOC) reports are internal control reports on the services provided by a service organization providing valuable information that users need to assess and address the risks associated with an outsourced service.
- PCI Compliance—The Payment Card Industry Data Security Standard (PCI DSS) is a set of requirements designed to ensure that all companies that process, store, or transmit credit card information maintain a secure environment.
- ISO 27001 Certification—specifies requirements for the establishment, implementation, monitoring and review, maintenance, and improvement of an information security management system.
- FED RAMP Certification—The Federal Risk and Authorization Management Program (FedRAMP) is a government-wide program that provides a standardized approach to security assessment, authorization, and continuous monitoring for cloud products and services.[20]
- Privacy Risk Management—The framework that guides the collection, storage, protection, and use of personal data, including personally identifiable information (PII).

---

[20] "FedRAMP," http://www.fedramp.gov (accessed 2/11/2014).

XXXX Social Media Risk Assessment

Foreseeable Risk	Causes of Risk	Existing Controls	Recommended Controls or Actions	Likelihood	Impact	Comments
Part 1	Use of Social Media by the Public (Including Customers)					
Reputational	The bank's name is being associated (accurately or not) on the Internet in unflattering posts	•	• Implement social listening program • Develop social response protocol	•	•	
Reputational	Disgruntled customer uses social media to criticize the bank	•	• Implement social listening program • Develop social response protocol • Make sure online complaint process is accessible to customer	•	•	
Reputational /compliance	A customer posts debit card details to a social media site exposing data covered by Payment Card Industry security standards.		• Develop rules for employees to follow if this were to occur. • Rules around how to handle these cases, from customer response to purging of data from social media site are required (if applicable) • Customer education regarding confidential information	•	•	
Legal (domestic and foreign	Bank may be subject to international jurisdiction due to social media activity by non-US		• Implement disclaimers that bank-managed social media accounts are governed by US	•	•	

FIGURE 1.2 Socially Legal Audit™ (SLA) Social Media Risk Assessment Matrix.

- HIPAA/HITECH Compliance—Health Insurance Portability and Accountability Act and the Health Information Technology for Economic and Clinical Health (HITECH) Act, enacted as part of the American Recovery and Reinvestment Act of 2009.[21]
- U.S. Safe Harbor Agreement with European Union (EU)—provides a streamlined and cost-effective means for U.S. organizations to satisfy the EU's directive's "adequacy" standard for privacy protection.[22]
- Data Management—Administrative process by which the required data is acquired, validated, stored, protected, and processed, and by which its accessibility, reliability, and timeliness is ensured to satisfy the needs of the data users.[23]
- Information Technology Internal Audits—address the internal control environment of automated information systems and how these systems are used. IT audits typically evaluate system input, output, and processing controls, backup and recovery plans, and system security.[24]
- Information Technology Governance—The framework of how decisions are made regarding IT Strategic Alignment, IT Value Delivery, IT Resource Management, IT Risk Management, and IT Performance Management.

Many of these control standards require companies to develop and institute various policies in regard to the numerous factors of security risk and management. Policies are basically a statement of intent by a company as to how certain issues are to be addressed by the company and its employees. In many cases, policies also extend to representatives of the company such as freelance or independent contractors, vendors, suppliers, advertising affiliates, etc. Policies list the express rules that will govern certain decisions the company makes and how violations of these rules will then affect employees and those subject to the policies.

Certain policies relate specifically to technology use, and some even outline specific rules for online, digital, and mobile activity by managers, employees, and company representatives. Following is a short list of policies in alphabetical order:

- Blogger Disclosure Policy—this policy lays out guidelines for a company's bloggers to ensure that they reveal their relationship to the company or indicate whether a product/service they are reviewing was a gift from the company being reviewed. This is a requirement from the Federal Trade Commission (FTC) to avoid violation of the false advertising and/or misleading advertising guidelines.[25]
- Bring Your Own Device (BYOD) Policy—this policy outlines specific guidelines and rules employees need to adhere to if they use their own smartphone, tablet, laptop, etc. for company purposes. We will discuss this issue in more detail in Chapter 2.

[21] "HITECH Act Enforcement Interim Final Rule," http://www.hhs.gov/ocr/privacy/hipaa/administrative/enforcementrule/hitechenforcementifr.html (accessed 2/11/2014).
[22] "Export.Gov—US-EU Safe Harbor Overview," http://export.gov/safeharbor/eu/eg_main_018476.asp (accessed 2/11/2014).
[23] "What is Data Management? Definition and Meaning," http://www.businessdictionary.com/definition/data-management.html#ixzz2a4NPJ1b7 (accessed 2/11/2014).
[24] "Decosimo Accountants and Business Advisors Information Technology Internal Audit," http://www.decosimo.com/www/docs/413.4725 (accessed 2/11/2014).
[25] "FTC Staff Revises Online Advertising Disclosure Guidelines | Federal Trade Commission," http://www.ftc.gov/news-events/press-releases/2013/03/ftc-staff-revises-online-advertising-disclosure-guidelines (accessed 2/11/2014).

- Document/Social Media Retention Policy—here are specific laws regarding document retention, especially in regulated industries. Those laws are now taking into consideration digital imaging systems as a way to preserve the data. Companies may also have their own guidelines as to retaining certain information. This requirement is also extending to social media content, and new applications are offering this capturing of content service.
- E-Mail Policy—this policy outlines the use of electronic communication by employees using the internal company electronic mail delivery system. These policies usually contain prohibitions of private or personal use of the system by an employee.
- Employee Contracts/Agreements with Social Media Clauses—employment letters and agreements are now starting to include clauses that state acceptable and unacceptable use of social media and online activity, and indicating who owns the social media accounts themselves—whether the company or the employee—depending on the account name and the usage of the account.
- Intellectual Property (IP) Policy—this policy outlines the appropriate use of company-owned content: copyrights, trademarks, trade secrets, patents, etc. The IP policy may cover work-for-hire concerns, indicating that anything created by an employee during their scope of employment belongs to the company (including social media posts), as well as logo use on a social media account. We will discuss more on this issue in Chapter 6.
- Information Technology/Computer Use Policy—this policy lays out the guidelines for use of company computer equipment by an employee during their employment period. Certain restrictions, such as secure access to download certain apps, and if devices can be taken off-site, may be included.
- Mobile Device Policy—this policy outlines how mobile devices—tablets and cell phones (whether smartphones or not)—can be used if they are provided by the company or not, if the company does not have a BYOD policy.
- Password Policy—this policy is usually embedded into the computer use policy but it is sometimes helpful to keep separate to emphasize its importance. The policy should lay out the basics of password generation, the importance of why a strong password is a good defense against breach incidents, how often the password should be changed, etc. Considering that most data breaches have a human cause, this policy and the training of employees on all things password related is imperative.
- Privacy/Confidentiality Policy—in the online world, privacy policies usually outline what kind of data is collected and how the party collecting it will use that data. Confidentiality policies remind employees of the nature of certain types of information and the requirements to not disclose specific information to third parties as required for compliance and legal purposes.
- Social Media Policy/Protocols—this policy outlines how employees should use social media whether on behalf of the company or even on personal accounts. The National Labor Relations Board (NLRB) has a lot to say about whether certain clauses in these policies are valid or violate the National Labor Relations Act. Social media protocols are guidelines as to how certain social media posts/comments should be made.

We will review most of these policies in Chapter 4. The key here is to note whether the company has these policies or not and, if they do, are they consistent with each other and do not open up the possibilities of conflicts and therefore leave the company vulnerable to liability.

The SANS Institute also offers a list of 20 Critical Security Controls for Cyber Defense.[26] This list was developed by a group of government and private organizations:

1. Inventory of Authorized and Unauthorized Devices
2. Inventory of Authorized and Unauthorized Software
3. Secure Configurations for Hardware and Software on Mobile Devices, Laptops, Workstations, and Servers
4. Continuous Vulnerability Assessment and Remediation
5. Malware Defenses
6. Application Software Security
7. Wireless Device Control
8. Data Recovery Capability
9. Security Skills Assessment and Appropriate Training to Fill Gaps
10. Secure Configurations for Network Devices such as Firewalls, Routers, and Switches
11. Limitation and Control of Network Ports, Protocols, and Services
12. Controlled Use of Administrative Privileges
13. Boundary Defense
14. Maintenance, Monitoring, and Analysis of Audit Logs
15. Controlled Access Based on the Need to Know
16. Account Monitoring and Control
17. Data Loss Prevention
18. Incident Response and Management
19. Secure Network Engineering
20. Penetration Tests and Red Team Exercises

Security involves emotions, beliefs, models of behavior and other non-quantifiable factors which makes the 'how much?' question insufficient.[27]

STEP 4: RISK RESPONSE PLANNING

Once the repairs and remediation have taken place, a plan to outline incident response procedures is developed for future reference. This plan will provide specific action steps and reporting guidelines should a breach or other security incident occur. The goal here is to reduce the impact of any specific incident by reducing the time to identify the incident, to locate and contain the incident, to mitigate whatever damage has been caused by the incident, and to institute practices to eliminate the risk of the incident happening again.

A "Risk Register" or "Risk Response Plan" is a good tool to extend the Risk Assessment of Step 2 with the Remediation Process of Step 3. The Risk Register identifies the risks, quantifies the risk score, and then recommends controls and response strategies building a remediation road map based on the company's priorities.

---

[26] Used under Creative Commons Attribution-NoDerivs 3.0 Unported License from SANS Institute, "The Critical Security Controls," http://www.sans.org/critical-security-controls/ (accessed 2/11/2014).
[27] Jarno Limnell, Director of Cyber Security, Stonesoft, 7/1/2013.

Key Components to a Risk Response Plan (RRP)[28] include:

- List of identified risks
- Definition of who has the authority to act and who can be an owner of a risk to devise and apply the appropriate response
- Results from the qualitative and quantitative risk analysis
- Established responses for each risk
- Expected level of residual risk
- Specific actions required to implement the response
- Budget and timing of each risk response
- Description of any contingency or fallback plans

Based on research, experience, and prior knowledge, there may be a number of options as to how to respond to a particular risk. As the RRP is developed, each option needs to be vetted for feasibility to ensure that it is the best response for the company. Questions to ask to determine the best response option include:

1. What options are there?
2. What constraints are there to the particular project or security implementation?
3. Based on review of the option characteristics, which one offers the most effective way to achieve the business goal?

There are generally four responses to negative risks: avoidance, transference, mitigation, and acceptance. Avoidance is when you change the plan to circumvent the risk all together. It is usually used when the risk is too high and therefore considered unacceptable. Transference is a strategy for when you can shift the risk to another party, such as through insurance, contracts, warranties, etc. Mitigation is when you can reduce the likelihood of a risk occurring or of the damage being unacceptable. Acceptance implies that the risk is considered too low to justify spending any resources on it.

These responses can change during the life cycle of a security project or the company's technology and online activity. Risks that may have been acceptable in the beginning may turn into a risk that needs to be mitigated, and vice versa. The RRP should be a dynamic document and an integral part of monitoring the system (see Step 6).

An interesting note I ran across discusses using an RRP model for evaluating and responding to positive risks or "opportunities."[29] Three response strategies for positive risks are:

1. Share the ownership of the risk with others to ensure you can seize the opportunity.
2. Increase the likelihood of the opportunity coming to pass by enhancing triggers that can set it in motion.
3. Exploit the opportunity by dedicating resources to it, whether in terms of experts or tools.

---

[28] "IT Project Management: Determining the Most Appropriate Risk Response," http://it-project-guide.blogspot.com/2009/01/determining-most-appropriate-risk.html (accessed 2/11/2014).
[29] "Risk Response Planning by AntiClue," http://www.anticlue.net/archives/000820.htm (accessed 2/11/2014).

On a final note for this section, I would like to mention Bailey and Brandley's *Ten Principles to Guide Companies in Creating and Implementing Incident Response Plans*[30]:

1. Assign an executive to take on responsibility for the plan and for integrating incident-response efforts across business units and geographies.
2. Develop a taxonomy of risks, threats, and potential failure modes. Refresh them continually on the basis of changes in the threat environment.
3. Develop easily accessible quick-response guides for likely scenarios.
4. Establish processes for making major decisions, such as when to isolate compromised areas of the network.
5. Maintain relationships with key external stakeholders, such as law enforcement.
6. Maintain service-level agreements and relationships with external breach-remediation providers and experts.
7. Ensure that documentation of response plans is available to the entire organization and is routinely refreshed.
8. Ensure that all staff members understand their roles and responsibilities in the event of a cyber incident.
9. Identify the individuals who are critical to incident response and ensure redundancy.
10. Train, practice, and run simulated breaches to develop response "muscle memory." The best-prepared organizations routinely conduct war games to stress test their plans, increasing managers' awareness and fine-tuning their response capabilities.

STEP 5: EDUCATE

Plans and policies may look great on paper, but getting them to be of optimal benefit to the company implies that they have to be implemented effectively. Part of that implementation is the training phrase that should be part of any security and risk management program. The company needs to outline who needs to be trained and what they need to be trained on. A good place to start is on the employee's role in the company and to determine whether they need access to certain information and how they need to access that information digitally and/or via online. However, even though not all employees require access to all company data, there are some basic security issues all employees (including top managers and executives) need to know to keep company data protected and safe.

"Security awareness" training for the general employee population has become an essential component to any security and risk management initiative. It consists of two components: security issues (the content) and adult learning theory (the context). Malcolm Knowles, an American practitioner and theorist of adult education, in the 1970s identified six principles of adult learning[31]:

- Adults are internally motivated and self-directed
- Adults bring life experiences and knowledge to learning experiences
- Adults are goal oriented

---

[30] Tucker Bailey and Josh Brandley, "Ten Steps to Planning an Effective Cyber-Incident Response," Harvard Business Review, http://blogs.hbr.org/2013/07/ten-steps-to-planning-an-effect/ (accessed 2/11/2014).
[31] "Adult Learning Theory and Principles," http://www.qotfc.edu.au/resource/?page=65375 (accessed 2/11/2014); "Infed. Org | Malcolm Knowles, Informal Adult Education, Self-Direction and Andragogy," http://infed.org/mobi/malcolm-knowles-informal-adult-education-self-direction-and-andragogy/ (accessed 2/11/2014).

- Adults are relevancy oriented
- Adults are practical
- Adult learners like to be respected

Rose McDermott, professor at the University of California, Santa Barbara, gives us a crucial factor to add to this list when the content in the training relates to security and threats. In an interview regarding a paper she wrote for Association for Computing Machinery (ACM) in 2012 entitled "Emotion and Security,"[32] she cautions IT professionals to learn how to train non-IT people. "People will listen to a conversation that is valid, salient, concrete and emotionally engaging. Abstract, pallid, statistical arguments tend to make people's eyes glaze over."[33] If you are going to communicate about a threat you should:

- be an expert and a trustworthy source,
- be focused on a specific anticipated attack,
- motivate respondents to act, and
- provide specific concrete actions individuals should take to counter the threat.

In addition to the above, I would like to bring to your attention Ira Winkler and Samantha Manke's list of seven key elements for a successful awareness program[34]:

1. Get executive-level support from chief officers (C-suite)—this will provide you with additional funding and support.
2. Partner with key departments that have mutual interests and can carry their own level of influence (such as the legal or compliance departments).
3. Be creative in terms of the curriculum and activities; engagement is the key to learning.
4. Make sure to set up metrics beforehand to be able to measure success of the program via change of behavior, attitudes, etc.
5. Educate people about how they can do something instead of just focusing on what they are prohibited from doing.
6. Put your program on a 90-day cycle to ensure information is relevant, current, and reinforced as required.
7. Be multimodal in your program. Use different formats and delivery methods to spread the message of security awareness—from online games and apps to traditional newsletters and posters—offering something for everyone.

Connecting those seven factors, Ira continues: *The mere act of providing a set body of knowledge does not change behavior. Information must be provided in a way that relates to how employees think and behave. There must be a personal association of how the knowledge would impact their actions. There is also a difference in providing an individual information on a one time basis, and delivering information in different formats over the course of time to effect change.*[35]

---

[32] "Communications Magazine of the ACM," Vol. 55, No. 2 (February, 2012), pp. 35–37.

[33] "Ignoring Security Advice from the Pros: The IT-User Disconnect—TechRepublic," http://www.techrepublic.com/blog /it-security/ignoring-security-advice-from-the-pros-the-it-user-disconnect/ (accessed 2/11/2014).

[34] "The 7 Elements of a Successful Security Awareness Program—CSO Online—Security and Risk," http://www.csoonline-.com/article/732602/the-7-elements-of-a-successful-security-awareness-program (accessed 2/11/2014).

[35] "7 Reasons for Security Awareness Failure—CSO Online—Security and Risk," http://www.csoonline.com/article/736159/ 7-reasons-for-security-awareness-failure (accessed 2/11/2014).

STEP 6: MONITOR

The three certainties of life: Death, Taxes, and Getting Hacked.[36]

Having done a risk assessment once does not mean you are finished. Continuous monitoring involves the identification, analysis, planning, and tracking of new risks, constantly reviewing existing risks, monitoring trigger conditions for contingency plans, and monitoring residual risks, as well as reviewing the execution of risk responses while evaluating their effectiveness.[37] Various tools used to accomplish this daunting task include:

- Risk Audits—the process of investigation, evaluation, and assessment of the actual, perceived, and projected risks that a company may face. These audits can be performed by an internal company professional or an external third party or company.
- Variance Analysis—this process looks at what was projected to occur and what actually occurred, whether financial (budget targets) or operational (performance goals), as well as the causes of the differences between the two.
- Trend Analysis—the evaluation of information from a designated period of time of a specific factor to identify patterns and relationships between factors and to use that data to project what may occur in the future.
- Technical Performance Measurements—reviewing specific indicators that the company has identified to determine whether the strategies and/or tools being implemented are achieving the desired results.
- Reserve Analysis—the process of reviewing the physical and financial status of equipment, tools, and other resources relating to the online and technology activity of a company, including costs to repair and/or replace those resources.
- Status Update/Review Meetings—risk management and security strategies need to be reviewed and the RPP and other risk management/security documents updated. It is important to keep the security and risk management teams up to date on any incidents that may occur, the response to the incident, new tools available for responding to incidents, new trends in security concerns, etc.

Keep in mind that if you set up policies as part of your controls, you need to ensure that you are enforcing them. Periodic policy reviews and enforcement reviews will provide you with data to determine whether the policy implementation has been successful or not.

Corporations will spend around $68 billion worldwide this year on IT security measures including firewalls, network monitoring, encryption and end-point protection.[38]

---

[36] James Christiansen, "The Three Certainties of Life: Death, Taxes, and Getting Hacked | ID Experts," http://www2.idexpertscorp.com/blog/single/the-three-certainties-of-life-death-taxes-and-getting-hacked/ (accessed 2/11/2014).
[37] RobustPM Home page, http://www.robustpm.com.
[38] Kyle Marks, "The Most Overlooked Part of Your Data Security," Harvard Business Review, http://blogs.hbr.org/2013/06/the-most-overlooked-part-of-yo/ (accessed 2/11/2014).

STEP 7: RESPOND

Keep in mind that what hackers are usually after with a breach is the data and not necessarily the device the data was on. The device serves as an access point, a critical one that needs to be watched and protected.

When responding to an incident, the goals are simple: limit the damage; increase the confidence of external stakeholders; and reduce recovery time and costs.[39]

Responsiveness to an incident focuses on time. The basic stages of a breach include:

- Incursion—the moment the unauthorized enters the system
- Discovery—the period of time the unauthorized takes to map out the system and discover where the data is
- Capture—the stage where the unauthorized commandeers the data using root kits or other tools at their disposal
- Exfiltration—when the data is sent back to the unauthorized; data is not necessarily removed from the system but copied to another location[40]

These stages present three critical points for responding to the incident to mitigate the damage and repair the breach:

- From the point of entry to the compromise
- From the compromise to discovery by the company
- From discovery by the company to remediation

An incident response team with specified members is a must and should be summoned as soon as an incident is discovered. Each member of this group should have and understand his or her role in the upcoming investigation and the remediation of the damage. Internal company members to this elite group should include representatives from the following departments:

- IT Security
- IT Operations
- Data Collection and Monitoring Division (if applicable)
- Physical Security
- Human Resources
- Legal Department
- Compliance Department
- Public Relations
- Management/Executive Level

In addition, third parties or individuals from outside the company may be called in an advisory role to the team and to ensure objectivity in terms of development and implementation of security and risk management systems.

---

[39] Bailey, Tucker and Josh Bradley, Harvard Business Review Blog, "Ten Steps to Planning an Effective Cyber-Incident Response," http://blogs.hbr.org/2013/07/ten-steps-to-planning-an-effect/, July 1, 2013.
[40] Blue Wave Computing Panel Discussion on "The World of Information Security," June 18, 2013, Gwinnett Technical College, Georgia.

BEST PRACTICES FOR INCIDENT RESPONSE

- Devote time to incident response planning before something bad actually happens. The millions saved by avoiding a breach justify the money spent on planning and preparation.
- Make sure your incident response team has the appropriate skills to deal with an incident, both technical and soft—such as being able to maintain calm, reduce panic—can mobilize individuals to take appropriate action, and effectively communicate with executives, the media, and employees.
- Do dry runs of the incident response to catch unanticipated obstacles and to ensure the response is appropriate.
- Make sure your incident response team is trained on how to identify and preserve physical and digital evidence.
- Determine the facts of the incident: what data was involved, was the data encrypted, the timeline of the incident, etc. It is important to get all the details before you notify or make an announcement of the incident, especially to the press.
- Make sure the message you do decide on is consistent across the board—from internal to online to clients to media to stakeholders. Determine who will be the point person for incoming calls and how the calls will be handled.
- Practice customary examination techniques such as interviewing the relevant individuals related to the incident and conducting technical and forensic investigations.
- Prepare to notify, and then actually notify, as required based on state and federal laws governing data protection and privacy. Record the incident in appropriate logs and registers, including remediation solutions and outcomes.
- Plans need to be reviewed and revised to keep up to date at least annually, and especially after an incident has occurred. Reinforce employee awareness of security.

BONUS: TEN IT SECURITY MYTHS

It is interesting what we in the security field believe when it comes to security, risk, and our own companies and capabilities. The following table outlines Ten IT Security Myths compiled by various online posts by various IT security professionals (Table 1.2). Do any of these ring true to you?

Table 1.2 Ten IT Security Myths		
	Myth	**Comment**
1	I'm an IT professional, it won't happen to me.	No one is infallible, and it is those of us who practice in this area that sometimes have a "God complex" and are most susceptible to cutting security corners. How strong are your passwords?
2	We have backups and backups. We are OK.	When was the last time you verified the data on the backups and made sure that the backup system was doing what it is supposed to do?
3	This system is secure. I implemented it.	How long ago was it implemented? Have there been any changes to the systems such as additions of access points for mobile devices? Probably time to review.

Continued

Table 1.2 Ten IT Security Myths—cont'd

	Myth	Comment
4	We detected the incident 5 min ago. We don't know what caused it, but we have it under control.	Really? How do you know? Who are you telling this to? Will you have to take any of this statement back?
5	We are not a target. Our data is not important.	But your data connects with client data and other data that can be very important and very valuable to the criminally minded or just a disgruntled employee.
6	Compliance is security.	Compliance sometimes is just paperwork. It can serve as a starting point for a comprehensive security and risk management system, but it should not be the final checkoff.
7	We've got the latest and greatest in information security and risk management tools. We are safe.	Software, policies, USB keys, etc. are all great—but don't forget the human element. According to security expert Jack Daniel: "Having the right people is more important than having the right tools. And that requires hiring the right people, investing in them, and retaining them—three processes we often get wrong."[41]
8	We have a firewall. Our data is secure.	Randy Rosenbaum, executive partner at Alert Logic, stated in a recent technology forum that "Breaking into a firewall you can learn with 20 minutes of YouTube."[42] Firewalls may slow a hacker down, but it does not stop the attack from coming.
9	Any and all vulnerabilities need to be addressed as a priority over business operations.	Even though security and risk management is considered a strategic business concern, it should not overtake the primary purpose of the business being in existence. Careful risk analysis, including financial considerations, must help guide decision making as to where the risks and remediation fit into the larger picture of the business acumen.
10	Security people know their stuff and business people just need to listen and give the money.	One of the key concerns in security and risk management is the dialogue between IT security personnel and upper management—a lot seems to get lost in the translation from technical to strategic. Security needs to be able to speak the business language to justify the funds it is requesting.

SECURITY/RISK MANAGEMENT APPS

Here is a table of some of the risk management and security-related apps available for current digital and mobile devices (Table 1.3). Security apps will be discussed in Chapter 2 as they focus on securing and protecting mobile devices, and not enterprise security. New apps are constantly being developed, so periodic searches to see what is new in the market is recommended. Each application has pros and cons, and you should evaluate each (as well as have your security and risk management team review) before selecting it to download and/or purchase.

---

[41] David Spark, "Top 25 Influencers in Security You Should be Following | the State of Security," http://www.tripwire.com/state-of-security/security-data-protection/top-25-influencers-in-security-you-should-be-following/ (accessed 2/11/2014).
[42] The World of Information Security, Gwinnett Technology Forum, June 18, 2013, Georgia.

Table 1.3 Security/Risk Management Apps

Name	Compatible Devices	URL	Price
Citicus MOCA	iPhone, iPad, iTouch	http://www.citicus.com/citicusmoca.asp	Free
Citicus™ Limited: Risk Assessment Checklist Mobile App	iPhone, iPad, Android, Blackberry Playbook, Windows Mobile	http://www.citicus.com/citicusmoca.asp	Free
Canvas: Risk Report	iPhone, iPad, iTouch	http://www.gocanvas.com/mobile-forms-apps/3257-Risk-Assessment-Checklist	$2.99
Risk Management Services: Breach Support	iPhone, iPad	http://www.risk-management-services.biz/Risk_Report.html	Free
Strategy and Risk Studio	iPad	http://strategyriskstudio.com	$25.99
Risk Calendar Chart Tool	iPhone, iPad	https://www.quixey.com/app/2400208252/risk-calculator-chart-tool	$.99
Marsh Risk Management Research App	iPad	http://usa.marsh.com/NewsInsights/MarshRiskManagementResearch.aspx	Free
SG Risk Log	iPad	http://www.simplegeniussoftware.com/sg-risk-log-ipad.html	$9.99

INTERNAL AND EXTERNAL RISKS

IT departments must ensure reliability, security and scalability for a wide range of devices as users' work migrates from PCs, laptops, local applications, and wired local networks to smart devices, cloud applications, and wireless access.[1]

In Chapter 1 we established that *risk* is a four-letter word that needs to be identified and remediated for the company to achieve its business mission.[2] Let us now take a more in-depth look at specific internal and external risks related to digital and online activity. The distinction between internal and external usually focuses on the locus of control for reducing or limiting the risk, or how the risk comes to be. However, one thing to take note of as we review these is that many of the risks related

---

[1] Aerohive Networks, "The iEverything Enterprise," (Whitepaper, 2012), http://www.aerohive.com/pdfs/Aerohive_Whitepaper_iEverything_Enterprise.pdf.

[2] As an aside, four-letter words are not all necessarily negative.

to digital and online activity may only seem to be under internal control; in reality, they overflow to the external and the company may not have all of the control it thinks it does. So much of what happens online is interrelated and interdependent with other factors, therefore this distinction between internal and external may not always fit neatly within the lines. In fact, it may be more appropriate to say that the digital and online nature of these activities makes these risks hybrids, with both internal and external variables affecting their effective management. I will comment on this as I review them. In addition, the following risks are not listed in any particular order or sequence of importance. Depending on where the company finds itself, different risks will become the center of focus at different times.

INTERNAL RISKS

One of the keys to successful risk management and security is the idea that certain risks are more under the control of the company to reduce and/or eliminate than others. The concept of internal risks, which lie within a company's purview, whether in its resources, processes, or people, can be comforting to some executives since they believe they can manage the potential threats more effectively and make definite decisions governing command of these without outside factors influencing or delaying the process.

INTERNAL RISK 1: SECURITY PERCEPTION, PRIORITY, AND BUDGET

As a risk management or security professional one likes to believe they are in control of the situation. In fact, there is a belief by many in the corporate level (C-suite) that the Chief Information Security Officer (CISO) is the only one responsible for information and online security—it is the CISO's job after all. That perception can make it difficult for the C-suite and members of a company's board to understand that security is a business function and needs to be aligned with business goals so they are an integral part of the security and risk management solution. On the other hand, CISOs also find it difficult to communicate security needs to executives in a language the executives understand. The lack of attention, on behalf of executives because it is someone else's problem, and the lack of effective dialogue between security professionals and executives, lead to the risk of underfunding and underallocation and/or misallocation of essential resources for security and risk management.

"Tell me where you put your money and I'll tell you what your priority is" is an observant rule of thumb. Research shows that spending on security and risk management is increasing, and for some companies security is its own line item outside the traditional budget for information technology (IT). But is it enough? Double of $0 is still $0, and sometimes doubling an insignificant budget that could not do the job before just seems like an empty gesture. The question that will always come up from the C-suite is, "Why do you need all this money for more people, more resources, more anything? Shouldn't digital mean you can do more with less?"

As a security professional, how do you explain that digital for security and risk management is not the same as digital for making a home movie or music recording? Digital in the risk environment has opened up that proverbial Pandora's box, unleashing a myriad of security concerns that did not exist when all was analog and we were dealing with isolated information systems that rarely connected to the outside world. So what can the security professional do to have this urgent message heard?

1. Recognize that there is a cultural disconnection between security and the C-suite. It is not wrong, and it is not a problem; it is a point of fact that, once acknowledged, allows you to get over it and focus on how to effectively communicate with "the others" of the C-suite.

2. Set as one of your security goals the creation of a risk-aware culture in the company—from the administrative assistant to the chairman of the board—each person is a potential break, so each one must also represent a piece of the solution.[3] The key is to help the company understand that security is NOT JUST a technology-based problem that needs to be limited to the technical people.

3. Prepare your presentation on security and risk management resource requests based on tangible business impact. The standard fear, uncertainty, and doubt (FUD) approach is not as effective as it once was, if it ever was.[4] You need to know: What is important to the board? What is the pain point they want to avoid? It could be a loss of a specific amount of revenue, products, or productivity time. Make the metrics mean something real and tangible.

4. Do not wait for a formal presentation to make risk management and security needs known. Informal lunches, rides in an elevator, drinks after work, all are opportunities to lay the groundwork for resource requests. Of course the key is to know how to do so tactfully and not to be annoying. Knowing when not to ask for something is a related important and less-common skill.

INTERNAL RISK 2: TRADITIONAL AND SHADOW IT

Once upon a time IT managers knew every piece of technology equipment that was purchased, owned, and used by the company, as well as to whom the equipment was assigned and for what purpose. Most technology purchases were centralized because they came out of the IT department's budget or it was the IT professionals who knew what specifications were required for the job. IT centralized not just purchasing but standards of technology, policies, and employee technology knowledge via training.

Today the scenario is quite different—often employees (especially managers) believe they know more about technology than the IT professionals or at least enough that they can make their own decisions about what is best for completing their tasks without depending on the company's IT expertise. There is so much information on the Internet, and most professionals feel confident in their capacity to understand and, to IT's chagrin, apply what they learned without necessarily going through official company channels. Search via Google and YouTube has made experts of us all. If you do not know how to do something, you can quickly search and find a video on YouTube that will go through it step by step—and in living color!

Budgets have become more territorial and compartmentalized, each department having a specific amount for their own technology needs. With the wallet comes the desire and authority to want the technology that is best and most effective for them, and considerations of how this technology

---

[3] Linda Phifer, "Top 10 BYOD Pitfalls to Avoid if You Allow Personal Devices," (June 10, 2013), http://searchconsumerization. techtarget.com/tip/Top-10-BYOD-pitfalls-to-avoid-if-you-allow-personal-devices.
[4] Hamish Barwick, "How to Present Security Issues to a Board," *CIO - Gartner Security RSS Feed*, (August 19, 2013), http:// www.cio.com.au/article/524044/how_present_security_issues_board/.

integrates with the overall company IT plan is not usually a priority, especially when each department has a very real goal of justifying itself against the others.

These factors have led to "Shadow IT"—technology decisions made solely on a business basis within a narrowly defined set of circumstances outside of IT's central control, and sometimes outside of IT's knowledge. Yet, the dilemma is that the business units still expect that the IT department will support the technology they purchased AND guarantee the security of the technology and the company data being stored and processed on it. Add to this that the security funding may not even be in the IT department's budget but might be allocated to a separate entity altogether. Gartner "predicts that a full 35% of IT spending will take place outside of IT by 2015…and by the end of the decade, Gartner says that figure will hit 90%."[5]

Simple examples of this are the decision to go with a cloud service that seems innocuous enough, such as Dropbox, for the transfer of extremely large files; or the use of collaborative applications, such as Google Docs, to assist on completing shared tasks, such as compiling annual reports. It is easy to set up accounts for Dropbox and Google Docs, and the business units may do so quickly without wanting to wait on the backlog of the IT help desk. But should a file transfer go wrong and the data loss or a Google Docs account with confidential information is hijacked, IT is under pressure to right the wrong, and sometimes even to have known that such a thing may happen—even if IT did not know the unit was using such digital tools! Managing unrealistic expectations is extremely difficult if you do not know they exist in the first place.

IT and security professionals walk a delicate line with the business units on the issue of shadow IT. Understanding that it exists in your company and is inevitable is a good place to start. It is then important to have a conversation with the business unit leaders. Give them guidelines and open a communications channel with them so they can see the IT and security departments as resources—resources that can help them make decisions that not only cover their needs but keep them secure and integrated to the rest of the company's IT structure. Assign business unit liaisons that periodically go out to the units themselves and offer assistance. This also works as a reconnaissance exercise, for the liaisons can bring back information about the technology, apps, and software the units are using and how they are being used, so the IT and security departments can prepare themselves to support and secure them. Or each unit can assign a liaison and the IT and security departments can have periodic meetings with the liaisons for updates, resource sharing, and specific training if required.

Communication is key for managing this risk, but it is also imperative to use the information once it is received. If lists of business unit technology are compiled but no one reviews them and follows up to ensure security and compliance measures are implemented, followed, and maintained, it is not worth the bytes it is taking up on some lost, isolated server—whether in-house or on the cloud.

Let us touch briefly on traditional IT security procedures. They have a place in online and digital security and should not be looked at as a lesser priority or belonging to a different risk scheme. For example, processing and sanitizing retired IT assets are an important strategy for online and digital activity security, but keep in mind that those assets now include mobile devices such as phones, laptops, etc. Making sure to remove SIM cards, clicking the reset and/or reformat buttons, and wiping out apps, access, and identification content are prudent best practices. Logging a chain of custody of each device can provide for a foundation for indemnification and transfer of liability should a breach occur.

---

[5] CSO, White Paper: "The 4-Step Guide to Cloud Data Security," (August, 2013), http://www.csoonline.com/resources/.

INTERNAL RISK 3: MOBILE

Data traveling from corporate servers to unsecured personal devices to apps and into the cloud leaves a digital paper trail of copies everywhere along its route.[6]

Smartphones, tablets, flash drives—collectively understood under the label of "mobile"—if you believe the myriad of news articles, white papers, and industry blogs, these devices send shock waves of terror into the hearts of security and risk managers. "Mobile security" is a buzzword that tries to encompass the emerging trend of personal portable devices that have made their way into everyday business operations, routines, and transactions. The statistics are staggering (see Figure 2.1), and more are published everyday.

In the past, some of these devices, such as the tablet or the personal device assistant (PDA) (remember those?), were confined to the area of field force automation (FFA). UPS and FedEx still rely on that kind of technology as the carrier stands there waiting for you to sign on a device that captures your signature and inserts it into a database to verify delivery and receipt. These customized handhelds had a very narrow specific purpose. They did their job and they did it well. But today's devices add the "smart" element, meaning that the device is multipurpose and the data it collects can be manipulated in a number of ways for a number of business ends. The new devices also do not have to be customized (an expensive proposition) but can be "programmed" through apps, a much less expensive option considering the off-the-shelf tools, app developers, and interns readily available to assist in their creation if they have not been created already. The phrase, "There's an app for that," rings more true than ever.

Employees, managers, executives, vendors, clients—they all bring these devices with them wherever they go. Public television (PBS) has aired a couple of documentaries now showing how society has adopted these smart technologies and has integrated them into every aspect of their lives—personal and professional. When was the last time you left your cell phone at home? For many it has become automatic and an attachment that is an extension of themselves. They feel lost without it, and for business, this means that they also feel less productive. This fact is backed up with statistics that demonstrate what mobile technology is being used for.

SearchSecurity.com polled 768 IT and security professionals in April 2013.[7] Its findings showed that 79% of the respondents used mobile for personal e-mail, instant messaging, and chat; 68% for web browsing and productivity tools; 59% for accessing social media; 49% for accessing their corporate intranet; and 41% for corporate applications. In addition, according to a 2013 Forrester Research report, 37% of employees are working from multiple locations and 82% are using mobile apps for that purpose.[8] As the numbers indicate, there is a lot of potential for corporate security concerns via multiple unsecured access points that have access to confidential and important corporate data and applications.

---

[6] Caleb Sima, "5 Approaches to Securing Your Company's Mobile Data," Venture Beat, (June 3, 2013), http://venturebeat.com/2013/06/03/mobile-data-security-approaches/.

[7] Kris Lovejoy, "10 Security Essentials Every CIO Needs to Know," Security Intelligence Blog (September 4, 2013), http://securityintelligence.com/10-security-essentials-every-cio-needs-to-know/?goback=.gde_80784_member_270966702#.

[8] "Managing the 21st Century Workforce: How Mobility is Transforming the Enterprise," (August 21, 2013), ITProPortal.com, http://www.itproportal.com/2013/08/21/managing-the-21st-century-workforce-how-mobility-is-transforming-the-enterprise/.

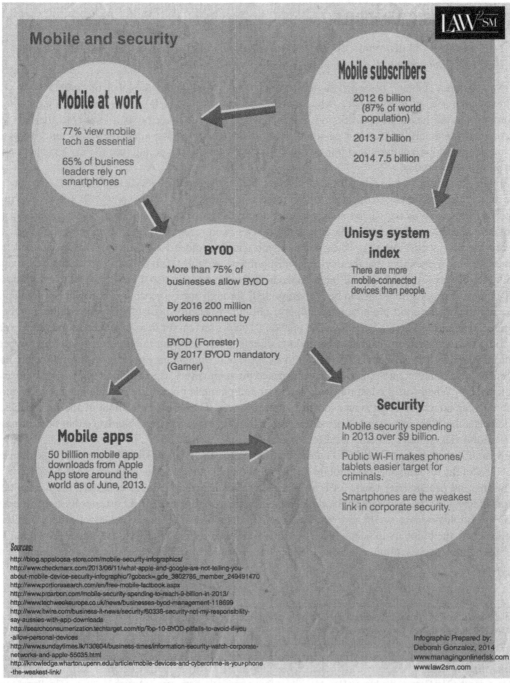

FIGURE 2.1

This new world of Bring-Your-Own-Device (BYOD), Bring-Your-Own-Apps (BYOA), Bring-Your-Own-Network (BYON), and Bring-Your-Own-Anything (BYOx) puts additional pressure on security and risk management professionals to figure out how to protect the company, the devices, and, most importantly, the data from being digitally whisked away. Concerns range from lost or stolen devices, to malicious apps, to Wi-Fi hijacking, to data theft, and more. A recent SearchSecurity.com survey indicates that the top mobile security fears include data leakage (45%); unauthorized access (41%); device loss/theft (40%); application security (38%); and compliance/malware concerns (tied each at 28%).[9] In addition, "79% of business in the United States, Canada, United Kingdom, Germany, and Japan had a mobile security incident in the past year, with the costs proving substantial."[10]

With these kinds of risk concerns, why do businesses permit BYOD, etc.? According to a 2013 BYOD & Mobile Security Report by Holger Schulze, which surveyed over 160,000 information security professionals, three key reasons topped the list: greater employee satisfaction (55%), improved mobility (54%), and increased productivity (51%).[11] Regarding employee satisfaction, Claire Hatton, Google's Industry Director, puts it this way: "People want to work the way they live…happy employees are loyal employees."[12] Improved mobility brings up the interesting new employee demand for the ability to "swarm," which is useful when required to complete an urgent task, respond in a timely manner to take advantage of a business opportunity, or resolve a customer problem via collaboration tools. Mobile connectivity goes beyond just telecommuting and does bring up the issue of the blurred line between personal and professional time. As for productivity gains, a survey sponsored by Citrix and conducted by YouGov of 1250 small businesses across Europe, North America, and Australia found that "almost one in five (18 percent) small businesses are achieving productivity gains of more than 30 percent by adopting mobile work styles, enabling people to work whenever, wherever and however they choose."[13]

Thus, with justifiable business reasons to allow BYOD, including its inevitability, approaches for security, protection, and risk management focus on the device, the app, the user, and/or the data. Let us look at these risks and some solutions currently in use in more depth.

MOBILE DEVICE MANAGEMENT

Mobile device management (MDM) can take on a variety of looks, from inventory controls to containerization, which consists of setting up separate zones for business and personal on the device itself. MDM focuses on looking to secure the device itself, so if lost or stolen, remote wipe applications are usually employed to protect confidential data and remove the risk of unauthorized access. MDM does require monitoring of the unique device identifier (UDID). Signature detection technology via intrusion

---

[9] Kathleen Richards, "Enterprise Mobile Security by the Numbers," *TechTarget*, (August 1, 2013), http://searchsecurity.techtarget.com/feature/Enterprise-mobile-security-by-the-numbers.

[10] "Managing Mobile Security in South Africa," IT News Africa, (June, 2013), http://www.itnewsafrica.com/2013/06/managing-mobile-security-in-south-africa/.

[11] "Bring Your Own Device: Risks and Trends in Mobile and BYOD Security," Via Resource (2013), http://www.viaresource.com/media/20307/byod–risks_-trends-and-skills-in-byod-security.png.

[12] Spandas Lui, "Mobility's Lesser-Known Fact: It's Not just about BYOD," ZDNet (June 17, 2013), http://www.zdnet.com/au/mobilitys-lesser-known-fact-its-not-just-about-byod-7000016866/.

[13] Nathan Eddy, "YouGov Study: European Businesses Lead US on BYOD Management," (June 11, 2013), http://www.techweekeurope.co.uk/news/businesses-byod-management-118699.

prevention systems (IPS) can also be deployed. One last issue to keep in mind with MDM is device compatibility for seamless access to the company's network as well as for technical support. There are a number of mobile device brands with multiple models and operating systems. Employees will select a personal device based on their needs and the features they want personally, not necessarily considering what will integrate best with the company's systems. IT and management need to have the conversation if there will be limitations to which brands and models will be supported by IT or if the company would need a support service agreement with the mobile service provider. If IT is expected to support all the brands in-house, IT will need the resources for staff, training, and tools to prepare to support these devices. We know that resources are not unlimited, so where the funding for this comes from can become a budget concern that was completely overlooked by all parties involved. In addition, each device has its own security concerns that then adds another level of security complexity.

MOBILE APP MANAGEMENT

Mobile app management (MAM) leaves device control up to the user and instead focuses on ensuring that the apps being used are free of security concerns such as malware and botnets. Companies have taken different approaches to this, from setting up company enterprise app stores with a selected inventory of approved apps, to providing a list of approved and blacklisted apps from open marketplaces such as the Apple App Store or the Android Marketplace. Antivirus software is an important component to MAM. It is important to make sure that you choose security software that caters to all operating systems such as iOS, Android, Windows, etc. According to NQ Mobile's 2013 Midyear Mobile Security Report, there were over 51,000 new mobile malware threats infecting 21 million mobile devices in the first half of 2013 alone.[14] One issue that connects MDM and MAM is the UDID—"78% of the most popular free Android apps identify the user's UDID and 6% of iOS apps do similar."[15] Using this information can allow for security incidents.

MOBILE DATA PROTECTION

Considering that the major concern with mobile device usage in business is data loss, some security professionals are focusing their efforts on protecting the data itself, using mobile data protection (MDP) strategies, also known as mobile content management (MCM). Encryption, which is coding information to prevent unauthorized views of the data and to ensure secure data transfers while preventing data loss or theft, is a predominant strategy of MDP. Encryption is not to be considered the sole silver bullet, however, and at the 2013 Black Hat Conference in Las Vegas, a session declaring a "cryptopocalypse" on the horizon emphasized the need for stronger keys and protocols.[16] Another strategy focuses on not allowing any data to reside on the device itself, only allowing the device to serve as a dummy access terminal to an internally secure intranet. The use of data/content lockers—software that creates

---

[14] Jeff Goldman, "51,000 New Mobile Malware Threats Uncovered in First Half of 2013," eSecurity Planet (July 29, 2013), http://www.esecurityplanet.com/mobile-security/51000-new-mobile-malware-threats-uncovered-in-first-half-of-2013.html.
[15] "Infosecurity—83% of Mobile Apps Exhibit Risky Behavior." (July 31, 2013), http://www.infosecurity-magazine.com/view/33726/83-of-mobile-apps-exhibit-risky-behavior/?goback=.gde_3802786_member_263448233.
[16] Patrick Lambert, "Are we Heading for a 'Cryptopocalypse'?" (TechRepublic, August 28, 2013), http://www.techrepublic.com/blog/it-security/are-we-heading-for-a-cryptopocalypse/.

corporate content containers that provide a central location for needed documents, reports, etc.—is one way to achieve this. An example is the AirWatch Secure Content Locker™ (SCL) from the AirWatch, LLC,[17] which can be used by employees as an app on their iPhones, iPads, and iPod Touch devices. In addition, the implementation of virtual private networks (VPN) can lead to security enhancements.

MOBILE USER MANAGEMENT

A recent LinkedIn discussion group focused on information security asked the question of whether we can firewall human nature. The answers varied but seemed to form around two distinct attitudes toward end users—either they were a security professional's worst nightmare or they were the answer to making security nightmares go away. The first school of thought leads one to believe that only technological solutions to mobile security will ensure protection for the company, as humans cannot be trusted, are self-interested, and will circumvent any controls you put into place for their own end; the second school of thought believes technology is not enough because humans cannot be trusted, are self-interested, and will circumvent any controls you put in place for their own end, and therefore the only way to protect the company is to make the users the solution (see the box below). I believe both approaches have truth in them, but are not comprehensive enough if used to the exclusion of the other, and so need to be used in parallel.

2013 Harris Interactive Mobile User Behavior Survey[18] findings, commissioned by CTIA[19]
- Less than 50% of wireless device owners use passwords or PINs on their devices
- Only 50% encrypt financial data when conducting online banking
- Less than 1/3 use antivirus software on mobile devices
- 45% do not see cybersecurity on their mobile devices as a threat in the same way they see it on their computers

[18]"Mobile Devices and Cybercrime: Is Your Phone the Weakest Link?" (June 5, 2013), Knowledge@Wharton, http://knowledge.wharton.upenn.edu/article/mobile-devices-and-cybercrime-is-your-phone-the-weakest-link/.
[19]"CTIA-the Wireless Association Home Page." accessed February 23, 2014, http://www.ctia.org/.

Passwords

We have seen the presentations full of statistics of the most common passwords—"password," "123456," and others. We know as risk management and security professionals how much we emphasize the importance of strong passwords. We create masks for passwords, with specific requirements (capital letters, symbols, numbers, and letters). We relate to users the horror stories of using the same password for multiple accounts while at the same time acknowledging that there is a limit as to how many passwords an individual can really remember without having some kind of reminder system (Post-it notes or a password file entitled PASSWORD.DOC) that lead to other security concerns. We offer suggestions using mnemonics and rebuke the use of family and pet names. We send out reminders every 3–6 months requesting they change the passwords they no longer remember, since they enable "remember me" and automatic log-ins for all the security log-ins (although we had recommended otherwise). And yet, cracking passwords is one of the most common ways hackers enter our secured

---

[17] "Enterprise Mobility Management." accessed February 23, 2014, http://www.air-watch.com/.

systems. Does this bear truth to the idea that passwords are really only "security theater," much like the pat downs by the Transportation Security Administration (TSA) officers at our airports?

Acknowledging the limits of passwords, various substitutes have been offered and are currently under development:

1. Long Passwords—Composed of 50 characters or more, they have been proven not to be unbreakable, and psychologically users cannot even fathom the idea of memorizing such a long key.
2. Passphrases—Instead of just one series of numbers or combination of numbers and texts, the passphrase is composed of a series of words converted into a password that would be hard to guess.
3. Multifactor Authentication—The requirement of more than one level of verification for access to a device, app, and/or data. It requires users to provide at least two identification factors— could be something they have (ID card, flash drive), something they know (password, security question answer), something they are (biometrics), and/or something they receive (such as an access code sent via SMS text to their mobile devices).[20]
4. Picture Gesture Authentication—Prof. Gail-Joon Ahn, at Arizona State University, is leading a project to create an authentication process that bypasses traditional passwords and have "users select images to create unique three-part patterns for access…using gestures such as a tap, a circle, or drawing a line on an image."[21]
5. Biometrics—The use of physical and/or behavioral characteristics to verify an individual's identity as a security measure has taken on a new urgency considering the lack of protection of passwords and encryption keys. Fingerprint analysis, eye retina scans, and voice pattern recognition have all been explored in the real world and in science fiction (remember the movie *Minority Report* and Tom Cruise's eye replacement incident?). The Apple iPhone 5S was announced with additional fanfare because it offered fingerprint sensor authentication to open the phone and buy products.[22] The sensor is embedded on the "Home" button of the phone and the biometric is only stored on the device itself, making it unavailable to other apps or servers. But biometrics is set to come of age, as smart devices become more advanced and nuanced via specific apps and connected plug-ins. Take, for example, Nymi,[23] a wristband that contains a voltmeter to read a heartbeat. According to a recent *New York Times* article, Karl Martin, one of its creators from the University of Toronto, states that one of its most secure features is that while a heart can be broken, a heartbeat cannot[24] (paraphrased). Another example is the work being done at the University of California, Berkeley, on a cheap headset that will be able to read your brain waves to verify your thoughts and, so, the password that you are thinking of.[25] Another

---

[20] What Apple and Google are Not Telling You about Mobile Device Security (Infographic), (June 11, 2013), http://www.checkmarx.com/2013/06/11/what-apple-and-google-are-not-telling-you-about-mobile-device-security-infographic/?goback=.gde_3802786_member_249491470.

[21] Joe Kullman, "Picture Password System Promising to Strengthen Online Security," (Arizona State University, August 7, 2013), http://fullcircle.asu.edu/2013/08/9316/.

[22] Robert Lemos, "iPhone 5S, 5C, iOS7 Provide New Mobile Security Features," eweek (September 10, 2013), http://www.eweek.com/security/iphone-5s-5c-ios7-provide-new-mobile-security-features.html/.

[23] For more information, see http://www.getnymi.com.

[24] Somini Sengupta, "Machines Made to Know You, by Touch, Voice, Even by Heart," NYTimes Blog (September 10, 2013), http://bits.blogs.nytimes.com/2013/09/10/beyond-passwords-new-tools-to-identify-humans/?_php=true&_type=blogs&_php=true&_type=blogs&goback=.gde_80784_member_272483256&_r=1#!.

[25] Ibid.

concept being considered for development is the "password pill" that contains a microchip and battery and is activated by stomach acid and would emit a radio signal.[26] A small, ingestible microchip was revealed by Regina E. Duncan, former Defense Advanced Research Projects Agency director and current Google executive (2014). She called it an "electronic tattoo."[27] It is interesting to note that in that same article that quoted Ms. Duncan, the journalist Christina Sarich also offers up a tidbit that microchipping is being included in health care bills, specifically the Health Care Affordability Act. This turned out to be an untrue rumor based on a post that appeared in NationalReport.net, a satirical news publication.[28]

6. Hard Keys—Securing a physical device to secure your mobile device seems a little oxymoronic, but it does offer another level of security. The problem is, how many "things" do users want to carry and how convenient is it to always connect the "things" before being able to get to do what you need to do on the phone or tablet? This convenience question applies to all of these password substitutes. The International Association of Information Technology Asset Managers (IAITAM) produced an infographic on mobile security, which states that "the challenge is to keep an easy access and high level of user experience with a high level of security in order to maintain the best mobile usage adoption, engagement and productivity."[29] What if the "thingy" is worn by the user, such as a personalized coded finger ring?

As we leave the password discussion, one last example of password fallibility comes to mind. In March 2014, Kashmir Hill, Forbes blogger on all things related to technology, virtual currency, and security, put out a cautionary notice regarding the address labels on the *New Yorker* magazines that were mailed out. Apparently, the user's online password was on the address label. This has since been fixed, but at last review the last four digits of the person's credit card was still present on the label.[30] If your company still mails hard copies out, what is on the mailing label? If your company executives receive magazines, etc., what is on that mailing label?

Hot spot issue

How many of our employees, including high-level executives, meet up with clients, potential clients, third-party vendors, etc. at a coffee shop or restaurant that touts free Wi-Fi connection for its patrons? These "hot spots" offer access, but do so without security, leaving the Wi-Fi connection open for malicious interference.

---

[26] Concept discussed by Motorola's head of research, Regina Dugan, who equates it with taking a vitamin every morning. Robert MacPherson, "'Password Fatigue' Haunts Internet Masses as Experts Ponder the Future of the Password," (The Sidney Morning Herald, June 26, 2013), http://www.smh.com.au/digital-life/consumer-security/password-fatigue-haunts-internet-masses-as-experts-ponder-the-future-of-the-password-20130626-2ovxw.html.

[27] Christina Sarich, "Getting Ready to Microchip the Entire Human Race," (March 31, 2014), http://naturalsociety.com/getting-ready-microchip-entire-human-race/.

[28] Sally Dennen, MSN News, "Rumor: Obamacare Requires Microchip Implants", (July 22, 2013), http://news.msn.com/rumors/rumor-obamacare-requires-microchip-implants.

[29] Tristan de Broucker, "Mobile Security Infographics," Appaloosa-Store Blog (June 14, 2013), http://blog.appaloosa-store.com/mobile-security-infographics/.

[30] Kashmir Hill, Forbes blog, The Not-So-Private-Parts, "Why You Need to Rip the Mailing Label off Magazines As Soon As They Arrive," (March 7, 2014), http://www.forbes.com/sites/kashmirhill/2014/03/07/why-you-need-to-rip-the-mailing-label-off-magazines-as-soon-as-they-arrive/.

As security and risk management professionals strive to accommodate the need for on-demand, off-company-site network access, IT needs to consider how to create the right wireless access infrastructure that can "scale to support many high-speed devices without service interruption; easily integrate users' diverse devices; provide secure, reliable access to enterprise applications based on user's identities; and help eliminate inconsistent wireless performance."[31]

Working with what wireless service providers already have available, one solution is the requirement of secured hub spots, available on the device itself either through a mobile modem or an app. For some regulated industries, this is not just a recommendation but a requirement for compliance in terms of the duty to maintain client information security and confidentiality.[32]

Talking loudly

Talking loudly is more than just rude behavior when the talk is on a mobile device, in a crowded venue, and the dialogue consists of company data—it is a full-fledged security threat.[33] Overheard conversations, or its more negative label—eavesdropping—can provide a way for someone to steal your information. Reminding employees of this little overlooked fact can go a long way. If the conversation is meant to be private, then some precautions should take place, such as trying to find a more private location to continue the discussion or put it off until you can get to it. Also remember, as Ken Hess says in his blog, "restrooms are not private."[34] Cover your mouth as you give certain personal and private information—yes, hackers can read lips! Certain information (account numbers, security answers) should not be disclosed via phone (or e-mail for that matter), and needs to be face to face or another secured channel.

Policies

In Chapter 1, I described how policies can help lay out expectations for everyone in the company. This is especially true for mobile and BYOD policies as the device use blurs the line between personal and professional many times. However, currently less than 14% of companies have a fully developed mobile security policy[35] and 60% of companies do not have a BYOD policy in place.[36] The last statistic is from the Acornis 2013 Data Protection Trade Research Report conducted by the Ponemon Institute in July 2013. The report also found that 80% of organizations have not educated employees on BYOD best practices, risks, or procedures, and that nearly a quarter of the 40% that did have BYOD policies made exceptions for executives.[37]

---

[31] Aerohive Networks, *The iEverything Enterprise*, (2012), http://www.aerohive.com/pdfs/Aerohive_Whitepaper_iEverything_Enterprise.pdf.

[32] An example would be for attorneys, those who do not use a secure hub are in violation of the American Bar Association's Model Rules of Ethics, as well as potentially in violation of their own state bar association code of conduct, which in turn could lead to a penalty and even disbarment.

[33] Ken Hess, "Overheard Conversations: When Heightened Mobile Security Fails to Protect," ZDNet (July 9, 2013), http://www.zdnet.com/overheard-conversations-when-heightened-mobile-security-fails-to-protect-7000017834/.

[34] Ibid.

[35] Dan Gendro, "Mobile Security Policies at 14% of Companies," (Mobile Commerce Press, August 29, 2013), http://www.mobilecommercepress.com/mobile-security-policies-in-place-at-only-14-percent-of-businesses/858463/.

[36] Chris Preimesberger, "Scary BYOD Data Protection Trends: 10 Common Problems," eweek (July 22, 2013), http://www.eweek.com/storage/slideshows/scary-byod-data-protection-trends-10-common-problems/.

[37] Ibid.

EXAMPLE OF A MOBILE/BYOD POLICY

(The following list of considerations for creating a BYOD policy comes from the Digital Government Toolit[38] Web site. Where it indicates "government," you can substitute with the appropriate business entity label, company, organization, etc., with minor modifications.)

- Technical approach
    - Virtualization
    - Walled garden
    - Limited separation
- Roles and responsibilities
    - Agency
    - User
    - Help/service desk(s)
    - Carrier technical support
- Incentives for government and individuals
    - Survey employees on benefits and challenges
    - Consider voluntary versus mandatory participation in BYOD program and impact on terms of service
- Education, use, and operation
    - Establish orientation, training, and user agreements
    - Establish associated policies collaboratively with union representative
    - Ensure compliance with Fair Labor Standards Act (FLSA) requirements (e.g., institute policies to ensure nonexempt employees do not conduct work after hours unless directly authorized/instructed)
    - Consider impact of connectivity and data plan needs for chosen technical approach (e.g., virtualization) on employee reimbursement
    - Implement telework agreements consistent with the Telework Enhancement Act and Office of Management and Budget implementation requirements
- Security
    - Assess and document risks in:
        - Information security (operating system compromise due to malware, device misuse, and information spillover risks)
        - Operations security (personal devices may divulge information about a user when conducting specific activities in certain environments)
        - Transmission security (protections to mitigate transmission interception)
    - Ensure consistency with government-wide standards for processing and storing Federal information
    - Assess data security with BYOD versus the devices being replaced
    - Securely design systems for interoperability (government data vs personal data)
- Privacy
    - Identify the right balance between personal privacy and organizational security
    - Document process for employee to safeguard personal data if/when government wipes the device
- Ethics/legal questions
    - Define "acceptable use" from both government and individual perspective
    - Address legal discovery (including confiscation rights) and liability issues (e.g., through predefined opt-in requirements in terms of service)
    - Consider implications for equal rights employment (e.g., disparity in quality of personal devices)
- Service provider(s)
    - Identify companies that could offer discounts to government employees
    - Assess opportunities to leverage the Federal Strategic Sourcing Initiative
    - Assess tax implications for reimbursement
- Devices and applications (apps)
    - Identify permitted and supported devices to prevent introduction of malicious hardware and firmware
    - Define content applications that are required, allowed, or banned, and consider use of MDM and mobile application management (MAM) enterprise systems to enforce policies [4]

Continued

EXAMPLE OF A MOBILE/BYOD POLICY—cont'd

> Adopt existing app development best practices to support device agnosticism and data portability across platforms
> Address app compatibility issues (e.g., accidental sharing of sensitive information due to differences in information display between platforms)
> Recommend approach to content storage (cloud vs device)
> Clarify ownership of the apps and data
> - Asset management
>   Disposal of device if replaced, lost, stolen, or sold, or employment is terminated (must remove government information before disposal)
>   Reporting and tracking lost/stolen personal devices
>   Replacement of personal lost devices if employee chooses not to replace with personal funds
> - Funding for service and maintenance

[38]"Bring Your Own Device," The White House, accessed February 23, 2014, http://www.whitehouse.gov/digitalgov/bring-your-own-device.

INTERNAL RISK 4: PEOPLE

We started looking at the human risk in the discussion concerning mobile user management (MUM) and will continue with an in-depth look at the new workforce in Chapter 4. This section will discuss a few outlying issues that do not fall neatly into either category as a stand-alone but do need to be acknowledged and addressed.

EXECUTIVES

A security risk that is often overlooked in many companies is when executives are allowed exceptions to the security rules. Whether the result of perceived authority of the executive on behalf of IT, a power play on the part of the executive over IT, a deliberate decision on behalf of the executive team, or an oversight that grows in scope by each "special" request by an executive, these exceptions are an increasingly concerning security threat. This is the kind of threat that needs to be managed tactfully on behalf of IT, and with the full understanding, cooperation, and support of the executive level. One exception can create a slippery slope. On the other hand, sometimes exceptions have to be made. In such circumstances, it is essential that the IT team has the appropriate security measures in place, works with the executive to ensure the measures are not circumvented, and limits the time that the exception can exist, if possible.

THIRD PARTY ACCESS (VENDORS, CUSTOMERS)

Companies do not necessarily function in a vacuum. There are situations where a third party requires a certain amount of access to the company's network. IT plays a vital role in making sure business units understand that this can be a security/risk management issue and that IT needs to be involved in order to grant the access with the security measures required. Sometimes an individual in the unit may think nothing of just putting in their own ID and password to grant the vendor access, especially if it is for a one-time instance or a short period. As an added measure, this should be addressed in the appropriate IT policy.

In this digital age, companies are also striving to develop client or customer portals, allowing a certain amount of self-help without the need of company staff, such as access to a customer's account, etc. Security and risk management measures need to be in place to ensure that they only get the information that pertains to them, that it is only the information they need for a particular transaction, and that whatever input they make can be scanned for accuracy, integrity, and potential risks (such as malware). Sometimes companies may be concerned about security measures making it too inconvenient for customers and demotivating the use of the portal, but something to keep in mind is MacDonnell Ulsch's[39] message of caution: "A customer's toxic IP address is every bit as dangerous as a malicious IP address originating directly from a hacker."[40]

IT/SECURITY PROFESSIONAL SHORTAGE

It is estimated that the so-called cybersecurity talent crunch will soon reach crisis mode. According to an article about the scarcity of IT security professionals, cybersecurity specialist James Gosler, chief technology officer at Dell SecureWorks and a former CIA employee, believes that "no more than 1000 people (in 2012) had the necessary skills to tackle tough cybersecurity tasks. The nation's companies and government agencies need at least 30,000 to secure their systems, he estimates. According to assessments by the International Information Systems Security Certification Consortium, or (ISC)2 more than 300,000 trained cybersecurity professionals are needed (worldwide)."[41] This impending crisis can also seem like a golden opportunity for individuals looking for a new career and/or a career change, as well as the educational institutions that will prepare them. Of course time is not on anyone's side, as preparation takes a specific period of studying time and the most skilled security professionals have developed their talent over many years of on-the-job experience or cultivation.

But new cybersecurity professionals are needed, not just for the everyday security tasks that will keep our businesses and governments operating but also for the long-term, high-level, security strategic thinking required for the changing nature of information security leadership.

So what can companies do to ensure that they have the professionals with the right security and risk management skills?

- Use aggressive recruiting tactics
- Create in-house farm teams to develop internal talent
- Offer in-house security certification preparation programs
- Develop partnerships with universities and other educational institutions to assist with curriculum development and internship opportunities
- Offer higher salaries to those professionals already in-house and treat them really well
- Poach from competitors (beg, borrow, or steal talent approach)
- Offer hacking and cyber-defense competitions at various educational levels to help identify rising security talent

---

[39] CEO and chief analyst at ZeroPoint Risk Research, LLC, a Boston-based consultancy focused on global risk management and related services.
[40] Kathleen Edwards, "Cybersecurity: Global Risk Management Moves Beyond Regulations," *TechTarget*, http://searchsecurity.techtarget.com/feature/Cybersecurity-Global-risk-management-moves-beyond-regulations, September 2013.
[41] Robert Lemos, "Bridging the IT Security Skills Gap," *TechTarget*, http://searchsecurity.techtarget.com/feature/Bridging-the-IT-security-skills-gap, September 2013.

- Use cloud managed and managed security services to lessen demand of internal security personnel
- Work with the military and/or government for training and "co-use" of security personnel

As for leadership, discussions concerning the roles of Chief Information Officer (CIO), Chief Privacy Officer, IT Manager, Data Manager, and now, Chief Digital Officer (CDO) are changing the landscape of responsibilities, expectations, and compensation. George Westerman offers some insight in a *Harvard Business Review* blog post about whether your CIO should be the CDO.[42] Just what should a Chief Digital Officer do in a company?

- Create a compelling and unifying digital vision
- Energize the company around digital possibilities
- Coordinate digital activities
- Coordinate digital investments
- Help to rethink products and processes for the digital age and foster digital innovation
- Provide critical digital tools and/or resources
- Energize a busy workforce regarding digital use
- Generate shared understanding of digital concerns with the senior executive team
- Emphasize the importance of governance and policy in the digital space
- Devise appropriate synergies
- Help build a clean digital technology platform[43]

As you read the above list, does it outline things that a CIO should not be involved in or accountable for? Is it a better strategy to keep the CIO and CDO functions separate? Can they work together effectively and peacefully, each in their own lane, or is there too much overlap that would lead to a power struggle and delays on decision making and project completion? It may be too early to tell. We do not have many CDOs out there yet, but in 2012, Starbucks Coffee Company hired Adam Brotman as its CDO. If we Google him today is he still in the position? How has he done? Are there now other CDOs?

One major responsibility lacking in Westerman's list is that it does not mention anything regarding security and/or risk management in the digital space. Does that mean that security is a separate function outside of the domain of the CDO, or is security so inherent it is implied in the list, or was it just an oversight by Westerman? Regardless of the answer, my recommendation would be to add it on.

EXTERNAL RISKS

Outside of the company technologies are being developed, created, modified, changed, and adopted that can present security risks that will affect a company's security even if they were not foreseen by the company. On one hand, because of digital technology, the information regarding these impending threats is available in a variety of formats and price points. On the other hand, because of digital technology, the amount of information can be overwhelming and cause IT departments to struggle with how to read, consume, analyze, and take advantage of the information while being constrained by staff, budget, and resource limitations. We review some basic external risk categories below, but the specific types within each category of external risks grow everyday.

---

[42] George Westerman, "Should Your CIO be Chief Digital Officer?" (Harvard Business Review, August 2, 2013), http://blogs.hbr.org/2013/08/should-your-cio-be-chief-digit/.
[43] See note 42.

EXTERNAL RISK 1: TECHNOLOGY ADVANCES

The news and trade reports are full of announcements of new technology and digital gadgets. Most of them are developed with the understanding that mobile connectivity is an essential component. Nothing stands alone anymore. Our devices need to "talk" to each other to be able to enjoy their fullest benefits. However, this connectivity also provides opportunities for security concerns to develop.

- Google Glass (GG)[44]—the eyewear of the future that records what you see and then allows you to share it with anyone and everyone via digital channels. This is just one of a series of wearable computing devices currently available but by no means the last word on this genre of digital tool, as many more are in development. It has made headlines with privacy concerns and security concerns, including a bug that was recently corrected by Google in terms of the possibility of the glass reading a malicious QR code and wrecking havoc on an internal network system. The GG also requires automation and there are no true access restrictions measures in place. But apps for GG are being developed and more will come.
- Smart TV—your television is watching you. If a smart TV behaves like a personal computer (PC), shouldn't it be viewed through the lens of technology security just like a PC? Also, where the TV is located is an interesting factor for the security question. If it is in the home, is it safe? Or is it just outside of the company's security control? If it is a smart TV at home and the employee (including an executive) is using it for business-related work, does it fall under any current IT policy—including BYOD—to help guide its use and safeguard company data? If the smart TV is in a business conference room, or a hotel conference center, or a vendor's or customer's office venue, but company data is being accessed from it, are security measures in place?
- Home/Office Security Systems—sensor networks that deliver real-time information via digital networks. As companies strive to do more with less, using technology to gather information and digitally process it to produce certain outcomes (such as locking doors), new access points into the corporate information system are often created that are often overlooked. It is vital for these systems to have limited access into, if at all, the main company's IT systems so as to limit potential exposure and security breaches.
- Medical Implants—personal access to personal data. The vulnerabilities of implanted medical devices were supposed to be the subject of a major presentation at a recent Black Hat Conference. But the scheduled speaker, Barnaby Jack, died before the session took place.[45] Just having the presentation title on the program, however, brought a new topic of discussion into security circles. The implications that medical implants that are digitally connections to information systems outside the physical body could provide security breaches leading to loss of medical records or even worse, death, was not something many had thought about. Add to this that the medical and health care industries are adopting IT at an increasing rate, using it to digitize patient records, lab results, drug prescriptions, surgery schedules, etc. My current physician walks into our appointment with a laptop, and another one with a tablet. Everything is right there in front of the doctor, so I cannot fib and say I do not remember what he told me the last time. How is this relevant to corporations? Consider that most high-level executives, as

---

[44] "Google Glass," accessed February 23, 2014, http://www.google.com/glass/start/.
[45] Chenda Ngak, "5 Scariest Cybersecurity Threats at Black Hat, Defcon," CBS News (August 7, 2013), http://www.cbsnews.com/news/5-scariest-cybersecurity-threats-at-black-hat-defcon/.

they age, may require medical assistance. Sometimes the very information that they are getting medical help can start a series of assumptions in the marketplace regarding the stability of the company itself. If medical systems are interconnected, there is the possibility of medical espionage to ensure a certain medical outcome for the executive that can determine a certain financial outcome for the company. I know, so *Bourne Identity*, but it can happen.

EXTERNAL RISK 2: CLOUD STORAGE

The concept of storing data, files, and other important and/or sensitive information off-site from a company's premises is not new. It offers protection via distance and redundancy, with the idea that two security incidents (whether disaster or breach) cannot happen at the same time in two different places relating to the same data—and if you lost it once, you still have a copy to restore from in fairly close proximity. The difference is that today's technology storage takes place digitally through file transfer via the cloud (Internet) instead of through physical transfer on CDs, tapes, cartridges, etc. Copies of important files can be transported to a second and/or other multiple locations in a relatively short amount of time—minutes even—without the use of a secured van with security guards. On top of that, because it is all in a digital format, the copy is as good in quality as the original.

Upload is quick and easy, and so is the access and restoration of data if it is compromised, saving time, money, and resources and getting the company back on track as soon as possible. That is the promise of cloud computing. But as Jaime Titchener points out in his *IT Governance* blog, "effective cybersecurity is a balance between people, processes, and technology."[46]

The National Institute of Standards and Technology (NIST) defines the cloud as "a model for enabling ubiquitous, convenient, on-demand network access to a shared pool of configurable computing resources (e.g., networks, servers, storage, applications, and services) that can be rapidly provisioned and released with minimal management effort or service provider interaction."[47]

From that definition, we can extract that the cloud has five general characteristics: On-demand self-service; Broad network access; Resource pooling; Rapid elasticity; and Measured service. It can be offered with a variety of options depending on the amount of control and risk a company is comfortable with:

- Software as a Service (SaaS)—the client uses the provider's applications on the provider's infrastructure
- Platform as a Service (PaaS)—the client uses its own applications on the provider's infrastructure
- Infrastructure as a Service (IaaS)—the client uses its own resources over the provider's infrastructure

Lastly, the cloud can be provided in a variety of deployment methods: private, community, public, and/or hybrid, each one defined by the ultimate classification of user of the cloud service, from private entity to academic or government institution.

Security concerns with cloud computing usually fall within four categories:

1. Egress policies governing input or upload devices into the cloud as well as preventing unauthorized uploads of malware, via firewalls, proxies, etc.

---

[46] Jamie Titchener, "Is Effective CyberSecurity a Balance Between People, Process and Technology?" (August 29, 2013) http://blog.itgovernance.co.uk/is-effective-cyber-security-a-balance-between-people-process-and-technology/.

[47] "The NIST Definition of Cloud Computing," NIST, accessed February 23, 2014, http://csrc.nist.gov/publications/nistpubs/800-145/SP800-145.pdf.

2. Protecting data once it is uploaded to the cloud to prevent leakages and ensure integrity of the data.
3. Evaluating cloud provider risk and usage, including the provider's security responsibilities and controls.
4. Protecting data from being downloaded from the cloud by whom it should not be, whether that is by locating compromised users, eliminating backdoors, or preventing tracking attacks.[48]

One of the currently evolving principles in the cloud environment is the concept of shared security responsibility between the cloud service provider and the client or cloud tenant so the four categories above are covered. Part of this reasoning comes from the client not feeling totally confident in the provider's ability to protect the client's data, so they feel "sharing" the responsibility gives them more control over the risks. However, a study conducted by the Ponemon Institute examining the perceptions and current practices relating to security and the cloud found that over 60% of the respondents felt that the cloud provider was primarily responsible for protecting data, especially if the client was using SaaS.[49] It is for this reason that Eric Holmquist, managing director at Accume Partners, a governance, risk, and compliance management firm, emphasizes that "it is very important to have very clear processes, policies, procedures and expectations about how things are going to be managed."[50] For client companies, this means understanding that by using the cloud you have a security "movement from a technologically managed solution (in-house IT) to a contractually managed solution (with a cloud service provider)."[51]

This can make some risk management and security professionals a little concerned since some aspects of security control are now out of their hands. To prepare for this transition, some due diligence is required: establish a cloud computing policy with protocols and guidelines, and determine roles and responsibilities within the company and the liaison with the provider; read and review all documents provided by the cloud provider, including any certifications and third-party audit reports; find out if there are any third-party dependencies on the part of the provider; conduct an on-site visit to see firsthand what security measures are in place and how the site is maintained; make a trial with some data to test if the interface and access controls meet your needs; and maintain in-house technical expertise who can oversee the cloud computing process with the company's best interests in mind.

A cloud computing policy helps outline the who, what, when, where, why, and how of a company's use of cloud computing within a business impact context. Some basic questions to consider when developing the policy are listed below. They have been compiled from various sources including Dasha Bushmakin's EECNet Blog:

- Identify why and how the company is using cloud computing—what benefits does it hope to reap from this kind of technology, whether for storage, additional computing power, decentralized data access, etc.
- Identify the kinds of data, applications, files, and information that will be stored in the cloud.
- Identify who is responsible for cloud computing, including administrative management.

---

[48] "The 4-Step Guide to Cloud Data Security," accessed February 23, 2014, http://info.skyhighnetworks.com/4StepGuideTo DataSecurity_registration.html.
[49] "Attitudes Towards Data Protection and Encryption in the Cloud," Help Net Security, (June 27, 2013), http://www.net-security.org/secworld.php?id=15149.
[50] "Video: Asking the Right Questions Key to Managing Cloud Security Risks," *TechTarget*, (March 15, 2013) http://searchcompliance.techtarget.com/video/Video-Asking-the-right-questions-key-to-managing-cloud-security-risks.
[51] "Cloud Data Security: Customers and Providers Share Responsibility," *TechTarget*, http://searchcloudapplications.techtarget.com/tip/Cloud-data-security-Customers-and-providers-share-responsibility, 2013.

- Identify who will have access to the cloud data and how that access is granted.
- Define who can negotiate the service level agreement (SLA) and who can make changes to the SLA and/or the service security controls.
- List any other existing company policies that may be relevant to cloud computing.
- List any compliance and/or regulatory issues related to the company's use of cloud computing, such as privacy concerns, disclosures, etc.
- Is there an exit strategy and policy for removing data or application from the cloud and terminating the agreement with the service provider?[52]

CLOUD SERVICE LEVEL AGREEMENT POINTS FOR CONSIDERATION:

- Does the agreement allow for an annual security audit and certification by a third party?
- Does the agreement grant an option to terminate the agreement in the event of a security breach if the provider fails on any material measure?
- Does the provider use any assessment tools with control objectives, and can you as a client view the results?
- If the provider does not use any assessment tools, can it be required to respond to findings from a third-party assessment tool, such as the Cloud Security Alliance (CSA) Cloud Controls Matrix?[53]
- Are regular vulnerability tests run on the platform?
- What kind of security measures does the provider have in place?
- What kinds of authentication methods are in place for access to the stored data?
- What does the provider state is its responsibility in terms of recovery of lost data?
- What are the recovery time terms, recovery point objectives, and data integrity measures the provider has committed to? Are there any penalties if these are not met?
- If the penalties are based on fee liabilities, how many months are covered—12, 24, 36?
- Does the provider carry cyber liability insurance? Does that insurance cover clients' losses as well?
- Does the service being provided adhere to any regulations the company must be compliant with?
- What is the incident notification time frame from the provider to the client?
- Where are the servers located versus where are the cloud provider offices located and registered for jurisdictional purposes, should the need arise for litigation?
- Does the agreement outline rules for requesting and granting preservation of evidence and litigation holds of data and/or other cloud forensic legal issues?

[53]"Cloud Control Matrix (CCM)," accessed February 23, 2014, https://cloudsecurityalliance.org/research/ccm/.

EXTERNAL RISK 3: HACKING

[Companies] have firewalls, anti-viruses, various protections and highly skilled IT people. But hackers somehow infiltrate and access their data. Hackers, as many assume, are not isolated individuals who wear black jackets and gloves and have long hair. They are very smart, well-funded, and well organized. They do their homework and they know exactly what they are doing. And most importantly they know where the money is.[54]

---

[52] Dasha Bushmakin, "Creating a Cloud Security Policy," http://blog.eecnet.com/eecnetcom/bid/98520/Creating-a-cloud-security-policy, 2013.
[54] "94% of IT Security Breaches Go Undetected!" The Nation, (August 4, 2013). http://www.nation.lk/edition/biz-news/item/19776-94-of-it-security-breaches-go-undetected.html.

Do you remember the movie *Hackers* with a young Angelina Jolie and Johnny Lee Miller as teenage do-gooders who use skills to infiltrate top-secret information systems to expose the bad guys? Whether for good (ethical hacking) or for illicit intentions (criminal hacking), the process is the same—gain access; steal, move, or modify content; then exit with very little trace. Today's hacking scenarios adds two new dimensions: automation and community. These two create a third dimension—speed—that makes time more valuable a commodity than ever: time to detect the hack, time to remediate the breach, and time to protect the system. Just as technology has evolved to protect systems, technology has also evolved to break into systems. Hackers do not need to sit at their computers or desks anymore, they too are mobile. Most of their tool kits can be set to automatic, and so their equipment can actually be left on its own while the hacker takes on a secondary task. Hackers are not isolated anymore. The "malspace"[55] ecosystem is full of hacker forums and community hubs, even hacker marketplaces. Hackers also have a number of motives for their endeavors, such as making money, getting noticed, causing societal disruption, taking down corporations and governments, etc.

MALWARE

Malware is software that has a malicious intent to cause damage to computer systems. Sometimes the malware is an unintentional backdoor because of flaws, errors, or bad code. Sometimes the malware takes advantage of an intentional backdoor that was in place for maintenance and upgrades. Malware can be found on Web sites, mobile devices, and applications. It is interesting to note the existence of extensive malware headquarter organizations that "act like any other large business…they provide customer support, post regular newsletters, report downtime or new features, and even run regular contests to keep their affiliates engaged and motivated."[56]

a. Trojan Horses—harmful code contained inside apparently harmless programing or data in such a way that it can get control and do its chosen form of damage.[57] They are risky because they steal data without a victim's knowledge.

b. Ransomware—software that holds the user's data and/or system unstable until a payoff is made. Most of the time the system and/or data are not returned even after the ransom is delivered. Usually these are browser based, such as hidden iFrames or malicious Java code.

c. Spyware—software that serves in a monitoring function for surveillance and intelligence gathering. This is an area where the personal and professional overlap; a new type of spyware targeted to spouses or significant others who want to know what their mate is doing or where he/she is doing it. Many of them are available for download for the Android from the Google Play store, such as "Boyfriend Tracker" and "SMS, Whatsapp & Locate Spy."[58] This should be addressed in employee training.

---

[55] Online environment inhabited by hacker groups, criminal organizations, and espionage units. Steve Durbin, "Managing the Risks of Cyberspace," CIO Insight, (August 15, 2013), http://www.cioinsight.com/it-management/expert-voices/managing-the-risks-of-cyberspace/?utm_content=buffer5bf5a&utm_source=buffer&utm_medium=twitter&utm_campaign=Buffer&goback=.gde_38412_member_266878082#!.

[56] Agence France-Presse, "Russian 'Mobile Malware' Industry could Spread to Other Countries," (The Raw Story, August 2, 2013), http://www.rawstory.com/rs/2013/08/02/russian-mobile-malware-industry-could-spread-to-other-countries/.

[57] Santichai Dumpprasertkul, "What is Trojan Horse? - Definition from WhatIs.Com," accessed February 23, 2014, http://searchsecurity.techtarget.com/definition/Trojan-horse).

[58] Max Eddy, "Mobile Threat Monday: The Good and Bad of Android Bitcoin Apps," (Ziff Davis Media Inc, September 9, 2013), http://securitywatch.pcmag.com/mobile-security/315645-mobile-threat-monday-fantasy-football-dangers-spousal-spyware-and-trojan-bloons.

BOTNETS

Botnets are a group of computers controlled by a single source and that runs related software and scripts, usually for an illicit purpose. See Figure 2.2 for more information on Botnets.

> *Distributed Denial of Service Attacks (DDoS)—a type of Botnet attack that targets a single victim and overloads it so legitimate users are denied service. There are two types of DDoS attacks: "a network-centric attack which overloads a service by using up bandwidth and an application-layer attack which overloads a service or database with application calls."*[59]

ADVANCED PERSISTENT THREATS

An advanced persistent threat (APT) is a network attack in which an unauthorized person gains access to a network and stays there undetected for a long period of time.[60] As reported by Michael Cobb, the APT life cycle consists of 6 phases: reconnaissance, spear phishing attacks, establishes presence, exploration and pivoting, data extraction, and maintaining persistence.[61]

a. Phishing—the creation of fake popular Web sites; targets include online game services, online payment services, banks, and credit and financial organizations. These are effective and destructive because Web sites are "mission-critical pieces of an organization's operations."[62] Phishing attacks that are targeted are called "spear phishing," and hackers spend a lot of time getting to know the target's communication methods and the look and feel of their missives in order to impersonate accurately. Phishing is usually used with an additional communication channel such as e-mail to entice the user to go to the malicious Web site. Discovering a phishing attack is just the first step to remediating the threat. Communication with employees and other related company personnel is very important. "Don't Open the E-mail" e-mails need to be sent out. Then a little investigation is required to discover who attacked you, what tools they are using to attack you, where the attack originated from, when the attack began, and why they attacked you, or what was the motive, the goal of the attack?[63]

b. Watering Hole Attacks—using a phishing attack as a foundation, the "watering hole" attack studies who visits the site and why and then places malware to target future visitors in a "wait and pounce" mode. A recent example comes from San Francisco and a big oil company (name not disclosed). According to Nicole Perlroth, a *New York Times* journalist, "Hackers infected with malware the online menu of a Chinese restaurant that was popular with the employees [of

---

[59] "What is Distributed Denial-of-Service Attack (DDoS)?—Definition from WhatIs.Com," *TechTarget*, accessed February 23, 2014, http://searchsecurity.techtarget.com/definition/distributed-denial-of-service-attack.

[60] "What is Advanced Persistent Threat (APT)?—Definition from WhatIs.Com," *TechTarget*, accessed February 23, 2014, http://searchsecurity.techtarget.com/definition/advanced-persistent-threat-APT.

[61] Karthik, "Advanced Persistent Threats—Attack and Defense—InfoSec Institute," (Infosec Institute, June 13, 2013), http://resources.infosecinstitute.com/advanced-persistent-threats-attack-and-defense/.

[62] "Infosecurity—Businesses Lack Awareness of Poor Security Consequences," *Infosecurity*, (June 25, 2013), http://www.infosecurity-magazine.com/view/33117/businesses-lack-awareness-of-poor-security-consequences/?goback=.gde_38412_member_253010245.

[63] "Five Ws of Phishing Intelligence," *Malcovery Security*, (2013), accessed February 23, 2014, http://www.malcovery.com/the-five-ws-of-phishing-intelligenc/.

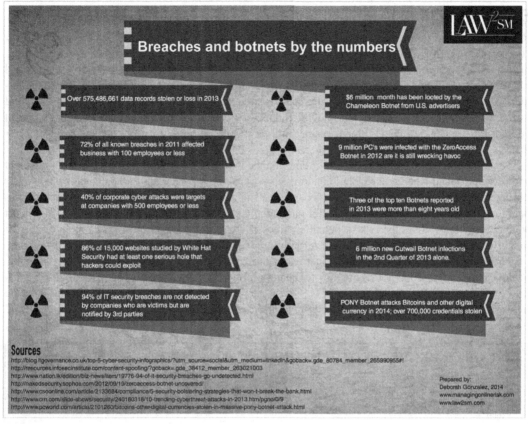

Breaches and botnets by the numbers

Over 575,486,661 data records stolen or loss in 2013

72% of all known breaches in 2011 affected business with 100 employees or less

40% of corporate cyber attacks were targets at companies with 500 employees or less

86% of 15,000 websites studied by White Hat Security had at least one serious hole that hackers could exploit

94% of IT security breaches are not detected by companies who are victims but are notified by 3rd parties

$6 million month has been looted by the Chameleon Botnet from U.S. advertisers

9 million PC's were infected with the ZeroAccess Botnet in 2012 are it is still wrecking havoc

Three of the top ten Botnets reported in 2013 were more than eight years old

6 million new Cutwail Botnet infections in the 2nd Quarter of 2013 alone.

PONY Botnet attacks Bitcoins and other digital currency in 2014; over 700,000 credentials stolen

Sources
http://blog.itgovernance.co.uk/top-5-cyber-security-infographics/?utm_source=social&utm_medium=linkedin&goback=.gde_60784_member_265990955#!
http://resources.infosecinstitute.com/content-spoofing/?goback=.gde_38412_member_263021003
http://www.nation.lk/edition/biz-news/item/19776-94-of-it-security-breaches-go-undetected.html
http://nakedsecurity.sophos.com/2012/09/19/zeroaccess-botnet-uncovered/
http://www.csoonline.com/article/2133684/compliance/5-security-bolstering-strategies-that-won-t-break-the-bank.html
http://www.crn.com/slide-shows/security/240160318/10-trending-cyberthreat-attacks-in-2013.htm/pgno/0/9
http://www.pcworld.com/article/2101260/bitcoins-other-digital-currencies-stolen-in-massive-pony-botnet-attack.html

Prepared by:
Deborah Gonzalez, 2014
www.managingonlinerisk.com
www.law2sm.com

FIGURE 2.2

the oil company]. When employees browsed the menu, they inadvertently downloaded code that gave attackers a foothold in the business's vast computer network."[64]

c. DHTML Form Hijacking—a kind of content spoofing, this code gathers user-inputted data from a dynamic fill-in or log-in form that has been hijacked. Web developers can use basic best practices to try to avoid these kinds of attacks, such as (1) validate user input for type, length, data range, format, etc.; (2) encode any user input that would be output by a Web application; (3) before deploying Web applications, test and scan them for vulnerabilities. If your company has hired a third-party Web application developer, go over these measures with them before launching the Web application live.[65]

---

[64] Perlroth, Nicole, "Hackers Lurking in Vents and Soda Machines," (New York Times, April 7, 2014), http://www.nytimes.com/2014/04/08/technology/the-spy-in-the-soda-machine.html?emc=edit_th_20140408&nl=todaysheadlines&nlid=33425801&_r=0.

[65] Bhavesh Naik, "Content Spoofing," (InfoSec Institute, August 2, 2013), http://resources.infosecinstitute.com/content-spoofing/?goback=.gde_38412_member_263021003.

EXTERNAL RISK 4: REGULATION

Regulation can be defined as "a rule of order having the force of law, prescribed by a superior or competent authority, relating to the actions of those under the authority's control."[66] We often think of regulations coming from the government and/or government agencies such as the Securities and Exchange Commission (SEC) or the Federal Trade Commission. Sometimes we may also see recommended guidelines from a professional industry association as it strives to self-regulate in new and evolving environments, such as the Federal Financial Institutions Examination Council's[67] recent attempt to offer guidelines for financial institutions on the compliant use of social media by their firms.

The debate about regulation is whether compliance with a regulation is effective risk management and/or security and whether a regulation addresses security concerns at all. Performance-based versus documentation supporting compliance to a particular rule or requirement[68] has been argued by many as being one of the reasons regulations do not guarantee the security most companies require. But to not adhere to the laws raises the risk of penalties, fines, close scrutiny of business operations, seizure of property, termination of the business, and/or jail time for key company executives.

There are a number of regulated industries in the United States including the obvious (financial, health care, food) and the not so obvious (education, nonprofits). See the List of US-regulated industries for a more comprehensive listing of U.S.-regulated industries, keeping in mind that many of these industries are also regulated in the majority of countries around the world.

LIST OF US-REGULATED INDUSTRIES:

Accounting/CPA
Air Transportation (Aviation, Airports, Aerodromes, and Airlines)
Alcohol, Wine & Spirits
Banking
Biotech/BioPharma
Communication Systems (including Telephone, VOIP, ISP, Cable)
Construction
Education **
Financial Services (including investments)
Food Sources (FDA, Farmers, Distributors)
Health care (including dental and home care)
High Tech
Hospitality (Hotels, etc.)
Insurance
Legal
Kids and Family Targeted Businesses (COPPA, etc.)
Manufacturing

---

[66] "Regulation Legal Definition of Regulation. Regulation Synonyms by the Free Online Law Dictionary." accessed February 23, 2014, http://legal-dictionary.thefreedictionary.com/regulation.
[67] Accessed February 23, 2014, http://www.ffiec.gov.
[68] Ernie Hayden, Verizon.

LIST OF US-REGULATED INDUSTRIES:— Cont'd

Marine transportation (including ferry and port services)
Medical (doctors, equipment, hospitals)
Nonprofit **
Pharmaceuticals
Railway and Road Transportation
Restaurants **
Other

**Although not regulated per se, these sectors have special legal and industry requirements they must meet.

Each industry has its own set of rules and regulations. These rules cover more than just online and digital activity, but that is our focus here. So, for example, look at Table 2.1 relating to just social media use in the financial sector. This list is constantly evolving and being added to, and its rules are modified as the technology and the use of the technology by the industry changes.

Table 2.2 lists federal laws, state laws, country legal codes, professional and industry guidelines and regulations relating to social media use in the health care and medical sector.

Neither list should be viewed as 100% complete. However, they do demonstrate how heavy and overwhelming the issue of compliance can be in terms of security and risk management—and the above were only identified relating to social media online use.

There are some specific regulatory and legislative incidents regarding security and online digital activity that I would like to present as examples of things to be on the lookout for.

1. Cybersecurity Bill a5955 (Senate Panel).[69] This bill was introduced by Senate Commerce Committee Chairman Jay Rockefeller, D-W.Va., and ranking member John Thune, R-S.D. It was passed by a voice vote in July 2013 and is headed to the Senate floor, where it will be merged with other cybersecurity measures. The bill outlines voluntary IT best practices for industry.[70]

2. Federal Information Security Management Act.[71] This act was passed in 2002 and recognizes the importance of information security by requiring each federal agency to develop and implement information security plans. In 2013, Rep. Darrell E. IIssa, R-CA-49, introduced a series of amendments to the act in H.R.1163,[72] which was passed by a vote in the House.

3. Cyber Intelligence Sharing & Protection Act (House, April, HR 624, CISPA).[73] This act was introduced by Rep. Mike J. Roberts, R-MI-8, and "directs the federal government to conduct cybersecurity activities to provide shared situational awareness enabling integrated operational actions to protect, prevent, mitigate, respond to, and recover from cyber incidents."[74]

---

[69] Eric Chabrow, "NIST Unveils Draft of Voluntary Cybersecurity Framework," (July 3, 2013), http://www.govinfosecurity.com/nist-unveils-draft-cybersecurity-framework-a-5883.

[70] Eric Chabrow, "Senate Panel Passes Cybersecurity Bill—BankInfoSecurity," (July 31, 2013), http://www.bankinfosecurity.com/senate-panel-passes-cybersecurity-bill-a-5955.

[71] "FISMA," accessed February 23, 2014, http://csrc.nist.gov/drivers/documents/FISMA-final.pdf.

[72] H.R.1163 - 113th Congress (2013–2014): Federal Information Security Amendments Act of 2013, 2014, 2/23/2014 sess., http://beta.congress.gov/bill/113th-congress/house-bill/1163.

[73] H.R.624 - 113th Congress (2013–2014): Cyber Intelligence Sharing and Protection Act | Congress.Gov | Library of Congress, 2014, 2/23/2014 sess., http://beta.congress.gov/bill/113th-congress/house-bill/624.

[74] See note 73.

Table 2.1 Laws and Regulations Related to Social Media Use in the Financial Sector

Law/Statute/Regulation	URL
Bank Secrecy Act: The Currency and Foreign Transactions Reporting Act of 1970	http://www.fincen.gov/statutes_regs/bsa/
CAN-SPAM Act	http://uscode.house.gov/download/pls/15C103.txt
Children's online privacy protection Act (COPPA)	http://www.ftc.gov/privacy/coppa2/
Community Reinvestment Act	http://www.ffiec.gov/cra/default.htm
Federal Deposit insurance Act	http://www.fdic.gov/regulations/laws/rules/1000-100.html
FDIC, 12 CFR Sec 740.5 (NCUA)	http://www.ncua.gov/about/Documents/Agenda%20Items/AG20110519Item1b.pdf
FDIC, 12 CFR Sec. 328.3	http://www.fdic.gov/regulations/laws/rules/2000-5200.html
FDIC, Fair Housing Act	http://www.fdic.gov/regulations/laws/rules/6500-2510.html
FDIC, Regulation B, Fair Lending Laws: Equal Credit opportunity Act	http://www.fdic.gov/regulations/laws/rules/6500-2900.html
FDIC, Regulation DD, Truth in Savings Act	http://www.fdic.gov/regulations/laws/rules/6500-3250.html
FDIC, Regulation E, Electronic Fund Transfer Act	http://www.fdic.gov/regulations/laws/rules/6500-3100.html
FDIC, Regulation Z, Truth in Lending Act	http://www.fdic.gov/regulations/laws/rules/6500-1400.html
FINRA Regulatory notice 10-06	http://www.finra.org/web/groups/industry/@ip/@reg/@notice/documents/notices/p120779.pdf
FINRA Regulatory Notice 11-39	http://www.finra.org/web/groups/industry/@ip/@reg/@notice/documents/notices/p124186.pdf
FINRA Rule 1230(b)6	http://www.lowenstein.com/SnapshotFiles/635aed94-fcf4-42f6-9615-4681125010b1/NonSubscriber.snapshot
Federal Rules of Civil Procedure, title V, rule 34 (e-discovery)	http://www.law.cornell.edu/rules/frcp/
Gramm Leach Bliley Act (GLBA), Privacy Rules & Data Security Guidelines	http://www.ftc.gov/privacy/glbact/glboutline.htm
Investment Advisers Act of 1940, Rule 206(4)-1	http://www.sec.gov/about/laws/iaa40.pdf
NASD Rule 2210	http://finra.complinet.com/en/display/display_main.html?rbid=2403&element_id=3616
NASD Rule 2310	http://finra.complinet.com/en/display/display_main.html?rbid=2403&element_id=3637
PCI Date Security Standard	https://www.pcisecuritystandards.org/security_standards/
Sarbanes-Oxley Act (SOX)	http://uscode.house.gov/download/pls/15C98.txt
SEC Rule 17(a)-3	http://www.sec.gov/rules/final/34-44992.htm
SEC Rule 17(a)-4	http://www.sec.gov/rules/final/34-44992.htm

Table 2.2 Laws and Regulations Related to Social Media Use in the Health care/Medical Sector

Law/Statute/Regulation	URL
Academy of General Dentistry	http://www.agd.org
AlPha-ASP/AACP Pledge of Professionalism	http://www.aacp.org/resources/studentaffairspersonnel/studentaffairspolicies/Pages/professionalism.aspx
American Association of Boards of Pharmacy: Model Pharmacy Act	http://www.nabp.net/assets/board_member_manual.pdf
American Counseling Association Code of Ethics (to be adopted 2014)	http://www.counselor-license.com/articles/social-media-counseling.html
American Dental Association: Ethics & Conduct Code	http://www.ada.org/194.aspx
American Medical Association	http://www.ama-assn.org/ama/pub/physician-resources/medical-ethics/code-medical-ethics.page
American Pharmacists Association (APhA) Code of Ethics for Pharmacists	http://www.pharmacist.com/code-ethics
American Psychology Association (APA) Ethics Code	http://www.apa.org/monitor/2010/07-08/internet.aspx
American Veterinary Medicine Association/Confidentiality Laws	https://www.avma.org/Advocacy/StateAndLocal/Pages/sr-confidentiality-patient-records.aspx
CAN-SPAM Act	http://uscode.house.gov/download/pls/15C103.txt
Federal Drug Administration	http://www.fda.gov/drugs/guidancecomplianceregulatoryinformation/default.htm
Federation of State Medical Boards (FSMB) Social Media Policy Guidelines	http://www.fsmb.org/pdf/pub-social-media-guidelines.pdf
FTC Endorsement Guidelines	http://ftc.gov/os/2009/10/091005revisedendorsementguides.pdf
Health Information Portability & Accountability Act (HIPAA)	http://www.hhs.gov/ocr/privacy/
Health Information Technology for Economic and Clinical health (HITECH) Act 2009 breach notification rule	http://www.hhs.gov/ocr/privacy/hipaa/administrative/breachnotificationrule/index.html
HIPAA/hitech Omnibus rule Checklist	http://www.alston.com/files/publication/b0f28670-3458-405c-81f8-17dbce5723c9/presentation/publicationattachment/64f1e7cf-11aa-448f-8e54-1afccdccd09d/13-090%20hipaa%20checklist.pdf#page=1
National Association of Emergency Medical Technicians (NAMET) Conduct Code	http://www.naemt.org/about_us/emtoath.aspx
National Center for Complementary & Alternative Medicine: Social Media Policy	http://nccam.nih.gov/tools/commentpolicy.htm
Patient Bill of Rights	By state
Patient Privacy Laws	By state: Mental Illness, HIV, Genetic information, etc.
Pharmaceutical Research & Manufacturers of America: Best Practice: PhRMA	http://www.best-practice.com/best-practices-regulation/health-regulations/government-regulations-on-pharma-social-media/
Protected Health Information (PHI)	http://www.hipaa.com/2009/09/hipaa-protected-health-information-what-does-phi-include/
Stored Communications Act of 1986	http://www.law.cornell.edu/uscode/text/18/part-I/chapter-121
Veterinary Medical Board Regulations	http://www.vmb.ca.gov/laws_regs/index.shtml

4. SEC CyberSecurity Disclosure Requirements.[75] Originally issued in 2011, the disclosure requirements outline what companies must do in regard to disclosing information about their ability to defend against attacks on their networks.[76] In April 2013, Senate Commerce Chairman Jay Rockefeller, D-W.Va., sent a letter to the SEC to review and make the requirements stronger.

EXTERNAL RISK 5: NATURAL DISASTERS AND SQUIRRELS

Natural disasters are sudden events in nature that cause major destruction. There have been a number of these in recent years, from the 2005 Hurricane Katrina to the 2004 Indian Ocean Tsunami to the 2010 Haiti earthquake. Natural disasters come in different varieties: storms, volcanic eruptions, earthquakes, landslides, wildfires, floods, etc. Caused by the elements of wind, air, fire, and earth, they cannot always be predicted, but sensor systems to foretell these disasters are constantly being improved upon and developed.

Natural disasters as an external threat are interesting because, psychologically speaking, they are "unlikely events" and are usually listed under a "Force Majeure" clause in contracts. This clause limits the company's liability should an event occur that causes data or security failure of IT systems, including online and digital services. But they do occur and need to be prepared for.

Disaster recovery programs are a necessary component to ensure business continuity after a natural disaster. These programs usually consist of a plan that outlines process and protocols to be followed based on specific events, and different preparation activities such as simulations and training exercises to get everyone ready should the unlikely happen.

Natural disasters are not the only "natural" incidents that can affect digital technology systems. Wildlife, especially squirrels, seem to have an affinity for causing mayhem and chaos with technology. A review of some technology incidents of the NASDAQ stock market reveals two separate incidents where squirrels paid the ultimate sacrifice in pursuit of the perfect technology blackout: first, in 1987, a Connecticut squirrel touched off a power failure, shutting down the NASDAQ for 82 min (more than 20 million shares could not be traded); and second, in 1994, another Connecticut squirrel chewed though an electric company's power line, leading to 34 min downtime.[77] Understanding the physical environment the company's digital technology systems reside in can help identify and evaluate potential natural disaster and wildlife security risks.

This list of internal and external risks is not exhaustive. There are many more that are commonplace and that we know of as well as new ones that have not yet come into existence. As we continue our journey into online and digital security in this book, we turn now to specific risks to security, starting with reputation and digital identity. Do you know how your company is viewed online? Do you know who you are online?

---

[75] "CF Disclosure Guidance: Topic no. 2 - Cybersecurity," Division of Corporation Finance Securities and Exchange Commission, accessed February 23, 2014 http://www.sec.gov/divisions/corpfin/guidance/cfguidance-topic2.htm.

[76] John Mutch, "Beware the Coming SEC Regulations on Cybersecurity," (Forbes, May 15, 2013), http://www.forbes.com/sites/ciocentral/2013/05/15/how-to-prepare-for-when-the-sec-comes-asking-about-cybersecurity-risk/.

[77] William Alden, "Computer Bugs and Squirrels: A History of Nasdaq's Woes," (New York Times, August 22, 2013), http://dealbook.nytimes.com/2013/08/22/computer-bugs-and-squirrels-a-history-of-nasdaqs-woes/?nl=todaysheadlines&emc=edit_th_20130823&_r=0&pagewanted=print.

REPUTATION AND IDENTITY

*Identity will be the most valuable commodity for citizens in the future,
and it will exist primarily online.*[1]

REPUTATION

Reputation is commonly defined as "the beliefs or opinions that are generally held about someone or something."[2] This definition is interesting in that it implies reputation is based on perception and not fact. Of course, we can argue that a belief or opinion may be formed from a series of facts that had been presented previously, but it is not a requirement based on the definition. We hear about reputation all the time in today's news and how important it is to protect a company's reputation, or your own reputation. Every day we are inundated with news headlines of how a company or an individual has loss their reputation (here, the assumption is that the lost reputation was a good one)

---

[1] Eric Schmidt, Google Chairman, The New Digital Age (April 2013).
[2] "Reputation: definition of reputation in Oxford dictionary," accessed March 2, 2014, http://www.oxforddictionaries.com/us/definition/american_english/reputation.

and the negative impact that loss has had on the company and/or individual. How then do you protect reputation if reputation is someone else's beliefs or opinions? We live in a society where everyone is considered worthy of having their own opinions, although we do not need to all agree with it. So why are we so concerned that the opinions they have of our company, its products and/or services, or of us are positive? Perhaps because in the corporate world, according to a recent IBM study on representational risk, a "strong reputation generates stakeholder trust."[3] Add to this the knowledge that in today's digital environment reputation is a fragile thing. As Warren Buffet states: "It takes 20 years to build a reputation and 5 min to ruin it. If you think about that, you'll do things differently."

REPUTATIONAL RISKS

A reputational risk is a threat to the positive perception others have or should have about our company, our products or services, or about us. It can lead to a number of negative consequences including:

- Loss of current and potential clients.
- Loss of current and potential employees (talent).
- Loss of revenue.
- Bad will on behalf of the public.
- Additional scrutiny on behalf of government and/or regulatory agencies.
- Embarrassment/loss of face.

The causes of reputational risks are pretty standard—the company or individual did something that was or was perceived as "improper" and it came to light in a big way. People may even use the word "scandal" here. I use the word "improper" because the action (or inaction) causing the reputational risk could be something illegal or just morally wrong in the eyes of the public, for example, a disgrace causing dishonor and disbelief leading to public outrage. Before the Internet, discoveries of such indiscretions would only be mainstream water cooler conversation if it broke in the national media, usually television. In today's online and digital environment, the shame is on display for an exponentially larger audience in record time and if it is truly juicy, it goes viral, expanding the exposure and negative impact of the original incident. Who breaks the story has also changed. Sources for the revelations can include the company's employees, the company's customers, authorized third-party affiliates of the company, the company's critics, and any other stakeholder with an interest in what the company is doing and how it is doing it. These additional factors of increased number of sources and the velocity of information dissemination make building, protecting, and recovering reputations a more challenging task than ever for risk managers and security professionals.

In addition, information technology (IT) risks can pose threats to a company's reputation. These can include data breaches, system failures, data loss, compliance failures, Web site outages, insufficient

---

[3] "Reputational risk and IT," (IBM, 2012), http://www-935.ibm.com/services/multimedia/2012_Representational_Risk_Study.pdf.

disaster recovery measures, poor technical support, and others.[4] Most of these relate back to the customer service and/or support functions of the company and so can be directly experienced by a customer.

One additional finding in the 2012 IBM Survey quoted earlier was the response to the question of who is most responsible for managing the reputational risk of a company. The Chief Executive Officer (CEO) came out on top with 80% of the respondents identifying him or her as the executive to be held accountable, followed by the Chief Financial Officer at 31%, and the Chief Information Officer at 27%.[5]

DEFINING IDENTITY

When we talk about identity we are referring to "the fact of being who or what a person or thing is."[6] Everything begins with identity and being able to prove you are who you say you are. To understand someone or something's identity, such as a company, we have to take into consideration a series of internal and external characteristics that exist in a relationship of one thing to the other so as to define the person or thing (Table 3.1 and 3.2).

Let us look at the physical aspect a little closer. For an individual, this includes, but is not limited to, our facial features, our body structure, our health and age, and our gender and sexuality. For a corporation, the physical characteristics list may look like this: logo or brand imagery, look and feel of Web site and other online presences, business card and stationery layout, office building architecture, layout and division structure, etc. We should note these are the things that most people tend to notice first about us and our companies. The risk is that the physical allows for a lot of assumptions to be made because the physical does not provide the context for what most people are seeing. Take, for example, photographs. Most people will go on LinkedIn and look up an individual that they are about to meet for the first time. I do this specifically so I can see their picture and know what they look like. This is important so I am not waiting at the restaurant wondering if the next person to walk through the door is the person I am supposed to meet. However, the photograph in the LinkedIn profile is contrived—meant to convey a certain impression on the viewer, usually one of professionalism. The photograph may also not be current; it could be a younger version of the individual I have been communicating with. Many times the photograph leaves out a lot of the story of who this person is and if they truly are professional or not. I will first discover that when they arrive on time or not.

The same can be said about a company. Its logo may convey one message but whether its products and/or services are truly what I need depends on a lot more than just the colors on its business cards, the graphic on its logo, or the fancy mahogany table in its conference room. However, the physical is where we usually begin.

---

[4] See note 3.

[5] Ibid.

[6] "Identity: definition of identity in Oxford dictionary," accessed March 2, 2014, http://www.oxforddictionaries.com/us/definition/american_english/identity.

Table 3.1 List of Internal and External Characteristics of a Person's Identity

Internal	External
Physical appearance	Cultural characteristics
Emotional responses	Nationality
Intellectual abilities	Societal characteristics of family, career
Spiritual beliefs	Religion
Innate gifts, talents, strengths, capabilities	Gender
Personal preferences	Societal position expectations

Table 3.2 List of Internal and External Characteristics of a Company's Identity

Internal	External
Physical appearance (logo, office décor, etc.)	Cultural characteristics of management
Corporate responses	Geo-political characteristics of where located
Intellectual abilities of workforce	Societal characteristics of workforce
Innate gifts, talents, strengths, capabilities of workforce	Gender of workforce
Corporate values	Societal values
Corporate mission	Societal expectations

DIGITAL IDENTITY

Our relationship with the Internet is changing. Mobile devices, wireless connectivity, and our increasing virtual presence across multiple social media services have all but collapsed the boundary between being online or offline. Together the virtual and the real form the seamless space in which many of us live out our daily lives. We fashion the self through social interaction, community and network affiliations, and here come to construct our identities as well as interpret the identity of others.[7]

According to Stephen Fells, President of Follr.com, a digital identity is "the sum of all digitally available information about an individual."[8] (see box). I would add that this definition also applies to a corporation's digital identity. Another way to look at it is that a digital identity is data available online about a person, place, or thing (like a corporation) that is unique to them or it. One of the key factors of a digital identity is that it also contains information about how these unique factors are in relationships with each other. The words to notice are "unique" and "relationships." In other words, identity is

[7] Digital Identity Matters, (June, 2010), http://www.pontydysgu.org/2010/06/digital-identity-matters/.
[8] Accessed March 2, 2014, http://follr.com.

about you, digital identity is about your relationships to others. For companies, their identities are about them, and their digital identities are about their relationships with employees, customers, the public, etc.

There is much discussion over online identities and how they are, in fact, used. There is nothing to stop an individual from creating multiple personas for completing certain tasks, such as shopping.[9] We had one White House Security Council staff who was fired once it was discovered that he was the person behind the Twitter account @NatSecWonk where he released security information and criticized Washington and national political players.[10]

There is also much discussion as to where all these tidbits of data that form your identity can be found online: search engines, web browsers, Internet service providers, cell phone companies, and our mobile devices (from smartphones to tablets). It is almost impossible to pinpoint all the "input" points of information about ourselves. Even when we think we are only giving certain information for one specific purpose, it seems to get used for a number of other purposes and on other online sites. For example, when you get a driver's license, your information is put into the registry of potential jurors that is accessed not only by the court system of the county you reside in, but also marketers who purchase this kind of information for targeted marketing efforts.

From a technical standpoint, digital identity consists of certain core elements:

1. Authentication elements (identification (ID) #, internet provider address, email address, user name, password, etc.).
2. Data (original content posted by the individual or company).
3. Identifiers (photographs, avatars, logos, images, etc.).
4. Digital traces (contributions to blogs, links, etc.).
    a. The difference between data and digital traces is that digital traces are smaller comments in response to someone else's original content. For example, they could be comments to a blog.

All of these together make up the technological definition of identity needed for IT systems to identify and authenticate users to ensure security of data. In the InfoWorld Deep Diver Series about Identity Management, they remind IT professionals that digital identity management can "ensure with reasonable confidence that the people who access your network are who they claim to be and have the access privileges that they are trying to access."[11] Using these elements you can create a system of identifiers, controls, and security attributes.

---

[9] Bekezela Phakathi, "Consumers shed real-word identity for 'digital personas' online," (Business Day, October 4, 2013), http://www.bdlive.co.za/business/retail/2013/10/04/consumers-shed-real-word-identity-for-digital-personas-online.

[10] Leslie Larson, "White House Security Council staffer axed for spewing snark and secrets in parody Twitter account," (Daily News, October 23, 2013), http://www.nydailynews.com/news/politics/white-house-official-fired-twitter-account-leaked-security-secrets-article-1.1493751.

[11] "InfoWorld Deep Dive Series, Identity Management, Modernizing Enterprise Access Control," (2013), http://www.infoworld.com/d/security/download-the-identity-management-deep-dive-224064.

Industry Interview:

Stephen Fells (Figure 3.1) is the president and founder of Follr.com, a Web site that promises its users smarter professional networking and digital identity control by providing a venue for an end-user to combine all of their online digital footprints into one comprehensive and organized platform.[12] During a telephone interview, Stephen and I discussed the importance of digital identity in today's world for the personal and the professional and some recent trends in identity protection.

Is there a difference between identity and digital identity?

Currently, there is, but the lines are beginning to blur. I see digital identity as defined in two ways, the physical (as a replacement for a passport or credit card and the use of biometrics for authentication) and information based (provides marketing opportunities by marrying personal data to commercial services and products).

How does personal identity and professional identity relate to each other online?

This is also blurring. 75–85% of employers currently conduct online and social media background checks on potential candidates and use information they find as reasons not to hire.

How does an executive's digital identity and that of the company he works for relate to each other?

One way is the sharing of business information on personal accounts. However, it does not matter if it is an executive or a first day employee. I believe people are more disappointed when executives misbehave because they feel the executives should know better.

How does identity and reputation relate in today's online world?

Everything is relative. When we network, we search the person online and form an opinion about the person based on the information we found (their identity). Today, we have the ability to share and consume as much information as we want in real time. Therefore, anyone can interact with "your brand" and share it with an unlimited amount of people. This means that companies really do not control their brand (reputation) anymore, we the people do via social media posts, blogs, online review sites like Yelp, etc. Consumers have many ways to discuss a brand, product, and/or company. The other

FIGURE 3.1 Stephen Fells, CEO of Follr.com.

thing is you cannot opt-out of the online discussion. It is happening around you whether you participate or not. This is forming your identity and your reputation.

What issue is one of your top concerns in terms of identity and privacy?

Our children and their digital identity. Are we as parents creating problems for them in the future based on what we post about them on our online accounts? Our children themselves have no initial control of their own digital identities. Recently, I became aware of InBloom[13] an online data collection system being used by New York State schools to collect information about students, such as test scores, etc. I am concerned of how that data will be used, who will access it, and how it will affect our students later in their careers.

[12] See note 8.

[13] InBloom is a nonprofit organization working to make it easier for teachers, parents and students to get a coherent picture of student progress, give them more options to be involved and informed, and make learning more engaging for students, accessed March 2, 2014, https://www.inbloom.org.

LEGAL IDENTITY

Legal identity is defined as whether you have capacity to have legal rights and duties within a certain legal system based on how the law recognizes you—for example, a corporation once registered is considered its own legal entity separate from who may have formed the corporation to begin with. Under the law, it means the corporation can enter into contracts, be assessed taxes, enter into a lawsuit, etc. Digital identity can be affected by reputational risks, but the legal identity can be held liable for compliance violations and criminal sanctions based on those same reputational risks.

EXECUTIVE IDENTITY

Although this book is concerned with corporate risks, I recognize that individuals form the core of any corporation. In today's digital and online world, individuals, especially high-level C-suite executives and directors, can affect corporate reputation and identity in unprecedented ways. Mismanaging their own identities and reputations can lead to vulnerabilities their corporation does not need. An example to keep in mind is what happened to Brendan Eich, who stepped down from being Mozilla's CEO less than two weeks after taking the helm in 2014. Eich learned that hard way that (1) the past is never far away on the Internet, and (2) the personal does affect the business. Apparently, Eich had made a $1000 donation to an organization in support of proposition 8, a California ballot initiative to ban same-sex marriage back in 2008. This was discovered by Mozilla employees and then picked up by "an online dating site, OkCupid, who asked its Firefox users to boycott the browser."[14] At first, Eich wrote a blog post to assure that he would uphold non-discrimination policies at Mozilla. He also gave a response that his personal views should not be judged on the company. The second line of argument did not hold up and his resignation came quickly behind.

A fact of today's digital world is that there is a blurring of the professional and the personal online. An executive may have their own LinkedIn profile separate from the corporate page, but an affiliation between the two can come into existence by the public, whether founded or not. We have seen the news stories of customer loss of faith in a company because the chief executive made a comment that was not

[14] Karabin, Sherry, Law Technology News, "Mozilla Chief Resigns over Stand on Same-Sex Marriage," (April 7, 2014), http://www.lawtechnologynews.com/id=1396629025161/Mozilla-Chief-Resigns-Over-His-Stand-on-Same-Sex-Marriage?slreturn=20140314093530.

readily accepted by the public, or did something that raised public outcry. It is more important than ever for top level executives to understand they are the face of their companies and what they say and/or do can and will be held against them and their companies, whether it is right for the public to do so or not. So let us take a look at several issues that affect reputational risks and security.

FEDERAL TRADE COMMISSION AND ONLINE CREDENTIALS

Truth in advertising is the Federal Trade Commission's (FTC) mantra. Its purpose is to protect consumers from unscrupulous predators, fraudsters, scammers, data hackers, and identity thieves. Realizing that consumers make purchase decisions using online resources has made the FTC take a closer look at online profiles of companies and executives, in specific online credential listing and recommendations. As consumers rely on information they find online, they tend to expect that the information listed is accurate, truthful, and that the entity who posted it is trustworthy. Many potential clients may read a person's LinkedIn page as if it were an expanded resume or a minimized autobiography. Some may even make a decision to hire the individual based on what the individual has written on his or her profile, including his or her credentials, skills, and experience. Recognizing the reliance of consumers on this information and the potential for consumers to be misled by what is written or how the information is presented, the FTC has issued a notice in December of 2011 stating that it would hold individuals and companies responsible for inaccurate and misleading information in online profiles under false advertising rules.[15] The concern is that because so many online users base their decisions on what they read in these social media profiles, the FTC wants to make sure they do so based on legitimate and accurate information. To eliminate this risk, educate your executives and all employees about this requirement so that the company is not held in FTC compliance violation.

In addition, these social media profiles, online narratives, and/or personal biographies add an extra element to the concept of identity. For example, *New York Times* writer Teddy Wayne reviewed a number of Twitter bios of the famous and not so famous in a recent article. In his words, "The Twitter bio is a postmodern art form, an opportunity in 160 characters or fewer to cleverly synopsize one's professional and personal achievements, along with a carefully edits non sequitir or two."[16] It is also a place where the appropriate disclaimer can be made. My Twitter bio at @law2sm includes: "Tweets are not legal advice."

EXECUTIVE VISUAL REPRESENTATIONS

I spoke of the importance of photographs previously. Most executives will have professionally taken company-approved photographs for their "official" online profiles. What about for their personal accounts? It is interesting to note the phenomenon of online "selfies"—portraits taken of oneself by oneself by turning the camera lens around to face you. A recent *New York Times* article, *My Selfie, Myself*, by Jenna Wortham, examined why these images are more than just the work of vain individuals.[17] Clive Thompson, a technology writer, is quoted in the article. "People are wrestling with how they appear to the rest of the world. Taking a photograph is a way of trying to understand how people see you,

---

[15] Shear, Bradley, "The FTC May Soon Crack Down On Social Media Credential Fraud," (September 15, 2013), http://www.shearsocialmedia.com/2011/09/ftc-may-soon-crack-down-on-social-media.html.

[16] Teddy Wayne, "Twitter Bios and What They Really Say," *The New York Times*, (October 6, 2013), http://www.nytimes.com/2013/10/06/fashion/twitter-bios-and-what-they-really-say.html?_r=0.

[17] Jenna Worthman, "My Selfie, Myself," *The New York Times*, (October 20, 2013), http://www.nytimes.com/2013/10/20/sunday-review/my-selfie-myself.html.

who you are, and what you look like."[18] But are these the images of the executive the company wants out there? Is this again a matter of educating about thinking carefully of what to post before you post it?

Social media platforms have added not only a way to share these photographs and other content, but other technology, such as Facebook's facial recognition, is able to automatically identify individuals in the photographs. It is offered as a tool to assist users in captioning their photographs, but stalkers can use this tool to identify and locate a potential target.

However, photographs are not the only way executives may represent their likeness online. For example, I use a caricature of me for my private legal practice (see Figure 3.2). I use this on my business cards and my Web site to be less intimating as an attorney to potential clients who may have never met an attorney before or who may have a negative connotation about lawyers in general because of media portrayals or personal experience. In choosing this image, I did make sure it represented me in a way I wanted to be represented—professional, serious, wearing glasses, and juggling multiple matters.

Executives may also choose such a visual representation or the executive may be taking part in a virtual environment that requires the adoption of an avatar, which is a graphical representation of the executive. In video games, these can be quite fanciful in expression, such as in World of Warcraft,[19] or more realistic, such as in The SIMS.[20] These avatars are usually also 3-dimensional. The choices an executive uses to dress his or her avatar may become the basis for the public's opinion about the executive and therefore about the company. One best practice being adopted by some companies who permit the use of avatars for executives (and employees) is instituting an avatar dress code to reduce the risk of negative public opinion.

FIGURE 3.2 Caricature of Deborah Gonzalez, for Her Private Practice, The Law Firm of Deborah Gonzalez, Esq., LLC. www.dgonzalezesq.com.

---

[18] Ibid.
[19] Accessed March 2, 2014, http://us.battle.net/wow/en/.
[20] Accessed March 2, 2014, http://www.thesims.com/en-us.

In online communities and forums, the avatar may be a simple 2-dimensional icon or even the company's logo. This last option, the use of a company's logo, can have legal and other negative consequences for the corporation as it can be seen as a company endorsement of the executive's actions in the online forums, or that the executive is representing the company in these forums and therefore the company would be liable for the executive's actions.

EXECUTIVE TRANSITIONS

Executives rarely spend their entire careers in one company. Changes in an executive's professional live can also inadvertently or directly affect a company's reputation. It should come as no surprise to anyone that when a high-level executive changes positions in a company or changes companies altogether it does not go unnoticed. Changes in the company's stock may result, either upward or down, as investors make decisions as to how the change will impact the financial situation of the company. Wall Street news reports are full of executive transitions and predictions of what they mean. A leadership succession plan is not always prepared ahead of time, sometimes due to an unforeseen event or incident, such as a scandal.

Many companies like to control the message when such a transition occurs—especially when the transition is not voluntary on behalf of the executive. Unfortunately, in our digital society, this is not always possible, as leaks of what could be a very newsworthy story gets out to the media, the competition, the public, and, indeed, the world through a tweet or online post. When a message is leaked it runs the risk of being surrounded by gossip, rumors, inaccuracies, and/or even fanciful facts of what occurred that may have never happened. This misinformation once released can take on a life of its own, being shared and commented on and expanded upon at the velocity of a click or retweet, spinning out of control and ruining either the executive's or the company's reputation or both.

A company's public relations team needs to be prepared to address this kind of communications crisis. A crisis control plan is essential for all companies in this digital age (see Tips on effective crisis management).

TIPS FOR EFFECTIVE CRISIS MANAGEMENT

1. Anticipate crises and have a plan.
2. Identify your crisis communications team and your spokesperson(s).
3. Train the team and your spokesperson(s) and make sure all other employees know who to turn to when the media requests start coming in.
4. Establish notification and monitoring systems.
5. Get to know and establish relationships with traditional media and online media—do not wait until something bad happens.
6. Assess the crisis situation.
7. Respond according to your plan.
8. Engage your employees.
9. Take responsibility for what occurred and offer a resolution.
10. Follow-up on the resolution.
11. Do a post-crisis analyst for lessons learned.
12. Revise your crisis plan.
13. Retrain the team and spokesperson(s).
14. Keep monitoring for new incidents.

We are also beginning to see executive employment contracts with specific clauses governing social media use in the announcement of executive transitions—from specifying a date and time for the release of the information on social media platforms, to requirements for social media blackout periods for executives for a certain amount of time (about 3–6 months) to give the public a chance to disassociate the executive with one company as they affiliate with another. Some may argue that the company then needs to reciprocate with its own self-induced social media blackout relating to the executive's transition, but current labor laws, contractual agreements, and human resource best practices already address the issue of what a company can or cannot say when an employee (executive or otherwise) leaves the firm.

EXECUTIVE BEHAVIOR AND LIFE CHANGES

Being in the public eye puts one under the spotlight and subject to scrutiny. Cell phones abound and captured video of an executive misbehaving is hard evidence to refute. It is not unusual for companies to prohibit cell phones, cameras, and other photograph-taking digital devices from company parties and functions in an effort to prevent that unfortunate (or inappropriate) photograph or video from being released to the public and affecting the company's reputation. Even the Secret Service got caught when they were discovered to have hired prostitutes as they were preparing for President Obama's arrival in Colombia.[21] The fallout online did not let the story die and it became so infamous that Wonderful Pistachio Nuts parodied it for one of their commercials.[22] Based on one review, "The television commercial shows scantily clad Latina women, seated on the laps of men in suits and sunglasses, feeding them pistachios as the ad's narrator states, The Secret Service do it... and get fired for it."[23] President Obama's administration took a hit on this as well, as the public questioned the effectiveness of the intelligence community in protecting U.S. interests.

On the personal side of things, an executive's marital status and family life can become fodder for reputational risks. The more renown an executive is, the more investors and the public are interested in the details of their life and how they factor into the success or failure of the company. Ugly high-end divorces played out in the public media are nothing new. They offer a brief insight into an otherwise private setting and who does not like to know that those in the C-suite have their share of problems too. Instead of it being limited to the water cooler, today, the discussion surrounding the divorce and all its unpleasant details finds its way online through social media platforms and other digital forums, including online radio talk shows. As the company is focusing on its day-to-day operations and long-term strategic plans, it now finds itself and its decisions questioned because of the personal decisions of the executive that led to the divorce, leading to expenditure of additional resources, including time, labor, and money to address this new risk to its reputation.

When an executive's divorce is not amicable, other issues arise when ex-spouses continue to battle each other over custody, alimony, the house in the Hamptons, the dog, etc. The more colorful the

---

[21] Pierre Thomas and Jason Ryan, "Colombia Secret Service Prostitution Scandal Spreads to the DEA," (ABCnews, May 21, 2012), http://abcnews.go.com/US/colombia-secret-service-prostitution-scandal-spreads-dea/story?id=16399758.

[22] The commercial has been taken down from YouTube based on a copyright claim by Fire Station (Roll International).

[23] Erin Brown, "Inappropriate Pistachio Commercial Shows Prostitutes Feeding Secret Service Agents," (October 25, 2012), http://redalertpolitics.com/2012/10/25/video-inappropriate-pistachio-commercial-shows-prostitutes-feeding-secret-service-agents/.

arguments, and the more minor the subject of the argument is, the more people like to point it out and call that person's judgment into question if this is the fine mess they got themselves into. The opposite can also occur if the public sympathizes with the executive for being disgraced, shamed, or taken advantage of. One new strategy currently being used is a "social media/online no-posting clause" in the divorce agreement itself, which prohibits both parties from making any negative comments, sometimes any comments whatsoever, about the opposite party, in any online and/or social media forum. However, this leads to the question, can you do the same with an executive's children or grandchildren (or other familial relations)? Outside of contract law, this is still an open question.

One last issue I would like to bring up in terms of executive life changes is the reverse of the divorce: marriage. Marriage can cause a number of changes and minor chaos for the executive and the company. If the executive is a public figure, how would changing his or her last name be viewed by the public? Do you remember when Hillary Clinton became Hillary Rodham Clinton during her husband's first term in office? The media and social analysts had a field day as to what it meant, if she had a feminist agenda, if it should be seen as a precedent for other married women professionals, how it reflected on the administration, etc. Looking at today's digital society, where your name becomes your brand, how do name changes affect online digital and social media account names—does the Twitter handle need to be changed or the company email address? Will the public recognize the executive with the new name? Is this something the company needs to be concerned with or just be aware of? A recent U.K. Daily Mail article[24] looked at this name changing issue and offered some personal insights as the mainly female interviewees discussed their reasons for changing or not changing their online account names, even when their offline last names changed.

CORPORATE IDENTITY: THE BRAND

According to David Ogilvy, founder of the world famous Ogilvy Advertising Agency, a company's brand is "The intangible sum of a product's attributes: its name, packaging, and price, its history, its reputation, and the way it's advertised."[25] Many in the industry have since modified the definition to indicate that the brand is actually the company's identity, and in current marketing parlance, the term is now "brand identity." It also relates to how the consumer distinguishes one company (or product or service) from another in his or her mind.

Company brand identities are developed and carefully cultivated. Companies may pay a branding agency (or consultant group) a lot of money to come up with the right brand or to get the right message of the brand out to the public. Time is taken to review the company's mission, vision, values and corporate culture, market position, and value proposition to come up with the appropriate brand identity. Then strategies are put into place to foster and promote the brand identity in the public to make it recognizable and therefore increase its value. It is because of this outlay of time, money, and resources that brand identity is considered a major investment in the success of a company and why it is heavily guarded, monitored, and protected.

---

[24] Margot Peppers, "Changing your online identity after marriage is a modern minefield," (DailyMail, October 3, 2013), http://www.dailymail.co.uk/femail/article-2442919/Changing-online-identity-marriage-modern-minefield.html#ixzz2gr2NS4O1.

[25] "What is brand?" (TechTarget), accessed March 2, 2014, http://whatis.techtarget.com/definition/brand.

However, brand identities do include a company's reputation as a leading factor. In our current digital world protecting a brand's identity can become an advocacy role requiring brand champions inside and outside the company. Let us take a look at how this can play out in the online sphere.

BADVOCACY

It is said that out of all the people who will come across your brand's identity, about a third will love you (so you do not need to do anything), about a third will hate you (so doing anything with them would be a waste), and about a third will be on the fence about you (this is the group to focus on as they could change their minds). Not everything that is posted online about a company is good. Not everything posted online about a company is bad either. However, it is the bad stuff that keeps us up at night worrying about the company's reputation.

Badvocacy is when "someone" spreads negative comments about you or your company on online and social media platforms and networks. It seems as if they are on a mission to let everyone know the worst and they can be a customer, an employee, or a troll. Badvocacy can be small and sneak up on you or can be big and take you by storm. Why does Badvocacy happen? From a customer's perspective, their expectations have not been met. Therefore, for example, their customer experience was substandard: they had a bad customer service interaction; there was inconsistency across customer channels, they felt frustration in trying to get help to resolve their issue, or the reality did not meet their expectations or the hype (which can sometimes be perpetuated by the company itself, remember "vaporwear"?[26]).

Customers use the online forums as a new tool for consumer advocacy; all they need is a web connection and an input device, and smartphones are more pervasive than ever. A KRC Research Study found that 20% of the global online adult population were badvocates, "people who passionately criticize or detract from companies, brands or products."[27] How do they badvocate?

- Facebook postings.
- Twitter tweets.
- Old fashioned conversations in person, on the phone, via email.
- Calling into radio shows.
- Writing in their blogs or podcasts.
- YouTube videos.
- Wearing a button or apparel denouncing the company.
- And more…

One of the good points of news is that many of these badvocates can be turned around with the appropriate response and resolution of their problem (see What to do about badvocacy?). There is a group, however, that there is little to nothing you can do about them—trolls—individuals or groups that like to complain and have selected your company as a target. Obviously, there was something there for them to have identified your company as their "quarry." What can you do? The best strategy for dealing with them is "just don't feed the trolls." In other words, learn who a troll is and then do not engage them.

---

[26] This term was coined by a Microsoft engineer in the 1980's. It was subsequently used to describe software or others products that were hyped but never existed, (May 4, 2008). For a fun list of 15 top vaporwear products see: http://www.pcworld.com/article/145351/article.html.

[27] "The Good Book of Badvocacy," (Weber Shandwick, 2009), http://www.webershandwick.hu/download/BadvocacyBook_British_low.pdf.

WHAT TO DO ABOUT BADVOCACY?

- Be proactive.
  - Develop procedures and policies.
  - Establish guidelines for employees and train them how to use social media on behalf of your company, such as a Social Media Policy.
  - Register email addresses and domain names that may be detrimental to your company.
  - Assign social media to key employees only (i.e., reputation manager, etc.).
  - Find the badvocates.
  - Search your company names with words like "hate," "sucks," "bad," "doesn't care," etc.
  - Listen (read) what is being said, who is saying it, who they are saying it to, and what responses they are getting.
  - Cultivate loyal fans and advocates. (Reward them.)
- Respond.
  - Find out what the true issue is.
  - Reach out publicly first, and then take the issue privately with the complainer.
  - Respond quickly—be careful of time zones; monitoring needs to be as comprehensive as possible.
  - Do not make it personal; do not attack the badvocate.
  - Apologize and offer to help.
  - Be patient. Do not get upset or angry. Chill.
  - Take action—resolve the issue.
  - Make it a WOW moment.
  - Post the resolution.

If you mistweet, misfire or misrepresent then take the time to think of an appropriate response. Acknowledge, apologize and be authentic.[28]

One type of badvocate, sometimes identified as a troll, is a hacktivist. Hacktivists use computing systems, including social media and digital online forums, to make a political statement or achieve political ends, promoting, for example, free speech, human rights, etc. One of the most popular of hacktivist groups is Anonymous.[29] Hacker history has it that the group began organically as part of an image board in 2003, but it did not become a full-fledged hacktivist group until 2008 when it launched a campaign against the Church of Scientology. One of the complexities of Anonymous is that it is not a centrally organized group of hackers. Their targets are diverse, and their "cause celebre" changes with the latest injustice that is perceived by the public or the media. Targets have included PayPal, BMI, SONY, Amazon.com, The U.S. Copyright Office, and the Federal Bureau of Investigation (FBI), among others. In August 2013, the FBI released a statement that it had shut down Anonymous by arresting five hackers who belonged to a splinter group.[30] However, as with most information relating to Anonymous, this has not been confirmed.

---

[28]"Social Media Marketing Mistakes – Corporate Tweets Gone Wild," (Synnd, April 7, 2011), http://synnd.com/blog/social-media-marketing/social-media-marketing-mistakes-corporate-tweets-gone-wild/.

[29]A documentary has been made about the group and its activities, accessed March 2, 2014. For more information see: http://wearelegionthedocumentary.com/about-the-film/.

[30]Shaya Tayefe Mohajer, "FBI Agent Claims Hacking Group Anonymous Is on Lockdown," (takepart, August 22, 2013), http://www.takepart.com/article/2013/08/22/fbi-agent-claims-hacking-group-anonymous-lockdown.

REVIEWS AND RECOMMENDATIONS

Olivia Roat is a marketing consultant. She wrote an article entitled "All About Fake Online Reviews: The Problem of Separating Fact from Fiction."[31] In the article, Ms. Roat discusses that fake reviews undermine the credibility of the Internet. Yet, Main Street Host, Ms. Roat's company, was one of 19 cited by New York Regulators as having engaged in astroturfing—writing false reviews in online review sites—for over 30 clients and was fined $43,000.[32]

Yelp,[33] Citysearch,[34] Urbanspoon,[35] and Angie's List,[36] are just a few of a multitude of service and product review sites that consumers can go to become informed about a place, service, or product and make a decision as to whether to spend their money with that business or not. They are trusted because of one of the core principles of online conduct—transparency—the idea that it is the person who says who they are when they say it is them—whether that is when writing a review of a new restaurant or lauding the latest victory by a law firm. Consumers do not trust advertisements, but they trust their friends and people they know (in one way or another) and so will put more weight on these types of reviews and recommendations.

However, as the Main Street Host example illustrates above, a good review can be purchased and a consumer's trust can be bought. According to a Harvard Business School Study, the risks of being caught might well be worth the deceit, as it "found that restaurants that increased their ranking on Yelp by one star raised their revenues by 5 to 9 percent."[37] It seems the number of fake reviews continue to increase. In 2012, Garner, Inc. released its findings that "10–14% of social media reviews would be fake and/or paid for by companies."[38] But the consequences can be significant as well. From fines to loss of client confidence, to compliance violations, such as against the Truth in Advertising Act enforced by the FTC, all of which lead to risks against the company's reputation.

VALUE AND WORTH OF IDENTITY

Our worth as an executive or as a company is determined by a variety of identity characteristics in good part by others and their perceptions. However, there are new tools and technologies that are impacting those perceptions.

---

[31] You can read her article on her company's blog: Olivia Roat, "All About Fake Online Reviews: The Problem of Separating Fact from Fiction," (Mainstreethost, September 25, 2012), http://blog.mainstreethost.com/all-about-fake-online-reviews#.Um6GN6VJfy8.

[32] David Streitfeld, "Give Yourself five Stars? Online, It Might Cost You," *The New York Times*, (September 23, 2013), http://www.nytimes.com/2013/09/23/technology/give-yourself-4-stars-online-it-might-cost-you.html?_r=0.

[33] http://www.yelp.com.

[34] http://atlanta.citysearch.com.

[35] http://www.urbanspoon.com.

[36] http://www.angieslist.com.

[37] "HBS Study Finds Positive Yelp Reviews Boost Business," (Harvard Magazine, October 2011), http://harvardmagazine.com/2011/10/hbs-study-finds-positive-yelp-reviews-lead-to-increased-business.

[38] "Gartner Says By 2014, 10-15 Percent of Social Media Reviews to Be Fake, Paid for By Companies," (Gartner, Sept 17, 2012), http://www.gartner.com/newsroom/id/2161315.

SOCIAL SCORING

One such tool is the measurement of online social proofs by sites such as Klout,[39] PeerIndex,[40] Kred,[41] and others. These sites claim to measure a person's social influence via an algorithm that takes into consideration a person's online activity across a multitude of social networks and platforms. If we take Klout, for example, your score can range from 1 to 100, but, according to Mark Schaefer in his 2012 book *ROI: Return on Influence*, if it is below 50, you are not worth connecting with, receiving a post or Tweet from, or otherwise waste valuable time with. Does this sound harsh? Superficial? Ridiculous?

Schaefer does have a whole chapter dedicated to the arguments against social scoring—including how the system can be gamed, how the system does not (and cannot) take the offline into account for the final score, how social media celebrities do not acknowledge its validity, and how it is elitist. In fact, on the last page of the book Schaefer declares, "By definition, influence is elitist. So by assigning numbers to people and stacking them up in order, the system institutionalizes a culture of haves and have-nots." So now, discrimination is digital.

What can be more distressing is a quote in Schaefer's book by Paul Saarinen, Director of Digital Insights and Culture for Bolin Marketing, "what I would really love to see is a data mash-up between Klout and 23andMe, a company that does genetic testing for health, disease, and ancestry."[42] So blood tests give me the genetic information as to whether you will be healthy or a drain on a company's health insurance payments (or a society's welfare system) + the social score gives me the digital information as to whether you are a valuable content producer in this society, and where does it stop before we justify the ending of a life (or a career, or an academy journey) before it has begun?[43]

Also, remember that I mentioned previously that the FTC issued a notice that it would prosecute individuals who list false credentials in their social media profiles under false advertising. Should these scores not be held to that standard too and therefore is illegal in their concept? Are these scores not falsely misleading? Also, if I hire you or purchase your product because of your high Klout score, and the product and/or you are defective, have I not been harmed to my detriment because of false advertising? Should Klout then be liable because I relied on its score? P.S.—Klout claims it keeps its algorithm a secret so people do not learn to game the system. However, it also means no one else can validate what Klout is doing.

Does your company use Klout scores or other social scoring as criteria for recruiting, hiring, promoting, awarding prizes to consumers, etc.? How will its use affect the reputational risks to your company?

INFLUENCE AND FOLLOWERS

As a recent LinkedIn innovation to its service, it introduced the concept of LinkedIn Influencers, a way of identifying "trusted industry influencers to get essential professional insight and career advice."[44]

---

[39] http://klout.com.

[40] http://peerindex.com.

[41] http://kred.com.

[42] Schaefer, Mark, "ROI: Return on Influence: The Revolutionary Power of Klout, Social Scoring, and Influence Marketing," (2012), pp. 173.

[43] Remember the movie GATTACA with Ethan Hawke about a dystopia where humans are engineered and "free-love" children are given the lowest paid jobs and marginalized from the moment of birth thanks to a simple blood test?.

[44] "Pulse," LinkedIn, accessed March 2, 2014, http://www.linkedin.com/today/influencers?trk=corpblog_0713_influencers.

Being identified as an industry leader has been a goal for many executives as it enhances their own company brands and adds credibility and value for their company's stakeholders. Looking at the LinkedIn Influencers board, you find evidence of another social scoring metric—number of followers. At the time I am writing this chapter, Richard Branson, founder of the Virgin Group, leads the pack with 2,805,484 followers. Not so closely behind is Jack Welch with 1,275,764, then Deepak Chopra with 1,258,409, and rounding out the million-and-over-followers club is Arianna Huffington with 1,049,088.[45] Will you follow any of these now because of all the others who are following them? What is the financial worth of these followers? For one LinkedIn Influencer, the value was the increase in the number of readers to his articles—from about 10,000 to over 123,000 on average. That means more exposure, more reach, more credibility, more influence. He also noted he was having fun and that "leading is more fun with followers."[46] But no financial numbers were mentioned.

Is there a responsibility regarding what you write when your influence is so broad? Will the public have a reason to sue the executive or the company for "following" bad "advice" that was posted by the influencer? Appropriate disclaimers are a must in this kind of a scenario and prompting executives and all employees to distinguish when they speak on their own behalf and when they speak on behalf of the company.

BADGES AND ONLINE CREDENTIALS

The Good Housekeeping Seal of Approval became a symbol to let people know the product or service being advertised or reviewed in the Good Housekeeping magazine met certain criteria as to be recommended by the magazine and that the magazine would stand behind its recommendation by guaranteeing a consumer a refund or replacement of the item should it need to be replaced within two years of the bestowing of the seal.[47] The seal is just one of a series of symbolic icons to inspire consumer confidence.

In the online and digital environment, badges serve a number of functions, from certifying certain capabilities to certifying that the Web site or provider of the services of the Web site meets certain criteria to justify an affiliation or endorsement. In the security arena, we have McAfee Secure, SiteLock Secure, Truste Certified Privacy, VeriSign Secured, among others (see Figure 3.3). Their graphical expressions are familiar to those in the information security field and help form the foundation for credibility.

For regulated industries, this can take on other significances as there are certain logos and badges required to be present on Web sites and online forums in order to be in compliance (such as an FDIC or Equal Housing Lender icons for banks).

It is a good idea to do an online badge/credentials inventory. Take a look at the badges on your company's Web site(s) and other online or digital platforms to ensure they are current and accurate. Also review in case new standards have been released to update badges, apply for new ones, or remove badges that are no longer valid. Badges convey certain messages to consumers so making sure your badges are an accurate reflection of your capabilities and controls can help prevent compliance violations, such as the FTC false advertising rules (yes, that again).

---

[45] LinkedIn Influencer's site accessed October 27, 2013.
[46] Dharmesh Shah, "The Surprising Brilliance of The LinkedIn Influencers Program," (LinkedIn, August 6, 2013), http://www.linkedin.com/today/post/article/20130806143440-658789-the-brilliance-of-the-linkedin-influencers-program.
[47] "About the Good Housekeeping Seal," accessed March 2, 2014, http://www.goodhousekeeping.com/product-reviews/history/about-good-housekeeping-seal.

FIGURE 3.3 Examples of Security Badges Found on Web sites.

There may be a time that a company may design a badge themselves to award to others through a certification program or other kind of review. It is important to understand what the badge signifies and what it warrants to consumers and those in the industry. Is it a standard that will be adopted by others, endorsed by others, such as a professional association, or is it a stand-alone icon with little value other than the value the company who created it gives it? Will the company be liable to consumers or others if the entity it awarded the badge to fails to live up to its designation?

The last I will speak of badges brings it back into the individual arena—badges are used throughout the online and digital world through gamification methods, the use of incentives to encourage continued interaction with an application or system. Good examples of these are the Four Square badges. Four Square[48] is a geo-location application that allows users to "check in" to different venues they are located at. By checking in users can accumulate points that can lead to rewards and incentives, such as becoming mayor of a venue or earning a badge for checking in to certain categories a number of times (see Figure 3.4 for examples). It is interesting to note who may have what badges as it conveys information regarding a person's preferences as well as certain behavioral patterns. This last can be used for social engineering attacks against an executive permitting unauthorized user's access to company data. Four Square and other geo-location applications have also brought to light the dangers regarding the physical safety of individuals as it puts information about an executive's whereabouts in a public sphere. In addition, you do not necessarily have to be someone's "friend" in Four Square to find out location information. I was surprised at a recent trip to Turkey, the Four Square "friends" invites I was getting as I viewed the Hagia Sophia, an ancient church and mosque that is now a museum, from Turkish nationalists. I was not even checking in. Just the fact that I had a Four Square account was enough to let other Four Square users know I was in the area.

---

[48] https://foursquare.com.

FIGURE 3.4 A Screen Shot from My iPhone of Some of My Acquired Four Square Badges.

Please do not judge.

IDENTITY VERSUS REPUTATION

The Internet now provides the opportunity for millions of additional people to gain exposure to Identity. It's what pops up when employers, dates, colleagues, friends, and pretty much anyone who meets us for the first time, searches for us online.[49]

Based on the discussion in the preceding pages, reputation is an opinion, identity is a fact. Why the distinction? Does it have to do with being able to control what I put out online as my "identity" versus

---

[49]Zuckerberg, Randi, "Your Child's Digital Identity Begins Long Before Birth," (Dot Complicated Blog, February 17, 2013).

what others may say about my "reputation"? Perhaps it may be more correct to say that reputation is a component of identity that is added by others based on the online information available about the individual in question. However, we still have not addressed one component of the identity/reputation dichotomy. Not everyone is presented with the same identity information on which to base an opinion of an individual's or an entity's reputation. Why? It has to do with the way search engines, like Google, work. It creates an algorithm based on previous searches and customizes search results based on data they have on you and how they analyze it. Therefore, technically, you and I can both search a company name and yet get different search results because of our search history. Can we then say that Google and other search engines are providing the building blocks for forming an opinion of reputation for a person, place, or thing?

Therefore, to mitigate reputational risk, an important strategy would be the implementation of Search engine optimization (SEO), to ensure that the preferred results show up on top as most users will not scroll down after page three to get the information they were seeking. SEO is a process of using various techniques to improve the visibility of a Web site in a list of search results. The use of Meta Tags, or descriptive and strategic keywords in Web site descriptions is one such strategy.

SEO has been promoted for marketing purposes, but has gained renown for being one of the few options available to negate the impact of negative online information about an individual or company. Unfortunately, we do not have the technological option of removing or deleting information completely from the online space. There are cached copies and backups on various servers as the Internet is decentralized and open servers are used on an availability basis to move content from one location to another. In addition, friends, family, colleagues, and strangers "tag" photographs and other online content with an individual's name and create a duplicate of the original content, sometimes unbeknownst to the original subject.

There are initiatives trying to provide solutions for evidence of past mistakes that now have permanent residence online. The European Union is fighting for what it believes is a basic right being threatened by today's digital and social media giants—the Right to be Forgotten (in French *le droit à l'oubli*—or the "right of oblivion"). It is based on the idea that people may put something up that they later regret and should have the right to delete it—or more to a public interest concern—that criminal records and really, really bad mistakes that people commit should be "forgiven" and "forgotten" and deleted from the Internet once they paid for it. *The Stanford Review* gave an example of a possible effect of the law if passed: "The right to be forgotten could make Facebook and Google, for example, liable for up to two percent of their global income if they fail to remove photos that people post about themselves and later regret, even if the photos have been widely distributed already."[50] This proposed law, more than any other, really brings to light the clash between the United States and the rest of the world in terms of privacy and free speech. For now, the rule in the United States is that what you post and put out there is permanent. There are backups to backups, memory caches, copies sent to friends, etc. As they say "What happens in Vegas ends up on Facebook"—and most times it is because we put it there. If we do not want people to see it—do not put it up.

Another initiative is based in California, which recently passed a bill allowing minors (under the age of 18) to remove content or provide a notice for removal of content to Web sites. The law, which takes

---

[50] Rosen, Jeffrey, Stanford Law Review, " The Right to Be Forgotten," (February 13, 2012), http://www.stanfordlawreview.org/online/privacy-paradox/right-to-be-forgotten.

effect in January 2015, has been nicknamed the "Digital Eraser" law.[51] A closer look at the language of the law shows that it is limited in scope, for example, minors can only remove content that they post, which most Web sites allow already, but cannot remove content placed by another, even if it is about them, and even if they put the content up first. Therefore, awareness and critical thinking training of what to post in the first place is still essential.

As we look at the issue of minors and online content, we realize the concern is that the minors grow up and become adults, hopefully productive and contributing adults, to our economy and business world. Should their futures be held hostage by digital content of events that occurred while they were still children? What about the fact that in today's digital society, parents are creating their children's digital identities, sometimes even before they are born. One Facebook profile showed a sonogram of a fetus with a status posting of "just swimming" and who attends "Tummy University."[52] Facebook subsequently took the profile page down.[53] However, parents continue to post information about their children—funny things they do or things that were not so funny. We have even noticed a trend in choosing a baby's name based on an available .com URL address. In essence, these parents are creating their child's digital legacy without the child having any say in the matter. Can the child later sue the parents for this behavior if they are turned down for employment due to these postings?

Add this to two recent studies regarding minors and mobile technology. The first is discussed at length in a book entitled *The App Generation* (Yale University Press) by Harvard Professor Howard Gardner. In it he and his co-author, Katie Davis, a digital-media scholar at the University of Washington, puts forth the theory that children's identity are being shaped and pigeon-holed by applications that emphasize a certain way of doing things for achieving success and to becoming more risk-averse,[54] which may not be attributes a company requires for its workforce.

The second study was conducted by Common Sense Media, a San Francisco based nonprofit organization that examines children's interaction with technology. The study "Zero to Eight: Children's Media Use in America 2013" surveyed 1463 parents with children under 8 years old. The study found that "among children under 2, 38% had used mobile devices like iPhones, tablets, or Kindles" and that "forty percent of families now own tablets, seven percent of the children had tablets of their own."[55]

How does this relate to security? Many executives have children. Cautioning executives about what they post online regarding their children is a prudent strategy as information can used to target the child or even the executive. Children do not always concern themselves with safety issues when they post updates, such as "on vacation with mom and dad, who happens to be the top guy at XYZ Company," or upload photographs that still contain geo-tagging information, identifying exactly when and where the photograph was taken or playing around with the tablet touch screens. The company and the company's data can be compromised through the executive's mobile devices regardless of where the executive is

---

[51] Fran Berkman, "New California Law Lets Teens Press 'Eraser Button' Online," (Mashable, September 24, 2013), http://mashable.com/2013/09/24/california-law-delete-posts/.

[52] Elizabeth Johnson, "Unborn child has Facebook profile," (CNN, May 31, 2011), http://news.blogs.cnn.com/2011/05/31/unborn-child-has-facebook-profile/.

[53] Lincoln Ware, "Fetus With 300 Friends' Page Deleted From Facebook," (June 3, 2011), http://thebuzzcincy.com/1033091/fetus-with-300-friends-page-deleted-from-facebook/.

[54] Marc Parry, "Young People Let Digital Apps Dictate Their Identities, Say two Scholars," (The Chronicle of Higher Education, October 28, 2013), http://chronicle.com/article/Growing-Up-Theres-No-App-for/142655/.

[55] Tamar Lewin, "New Milestone Emerges: Baby's First iPhone App," *The New York Times*, (October 28, 2013), http://www.nytimes.com/2013/10/28/us/new-milestone-emerges-babys-first-iphone-app.html?_r=0.

located. However, hackers and others with malicious intentions use social engineering to create targeted attacks and children's online accounts can be another point of entry or source of information.

PROTECTING IDENTITY

The FTC defines identity theft as "a fraud committed using the identifying information of another person."[56] The U.S. Department of Justice (DOJ) goes a bit further "Identity theft and identity fraud are terms used to refer to all types of crime in which someone wrongfully obtains and uses another person's personal data in some way that involves fraud or deception, typically for economic gain."[57] Both definitions emphasize that it is an illegal act and therefore subject to enforcement under the law.

For companies, it is also a security risk as identity is a key to access and sometimes control of a company's data systems. Some current statistics regarding identity theft are quite revealing.

- Fifty-five percent of companies are concerned with identity theft.[58]
- Online fraud cost totaled $3.5 billion in 2012 for e-retailers.[59]
- Identity theft generates $1 billion a year for the thieves.[60]
- Approximately 11.5 million United States residents have their identities used fraudulently.[61]
- Approximately 7% of all adults have their identities misused with each instance resulting in approximately $4930 in losses.[62]
- An identity fraud incidence happens every 3 s.[63]

The types of fraud based on identity theft are not surprising. Based on the U.S. Department of Justice 2013 Report, the top three include misuse of existing credit card (64.1%), misuse of other existing bank account (35%), and misuse of personal information (14.2%).[64] The states with the highest identity theft complaint rate include Arizona (149 victims out of 100,000); California (139.1); Florida (133.3); Texas (130.3); and Nevada (126). The states with the lowest identity theft complaint rates include South Dakota (33.8); North Dakota (35.7); Iowa (44.9); Montana (46.5); and Wyoming (46.9).[65]

Does this suggest a factor for company location decision-making? Not necessarily, as company customers come from all over the country. So even if you are located in a low complaint state, like South Dakota, it may be a good idea to see where the majority of your customers are located in case it is a high complaint state, like Arizona, so you can take appropriate precautions as you transact business with those clients.

---

[56] Federal Trade Commission, "FTC Issues Final Rules on FACTA Identity Theft Definitions," (October 29, 2004), http://www.ftc.gov/news-events/press-releases/2004/10/ftc-issues-final-rules-facta-identity-theft-definitions-active.

[57] Accessed March 2, 2014, http://www.justice.gov/criminal/fraud/websites/idtheft.html.

[58] "An Overview of Web Security," (October 3, 2013), http://fr.slideshare.net/Bee_Ware/an-overview-of-web-security#.

[59] Ibid.

[60] Ibid.

[61] "Identity Theft/Fraud Statistics," http://www.statisticbrain.com/identity-theft-fraud-statistics/(June 18, 2013).

[62] Id.

[63] Erik Grueter, "Identity Theft Protection 101: Who's Spying On You?" (July 16, 2013), http://www.doctrackr.com/blog/bid/317379/Identity-Theft-Protection-101-Who-s-Spying-on-You-Infographic?utm_source=linkedin&utm_medium=social&utm_content=775219.

[64] "Identity Theft/Fraud Statistics," (June 18, 2013), http://www.statisticbrain.com/identity-theft-fraud-statistics/.

[65] Ibid.

The FTC,[66] DOJ,[67] and even the FBI[68] offer information and resources for consumers and businesses regarding how to identify identity theft and what to do about it should you become a victim. All suggest active and periodic monitoring of online accounts (especially financial ones, such as online banking) to see if any unusual activity shows up, such as charges you did not incur or medical bills being denied. They all also provide checklists or suggested steps to take to recover from the fraud (see If you are a victim of ID theft).

IF YOU ARE A VICTIM OF ID THEFT:

- Place an initial Fraud Alert with the FTC.
- Order your credit reports.
- Create an identity theft report.
- Change your passwords to all online financial accounts (even the ones not affected in case you used the same password).
- Document any irregular activity and the actions you take to correct the situation.
- Contact the U.S. Postal Service if you believe part of the fraud changed your mailing address.
- Contact the Social Security Administration if you believe your Social Security number has been used fraudulently.
- Contact the Internal Revenue Service if you believe your identification information is being used for tax violations.
- Contact all your financial institutions and creditors to alert them to the theft.

Even with a plan for what to do if identity theft happens, it is still important to try to prevent it or at least limit the likelihood that this could happen to your company's employees (especially executives). Providing them with training and supporting materials can be helpful. The FTC provides information brochures (and bookmarks) for free that you can then distribute to employees as an added benefit to increase their knowledge base and to decrease the security risk.[69] Companies have also looked at instituting a policy of the use of digital lockers especially for executives to protect their online access credentials.

Below, I list some best practices when it comes to protecting identity online, some of which are repeated from other best practice lists previously listed in this book.

- Be careful what you post online.
- Be careful of who you allow to post online on your behalf.
- Use strong passwords.
- Do not use the same password for multiple accounts.
- Use two-factor verification when available.
- Make good use of your security questions.
- Do not accept invitations from strangers.
- Be aware of your privacy settings and use them when available.

---

[66] "Identity Theft," (FTC), accessed March 2, 2014, http://www.consumer.ftc.gov/features/feature-0014-identity-theft.

[67] "Identity Theft and Identity Fraud," accessed March 2, 2014, http://www.justice.gov/criminal/fraud/websites/idtheft.html.

[68] "Identity Theft," (FBI), accessed March 2, 2014, http://www.fbi.gov/about-us/investigate/cyber/identity_theft.

[69] "Identity Theft Resources," (FTC), accessed March 2, 2014, http://www.consumer.ftc.gov/features/feature-0015-identity-theft-resources.

- Take a digital inventory.
- Do a digital identity audit.
- Use privacy preference settings on ALL your online accounts.
- Use secure hubs and not public Wi-Fi.
- Secure your mobile.
- Set up Google Alerts to monitor the conversation regarding your name and your company name.
- Unsubscribe from newsletters, RSS feeds, etc., that you do not read.
- Clean up abandoned accounts.

PROTECTING REPUTATION

A company's reputation can be a tenuous thing. Common reputation management problems come from: squatted usernames, squatted domains, job changes, name changes, negative comments, false information, fake profiles, trademark infringement, bad news coverage, complaint and/or hate sites, personal and/or corporate scandals, negative media coverage, etc.[70]

There are companies who offer services to protect or repair a company's reputation. At one time, they were concentrated in your Public Relations department or Public Relations agency, those spin doctors who knew what words to say, how to phrase them, and what medium to send the message on. Today, they are online and their focus is managing your company's online reputation. Brand.com[71] and Reputation.com[72] are just two focusing on the online and digital sphere. Brand.com clients include Fortune 500 businesses, while Reputation.com offers services for both individuals and companies. Reputation.com offers specific services, such as "tracking, analyzing, and improving online reviews, social media, business listings, and local search visibility for all of your business locations across the entire Internet."[73]

These services cost money and so need to be strategically thought of in terms of where do they fit in the budget (public relations or security), who or what needs to be covered (company, executives, both), what service provider to use, etc. For example, Reputation.com not only has different pricing models for personal, small business, and enterprise, but within each category there are different options. For the personal, they go from a basic service at $99 to a white glove service of over $500.

Part of the necessity for this service or at the very least the function of online reputation management (ORM) is "the need to increasingly curate our increasingly visible digital lives"[74] whether that be an executive's or an artificial entity like a company. At the beginning of this Chapter, I postulated that what one does personally can definitely affect a company's reputation. The challenge for risk management and security professionals is laying this out in an argument that resonates with board members

---

[70] "The Online Reputation Management Guide," Outspoken Media, (2010), accessed March 2, 2014, http://outspokenmedia.com/guides/orm-guide/.

[71] http://www.brand.com.

[72] http://www.reputation.com.

[73] See note 72.

[74] "Digital Identity Matters," Rhizome, http://digitaldisruptions.org/rhizome/wp-content/uploads/2010/06/rhiz08_DigitalIdentityMatters.pdf.

and those who control the financial resources of a company to assign funds to this task by recognizing its value to the company.

In the meantime, the following are some tips to ORM to help begin the process:

- Accept that all employees are part of the company and part of the brand. Every interaction they take on behalf of the company enhances or detracts from the company's reputation. Treat them well and educate them about their role in regard to the company's reputation.
- Be consistent between online and offline practices.
- Provide great customer service.
- Have a social listening program in place to monitor the conversation about your company so you can address concerns as they arise.
- Use tools such as Feed Reader, Google Alerts, Yahoo Alerts, Twitter Searches, etc.
- Know where your brand advocates are and nurture them.
- Know where your competition is online and monitor them.
- If you see something negative on another site, send a request for removal to the site Webmaster. They may or may not take it down, but it usually does not hurt to ask.
- Publish quality content and promote it so that they rank high in the results and the negatives are pushed down.

THE NEW WORKFORCE

"All of a sudden Human Resources is at the table in innovation. Why? Having the right people, having the right environment, defining the behaviors, having leaders role model the behavior, training—all of this is mission critical if you want to be an innovative company."[1]

No one will dispute the importance of Human Resources (HR)[2] in the business environment. Businesses need employees, and finding the right ones can be decisive to a business' success, as noted in the quote above. However, HR's role in an organization is transitioning from back-office procurement of talent to front-line strategic resource allocation. It is because of this transition that HR is now being

---

[1] Darden Hess, quoted in "The New Recipe for Workforce Innovation," (Jan 17, 2013), http://www.workforce.com/articles/the-new-recipe-for-workforce-innovation.

[2] Human Resources (HR): these two words, which can be the name of a department with the specific focus of activities related to employees, can also be recognized as two words that identify the employees themselves as an asset to that business. This chapter will review risks associated with both, so to minimize confusion I will use "HR" to identify the department and "workforce" to identify the employees.

looked upon as a partner in risk management and security, especially in the online and digital arenas where employees are conducting their tasks.

Most would say that HR's primary role is to attract top talent that fits the organization's culture[3] (see Box for list of core HR responsibilities). However, "fit" is not the only criteria. HR is looking for the "right" talent, with the right knowledge, skills, and ability required for a specific business function. In looking for that kind of talent, we see an HR department that is using a diversity of tactics, tools, technology, and strategies, some old some new, including greater use of strategic alliances, to ensure an invaluable asset to the company. However, each of these can pose their own risks to the company—from potential liability of discrimination, to leakage of confidential information to unauthorized third parties.

CORE HR RESPONSIBILITIES

- Organization design (hierarchy/authority)
- Workforce planning
- Talent acquisition
- Retention
- High performance standards
- Learning and development
- Leadership development
- Succession planning and implementation
- Labor relations
- Risk management
- Employee security and safety
- Worker's Compensation
- Benefits (medical)

EMPLOYMENT CYCLE

HR is involved in every step of the employment cycle, which is the different stages of an employee's tenure at the company (see Figure 4.1). New technology and the current use of social media and digital online activity in each of these stages by HR, job candidates, and employees, have increased the likelihood of certain risks and/or created new risks that information technology (IT) and security did not need to contend with before. The risks at each of these stages include reputational risk of the company's brand, organizational, such as data and confidentiality, and legal, for compliance, etc. The risks will be discussed in more detail in their appropriate sections within this chapter. These sections are:

1. Workforce planning. The first stage looks at the requirements the company has for employees.
2. Recruitment. The second stage contains the strategies for sourcing an employee and how to advertise.
3. Hiring/orientation. The third stage begins the process of the employee's actual affiliation with the company. Things such as the job offer, employee agreement, and welcome orientation fall within this process.

---

[3] "Workforce for the Future," (2010), accessed March 5, 2014, http://www.mwdh2o.com/BlueRibbon/pdfs/Workforce-Future.pdf.

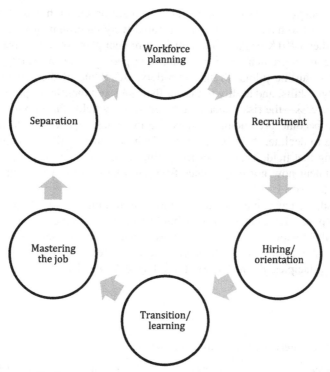

FIGURE 4.1 The Employment Cycle.

4. Transition/learning. The fourth stage looks at the time the employee takes to acclimate to the company, its environment and culture, the job, the colleagues, etc. For each employee, this stage may last a different period of time depending on the skills and knowledge required by the job and the employee's capability.

5. Mastering of the job. The fifth stage assumes the employee has reached a level of proficiency or mastery of the skills, knowledge, and capability required by the position for which they were hired. This may be indicated by promotions, awards, or other recognitions. Not all employees will reach this level.

6. Separation. The sixth stage marks the end of an employee's affiliation with a company. It could be voluntary (resignation or retirement) or involuntary (firing or death).

WHO IS THE WORKFORCE?

Because HR's focus is employees, it is important to understand who makes up the workforce and how that workforce is changing. Let us start with demographics. We have a few factors at work here. Depending on your perspective, we either have to concern ourselves with a retirement bubble or with older employees staying on the job longer. I believe it is a combination of both plus a new generation.

On the retirement angle, we have some workers who are on the high end of the retirement age who are some of the last to have worked in a structured work environment with guaranteed retirement benefits—whether a 401K or other alternative retirement plan. We also have some older workers in fields that require retirement after a certain time period to ensure safety of customers and property, for example, airline pilots, flight controllers, etc. Some of these workers take years to acquire the knowledge, skills, and ability to master their jobs and their leave poses a gap in essential talent for business success—the risk management and security fields fall into this scenario. Besides the required time to become proficient, the decrease in wages, and with birth rates in developed countries continuing to decline, there is the issue of whether there will be enough people who are interested in pursuing that field. These questions bring in the element of globalization and a more diverse workforce: talent now not only comes from anywhere in the world, but also works from almost anywhere in the world.

On the other hand, we have an economic situation that has made it almost mandatory for certain older workers to postpone retirement, or to come out of retirement and reenter the workforce to be able to meet their financial obligations. In some companies, you may have as many as four different generations comprising the labor pool. This multigenerational workforce poses challenges and risks as traditional management principles do not work for all (see Table 4.1: Workforce Generations and Characteristics).

Table 4.1 Workforce Generations and Characteristics

	Veterans	Boomers	Generation X	Millennials
Born	Before 1946	1946–1964	1965–1979	1980–2000
Age today	68+ years old	50–67 years	35–49 years	34–14 years
Characteristics	Sacrifice, hard working, and loyal. Reluctant to speak up or buck the system. Comfortable with delayed rewards.	Service-oriented, team players, idealistic. Systems, forms, and structures	Independent, impatient, not intimidated by authority. Wary of sugar-coated messages.	Tech savvy. Globally aware. Want up-to-the-second feedback and direction. They want guidance and mentorship.
How is work completed?	Hard work	Team work	Network	Social
What should work provide	Safety and security	System and structure	Challenge and risk	Reward and satisfaction
Management attitude	Management is king	Management is respected	Management needs to be competent to earn respect	Management + employees make decisions.

Adapted from Green, 2009.[4]

[4] Marnie E Green, "Managing the Workforce of the Future" (October 14, 2009), http://www.slideshare.net/mgreen1965/managing-the-workforce-of-the-future.

MILLENNIALS

Depending on the article of the day, they are either "the most risky employee a company can have"[5] or they are the salvation of a company with their technological savvy and appetite for learning. They are called Generation Y or millennials, because they were born at the time of the millennium (between 1979 and 2000), they include approximately 70 million people in the United States alone, and will form 47% of the U.S. workforce by 2014.[6]

These digital natives, like the social media and wearable technology they conduct their lives with, are here to stay. So how are they as employees? To understand them we need to remember how they were raised—with unlimited options but with structured lives,[7] very independent and self-sufficient,[8] information always at their fingertips through computers at home, school, libraries, etc., always consulted with about decisions, had their opinions valued, and always told they could make a difference. It is this last factor that makes them the most civically engaged generation yet.

With this in mind, looking at the list of attributes for millennial employees makes a lot of sense. They are hungry for technology and learning, "more motivated by personal satisfaction with their jobs then with money, they want to grow in their positions, they want to be challenged, they want to have the opportunity to be included in decision-making and offering solutions to business problems, they want to be heard, they are results-driven, and will change jobs more often seeking companies that will offer them what they want."[9] But they are also "used to working in teams, are positive and confident with a "can-do" attitude, want variety in their work, and want to know where their career is going ad exactly how to get there."[10] The final group of attributes speaks to their social-mindedness; "they want to make friends at work and they want flexibility in scheduling because they want a life away from work."[11] It is these characteristics that have also garnered them the nickname of NANOBOT: nearly autonomous, not in the office, and doing business in their own time.[12]

Things are seldom one-sided and along with their positive traits, some have noted that these can actually take on a negative connotation in the extreme. New York Times reporter, Keshav Nair, recently wrote "millennials are the most at risk generation due to the higher rates of observing

---

[5] Keshav Nair, "Ethics Training Essential with New Workforce Behaviors, Characteristics" (July 25, 2013), http://www.tnwinc.com/4220/risk-assessment-tools/.

[6] Brian Solis, "The Disconnect between Aging Management and the Younger Workforce" (August, 2013), http://www.briansolis.com/2013/08/the-disconnect-between-aging-management-and-the-younger-workforce/.

[7] Susan M Healthfield, "11 Tips for Managing Millennials", accessed March 5, 2014, http://humanresources.about.com/od/managementtips/a/millenials.htm.

[8] One article offered that the independence comes from the fact that most millennials were latch key kids; their parents worked and so they had to fend on their own.

[9] Joan Gerberding, "Managing and Keeping the New Workforce" (July, 2013), http://performinsider.com/2013/07/managing-and-keeping-the-new-workforce/.

[10] See note 7 above.

[11] Ibid.

[12] WSJ Podcast 2008 (December 12, 2008), http://podcast.mktw.net/wsj/audio/20081212/pod-wsjjrnano/pod-wsjjrnano.mp3.

misconduct and experiencing retaliation for reporting incidents."[13] He lists three risk and security concerns:

- Millennials are open and transparent and more likely to share information about their work with others, which can put the company at reputational risk.
- Millennials are more likely to keep copies of confidential company documents after they had need of them and may not consider safety precautions for storing them.
- Millennials may be more flexible with moral standards and consider the end justifies the means if it means saving their job.

Nair offers the solution that ethics training is essential for this group of employees to reduce the above-listed risks, as well as others.

CHANGING OF THE GUARD

As we look at the challenges of managing millennials, another challenge is apparent, that of millennials as managers. With the retirement bubble scenario, are we seeing millennials being given higher levels of responsibility earlier in their careers than previous generations?[14] Could this be causing risks because they are not yet ready to manage these responsibilities? In addition, do younger supervisors managing older workers provide more opportunities for discrimination against older workers because younger supervisors are not sure about managing those who may have more experience than them? Does the perception of millennials by the older generations as more demanding because they feel informed, connected, and empowered, provide occasions for bullying by millennials? Does the demanding nature of the millennials fuel pressure onto the older generation to adjust to higher level technology usage even though the older generation is not ready leading to risks due to inappropriate and insecure use of these technologies? As with the ethics training question posed by Nair, later in this chapter we will explore whether specific management training will assist in reducing these risks.

RECRUITMENT

If employees are one of the biggest security risks for a company, as we have discussed in previous chapters, then it makes sense that a major strategy to reduce that risk is to ensure that the recruitment process of identifying and selecting candidates keeps security and risk management as one of its parameters (see Figure 4.2). Here is an opportunity for HR and security personnel to work together to better secure success for the business in the long term.

PLANNING

HR begins by developing a workforce plan based on an organization's strategic plan and current organizational structure. Expanding the workforce may be the result of a change in the business model, creation of a new business line, or business reorganization. In addition, workforce issues may come up

---

[13] See note 5.
[14] See note 6.

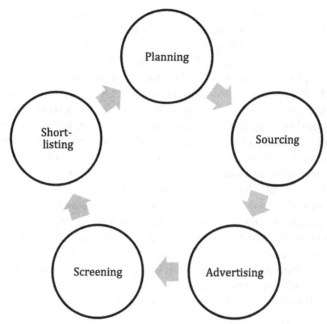

FIGURE 4.2 The Recruitment Cycle.

because of a changing external environment outside of the company's direct control and influence, such as a labor supply shortage, budget cuts, or changes in legislation. The last group of issues workforce management is concerned with is the maintenance and improvement of the existing workforce, such as regular training, business continuity planning, etc.

Whatever the cause, HR must ensure meeting with the appropriate internal stakeholders to understand the needs for new employees. These needs cover budget concerns, such as salary ranges, skills required, and levels of authority for the new employee, and position and work location of the employee. For example, is it a full-time position, part-time, contingent, virtual, free agent, independent contractor, consultant, or other?

Part of the planning to meet workforce objectives to fulfill company needs consists of job analysis, ensuring that job descriptions fit what the worker is actually required to do, and headcount forecasting, comparing future workforce needs with the current workforce profile to identify gaps or opportunities to transition existing employees.

SOURCING

Once HR knows what kind of employees it is looking for, they turn to where they can find them or who can help them find the right talent. Today, HR has different options to source a position. Some companies have a tradition of looking within the company at existing talent and seeing if there is a match for promotion. Alternatively, HR may use the internal workforce as ambassadors to help personally recruit individuals they may know who will fit the job and the company culture. It is not unusual in that scenario that the referring employee receive a fee or other benefit for helping to fill the position.

Recently, a financial organization had a question regarding permitting employees to post the employment opportunities on their personal social media accounts. Would this open them up to the risk of a discrimination lawsuit or could it be perceived as the employer endorsing the rest of the employee's social media content, subjecting the employer to other risks of legal violations, such as copyright infringement on that employee's account? This becomes an important issue because of the prevalent use of LinkedIn and LinkedIn groups as a sourcing resource. It is safe to say that letting employees know that the opening exists and suggesting that if they want to post it on their social media or other online digital accounts to do so via a link to the company's official employment opportunity page is one way to control the actual content of the job posting. This way they could still get credit if a new employee is hired because of their online referral. You do, however, want to discourage any elaboration on the part of the current employee about the position or the qualifications for the position. That could lead to legal trouble. LinkedIn also has a feature called "Work With Us" that identifies the individual's employer, checks to see if the employer has any job openings listed on its official LinkedIn company page, and lets viewers of the individual's profile see the opportunities available.

HR can also turn to third-party staffing vendors, such as freelance headhunters, executive recruiting firms, and employment agencies. Most of these will encourage some kind of technology-enabled system to announce the position, identify talent, solicit interest, and screen candidates. From a risk management and security standpoint, keep in mind the following: inquire as to whose system will be used—yours or theirs? If theirs, then ask the appropriate security questions:

- What kind of data will be collected?
- How will data be stored and protected?
- Who has access to the data?

HR may also conduct its own search to identify and attract potential talent. Social media sites, such as LinkedIn and Twitter, are mined by HR professionals looking to fill positions. LinkedIn has an application called "Recruiter Mobile" to help HR do just that. HR does have to understand how these tools work; for example, what would be an appropriate hashtag on Twitter to use when announcing a job opening to get the best candidates? Posting a job online is not that new—Monster.com and other websites have been offering this option for a while. However, posting a job on the new social media platforms is new. LinkedIn may seem like the most appropriate, due to its professional nature, but you can also use Tweetajob.com, and it looks like Facebook will be entering this arena as well. One thing to make sure you do before posting a job on these platforms is to read their Terms of Service/Use to make sure you are not violating any of their rules.

One of the concerns with sourcing is that even though the digital environment allows you to reach out to millions of potential employees, it also allows employers to limit who will see the listing. Again, this is not something new. Companies have always had to decide where to post a position as some of them require a payment and budgets are limited. However, when posting online, the possibility of discrimination (excluding a certain class of candidates) based on disparate treatment of where a position is listed is more probable than ever.

ADVERTISING

After HR identifies where to source, it creates the posting and advertises the position. It is interesting to note that with digital and online platforms, HR needs to concern itself with HR marketing and the branding of the employer as an attractive option for desired talent, especially in the fields where there is a labor shortage. There is an increased risk for reputation damage, depending on how the company is portrayed, intellectual property infringement, theft risk depending on how logos and other company identity-related imagery and text are used, and hacking opportunities due to social engineering (like phishing attacks) with the information provided in the job positing itself (such as contact info). Here is another opportunity where HR and security personnel can work together to ensure that the online advertising venues are reviewed for security purposes and the right precautions are put into place, such as a generic mailbox for submissions and inquiries so no specific employee names with their direct contact information are listed.

SCREENING

This part of the process actually occurs in three phrases: receiving the submissions, sorting the submissions, and screening the submissions to create a short-list of potentially qualified candidates to pursue to the next level.

When the resumes come in, they may not all look like traditional resumes. With so much competition for limited positions, candidates are trying to be creative and stand out. New formats are being introduced from quick response (QR) codes that open to a video profile, to data visualized resumes that appear more like an infographic than the standard listed details. You should specify if you will or will not accept these new formats. From a security standpoint, these new formats can cause concerns. Any link can be used by a hacker to redirect a viewer to a malicious Website or access unauthorized material. A reminder about phishing attacks to HR professionals (and interns or others who may be assisting them in reviewing the submissions) is important, as well as instructions to send the questionable material directly to security if something seems unusual.

Filtering through the resumes to prescreen qualified candidates will more than likely include a social media background check. It may be something as simple as looking up the candidate's name in Google and seeing what comes up, or contracting with a company that supplies a report without certain characteristics that can be viewed as discriminatory (i.e., gender, age, race, etc.). If your company/client plans to conduct these background checks, they should receive consent from the candidate.

There has been a lot in the media regarding employers requiring job candidates to give them their social media account passwords or to log into their accounts and allow the interviewer to shoulder surf and see what has been posted. The issue raises concerns over privacy and the separation between the professional and the personal. One professor who was interviewed online declared that it was "like giving the potential employer the key to your house," and questioned why that would be necessary.

As of this writing, there has not been a federal bill passed through Congress regarding this issue. However, in 2013, over 36 states had either passed legislation or had introduced legislation prohibiting employers from requesting the passwords or shoulder surfing job candidates.[15]

Companies are also comparing the resumes they receive to the candidate's social media profiles, like their LinkedIn accounts, and will question discrepancies or facts that do not seem to match or may

---

[15] *Employer Access to Social Media Usernames and Passwords*, accessed March 5, 2014, http://www.ncsl.org/research/telecommunications-and-information-technology/employer-access-to-social-media-passwords-2013.aspx, and *Bill Tracker: Social Media Bills*, accessed March 5, 2014, http://www.billtrack50.com/PublicStakeholder/VmSxMH7n9kCgyaPMoqbBtw/.

even contradict each other. This is a very important point in terms of is the person really who they say they are and do they have the credentials they say they do? The Federal Trade Commission issued a notice in late 2011 that they would crack down on fraudulent credentials in social media profiles under false advertising, especially for those in regulated industries.

Another series of issues have arisen in terms of "friending" during the recruitment and interview process—either by the candidate or by the interviewer. This can raise conflict of interests or bias (if the two are already friends) or duress/pressure to friend the interviewer because the candidate wants the job. It is good practice to remind those on the interview/search committee that they should not post about any candidate or about the job search process on any social media platform. Discretion and confidentiality are important. These posts and tweets can be introduced in court as evidence of bias or discrimination.

SHORT-LISTING

After the screening is done by comparing the submissions to the job requirements, an initial short list of potential candidates is identified. It is at this time that reference checks may take place to verify information submitted by the candidates and other sources of information that can be found online. This is a good place to note the role of endorsements in the digital space. For example, LinkedIn permits full-length recommendations and specific skills-based endorsements. Questions as to the appropriate, ethical, and legal use of these recommendations and endorsements have come up raising again the potential for reputational risk to the company and violation of labor laws. It is customary that when HR receives a call inquiring about a former employee, it can only give out certain information, such as if the person worked there and the time frame they were employed. Any other information is limited as it can subject the employer to liability either for defaming the former employee or misrepresenting the former employee's capabilities. There is debate as to whether online endorsements from co-workers can be held to that same standard, as more and more employers rely on the information they find online about candidates in determining whether to hire them or not.

In addition, LinkedIn allows contacts to add skills that the individual did not originally identify permitting the opportunity of skill-creep. Again, the concern is does the profile offer an accurate and not misleading picture of this person's qualifications and experience?

For risk management purposes, training HR professionals to then convey this kind of information and guidance to employees is important. One financial institution has gone so far as to design Financial Industry Regulatory Authority compliant look-and-feel templates for their employees to use (at their discretion) for their personal LinkedIn profiles.

HIRING

Social media-related risks continue once a candidate has been selected. These risks focus on inappropriate or untimely announcements relating to the job offer. Official announcements by the company should not be superseded by unofficial tweets and Facebook statuses, as these can sometimes affect stock prices and other business-related values and assets. As part of making the offer, HR should discuss with the desired candidate certain guidelines to follow to reduce the likelihood of these risks. For example, let the candidate know IF and WHEN it is appropriate for them to post about the new position and being selected. Some companies have a practice of issuing a press release for a certain level of hire. Giving the candidate the URL for the press release so that it can be linked to their personal tweet or status can help ensure the company's message is kept intact.

How the offer is made is also changing. Depending on the company culture and the level of hire, an email may go out instead of an officially mailed letter. I think it would be prudent to hold off sending offers via a tweet. Recent court decisions have held that a tweet can modify a contract, so it is in the company's interest that there should be no tweeting about the terms of the offer and the acceptance. Negotiation via social media is not ideal, especially considering that much of the negotiation will concentrate on confidential types of terms, such as compensation, benefits, options, etc., and social media is considered a public medium despite certain privacy preference settings.

The employment agreement may also take on different forms considering the technology available to us now. Digital documents requiring e-signatures are becoming more acceptable as original documents and binding to the parties involved. Here, the risk concern focuses on security and privacy of the document, making sure it goes to who it needs to go to and is accessed by only those authorized to do so. IT, security, and HR can work together to identify the right e-signature platform. This platform can also become the standard throughout the corporation, adding another level of security and risk prevention.

We are seeing some new terms making their way into the employment agreement relating to digital, social media, and online activity.

1. Social media account ownership. This term outlines whether or not there are official corporate accounts assigned to the employee for the duration of their employment with the company. It may list the actual social media and/or online digital accounts or it may leave that for future identification and setup, as well as account credentials (identification (ID) and password, for example), in collaboration with IT.
2. Social media activity guidelines. This term may simply refer to a social media policy or other documentation the company may have adopted to offer employees guidelines on social media activity use while they are employed by the company; or the term may actually spell out the guidelines themselves. I have also seen social media guidelines referenced by a "morality" clause that outlines certain behavior that the company will not permit from an employee, such as certain sexual behavior or drug use, that the company believes will denigrate the reputation of the company. In extension, photographs of the employee engaging in such conduct can be viewed as evidence in a disciplinary hearing. Including such a clause is seen as one way to reduce the likelihood of reputational risk.
3. Social Media blackouts. This term prescribes a certain amount of time (usually about 6 months) where the newly hired employee restrains from doing any online activity on social media platforms to create some distance from one former corporate affiliation to the new one.
4. Virtual/WiFi Work Environment. This term outlines the use of technology for corporate purposes outside the corporate offices or within using wireless networks. Again, it may reference a separate policy the company already has in place. It will be even more important to lay out in the employee agreement if the hired employee will be part of an expanded or contingent workforce.
5. Virtual/Flex schedule. This term provides parameters as to the expectations of the company relating to the employee's physical time commitment to complete the job. We take note that the new incoming generation of millennials does not necessarily appreciate the nine-to-five structure of the pre-digital world. They understand that they may be more productive from

3 o'clock in the afternoon to 2 o'clock the following morning. Their goal is to complete the work, not necessarily complete it within traditional time parameters. This opens up security concerns as these employees may use their own devices (bring your own device (BYOD)) offsite to access company data and finish their work. IT and security should consider this as you lay out security guidelines for BYOD, in what could become a 24-7 access environment.

EMPLOYMENT

Many of the risks associated with online and digital activity that concern corporate security professionals happen within the employment period itself.

SOCIAL MEDIA POLICIES

There has been a bit of debate over whether a social media policy is a requirement and can offer protection from liability for a company or whether it is overdoing it. We do know that having a policy can be a first line of defense for a company against a wrongful termination suit. But, truth be told, it is not just having a policy, it is making sure the policy adheres to standards, is enforced consistently and across the board, and employees are trained so they know what is permissible and what can happen to them if they do not follow the rules.

Some key items for the social media policy include:

- It should be consistent with other company policies that relate to technology use, email use, privacy, and confidentiality of company data and clients, and any other policy dealing with communication and digital equipment (including mobile phones and tablets).
- It should identify benefits of social media.
- It should address the risks of social media.
- It should designate the contact person(s) for people to consult with in regard to this policy (name, title, and contact information, including telephone number, email address, and/or other communication contact).
- It should describe the firm's expectations, the fact that individuals are going to be responsible for their online activities.
- It should lay out the requirement of protection of client and firm confidences and address jurisdictional rules on advertising and disclosure to solicit new clients (especially for regulated industries).
- It should indicate that the company reserves the right to take disciplinary action against those who violate—and must outline what those actions may be.
- It should state that the company reserves the right to monitor use of social media by employees while the employee is using company equipment, if that is the case.

The National Labor Relations Board (NLRB)[16] has issued three memorandums outlining its reasoning behind several social media termination cases in determining whether the social media policies the

---

[16] "Acting General Counsel releases report on social media cases" (National Labor Relations Board, August 18, 2011), https://www.nlrb.gov/news/acting-general-counsel-releases-report-social-media-cases.

companies had implemented were valid or not. One thing to keep in mind is "Employers should review their Internet and social media policies to determine whether they are susceptible to an allegation that the policy would 'reasonably tend to chill employees' in the exercise of their rights to discuss wages, working conditions and unionization."[17]

According to the NLRB, social media policies need to be narrowly construed, not overbroad, not use vague language, and can also include reminders to the employees to be respectful, fair, and courteous in their online postings, not to defame a company's products or services, that the company's anti-harassment and antidiscrimination policies apply online, and certain disclosure of confidential information can be prohibited.

SOCIAL + MOBILE WORKFORCE

We discussed BYOD in Chapter 2 as one of a number of new internal threats to a company's security due to online and digital activity. We emphasize again the need for a BYOD policy and mobile security strategy. As we take into account the millennials and how they rely on their devices to engage with the world around, then special attention must be placed on how this affects company risks and security concerns.

Another concern relates to the personal safety of the employee and those around them, including customers, vendors, or others. There has been recent debate about the distraction factor of these mobile devices, not just in terms of driving, but even pedestrian walking and fatal accidents.[18] If the company issues mobile devices or has a BYOD policy, it is a good idea to also look at providing Bluetooth or other hands free technology for vehicles. In addition, the company should include awareness training and remind employees about the dangers of being distracted by their mobile devices and the consequences that can occur. These distractions can cause accidents and major injuries, even fatalities that can lead to legal liability for the company if the employee was using company equipment and/or if the employee was distracted while within their scope of employment.

Millennials believe that they are great multitaskers and that what some people may call "distraction" they call "multitasking." However, a number of studies have outlined the fallacy of this belief. A case in point is the 2009 Stanford University study published in the Proceedings of the National Academy of Sciences "Cognitive Control in Media Multitaskers." Clifford Nass, one of the study's co-authors, notes that scholarship has remained firm in the overall assessment: "The research is almost unanimous, which is very rare in social science, and it says that people who chronically multitask show an enormous range of deficits. They're basically terrible at all sorts of cognitive tasks, including multitasking."[19]

It is also important for HR to note the pervasiveness of mobile devices where essentially an employee may never be "off" and subject to unrealistic expectations of QR times even at 2:00 o'clock in the morning. Recent articles are discussing the concerns of the psychological impact of social media use

---

[17] Jayne Navarre, "Do your law firm employees have a right to free speech on Facebook? Legal Case Filed by NLRB," (November, 2010), http://virtualmarketingofficer.com/2010/11/do-your-law-firm-employees-have-a-right-to-free-speech-on-facebook-legal-case-filed-by-nlrb/.

[18] "Pedestrian Deaths Linked to Texting and Walking" (ABCnews, August 26, 2013), http://abcnews.go.com/WNT/video/pedestrian-deaths-linked-texting-walking-20076570.

[19] John Wihbey, "Multitasking, social media and distraction: Research review" (July 11, 2013), http://journalistsresource.org/studies/society/social-media/multitasking-social-media-distraction-what-does-research-say#.

by individuals and how "social media-induced angst is on the increase."[20] From issues of self-esteem and self-depiction on social media sites to the recent slate of online workplace bullying, HR needs to be aware of the risks to an employee's state of mind, which, in turn, affects productivity and accuracy.

BullyingStatistics.org is a nonprofit organization that provides data and resources to combat bulling, whether in schools, the workplace, or online. On one of its pages, it lists some of the ways that companies suffer due to bullying including:

- High turnover, which is expensive for companies as they invest in hiring and training new employees only to lose them shortly thereafter, possibly to a competitor.
- Low productivity because employees are not motivated to do their best and are more often out sick due to stress-related illnesses.
- Lost innovations because the bully is more interested in attacking the victim than advancing the company, and the victims become less likely to generate or share new ideas.
- Difficulty hiring quality employees as word spreads that the company has a hostile work environment.[21]

SOCIAL MEDIA ACCOUNTS AND MONITORING

Companies are concerned that information that is posted by employees online and digitally can have adverse affects on the company's reputation and financial performance. To that end, companies sometimes institute monitoring programs relating to social media use. For example, IT may be able to block access to certain social media sites by employees using company equipment. This may be a little more difficult if the employee is using his or her own device. IT systems can also log URL's and site information of where an employee may have visited while on company equipment. These logs can be reviewed for time duration spent away from what is considered productive work.

In addition, such monitoring can help companies identify instances of twitterjacking or cybersquatting, false impersonations of the company or one of the company's employees, of company official social media accounts, and/or intellectual property theft. Upon discovery, the company can then take appropriate remedial action to remove or lessen the risk.

Monitoring in such a manner is considered realistic for an employer who needs to monitor its company assets for maintenance and capacity, etc., but guidelines require that the company inform employees that such monitoring is taking place. State labor laws and recent court decisions have addressed the issue of workplace monitoring before, through the lens of privacy, indicating that employees should not have an expectation of privacy at their workplace, including with some of their emails. There are cases where the opposite has also been held true, when an employee has a subjective expectation of privacy due to the use of passwords or other locking device.[22] It is important that HR has a number of discussions with the legal department to ensure compliance to the laws.

---

[20] Peggy Drexler, "Your Social Life is not your Social Media" *Psychology Today* (October 17, 2013), http://www.psychologytoday.com/blog/our-gender-ourselves/201310/your-social-life-is-not-your-social-media.

[21] "Workplace Bullying," *Bullying Statistics* (2013), accessed March 5, 2014, http://www.bullyingstatistics.org/content/workplace-bullying.html.

[22] Diane Vaksdal Smith and Jacob Burg, "What Are the Limits of Employee Privacy?" GPSolo, vol. 29, no. 6 (November/December 2012), http://www.americanbar.org/publications/gp_solo/2012/november_december2012privacyandconfidentiality/what_are_limits_employee_privacy.html.

Another aspect of keeping track of employees productivity relate to the company's knowledge of where an employee is during their hours of employment. Workforce Management IT Systems, which include functions, such as time cards or "checking into" a job, are becoming more sophisticated and integrated with other company HR and IT systems. In addition, third-party vendors, such as ADP Payroll Systems,[23] offer their own platforms with different functionality. As with all third-party software vendors, IT security needs to be part of the conversation to procure such services and ensure that security precautions are in place.

EMPLOYEE PRIVACY: BENEFITS AND DATA COLLECTION

We discussed one component of privacy in regard to employee monitoring above. Another privacy issue employees are concerned about is the use of their online content in determining benefit levels, such as health insurance premiums and coverage. For our discussion, privacy is "a person's right to control access to his or her personal information."[24] This legal definition of privacy can lead to a cause of action called "Invasion of Privacy," which "is the intrusion into the personal life of another, without just cause, which can give the person whose privacy has been invaded a right to bring a lawsuit for damages against the person or entity that intruded. It encompasses workplace monitoring, Internet privacy, data collection, and other means of disseminating private information."[25]

In September 2013, a story was published in the New York Times about a new health wellness program being instituted by Pennsylvania State University (PSU) for nonunion employees. "The plan requires a visit to the doctor for a checkup, to undergo several biometric tests and to submit to an extensive online health risk questionnaire that asks, among other questions, whether they have recently had problems with a coworker, or supervisor, or a divorce. If they don't fill out the form, $100 a month will be deducted from their pay for noncompliance."[26]

The faculty believes this plan is coercive and punitive and it was being reevaluated since it was also discovered that the HR department of PSU did not review the questionnaire beforehand. The New York Times article does go on to say that there are a number of other companies using wellness programs, the idea being that if their employees are healthier the health costs will go down, resulting in savings. However, most of these other plans use incentives to get employees to participate, unlike the PSU plan.

Other concerns regarding the program were where all these data about the employees and their health issues would reside and who would have access to it? PSU said the third-party vendor of the health program would take care of those issues, but PSU would still be liable for any breach of confidential information as the procurer of the service. This relates to a discussion in a previous chapter regarding the security risks of using a cloud service provider and what safeguards need to be put in place and in the contract for protection.

---

[23] Accessed March 5, 2014, http://www.adp.com.
[24] "Privacy Legal Definition," accessed March 5, 2014, http://www.duhaime.org/LegalDictionary/P/Privacy.aspx.
[25] "Invasion of Privacy Law & Legal Definition," accessed March 5, 2014, http://definitions.uslegal.com/i/invasion-of-privacy/.
[26] Natasha Singer, "On Campus, a Faculty Uprising over Personal Data" (The New York Times, September 15, 2013), http://www.nytimes.com/2013/09/15/business/on-campus-a-faculty-uprising-over-personal-data.html?nl=todayshead,252,es&emc=edit_th_20130915&_r=0.

PRODUCTIVITY TOOLS AND APPLICATIONS

One reason employees like using their mobile devices is the vast diversity of applications that they feel make them more productive. In Chapter 2, we outlined some security measures to take place to protect against the downloading of malicious malware contained in unsafe applications.

However, sometimes, employees do not realize the security risks of these applications. A good example is what occurred during a recent high-profile trial against George Zimmerman who was facing charges for killing a teenager, Trevon Martin. A witness, Zimmerman's former professor, was testifying via Skype. He was soon interrupted as "random users started calling into the conversation after Assistant State Attorney Richard Mantei's Skype username was displayed on courtroom video screens."[27] This incident reminded people that Skype is a social network not just a video conferencing tool and certain settings need to be in place to maintain privacy. Making HR aware of this point, so they can let employees know and offer other dedicated conferencing options, such as GoTo Meeting,[28] are good practices to put in place.

TRAINING

Training or professional development is a useful tool in reducing risks and shoring up security control in an organization. If done correctly, it does this by bridging two gaps in the traditional employee engagement model:[29]

- It effectively enables workers with internal support, resources. and tools, and
- It helps in creating an environment that is energizing to work in because it promotes physical, emotional, and social well-being.

New technology and the online digital space are allowing for different delivery methods and different forms of training so HR can be more responsive as to how employees actually learn and process information. This, in turn, enhances the effectiveness of the training and increases awareness and knowledge retention on the part of the employee.

One such method is the use of gamification in training programs. Gamification is defined as "the application of typical elements of game playing (e.g., point scoring, competition with others, rules of play) to other areas of activity, typically as an online marketing technique to encourage engagement with a product or service."[30] In our scenario, it is to encourage employee engagement with the training that is taking place.

According to a Forbes article, "It is human nature to play. We are programmed to do it from day one. Play enables us to explore new things, to stretch our abilities, to learn and adapt. The explosion of mobile and Internet-enabled technologies over the last decade means we have been able to create,

---

[27] Paresh Dave, "Skype blunder interrupts George Zimmerman trial" (Los Angeles Times, July 3, 2013), http://www.latimes.com/business/technology/la-fi-tn-george-zimmerman-trial-interrupted-by-skype-calls-20130703,0,6252431.story#axzz2l11Ia5es.
[28] Accessed March 5, 2014, http://www.gotomeeting.com.
[29] "Global Workforce Study," Towers Watson (2012), accessed March 5, 2014, http://towerswatson.com/assets/pdf/2012-Towers-Watson-Global-Workforce-Study.pdf.
[30] "Gamification: definition" (Oxford Dictionaries), accessed March 5, 2014, http://www.oxforddictionaries.com/us/definition/american_english/gamification.

participate and play in new ways. It has been a de facto legitimization of game play for adults."[31] Organizations are using this fact to engage employees. In that same article, Forbes reported that "according to Gartner, by 2015 over 50 percent of organizations will be using gamification to engage employees."[32] Currently, Delta Airlines, Deloitte, IBM, and Wall Street companies have used this method successfully[33] (see Box on Tips to Gamify Your Training Program). Besides the engagement factor, reduction of costs make certain trainings possible, such as case simulations.

TIPS TO GAMIFY YOUR TRAINING PROGRAM

1. Learn about the effective use of gamification. Research how it is being used in your industry and successful case studies.
2. Create a business case for integrating gamification in your training plan.
3. Pitch the business case to the executive level and get their buy-in. This is important so some employees do not resist the training because it is just a game.
4. Lay out your goals for the game and the training.
5. Determine whether you will use a vendor who designs and develops games in the corporate training context, such as Silly Monkey[34] in Georgia, and include this cost in your budget.
6. Make it interesting and engaging.
7. Create tasks that are challenging and achievable so employees do not lose motivation.
8. Explain the rules of the game to the employees and show how they can track their progress.
9. Get the word out and reward employees who help get the word out.
10. Ask for feedback from employees and incorporate when it makes sense to do so.

[34] Accessed March 5, 2014, http://www.sillymonkeyinternational.com.

TALENT MANAGEMENT VERSUS KNOWLEDGE MANAGEMENT

Usually, HR understands about the talent management part (managing employee contributions) and IT accepts within its purview the responsibility for knowledge management (managing company information). With the new digital and online technology available, here is another place for collaboration between the two departments. When I taught Management Information Systems, I would share with my students the following "data formatted is information, information analyzed is knowledge, knowledge applied is wisdom." Therefore, for me, knowledge management meant a series of steps to capture information relevant to the company's core mission and operations, and process it to be able to share it among those who require it so that they can problem solve with confidence of the wisdom of those who know.

There are a variety of approaches to knowledge management from conducting a knowledge assessment or audit to developing a project plan and measurement matrix. Companies implement an assortment of methods as well: storytelling, communities of practice, collaborative workspaces, knowledge cafes, etc. Even with these tools, it is often difficult to capture the expertise of an expert. One of the

---

[31] Adam Swann, "Gamification Comes of Age," *Forbes* (July 16, 2012), http://www.forbes.com/sites/gyro/2012/07/16/gamification-comes-of-age/.
[32] Ibid.
[33] "Gamification of Employee Training," HRthatWorks (November 15, 2013), http://www.hrthatworksblog.com/2013/11/05/gamification-of-employee-training/.

difficulties affecting Artificial Intelligence systems, as outlined by Professor Hubert Dreyfus, is that you cannot capture unconscious knowledge.[35] To illustrate, here is an old joke from my IT days—a company spends millions for a new computing system. After it is installed, it does not work. The company's internal guys spend months trying to figure it out and finally bring in an "expert." The expert circles the main system three times, takes out a little hammer, and hits the bottom right hand corner two times. The system boots up and everything is fine. The expert sends the company an invoice for $100,000, which the company refuses to pay without an itemized bill. The expert sends an itemized bill. "Hitting the system with a hammer $1. Knowing where to hit the system with a hammer $99,999." The company paid.

TERMINATION

An employee may separate from a company voluntarily by resigning or retiring, or involuntarily by being terminated. Many states are at-will employment states and there is usually no cause of action for being fired unless it was discriminatory in fact. However, the news offers many examples of employees being fired for a Facebook post or a tweet—and so many questions come up about being able to fire an employee because of what they posted online. If that firing does happen, make sure the company has adhered to its social media policy (if it, in fact, has one) and that the post does not constitute "concerted protected activity" as defined by the NLRB (see above). Make sure also to preserve any of the incriminating posts or tweets for evidence via screen prints that will have the date and time stamp on them (see more below for what to do when a dispute arises).

The company should follow its procedures for whenever an employee leaves the firm—disable IDs and passwords so they do not have access to company information, gather keys and equipment (laptops, cell phones, tablets, etc.), make an official announcement to clients the employee may have been servicing, etc. Also, make sure that the employee understands that they cannot tweet or post on any company social media account once they no longer represent the company. If they were in charge of social media for the company, they need to turn over the ID and password and the company should immediately change the password. It would also be a good practice to monitor the company accounts for a while after the employee left to offset any "badvocacy" or bad mouthing the employee may engage in. Remind the outgoing employee of any stipulations in the employment agreement regarding social media activity blackouts, etc.

It has been interesting taking note of how companies responded to certain employees' disassociation with the company, especially when that employee has become somewhat of a "celebrity employee" because of their online and digital activity. Take for example Lionel Menchaca. He was Dell's Chief Blogger for over 7 years and was one of the first to venture into the online social media space or Dell. When he left Dell in June 2013 for another position, Dell allowed him to post a farewell blog. When you read the blog you will understand why that was such a smart move for Dell. Lionel had a following. Permitting him to say goodbye also gave him an opportunity to endorse the company he had worked at for 18 years one last time; and what a send off it was. He praised the company and encouraged his followers to continue to follow Dell. He phrased his decision to leave as a positive advance forward for

---

[35] Stanley Fish, "Watson Still Can't Think" (The New York Times, February 2, 2011), http://opinionator.blogs.nytimes.com/2011/02/28/watson-still-cant-think/?_r=0.

himself and never made a negative statement about the company he was leaving. In addition, Dell also let him advertise that he changed his Twitter handle from @LionelatDell to @LionelGeek, but he does note @Dell as well. You can read the full farewell posting here: http://dell.to/190v2LC.

This was not the same fate as another Dell social media founder—Richard Binhammer of @richardatdell. When he left Dell, they terminated his accounts and the message "Sorry that page doesn't exist" began to be displayed on his eBlogger page.[36] He was not given the opportunity to say goodbye. The question that comes up is why and then does this have any risk implications—such as a violation of labor laws for not being consistent with all departing employees? Did Lionel offer something to Dell that Richard did not in a send off? As a last note, I searched Twitter and found @richardatdell. It seems to have been reclaimed by "Receiving Money" whose bio reads: "Participating in a Break off Tweeting due to I'm Gaining $650 each day doing business via the web at my home. All my aspirations now came to me."[37] This gives another reputational risk management lesson—reclaim the accounts with the company's name as part of the exit process to prevent the wrong message being sent out to customers and the public.

As a last example, let us look at what happened when Robert Scoble, a top blogger and technology evangelizer for Microsoft decided to leave and take a position with a start-up called PodTech Network, Inc., in 2006. Apparently, it was leaked before even Scoble was ready to make an announcement. A number of posts came out with a variety of assumptions, mainly against Microsoft because Scoble was known to criticize his company's products on his blog, the Scobleizer, unlike other Microsoft bloggers. Scoble wanted to set the record straight and on his blog he did so by laying out eight points to correct the misinformation going around the digital space. Like Lionel, Scoble praised his former company and promised to be a loyal fan. His tone is frank and straight-forward and at the end lets the reader know he is moving on and hopes they do too.[38]

WHAT TO DO WHEN A DISPUTE ARISES?

One of the first things to check is if the terminated employee had an exit interview and what they said, if anything, about the incident or the parties involved. Make sure to tell the company or employee not to delete any posts or tweets or content from the social media platforms as this can be construed as spoliation of evidence in a litigation matter. Make them aware that some information that may be personal in manner may actually be made public and disclosed during the litigation process. They can also decide to hire a company, such as i-Sight,[39] to conduct a social media investigation to secure evidence to be used in litigation.

Getting information, evidence, from social media platforms, is not always easy. The platforms rely on the Stored Communications Act that reads in part "a person who provides an electronic communications service to the public shall not knowingly divulge to any person or entity the contents of a communication while in electronic storage by that service... the exceptions include law enforcement, government agencies, subject to restrictions or other third parties—but only with the consent of the

---

[36] He now has a new blog, accessed March 5, 2014, http://richardbinhammer.com/blog/.

[37] Accessed November 19, 2013, https://twitter.com/richardatdell.

[38] "Correcting the Record about Microsoft," *Scobleizer* (June 10, 2006), http://scobleizer.com/2006/06/10/correcting-the-record-about-microsoft/.

[39] Accessed March 5, 2014, http://www.customerexpressions.com/cex/cexweb.nsf/HomeDisplay.

author or addressee." Facebook, Twitter, and Google, want you to get consent from the other party first before submitting a subpoena to them directly. They have made it easier though. Facebook has an online form you can fill out[40] but Twitter is not so interactive and still requires mail or fax.[41] Google, which is the parent of YouTube, will accept emails.[42]

Many things can occur in a courtroom related to social media use by attorneys, jurors, defendants, witnesses, judges, and gallery visitors that can affect the outcome of a trial, from contempt charges to a mistrial. The issues usually fall within one of four categories:

1. Defendant's constitutional right to a fair trial.
2. Privacy concerns of jurors, attorneys, witnesses, the judge, and the defendant(s).
3. Fourth Amendment search and seizure concerns.
4. Professional responsibility/ethics of the involved attorneys

So, keep the above in mind as you strategize with HR about protecting the company in the employment law arena and how IT and security is involved in the process (such as in preserving evidence through logs, etc.). Most importantly, remember that social media is public, permanent, and powerful. It is constantly evolving with new platforms and applications being developed and released all the time. You must keep yourself up-to-date and informed of these changes and how they can affect your risks.

OTHER

"Security is becoming less about technology and more about people—understanding their behavior, and protecting users as they do their work. The study shows that women tend to value skills such as communication and education—the skills that are currently in short supply."[43]

The above quote is from an article by Michael Kassner that came out in IT Security in 2013. He is discussing the gender gap in information security and why women are essential to the industry. It also showcases an issue I that highlighted previously; there is a shortage of IT security talent—male or female. In October 2013, TEKsystems Network Services surveyed IT and business leaders regarding their current information security practices. A key finding was that there is a pervasive human capital crisis:

- Half of the respondents believe the lack of qualified security talent is approaching a state of critical mass where their organizations are vulnerable to serious risk exposure.
- Only 15% of respondents are very confident that they have the security-related skill sets needed to meet evolving threat landscapes.
- Less than 20% are very confident their IT organization has an adequate allocation of information security resources in-house for security policy, identity and access management, and

[40] Accessed April 8, 2014, https://www.facebook.com/help/473784375984502/.
[41] "Guidelines for Law Enforcement", accessed March 5, 2014, http://support.twitter.com/articles/41949-guidelines-for-law-enforcement.
[42] legal-support@google.com
[43] Michael Kassner, "Gender gap: Why information security needs more women," TechRepublic (November 4, 2013), http://www.techrepublic.com/blog/it-security/gender-gap-why-information-security-needs-more-women/.

information risk management skills. Further, more than half say it is difficult to find and source resources for these skill sets.[44]

This is another key factor for HR and IT security to work together to ensure that the company can recruit necessary talent but also that the company does not lose talent because of other opportunities, not enough engagement, or negative reputation of the company.

In retaining talent, enhancing the leadership skills of the management and supervision team must be a priority. Considering that we have a new digital and online landscape, the skills that these new cyber-security leaders need have changed as well (see Box competencies that will be required for leaders of the future). In addition, the role of mentors or personal guides to counsel, validate, and offer support to employees has taken on a new importance.[45]

COMPETENCIES THAT WILL BE REQUIRED FOR LEADERS OF THE FUTURE[46]

- Accessibility
- Global and cultural acumen
- Transparency
- Authenticity
- Strategic flexibility
- Interpersonal agility
- Risk leverage
- Rapid decision-making
- Technological savvy

[46]"Global Workforce Study," Towers Watson (2012), accessed March 5, 2014, http://towerswatson.com/assets/pdf/2012-Towers-Watson-Global-Workforce-Study.pdf.

Women are not the only underrepresented group in cybersecurity. Workers from around the world are filling in the talent gaps. This presents another potential risk for HR—labor laws and IT laws of the different countries the workers may be working in physically as well as virtually. Standards of privacy and employee rights vary greatly from one country to another. HR and IT should review any proposed project with global implications with legal to ensure no laws anywhere are violated. An example is the use of a gamification-based employee training that was to show a scoreboard with each employee's running scores as a way to incentivize employee engagement with the training. In Germany, this was considered against the employee privacy law.

Another concern with international workers is the United States "deemed export" issue. A deemed export is when you disclose information to a foreign individual while you are in the United States. This has been converted into the question of do you need an export license if you put something in the cloud or send an email to a foreign worker? Apparently, that depends on whether you are following a

---

[44] "Study Reveals Shortage Of IT Security Talent Equals Abundance Of Risk" (October 20, 2013), http://www.darkreading.com/management/study-reveals-shortage-of-it-security-ta/240162859?goback=%2Egde_37008_member_5798090843084578818#%21.

[45] Rodd Wagner and James K. Harter, "12: The Elements of Great Managing" (April 12, 2011), http://www.bizsum.com/sites/www.bizsum.com/files/bbs_uploads/12_The%20Elements%20of%20Great%20Managing.pdf.

Department of State (DOS)[47] definition of technology or a Department of Commerce (DOC), Bureau of Industry and Security definition of technology.[48] The DOS focuses on defense articles and defense services. The DOC looks at dual use technologies and how-to-use information. An example of where deemed exports and security risks overlaps involves an employee's laptop that contains controlled technical data. The laptop is hacked and the data is sent to China. According to the DOC, this would be a deemed export—even though it was involuntary—and a voluntary disclosure to the DOC is required. A penalty may not be assessed on the company, however, if appropriate and reasonable security measures where in place, for example, encryption. A good best practice is to make sure IT security people and relevant employees understand and are aware of this issue to be able to put into place training and technological safeguards against this occurrence.

---

[47] Accessed March 5, 2014, http://www.pmddtc.state.gov.
[48] "Deemed Exports", accessed March 5, 2014, http://www.bis.doc.gov/index.php/policy-guidance/deemed-exports/.

BIG DATA

5

Big data is at the foundation of all of the megatrends that are happening today, from social to mobile to the cloud to gaming.[1]

DATA. The name of the character from the *Star Trek: Next Generation* television series and movies.[2] Played by actor Brent Spiner, Data represents an outsider's view of humanity as well as a futuristic possibility of the combination of the best of man and machine to achieve goals with empathy checked by logic and the need for efficiency and accuracy. Data is also known as a grouping of information that can be analyzed for decision making. Data, the character, had a memory capacity of 800 quadrillion bits

---

[1] Chris Lynch, former Vertica CEO, as quoted in "100 Greatest Data Quotes," accessed March 10, 2014, http://v1shal.com/content/100-greatest-data-quotes/?utm_source=rss&utm_medium=rss&utm_campaign=100-greatest-data-quotes.

[2] Yes, I am a sci-fi buff and enjoy Star Trek, Star Wars, etc. But I do not reach the level of "Trekky." It is, however, a goal that can still be achieved.

(~89 PB).[3] We, as data producers, created "2.8 zettabytes of [data] in 2012, a number that's as gigantic as it sounds, and will double again by 2015."[4] How many Datas would we need to hold our data if that was even an option?

But that is one of the basic questions for risk and security—where to put the data? Where we put it determines our security strategy, but before that we still need to know where is the data in the first place? In this chapter we will review the different security issues regarding data including specific concerns throughout the data cycle, the promise of bug data analytics for security and risk management, and the relationship between data and privacy. We end with a brief review of government surveillance and the NSA activities leak.

Maribel Lopez, Mobile Market Strategist, proposes three key data components for mobile security that I believe work well for all data, whether mobile or not: data in creation, data at rest, and data in transit.[5] Each of these poses a series of risks and security concerns, for example, data in creation brings up the issues of application design, coding, and minimizing malware threats; data at rest requires us to look closely at encryption and authentication, data storage, and data destruction; while data in transit reminds us that data can be dynamic as it moves or streams through our network or a series of digital channels demanding access controls and securing the channels.

Looking at the data issue from a strategic point of view, determining its value emphasizes the need to secure it. How much is the data worth? Actually, the more appropriate question really is how much is your business's data worth? The answer to that question depends on whether you can continue to do business without the data. More about this later in the chapter; for now, understanding that it actually has a bottom line impact should be enough to grab any C-suite executive's attention.

However, "big data" is a slightly different animal than just the traditional definition of data as information collected. Lisa Arthur in a Forbes article defined big data as "a collection of data from traditional and digital sources inside and outside your company that represents a source for ongoing discovery and analysis."[6] Well that sounds just like how we defined data. So what is the difference between data and big data? The sheer volume. According to analyst firm Gartner, 'Big data' is high-volume, -velocity and -variety information assets that demand cost-effective, innovative forms of information processing for enhanced insight and decision making."[7] Notice the 3 V's: volume, velocity, and variety. Ms Arthur refers to these too: 'volume' (the amount of data), 'velocity' (the speed of information generated and flowing into the enterprise) and 'variety' (the kind of data available).[8]

Protecting data at any stage requires a multilayered approach, sometimes comprising tiers of control with safety nets in case the previous control layer fails,[9] and where there is a failure, looking for compensating controls to offset the level of deficiency.[10]

---

[3] "Data," (Memory Alpha), accessed March 10, 2014, http://en.memory-alpha.org/wiki/Data.

[4] Patrick Tucker, "Has Big Data Made Anonymity Impossible?" (MIT Technology Review, May 7, 2013), http://www.technologyreview.com/news/514351/has-big-data-made-anonymity-impossible/.

[5] Maribel Lopez, "3 Key Components to Consider in Mobile Security," (July 18, 2013), http://networkingexchangeblog.att.com/enterprise-business/3-key-data-components-to-consider-in-mobile-security/#sthash.vXArpvdz.dpuf.

[6] Lisa Arthur, "What is Big Data?" (Forbes, August 15, 2013), http://www.forbes.com/sites/lisaarthur/2013/08/15/what-is-big-data/.

[7] Svetlana Sicular, "Gartner's Big Data Definition Consists of Three Parts, Not to Be Confused with Three 'V's," (Forbes, March 27, 2013), http://www.forbes.com/sites/gartnergroup/2013/03/27/gartners-big-data-definition-consists-of-three-parts-not-to-be-confused-with-three-vs/.

[8] See note 6.

[9] Nige, "Security Program Best-Practices," (Nige the Security Guy, June 14, 2013), http://nigesecurityguy.wordpress.com/2013/06/14/security-program-best-practices-2/?goback=%2Egde_80784_member_250044061.

[10] Ibid.

So this brings us to the concept of a Big Data Ecosystem[11] consisting of Infrastructure Security, Data Privacy, Data Management, and Integrity and Reactive Security as our core risk management and security concerns. Let us see how they play out.

DATA CYCLE

Data, like most other business assets, has a life cycle (see Figure 5.1) governing its transition in terms of substance and use. Its stage of evolution also determines its value at any given time.

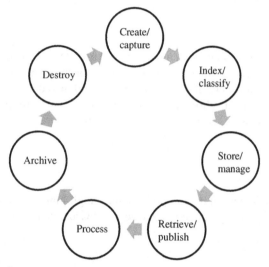

FIGURE 5.1 The Data Life Cycle.

CREATE/CAPTURE

We can create data or capture data that already exists. Risks include human error from a manual data entry process or a software failure in automatic recording of input (i.e., behavior such as typing keys or URL tunneling). Intellectual property risks concerning data creation will be addressed in Chapter 6.

INDEX/CLASSIFY

Indexing is a way to "point to the location of folders, files, and records. Depending on the purpose, indexing identifies the location of resources based on file names, key data fields in a database record, text within a file or unique attributes in a graphics or video file."[12] Classifying data, explored in more detail below,

---

[11] "CSA Releases the Expanded Top Ten Big Data Security & Privacy Challenges," (2013), accessed March 10, 2014, https://cloudsecurityalliance.org/csa-news/csa-releases-the-expanded-top-ten-big-data-security-privacy-challenges/?goback=%2Egde_1864210_member_251749458.

[12] "Indexing Definition," (PC Magazine), accessed March 10, 2014, http://www.pcmag.com/encyclopedia/term/44896/indexing.

allows us to categorize data by certain characteristics and/or formats for easier determination of value and access. Risks can include lost data based on nonexistent indexing or inappropriate resource allocation for security purposes because of misclassification of data that ends up devaluing its importance.

STORE/MANAGE (ENCRYPTION)

Data has to be held somewhere in an electromagnetic form that can be accessed by a computer processor once it is collected and/or compiled. Storage options include business-owned devices, cloud service providers, hybrids, off-site physical backup storage, etc. Risks can include faulty security practices, server/hardware failure, cloud service interruption, and data breaches.

RETRIEVAL/PUBLISH

Data needs to be extracted to be processed, analyzed, and used to make decisions. Queries can be set up to display information directly online (such as via apps) or in specific formatted reports (for later online sharing and/or actual printing). Risks can include unauthorized access, coding errors and bugs, redirection of electronic reports, misdirection of electronic information for printing or forwarding to a wrong device, errors and omissions from the published report, etc. We will discuss more on liability of publishing in Chapter 6.

PROCESS

This is the handling and treatment of data to produce meaningful information. Risks can include malware threats, coding errors and bugs, unauthorized access, inaccurate results, etc.

ARCHIVE

Data does have a certain lifetime. At some point it becomes outdated, obsolete, and/or replaced with new more relevant data. Considering the costs of data storage and the potential liability for outdated data getting out, a protocol should be developed to determine what data should be archived, when, where, and for how long. Risks can include authorized access, inability to access vital information when required, archive device failure, etc.

DESTROY

Destroy means to make the data unreadable. In today's online digital environment can data really be destroyed never to be seen again?[13] Cache systems, multiple backups, tagging by others, computer forensics, and other technology practices sort of hint at "not possible." However, that does not stop businesses from attempting to clear out data storage and retire old devices (or even giving devices away without deleting the data it contained, such as in copiers with hard drives). Risks can include data in the wrong hands, stolen disposed of devices, violation of legal holds and discovery requests for litigation, etc.

---

[13] Dell actually offers a Certified Data Destruction Service, (May 31, 2008), http://www.dell.com/downloads/global/services/Dell_ProSupport_Certified_Data_Destruction_GLOBAL_FINAL.pdf.

DATA MANAGEMENT PLANS

Database Management System: a complex set of inter-relational data structures allowing data to be lost in many convenient sequences while retaining a complete record of the logical relations between the missing items.[14]

The quote is from Stan Kelly-Bootle's *The Devil's DP Dictionary*, so it is meant to be cynical. But in humor can lie a bit of truth—it recognizes that systems put in place, though logical, can lead to disastrous results, or at least not the results we desired.

Most data management plans (DMP) focus on the different stages of the data life cycle, from data collected to stored to accessed to managed to destroyed. At each point risk management and security professionals are challenged to keep the data protected from corruption and unauthorized access. Add to that the requirement of ensuring privacy while protecting persona and/or corporate data.

Besides the basics already discussed above, there are six additional factors to DMPs in an online environment: data growth, corresponding costs, server space, data security, peak time, and upgrades.[15] We know data creation and capture is expanding exponentially. This leads to the issue of the costs to store and process this data. One reason so much data is being captured and kept is that the cost of storing the data has also decreased exponentially. In 1980, storing 1 GB of data cost about $193,000.[16] In 1990, that cost dropped to $9,000.[17] By the year 2000, storing that same 1 GB of data was down to $19.70.[18] And today, I can get 1 GB of storage for as low as $1.81 on Amazon.com.[19] With the cost so diminutive, why not keep it around just in case?

As a side note, new technologies for data storage and access are continuing to be developed and tested. One risk concern with storage technology is whether the technology will become obsolete, thereby rendering the data on the storage devices no longer readable or retrievable. Remember the floppy disk or the 3.5 hard floppy? Can you find a reader for either of those now easily and conveniently? In all probability, even if you did, the cost would be unfeasible. One of the latest "breakthroughs" is the ability to store data on glass.[20] May I remind you of the scene from the 2002 movie *Time Machine* where Orlando Jones plays a librarian hologram, Vox, who is displayed via the glass panels in the new library as well as on the broken glass planes in the destroyed library?[21] Artificial intelligence, which Vox is comprised of, is considered to be a data storage glutton. We can only imagine

---

[14] Stan Kelly Bootle, "The Devil's DP Dictionary," accessed March 10, 2014, http://www.goodreads.com/quotes/759991-database-management-system-origin-data-latin-basus-low-mean.

[15] "4imprint Blue Papers: Guide to Managing Company Data," (2012), accessed March 10, 2014, http://info.4imprint.com/wp-content/uploads/1P-20-1012-Managing-your-companys-data.pdf.

[16] Matt Komoroski, "A History of Storage Cost," (September 8, 2009), http://www.mkomo.com/cost-per-gigabyte.

[17] "A Brief History of Digital Data," accessed March 10, 2014, http://viethuynh.com/66737/585130/works/a-brief-history-of-digital-data.

[18] Ibid.

[19] "1gb Usb2.0 Flash Memory Drive Thumb Stick Swivel Design Orange," accessed March 10, 2014, http://www.amazon.com/Usb2-0-Memory-Swivel-Design-Orange/dp/B0052WGDE8/ref=sr_1_2?s=electronics&ie=UTF8&qid=1387293424&sr=1-2&keywords=flash+drive+1 + GB.

[20] Sam Shead, "Will digital data outlive the human race?" (TechWorld, July 16, 2013), http://news.techworld.com/storage-/3457713/will-digital-data-outlive-the-human-race/.

[21] "Time Travel, Practical Application," accessed March 10, 2014, http://movieclips.com/U4kx5-the-time-machine-movie-time-travel-practical-application/.

how much data is in those panels to keep Vox functioning. The other supposition is that the glass panels use some kind of solar technology for power. Another concern for DMPs is the guarantee of a continuous power source to keep the systems functioning and the data accessible as well as secured.

One answer why you may not want to just keep accumulating and storing data is that physical server space is limited. Also the costs so far discussed are for physical do-it-yourself storage and does not take into account cloud service fees, which may be higher because of additional services beyond data storage that they offer, such as security controls. Security is another factor to DMP and a second answer against storing data forever and ever. Security controls and monitoring have associated costs and are getting expensive, considering that the labor talent is currently at a shortage and the volume of security risks and attacks are on the rise.

This brings us to the peak time factor. All data that is stored is not accessed at the same time or even during the same periods of time. There is a rhythm to the business cycle, and data follows the same flow. Peak time refers to the period of time where demand for the data is at its highest. This demands creates a few challenges of its own including allocation of resources, stretching of resource capacity, bandwidth throttling, and monitoring of access to ensure against unauthorized access just to name a few.

The last factor listed above for DMPs is the issue of upgrades. Upgrades can be as varied as the data itself. There can be upgrades to the physical technology, updates to the software and applications, upgrades to security features, or updates and/or revisions to policies and procedures for the data life cycle due to legislation, regulation, and or company reprioritizing. Upgrade and updates imply additional resource utilization, from the financial budget to the labor pool to the time crunch of deadlines. Failure to upgrade can lead to a number of risk and security issues including loopholes that permit unauthorized access from unfixed bugs and backdoors to compliance violations for unmet regulations. Considering that the online and digital world is constantly evolving, this issue of upgrades and updates can be a challenging one as it requires a continuous monitoring of new information, new trends, and new rules.

DATA CLASSIFICATION

> *Every day, three times per second, we produce the equivalent of the amount of data that the Library of Congress has in its entire print collection, right? But most of it is like cat videos on YouTube or 13-year-olds exchanging text messages about the next Twilight movie.*[22]

Every minute data is being created and uploaded into the digital space. According to Removeand Replace.com "there are 277,000 Tweets every minute, Google processes over 2 million search queries every minute, 72 hours of new video are uploaded to YouTube every minute, more than 100 million emails are sent every minute, Facebook processes 350 GB of data every minute and 571 new websites are created every minute."[23] Now this "fact" is dated March 13, 2013. How much does this data change? In June 2012, those numbers were slightly less: "YouTube users upload 48 hours of video, Facebook users share 684,478 pieces of content, Instagram users share 3,600 new photos, and Tumblr sees 27,778 new posts published."[24]

---

[22] Nate Silver, accessed March 10, 2014, as quoted in http://v1shal.com/content/100-greatest-data-quotes/?utm_source=rss&utm_medium=rss&utm_campaign=100-greatest-data-quotes.

[23] "How Much Data is on the Internet and Generated Online Every Minute?" (RemoveandReplace, March 13, 2013), http://removeandreplace.com/2013/03/13/how-much-data-is-on-the-internet-and-generated-online-every-minute/.

[24] Neil Spencer, "How Much Data is Created Every Minute?" (Visual News, June 19, 2012), http://www.visualnews.com/2012/06/19/how-much-data-created-every-minute/.

Table 5.1 Data Classification Schemes for Government and Private Entities[26]	
Government	**Private**
Unclassified	Public
Confidential	Proprietary/internal use only
Secret	Company confidential
Top secret	Restricted/highly confidential

[26] Table adapted from information in, "Three Steps to Successful Data Classification," (February, 2013), http://www.titus.com/resources/marketo/WEB_CLS_WP_3_Steps_Data_Classification.pdf?fulfilled=true.

This is a lot of data being put up in the digital space. But not all of it is relevant to your organization. Having a protocol to identify the valuable data that must be captured and stored can save resources and time from an IT perspective and a security standpoint.

Part of the protocol should be the classification of data. Many organizations also have data classification policies in place so all employees and members of the organization's community understand what kind of data is to be protected and to what extent. (Table 5.1) Carnegie Mellon University puts it succinctly: "data classification, in the context of information security, is the classification of data based on its level of sensitivity and the impact to the [University] should that data be disclosed, altered or destroyed without authorization. The classification of data helps determine what baseline security controls are appropriate for safeguarding that data."[25]

One of the biggest risks with data classification is the possibility of misclassification of the data itself. Classification level is usually associated with levels of access, sometimes referred to as security clearance levels. If the data is misclassified, it can be accessed by individuals who have no legitimate business need to access it and puts it in jeopardy of being leaked, hacked, stolen, or given away (unintentionally). Controls and protocols need to be put in place that ensure the appropriate data classification with checks and balances where the classification is periodically reviewed. There is more on data access best practices in the next subsection.

Many organizations will have in place a confidentiality and/or disclosure policy. This policy works hand in hand with the data classification policy (sometimes it is the same document). The idea is to lay out what each data classification is and how it is applied to the company's data so all employees are on the same page. It is also important to include some examples of what is and what is not considered confidential information. The following is from a current social media policy (written in 2013 to adhere to the National Labor Relations Board's recommendations regarding confidential information on social media sites):

Employees and [company] representatives are prohibited from disclosing information that is subject to protection under trade secret law, copyright law, confidential information as defined in the Confidentiality Policy, or the attorney-client privilege. Trade secrets may include information regarding the development of systems, processes, products, know-how and technology. Do not post internal reports, policies, procedures or other internal business-related confidential communications.

---

[25] "Guidelines for Data Classification," (Carnegie Mellon University, last updated: September 15, 2011), http://www.cmu.edu/iso/governance/guidelines/data-classification.html.

The next example comes from an Employee Code of Conduct manual for a financial organization.[27] It divides confidential information into two categories: customer information and information regarding the company.

CONFIDENTIALITY
Customer information
In accordance with the Gramm-Leach-Bliley Act (GLBA) of 1999, financial institutions are required to have administrative, technical and physical safeguards for sensitive customer information. As such, safeguarding the confidential financial information concerning the Company's customers is essential to maintaining the public trust. It is the policy of the Company that such confidential information acquired by a staff member through his or her employment must be held in the strictest confidence. Such information is to be held for Company purposes only and not as a basis for personal gain by any staff member. Such information must also be protected from misuse that could result in identity theft. Aside from routine credit inquires, information regarding a customer may generally only be released to private persons, organizations or governmental bodies that request it with the consent of the customer involved or upon receipt of legal process, such as a subpoena or court order. Information obtained about any Bank customer from any record of the Bank shall not be disclosed. This provision continues regardless of whether the individual who obtains the information ceases employment with the Bank.

Confidential customer information should never be discussed with anyone outside the Company, and only with those within the Company who have a legitimate business need to know. Such information should never be discussed in public places, even within the Company's offices. Staff members should be sensitive to the risk of inadvertent disclosure resulting from open doors, speakerphones, cellular phones, and when transmitting confidential information by fax or other electronic media.

Information regarding the company
Financial or other information regarding the Company, its operations, its customers or any aspect of its business may not to be released to any outside person or organization unless it has been published in reports to shareholders, otherwise made available to the public through authorized news releases. All news media inquiries must be referred to the President, the Chief Operating Officer or the Chief Financial Officer. The Company expects every employee to treat information concerning the Company and its personnel with the same confidentiality as information concerning customers of the Company and to observe, with respect to the Company, the same guidelines set forth in Paragraph A above.

DATA ACCESS
Data access determines who has the authority to use certain business information for certain purposes. Sometimes access is determined by the individual's position in the company, sometimes it is based on the project being worked on, and sometimes it is for a finite amount of time (such as with temporary workers). Levels of data access can change during the tenure of an employee with the company due to changes in position or work assignment. Data access needs to be managed and monitored so that

---
[27] Used with permission.

changes to the employee's authority are noted in the data access as soon as possible to avoid the potential risks of unauthorized access or malicious behavior against the company's data.

The following are a series of best practices and steps to minimize the likelihood of these risks:

1. Audit Data Access—the first step is to review data access protocols and policies.
2. Inventory Permissions—this step requires you to identify and list who has access to what data and why. You should then be able to refer to the data access protocols and verify if they have been followed or where there may have been exceptions.
3. Inventory and Prioritize Data—as you complete the audit and permissions inventory, you will also be identifying types of data that are in the company's systems. This will allow you to specify whether the data is stale and no longer useful or if the data is actual and dynamic.
4. Align Security Groups to Data—as you prioritize the data, you can determine the level of security control it requires and what strategies to put in place.
5. Identify Data Owners—most employees are data users, using data that is supplied by someone else. You do need to know who is supplying the data as well as who is being held accountable for the data. These data owners need to understand their responsibility toward data integrity and accuracy for the data they own as well as to be accountable to any changes in terms of authorized access to the data, etc.
6. Perform Entitlement Reviews—most IT and security professionals are familiar with the executive exception to many security controls that are put in place to protect company data due to internal political concerns. It is important to periodically (for example, annually) review any entitlement authorizations that have been given. This should be coordinated with any human resource changes (such as employee promotions, demotions, and/or terminations) to minimize unauthorized access risks.
7. Audit Permissions & Group Changes—internal company groups, usually by departments, are set up to facilitate messaging to a team of individuals who have a common concern or function within the company. These groups may be long-term or permanent (i.e., Human Resources) or ad hoc (i.e., a task force). Putting in a second factor of authorization to make a change to the access permission for a group can minimize the risk of unauthorized access to and/or breach of data.
8. Remove Global Access Groups—there are times when a message needs to go out to everyone in the company (i.e., benefit enrollment dates) or certain information needs to be accessed by all employees in a company (i.e., the employee handbook or code of conduct). But care needs to be taken and employees educated against the quick "Reply All" option to certain messages that may unintentionally leak confidential information to those who do not need to know. In regulated industries, such as finance and insurance, this could lead to a reporting requirement for a breach incident that can be time consuming, cumbersome, and easily avoided.
9. Lock Down, Delete, or Archive Unused Data—as you determine who owns the data, discuss with them the importance of data management and the data life cycle. At a certain point, the data they are using is no longer of value and needs to be taken off the live network to recoup resources and computing capacity. Assist them in determining when that may happen, and set up a protocol to identify the specific stale data and what should be done with it. For example, should it be archived for a specific period of time or can it be deleted? The idea of locking down certain data is to prevent reports or data that have been published and/or released to be manipulated and/or altered to the detriment of the company.

10. Clean Up Legacy Groups and Artifacts—groups that are formed ad hoc usually have a beginning and en end when they have completed their task. It is important to identify when the groups are no longer functional and to dismantle or deauthorize the group members. Their folders and data can be archived for future reference if required. This should also be set in a protocol so all groups will know what will happen to their data.

DATA ANALYTICS

> *Data is not information, information is not knowledge, knowledge is not understanding, understanding is not wisdom.*[28]

One of the benefits of all this abundance of data is what can be derived from it—knowledge that can be applied to "raise productivity, improve decision making and gain competitive advantage," as stated by Tim McGuire, a McKinsey & Co. director.[29] McGuire goes on to outline three specific challenges companies face regarding big data: "deciding which data to use (and where outside your organization to look), handling analytics (and securing the right capabilities to do so), and using the insights you've gained to transform your operations."[30] The analytical part requires a combination of the right technology to process the data and the insight of the human experience to make it applicable to the situation at hand.

For some big data is the conundrum, while for others big data offers a solution. Gary Marcus and Ernest Davis, writing for the *New York Times*, offered some basic cautionary tips regarding what they call the "nine problems with big data."[31] The underlying message is that big data is not a final solution or silver bullet but a tool and a resource. It has its advantages and its fallbacks, but at the end of the data you still need more than just the raw data to make informed decisions. When harvested and processed correctly, the analysis can be used to protect data via predictive analysis and data leakage protection and to discover the responsible parties for a breach via security event incident monitoring.

There is always the possibility of false positives in data analysis. Not every variable can be accounted for in every situation. But not many will challenge the wisdom of using data that is readily available to try to prevent security incidents from happening and, if they do, to try to prevent them from happening again.

In March 2013, Oracle issued a white paper on Big Data Analytics[32] discussing five key approaches to analyzing big data and generating insight:

- Discovery Tools—allow users to interact with structured and unstructured data from different sources in a simple way to understand and display data element relationships and then apply them to specific problems.

---

[28] Clifford Stoll, accessed March 10, 2014, as quoted in http://v1shal.com/content/100-greatest-data-quotes/?utm_source=rss&utm_medium=rss&utm_campaign=100-greatest-data-quotes.

[29] "Making Data Analytics Work: Three Key Challenges," (McKinsey & Company, March 2013), http://www.mckinsey.com/insights/business_technology/making_data_analytics_work.

[30] Ibid.

[31] Gary Marcus and Ernest Davis, New York Times, "Eight (No, Nine!) Problems with Big Data," (April 6, 2014), http://www.nytimes.com/2014/04/07/opinion/eight-no-nine-problems-with-big-data.html?emc=edit_th_20140407&nl=todaysheadlines&nlid=33425801.

[32] "Big Data Analytics," (Oracle White Paper, March, 2013), http://www.oracle.com/technetwork/database/options/advanced-analytics/bigdataanalyticswpoaa-1930891.pdf.

- Business Intelligence Tools—analyze transactional business data from a metadata perspective; much more technical than the data discovery model.
- In-Database Analytics—assist in finding patterns and relationships within your data by processing the data in the database itself to conserve resources.
- Hadoop—is a free, Java-based programming framework that supports the processing of large data sets in a distributed computing environment offered by the Apache Software Foundation.[33]
- Data Driven Decision Management (DDDM)—making decisions that are backed by data analysis, uses data predictive modeling, business rules, and self-learning.

One aspect I would add to this is the concept of "search" in terms of online and social media activity. Querying does not only happen within the company's database systems. Google has changed the way we look for and receive information, as well as how we organize that information. Douglas C. Merrill, former Google CIO, even wrote a user's guide to Google titled "Getting Organized in the Google Era" (2011). We can expect our employees to use Google to find answers, even research data to substantiate business decisions. It is important to educate employees regarding information and digital literacy in our current digital environment. Not everything that is posted online is accurate or true. Authors of online content can have a specific agenda, and understanding who is presenting the information and from what angle can greatly affect whether the information presented should be used in a business context or not. In a time where tweeting a URL to a story is made easier every day with tools such as Hootsuite,[34] is there liability should someone else depend on the information you tweeted? Is your tweet or retweet an endorsement of the content held at the link destination? How can the company verify the accuracy, integrity, and security of the content on that link that has been generated outside of the company's purview? For regulated industries, this adds a higher level of responsibility for compliance concerns.

But the query search is only one risk aspect of search engines. The other deals with search engine optimization (SEO) and some risky tactics agencies may be using to ensure that your company and/or brand is listed at the top of search engine result pages. Mike Morgan, founder and director of High Profile Enterprises and content director at TrinityP3, a creative agency, identified some of these risks in his June 2013 blog post[35]:

- Mass directory submissions to low quality directories that have no real users and many dubious listings. Google has banned the majority of these sites from its index.
- Article spinning or the use of synonyms to replace words in brackets and make the content unique to a specific audience.
- Comment spamming to hundreds of Web sites knowing that some will auto-approve.
- Paid links and advertorials are also in breach of Google's guidelines.
- Blog networks of fake blog sites.
- Keyword stuffing of meta-descriptions drafted for SEO rankings.

There was also the concern about using a competitor's trademark as a keyword for SEO purposes. The standard for trademark violation is likelihood of consumer confusion. If there is no relation between

---

[33] "What is Hadoop?" (Techtarget, August 4, 2010), http://searchcloudcomputing.techtarget.com/definition/Hadoop.
[34] Accessed March 10, 2014, https://hootsuite.com.
[35] Mike Morgan, "8 High Risk SEO Strategies Your Agency Might Be Using," (TrinityP3, June, 2013), http://www.trinityp3.com/2013/06/agency-seo-strategies/.

the product and/or service on the Web site and the trademark then it would be in violation. For example, using a trademark as a meta-tag for SEO purposes only is a violation. Hiding the trademark in the code is even more of a violation.[36] It is important to conduct due diligence on any SEO functions within the company or being employed on behalf of the company by a third-party provider, as the company can be held liable. Read more on this in Chapter 6.

PROTECTING DATA: BACKUP

Access controls assist in securing data by focusing on who is authorized to access data and what data they are authorized to access. Another key to protecting company data is the backup plan, a documented procedure to create a duplicate version (or versions) of important company data that is secure and can be accessed easily should the need arise. The backup is the "in case of," "just to be safe," "planning for failure," strategy that minimizes the risk of data loss that cannot be recovered. Backup is not synonymous with disaster recovery but is a vital part of it. It is based on the idea that data duplication offers the safeguard of redundancy should something go wrong.

A backup plan should be simple, secure, and scalable. It needs to take into consideration factors such as the size of the company and the value of its data, current technology options available to the company, financial concerns, and employee behavior.

The plan will begin with identifying the kind of data that is to be backed up—documents, applications and/or programs, media files, operating systems—and where that data is located—hard drives, servers, laptops, mobile devices, cloud providers, etc.

Different methodologies exist for backing up data. In the beginning one of the only options was in-house, local backup storage consisting of "backup" hardware such as tapes. That expanded in scope to include backup removable drives, even flash drives for minimal or special data. There was a time when IT would send out backup reminders to employees, based on a manual system. Storing the tapes on site sometimes defeated the purpose of having a duplicate to restore, so off-site backup storage was developed, and transport of backup medium and tapes became another risk and security concern.

Automatic backups can be implemented with a predetermined schedule or routine. This alleviates the uncertainty of whether an employee remembers to set up the backup program to run or not when they leave the office for the day. It can be set up to run during the evening or down time so as not to interrupt business operations. The data repository for automatic backups may still be stored on-site or transported off-site.

Backup outsourcing or cloud backups are being touted as killing off the backup tape—but this may still be a few years away. Cloud backup providers offer the advantage that the data is not only backed up but the files can be synced and mobile access to the backed up data available for convenience. However, it is important to do some due diligence to ensure that your use of the cloud services are not leaving your company's data at risk. Bradley Shear recently wrote on his blog, Shear on Social Media Law, "clicking 'I Agree' when registering for a new digital account/service or when a digital service's policies have been updated may have major legal consequences…what may happen when you agree to

---

[36] Rechtsanwalt Christian Solmecke, "Ensuring SEO techniques comply with trademark law," (Wilde Beuger Solmecke, October 7, 2013), http://www.wbs-law.de/eng/ensuring-seo-techniques-comply-with-trademark-law-46873/.

terms and conditions you may not understand…an online British retailer once inserted a clause into its digital agreements that gave it the right to reclaim its customers' immortal souls."[37]

Your company's data may not be worth your immortal soul, but knowing what responsibilities the provider does or does not have in regard to that data should a loss occur on your watch may be. InTechnology offers some tips for choosing a data backup service and provider:

- Make sure they are reliable in terms of the technology they are using.
- What is the breadth of services they offer and can you customize to fit your company's specific needs?
- What kind of security controls do they have in place—for example, encryption—do they have any backdoor access to your data?
- Can they ensure that you are able to access your data right away should need be?
- Are they cost-effective? (Compare competitors)
- Do they know about compliance, and are they compliant based on your particular industry and current regulations?
- Do they provide disaster recovery solutions?
- What is their authentication procedure?
- What is their data recovery procedure should you terminate the relationship or the account gets suspended?
- Is the service easy to use?
- How is their customer support?
- Check references and other clients.[38]

With the mobile and BYOD revolution it is also important to educate employees about backing up their mobile devices. The Apple iOS is fairly simple with the use of the iTunes technology. Google Android has a restore function but does not guarantee that application data will be backed up and restored. Samsung has a Smart Switch program. HTC has its Sync Manager, and SONY has the Xperia Transfer. Just about every mobile system has a way to back up and restore certain amounts of data. As you look to setting up security controls for the mobile devices of your company's employees, do not forget about the backup function.

In addition, employees may be using their own backup utilities at home or even for business purposes. The use of Dropbox[39] and other personal cloud storage services is on the rise. Another one is Mozy,[40] which also offers an enterprise version. Carbonite[41] is another popular one. Some of these virtual backups also offer dynamic or smart backup technology—only backing up files and programs that have been updated or changed since the last backup.

If your company has a BYOD policy and employees are using their own devices, be sure to address these third-party backup services in the recovery and data breach protocols should a loss of the device or a breach incident occur. It does not secure the company's data if you do a remote wipeout of the device only to have the employee restore the majority of the data themselves with the cloud provider and outside the parameters of the company's security features.

---

[37] Bradley Shear, "The terms and conditions that apply to the storage of your data are important," (September 2013), http://www.shearsocialmedia.com/2013/09/the-terms-and-conditions-that-apply-to.html.

[38] "Top 10 Tips for choosing a Data Backup Service & Provider," (InTechnology), accessed March 10, 2014, http://www.intechnology.co.uk/resource-centre/top-tips-choosing-a-data-backup-provider.aspx.

[39] Accessed March 10, 2014, https://www.dropbox.com.

[40] Accessed March 10, 2014, http://mozy.com/#slide-8.

[41] Accessed March 10, 2014, http://www.carbonite.com.

LOSING DATA

Data can be lost in a number of ways. According to Online Backup Geeks (yes, that is their name) the most common reasons are[42] (Figure 5.2):

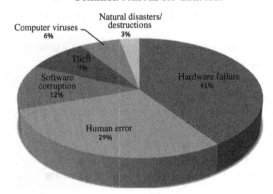

Common reasons for data loss

FIGURE 5.2 Common Reasons for Data Loss.

Preventing data loss from natural disasters and/or power failures/surges requires the acknowledgment that these can and will occur. Making sure power protectors are in place and backup protocols are implemented can alleviate the pain should and/or when the inevitable occurs. Another solution is to purchase backup generators or other alternative power source(s) that can kick in should the primary one malfunction. Keep in mind that these are temporary solutions at best. Full recovery is time constrained.

Theft of the devices themselves can also lead to data loss. One strategy to put into place is developing and implementing a protocol to document the chain of custody of laptops, mobile devices, and other company-assigned hardware—especially if the devices are portable and can be signed out or assigned to multiple individuals at different times. This is usually a standard inventory practice. Ensuring that the devices are physically secured is another best practice. Are they kept in locked offices or closets? Who has access to the keys?

Once the device is secured, is the data secured that resides in the device? Authorization to access the data in the device via passwords or another methodology, as well as making sure the data is encrypted, are not only good rules of thumb but can also be required by certain regulations and laws such as the Health Information Technology for Economic and Clinical Health Act of 2009.[43] In addition, hardware keys can be used that require a certain gadget to be attached to the laptop or other computing device in order to access the data or programs. These dongles are programmed with specific access codes or other cryptographic mechanisms for added security.

---

[42] April, 2013, http://www.onlinebackupgeeks.com/online-backup-blog/wp-content/uploads/2013/04/Backup-Battalion-Saves-World-From-Intergalactic-Data-Disasters.jpg.

[43] "Breach Notification Rule," (U.S. Department of Health and Human Services), accessed March 10, 2014, http://www.hhs.gov/ocr/privacy/hipaa/administrative/breachnotificationrule/index.html.

Another kind of theft involves hackers and intentional (although sometimes not malicious) data breaches. David McCandless, a journalist who operates the site Information is Beautiful, has compiled on a timeline a visualization of the world's biggest data breaches since 2004.[44] It is surprising to see who has been breached and even more concerning the number of records/users that were affected by these breaches. To name a few:

- Target (2013) 40 million
- Adobe (2013) 38 million
- Facebook (2013) 6 million
- Living Social (2013) 50 million
- Evernote (2013) 50 million
- Massive American Business (2013) 160 million
- Apple (2012) 12.3 million
- SONY Play Station (2011) 77 million
- UK's National Health Service (2011) 8.3 million
- U.S. Military (2009) 76 million

According to recent studies, the cost of a data breach is on the rise. Per capita in the United States, the average is $188. If the incident occurs in the financial sector, it goes up to $254. But the highest cost is in the health care industry at $304.[45]

Also, social media account information has value. Some current account numbers[46]:

- iTunes account for $8
- Fedex.com, Continental.com and United.com accounts for $6
- Groupon.com for $5
- Hosting provider Godaddy.com for $4
- Wireless providers Att.com, Sprint.com, Verizonwireless.com, and Tmobile.com for $4.
- Facebook and Ttter for $2.50

You can refer to Chapter 2 and the section on external threats for more information and best practices to minimize data loss via the hacking risk.

DATA RECOVERY

If you torture the data long enough, it will confess.[47]

There have been numerous stories in the news of companies that have gone bankrupt after a significant data breach. Most of these fail because the data lost could not be recovered in a timely manner, if

---

[44] "World's Biggest Data Breaches," (December 31, 2013), http://www.informationisbeautiful.net/visualizations/worlds-biggest-data-breaches-hacks/.

[45] Kyle Murphy, "Data breach costs decline, malicious attacks increase in US," (Health IT Security, June 14, 2013), http://healthitsecurity.com/2013/06/14/data-breach-costs-decline-malicious-attacks-increase-in-us/.

[46] "The business behind a hacked email account," (Security Affairs, June 13, 2013), http://securityaffairs.co/wordpress/15205/cyber-crime/business-hacked-email-account.html?goback=%2Egde_80784_member_249979886.

[47] Ronald Coase, Economist, as quoted in http://v1shal.com/content/100-greatest-data-quotes/?utm_source=rss&utm_medium=rss&utm_campaign=100-greatest-data-quotes, accessed March 10, 2014.

at all, leading to a cessation of business operations or a substantial fine from a regulatory agency. For example, the Federal Trade Commission (FTC) will aggressively police companies with control over large databases of personal information and is currently in a process against Wyndham Hotel Group for numerous data breaches that occurred in a short amount of time.[48] Wyndham on its part is appealing whether the FTC even has that kind of authority.

A key component to any backup plan is the restore function. After an incident is discovered, an incident report is usually compiled and logged indicating certain facts of the incident for later review and to become part of the institutional knowledge base in terms of security and risk management. If the incident involved a device that was recovered or a device with corrupted hardware, computer forensics, the use of computer techniques to collect data from digital and mobile devices, may be used to recover the data thought lost. A good example of this technique was when Arthur Andersen, the consulting firm, was found guilty of obstructing justice for shredding and destroying documents and e-mails relating to a case against Enron. It was later revealed that a significant amount was recovered from electronic backups.[49]

Computer forensics is also the technique used for collecting and analyzing digital evidence during electronic discovery (or e-discovery) in preparation for a trial. This is one of those factors you need to consider when sifting through old data and determining whether it can be destroyed or may be required later on and needs to be preserved for a legal proceeding.

There should be a restore and/or recovery protocol for your company. This protocol may be part of a larger document or restoration plan. Certain metrics will be defined in the plan to ensure that the company will be functional as quickly as possible after an incident.

- Restore/Recovery Time Objectives—the maximum tolerable length of time that a computer, system, network, or application can be down after a failure or disaster occurs.[50]
- Restore/Recovery Point Objectives (RPO)—the age of files that must be recovered from backup storage for normal operations to resume if a computer, system, or network goes down as a result of a hardware, program, or communications failure.[51]
- Network Recovery Objectives—this is the maximum tolerable length of time that the company network must be restored for the use of customers and/or clients.

Following are some additional metrics as outlined by Robert Levine in Wikibon, an online IT professional community[52]:

- Recovery Time Granularity (RTG) determines the time spacing between recovery points; whereas RPO is the last recovery point prior to a failure, RTG defines recovery point selection options prior to that recovery point.

[48] "Tug of Authority over Legal Gap in Online Privacy," (NPR, December 14, 2013), http://www.npr.org/2013/12/14/-251031687/tug-of-authority-over-legal-gap-in-online-privacy.
[49] Dan Ackman, "Accounting for Texans," (Forbes, January 16, 2002), http://www.forbes.com/2002/01/16/0116topnews.html.
[50] Margaret Rouse, "What is recovery time objective?" (TechTarget, August 2011), http://whatis.techtarget.com/definition/recovery-time-objective-RTO.
[51] See note 50.
[52] Robert Levine, "Recovery point objective – recovery time objective strategy," (Wikibon), accessed March 10, 2014, http://wikibon.org/wiki/v/Recovery_point_objective_-_recovery_time_objective_strategy.

- Recovery Object Granularity expresses the level of objects that a recovery solution is capable of recovering. For instance, object granularity may be a storage volume, a file system, a database table, a database row/column/field, a transaction, a mailbox, an e-mail message, etc.
- Recovery Event Granularity measures the ability of a recovery solution to track events and to recover an application or data to a specific event.
- Recovery Consistency Characteristics measure the usability of recovered data by the associated application.
- Recovery Location Scope defines where the protected data must be stored when recovery takes place (i.e., locally, remotely, on which media/storage tier).

The concern with each of these metrics is the risk of what happens if they are incorrectly measured or not met. Having these terms defined in a policy and/or checklist does not assist the company in its recovery efforts if the individual responsible for defining the metrics or meeting them does not understand them and/or does not have the resources, abilities, and/or capabilities to achieve them.

PRIVACY: TO USE OR NOT TO USE DATA DILEMMA

Data science is not voodoo. We are not building fancy math models for their own sake. We are trying to listen to what the customer is telling us through their behavior.[53]

In Chapter 4, we defined "privacy" as "a person's right to control access to his or her personal information."[54] We also indicated that this legal definition of privacy can lead to a cause of action called Invasion of privacy, which "is the intrusion into the personal life of another, without just cause, which can give the person whose privacy has been invaded a right to bring a lawsuit for damages against the person or entity that intruded. It encompasses workplace monitoring, Internet privacy, data collection, and other means of disseminating private information."[55]

In today's online digital world where substantial amounts of personal data are being collected and compiled, privacy has taken on a new sense of urgency for the end user, specifically consumers. What kinds of information are being collected? Basically anything a user is willing to give: browsing behavior (patterns/history sniffing), user preferences, user credentials, and even user locations (geolocation, 4Sqaure). How is the information collected? Via surveys, registration, permission allowances, Flash cookies, mobile apps, etc.

According to Oxford Dictionaries, a social graph is a representation of the interconnection of relationships in an online social network.[56] The value of the social graph is the diversity of data characteristics that it can collect on an individual, known as an actor or node. "Individuals and organizations, called actors, are nodes on the graph. Interdependencies, called ties, can be multiple and diverse,

---

[53] Kevin Geraph, (July 9, 2013), Head of Analytics 360i, as quoted in http://www.slideshare.net/TrueLens/top-10-marketing-big-data-quotes-e-book.

[54] "Privacy Legal Definition," accessed March 10, 2014, http://www.duhaime.org/LegalDictionary/P/Privacy.aspx.

[55] "Invasion of Privacy Law & Legal Definition," (USLegal), accessed March 10, 2014, http://definitions.uslegal.com/i/invasion-of-privacy/.

[56] "Social Graph," (Oxford Dictionaries), accessed March 10, 2014, http://www.oxforddictionaries.com/us/definition/american_english/social-graph.

including such characteristics or concepts as age, gender, race, genealogy, chain of command, ideas, financial transactions, trade relationships, political affiliations, club memberships, occupation, education and economic status."[57] Mark Zuckerberg, CEO of Facebook, used the term in a 2007 Facebook event giving it a more expansive definition of use, forecasting that the social graph is changing the way the world works and will be the way information gets targeted to individuals.[58]

Marketers insist that the more information they have the better they can satisfy consumer needs by customizing the user interface with the brand to eliminate nonrelevant advertising to the individual. In other words, the collection of personal data allows the marketers to not invade a consumer's privacy and annoy them less.

Consumers on the other hand are becoming leery of what else their personal information may be used for beyond the narrow consent that they gave for its use—or what they thought was a narrow consent for limiting its use and who can use it.

Privacy policies are everywhere on the Internet. One reason is that Google requires Web sites that use its Google Analytics program to have one: "Google Analytics collects information anonymously. It reports website trends without identifying individual visitors. All website owners using Google Analytics are required to have a privacy policy that fully discloses the use of Google Analytics."[59] The privacy policies serve two purposes: (1) to let consumers know what information is collected on them, how it will be used, and whom it will be shared with; and (2) to comply with disclosure regulations and requirements in regard to consumer personally identifiable information (PII). An example of the latter is the Health Information Portability and Accountability Act.[60]

Privacy policies consist of a number of essential components: notice to consumers of what information is collected, how it will be used, and by whom; choice to opt out of their information being collected or used in any manner beyond the original purpose it was collected for; access to the information to verify accuracy and to correct it if needed; security measures in place to protect the data that is collected and to prevent it from being breached and/or stolen; and enforcement mechanisms for noncompliance of fair information practices.

Having the privacy policies in place is one strategy to minimize the risk of a consumer invasion of privacy lawsuit or sanction by a federal agency such as the FTC. It is rumored that a single tweet can violate up to 17 federal privacy laws and over 100 state laws—88 in California alone! (See Federal privacy laws). Lawsuits against Facebook and Google regarding privacy concerns are not new. Facebook is currently being investigated by the FTC over its recent privacy policy changes.[61] But Facebook's legal privacy woes are international in scope and go back to its early days.[62] Google is facing the same with Dutch authorities who in November 2013 found Google in violation of its Private Data Protection Act.[63]

---

[57] "What is social graph?" (TechTarget, September 2010), http://whatis.techtarget.com/definition/social-graph.

[58] Ibid.

[59] "Google Analytics Overview," (Google), accessed March 10, 2014, http://www.google.com/intl/en_uk/analytics/privacyoverview.html.

[60] "Health Information Privacy," (U.S. Department of Health and Human Services), accessed March 10, 2014, http://www.hhs.gov/ocr/privacy/.

[61] Vindu Goel, "Facebook Privacy Change is Subject of F.T.C. Inquiry," (New York Times, September 12, 2013), http://www.nytimes.com/2013/09/12/technology/personaltech/ftc-looking-into-facebook-privacy-policy.html?_r=0.

[62] Maggie Shiels, "Facebook 'violates privacy laws'," (BBC, May 31, 2008), http://news.bbc.co.uk/2/hi/7428833.stm.

[63] Darrell Etherington, "Dutch Authorities Find Google Violates Its Private Data Protection Act," (TechCrunch, November 28, 2011), http://techcrunch.com/2013/11/28/dutch-authorities-find-google-violates-its-private-data-protection-act/.

FEDERAL PRIVACY LAWS

- Health privacy laws
  - 1974 National Research Act
  - 1998 Health Insurance Portability and Accountability Act (HIPAA)
- Financial privacy laws
  - 1970 Bank Secrecy Act
  - 1998 Federal Trade Commission—SEC
  - 1999 Graham–Leach–Bliley Act (GLB)
  - 2000 Sarbanes–Oxley Act (SOX)
  - 2003 Fair and Accurate Credit Transactions Act
- Online privacy laws
  - 1986 Electronic Communications Privacy Act (ECPA), pen registers
  - 1988 Stored Communications Act (SCA)
  - 1998 Children's Online Privacy Protection Act (COPPA)
- Communication privacy laws
  - 1975 Foreign Intelligence Surveillance Act (FISA)
  - 1984 Cable Communications Policy Act
  - 1986 Electronic Communications Privacy Act (ECPA)
  - 1994 Digital Telephony Act—Communications Assistance for Law Enforcement Act (CALEA), 18 USC 2510–2522
- Education privacy laws
  - 1974 Family Educational Rights and Privacy Act (FERPA)
- Information privacy laws
  - 2001 USA Patriot Act, expanded pen registers
- Other
  - 1974 Privacy Act
  - 2005 Privacy Act, sale of online PII data for marketing
- Proposed
  - 2011 Commercial Privacy Bill of Rights Act
  - 2011 Consumer Privacy Protection Act[64]

[64]Accessed March 10, 2014, Neither of the 2011 proposed bills has been enacted. But in February 2012, the White House determined that consumer privacy required an official statement from them and issued a report on their thoughts on future privacy legislation: http://www.whitehouse.gov/sites/default/files/privacy-final.pdf.

Having noted Google's and Facebook's international woes, it is a good time to look at the way the rest of the world perceives data privacy. To begin with there are currently over 50 international laws in place to protect personal data including "Canada's Privacy Act, Germany's Federal Data Protection Act, Argentina's Personal Data Protection Act, and Korea's Act on Personal Information Protection."[65] There are also data protection agreements between countries, for example, the bilateral treaty regarding data protection between the United States and Germany. In addition, the European Commission Justice Department has made a number of decisions regarding the adequacy of the protection of personal data in third countries (which for them included the United States):

The Council and the European Parliament have given the Commission the power to determine, on the basis of Article 25(6) of directive 95/46/EC whether a third country ensures an adequate level of protection by reason of its domestic law or of the international commitments it has entered into…

---

[65] Kimberly Madia, "3 Big Data Security Tips You Need to Know," (IBM), accessed March 10, 2014, http://securityintelligence.com/3-big-data-security-tips-you-need-to-know/?goback=%2Egde_80784_member_255760580.

The Commission has so far recognized Andorra, Argentina, Australia, Canada, Switzerland, Faeroe Islands, Guernsey, State of Israel, Isle of Man, Jersey, the US Department of Commerce's Safe harbor Privacy Principles, and the transfer of Air Passenger Name Record to the United States' Bureau of Customs and Border Protection as providing adequate protection.[66]

Consider the above in the light of the recent European Union's Data Protection Directive that is slated to be approved by mid-2014 and effective in early 2016. According to the analysis of the current language of the directive, it would require additional steps by companies collecting personal information to ensure compliance with the law:

- Businesses must provide better and more accurate disclosures about new uses of data.
- Businesses must provide better Web site security and address the invisible activity that occurs behind the scenes that consumers are not privy to.
- Businesses must adhere to stricter data breach response protocols for reporting and remediating the incident.
- For businesses of a certain size that collect a certain amount of data, they will be required to hire a data protection officer to ensure compliance with the directive and to protect the consumer's privacy.[67]

Your company may be headquartered and registered in the United States, but due to the online environment where borders are virtually nonexistent, not understanding how these laws affect your current consumer base (who may be international to a certain extent) and organizational operations are a risk that can hold your company liable and in violation of international law.

PROTECTING AGAINST LIABILITY FOR DATA/PRIVACY LOSS

I have travelled the length and breadth of this country and talked with the best people, and I can assure you that data processing is a fad that won't last out the year.[68]

We have discussed privacy policies above, but they are not the only safeguard or best practice companies are putting in place to reduce the risk of regulatory violation or legal liability.

INSURANCE

Errors and omissions insurance as well as cyber-liability insurance procurement by businesses is on the rise. Another new twist is the electronic data loss insurance. Hiscox currently offers a version,[69] Read

---

[66] "Commission decisions on the adequacy of the protection of personal data in third countries," accessed March 10, 2014, http://ec.europa.eu/justice/data-protection/document/international-transfers/adequacy/.

[67] Joel A Levy, "The EU steps up on data protection," (Business Review Europe, August 21, 2013), http://www.business revieweurope.eu/technology/the-eu-steps-up-on-data-protection.

[68] Editor in charge of business books for Prentice Hall, 1957: Tina Sieber, "8 spectacularly wrong predictions about computers and the internet," (March 15, 2011), http://www.makeuseof.com/tag/8-spectacularly-wrong-predictions-computers-internet/.

[69] "Electronic Data Loss Insurance," (Hiscox), accessed March 10, 2014, http://www.hiscoxusa.com/small-business-insurance/business-owner-insurance/data-loss-insurance/.

carefully what is and is not covered; for example, the Hiscox version covers data loss but not the liability due to the data loss; it will cover interruption of computer operations but not your mistakes or employee actions; and it is limited to $10,000 at the high end for most of these losses.

DISCLAIMERS/DISCLOSURES

The Securities and Exchanges Commission has continuously issued guidelines regarding appropriate disclosures and disclaimers for online content posted by financial institutions. The FTC recently released updated guidelines for disclosure in advertising, which include disclosure of endorsements, sponsorships and other payments from online endorsers, including bloggers.[70] The FTC originally addressed the issue of online disclosure in a 2009 report. The 2013 update is a must read for anyone who communicates online, especially if they blog and review products and/or services[71].

1. Proximity and placement

   The purpose of the consumer rules is to protect consumers by making sure they have all the information they need to evaluate content that is put online and that may affect their decision to purchase a product or service. The FTC wants to make sure that the disclosure is in a place that the reader will see—it cannot be hidden on an obscure tab, for example. The FTC uses the wording that the disclosure must be "conspicuous."

2. Truthfulness

   As it protects the consumer, the FTC requires that advertising be truthful, not unfair, and does not lead to deceptive practices. This is why the wording of the disclosure itself is important. Are you disclosing that the manufacturer gave you a free sample of their product so that you could review it? Did you win the product at an event? Are you (or your employees) disclosing that the product or service was a perk you acquired from your Klout score? The Klout perk is still considered a boon to you, so it must be disclosed.

3. Distracting factors in ads

   One core principle of content design is that it not be so busy—with graphics, images, texts, hyperlinks, etc.—that the message, and more importantly, the disclosure is lost. When you finish your blog, review it on the screen and see how it looks. It is also a good idea to view it on different devices, such as a tablet or smartphone. The FTC rules do take these devices into account as to whether the disclosure is effective or not.

4. Repetition

   Saying something once is good, but saying it a few times is better. You may need to repeat the disclosure in various places on your blog and throughout your Web site. Don't forget to repeat on your social media postings as well.

5. Understandable language

   One of the complaints I always hear as an attorney is why can't the legalese be in English? Well, the FTC agrees with you and requires that the disclosure be in "clear and understandable" language. What is clear and understandable language? Can a reasonable

---

[70] Stephanie Schwab, "Disclosures for Bloggers and Brands," (Social Media Explorer, April 24, 2013), http://www.socialmediaexplorer.com/social-media-marketing/disclosures-for-bloggers-and-brands/.

[71] ".com Disclosures," (Federal Trade Commission, March, 2013), http://www.ftc.gov/sites/default/files/attachments/press-releases/ftc-staff-revises-online-advertising-disclosure-guidelines/130312dotcomdisclosures.pdf.

person understand what you want to disclaim? By the way, the FTC does acknowledge that you can have not just visual—text—disclosures but also audio disclosures, so for those of you who podcast or YouTube your blogs, remember to put in disclosures there, too.

TERMS OF USE/SERVICE

Terms of use/service (TOU/S) are the rules for users to adhere to if they wish to use your Web site and/or service. It relates to the requirement of disclosure to consumers. You cannot assume that consumers know how to "act" on a Web site. We need to have the rules laid out for them. Many will claim that the users don't read the TOU/S anyway. Sometimes you see them presented as a first screen with an "I Agree" click button to continue. It is assumed that the user has read them, and regardless, unless found unconscionable, the user will be held bound by them.

SUBMISSION GUIDELINES

Data can come in the form of user-generated content (UGC): videos, articles, photographs, etc. Some Web sites and online platforms encourage their users to engage with the brand by uploading and/or sharing content through the brand's platform. The guidelines are important because they lay out the parameters of what can be submitted, how it can be submitted, and whether that submission will be subject to prescreening or not.

COMMUNITY GUIDELINES

These guidelines govern comments and responses by users to items that have been posted by the brand and/or other users. They serve an important purpose for many companies in reserving the right to monitor and remove certain UGC that may be seen as obscene or harassing, or otherwise objectionable. An example of defining objectionable material follows:

> *"Objectionable" means as to any content, information in any medium or format, including without limitation text, data, graphics, audio, or video, that:*

- *is libelous or defamatory, pornographic, sexually explicit, unlawful, or plagiarized;*
- *a reasonable person would consider harassing, abusive, threatening, obscene, or excessively violent, or*
- *constitutes a breach of any person's privacy or publicity rights, hate speech, or an infringement of any third party's intellectual property rights of any kind, including without limitation, copyright, patent, trademark, industrial design, trade secret, confidentiality, or moral rights; or*
- *violates or encourages others to violate any applicable law.*

It is interesting to note that one challenge is that of moderating UGC—a reason some use to argue against any moderation whatsoever. There are a number of comments that are posted to brand platforms that originate from nonhuman sources. In fact, according to a report released by Incapsula, an online security and bot-tracking firm, "nearly 61.5 percent of Web traffic is non-human...5 percent came from scrapers (bots responsible for content theft and duplication) and 4.5 percent came from hacking tools."[72]

---

[72] "While We Spend a Lot of Time on the Net, Most Traffic Is Non-Human," (Red Orbit, December 13, 2013), http://www.redorbit.com/news/technology/1113027605/most-internet-traffic-comes-from-non-human-sources-121313/.

Companies are using antispam applications, such as Akismet,[73] to automatically reduce the number of these nonrelevant comments. Akismet claims to "zap" over 147 million pieces of spam a day.[74]

DATA SURVEILLANCE

The commercial interest of technology companies and the policy interests of government agencies have converged.[75]

Do you know who Edward Snowden is? I am sure this will become a pop culture question in the near future. Mr Snowden was a former U.S. National Security Agency (NSA) contractor who leaked information regarding NSA's surveillance practices, which he found concerning.[76] His leak would reveal that the NSA had been spying on millions of individuals around the world, including American citizens and world political leaders, under a series of programs, such as PRISM, a massive data collection effort. The NSA claimed it was doing this in the interest of national security. Mr Snowden is currently residing in Russia to avoid prosecution in the United States. He was awarded the 2014 Ridenhour Prize, which was established by the Nation Institute and the Fertel Foundation, for truth telling.[77]

The Snowden incident brought to light how much information is out there and how it can be collected. These are facts that most individuals were aware of—the surprise was who was doing the data collection.

So who can be spying on us? Let us list who we know: government, employers, competition, head hunters, recruiters, spouses, friends/colleagues, strangers, and… this list is quite broad. Each of those entities has different reasons for wanting specific data on us and will use it for different purposes. Is it all bad or malicious? It is interesting to note that in a recent poll many Americans were not all that concerned about the government spying program.[78]

But the Snowden affair has brought some changes to the NSA in its operations and computer networks to prevent additional leaks, including "41 specific technical measures to control data by tagging and tracking it, to supervise agency networks with controls on activity, and to increase oversight of individuals."[79]

On the judicial front, a federal district court ruled in December 2013 that "the NSA program that is systematically keeping records of all Americans' phone calls most likely violates the Constitution" and

---

[73] Accessed March 10, 2014, http://akismet.com.

[74] Ibid.

[75] Evgeny Morozov, "The Real Privacy Problem," (MIT Technology Review, October 22, 2013), http://www.technologyreview.com/featuredstory/520426/the-real-privacy-problem/.

[76] "Edward Snowden Biography," (BIO), accessed March 10, 2014, http://www.biography.com/people/edward-snowden-21262897.

[77] Noam Cohen, "Snowden to Receive Truth-telling Prize," (New York Times, April 6, 2014), http://www.nytimes.com/2014/04/07/business/media/snowden-to-receive-truth-telling-prize.html?emc=edit_th_20140407&nl=todaysheadlines&nlid=33425801.

[78] "Fewer U.S. citizens now concerned about government Internet spying," (October 25, 2013), http://www.upi.com/Top-_News/US/2013/10/25/Fewer-US-citizens-now-concerned-about-government-Internet-spying/UPI-68281382720800/.

[79] "After 'cataclysmic' Snowden affair, NSA faces winds of change," (CNBC, December 14, 2013), http://www.cnbc.com/id/101273384.

ordered the government to stop collecting data on the two plaintiffs of the case.[80] Well, what about the rest of us?

On December 18, 2013, President Barack Obama received 46 recommendations from a panel of outside advisors who "urged [him] to impose major oversight and some restrictions on the National Security Agency," arguing that in the past dozen years its powers had been enhanced at the expense of personal privacy.[81] After reviewing the report, Obama and his administration unveiled a proposal to limit NSA's collection of data.[82] This did not end the controversy as less than a month later the "Heartbleed" bug, a security flaw in two-thirds of the world's Web sites, was discovered by researchers. As information came out about the bug, the NSA became a focus as to what it knew about the bug, when it knew about the bug, and whether it had exploited the bug to gain access and information it should not have. Although NSA has denied prior knowledge of the bug or any exploitation of it, Obama did make a statement that the NSA is allowed to keep some Internet security flaws secret "for a clear national security or law enforcement need."[83] Unfortunately, we have not heard the end of this.

DICTATORSHIP OF DATA

Data is the new oil!

Clive Humby, dunnhumby

Data is the new oil? No: Data is the new soil.

David McCandless[84]

Acxiom is a data broker.[85] It currently holds an average of 1500 pieces of information on more than 500 million consumers around the world.[86] They promote their technology as an "audience operating system for data and decision sciences."[87] They analyze the data they collect and sell it to companies who use it to advertise and target market to consumers. The data they collect includes names, addresses, credit card records, purchase histories, travel itineraries, etc. They are not the only one.

---

[80] Charlie Savage, "Judge Questions Legality of N.S.A. Phone Records," (New York Times, December 17, 2013), http://www.nytimes.com/2013/12/17/us/politics/federal-judge-rules-against-nsa-phone-data-program.html?nl=todaysheadlines&emc=edit_th_20131217&_r=0.

[81] David Sanger, "Obama is Urged to Sharply Curb N.S.A. Data Mining," (New York Times, December 19, 2913), http://www.nytimes.com/2013/12/19/us/politics/report-on-nsa-surveillance-tactics.html?nl=todaysheadlines&emc=edit_th_20131219&_r=0.

[82] Charlie Savage, "Obama to Call for End to N.S.A.'s Bulk Data Collection," (New York Times, March 25, 2014), http://www.nytimes.com/2014/03/25/us/obama-to-seek-nsa-curb-on-call-data.html.

[83] David Sanger, "NSA Allowed to Keep Secret Some Internet Security Flaws Officials Say," (New York Times, April 13, 2014), http://www.bostonglobe.com/news/nation/2014/04/12/obama-allows-nsa-keep-some-internet-security-flaws-secret-officials-say/E2VkNsH6G0mNQh0uvBipoM/story.html.

[84] Vishal Kumar, "100 Greatest Data Quotes," accessed March 10, 2014, http://v1shal.com/content/100-greatest-data-quotes/?utm_source=rss&utm_medium=rss&utm_campaign=100-greatest-data-quotes.

[85] Accessed March 10, 2014, http://acxiom.com.

[86] See note 4.

[87] See note 85.

Acxiom has been in the news recently. Facebook entered a deal with Acxiom early in 2013 to merge Facebook user data with Acxiom's data sets leading Acxiom's chief science officer to claim in an investor meeting that its "data could now be linked to 90% of U.S. social profiles."[88] The value of that data is the idea that companies would be able to predict different propensities of an individual.

How far can this predictive analysis go? A researcher at the University of Rochester and a Microsoft engineer "showed they could predict a person's approximate location up to 80 weeks into the future at an accuracy of above 80 percent...by mining 32,000 days of GPS readings taken from 307 people and 396 vehicles."[89] To me that seems like a really small sample and yet a high percentage of accuracy. Can you imagine receiving a message "in 2 weeks you will be passing XYZ store. Stop in and buy the [item] you want that will be on sale?" Sometimes I cannot imagine what I will be doing later in the day, but the technology seems to exist that will know before I do. The question then comes up—did I do it because I was going to anyway or did I do it because the idea was planted in my head? OK Oracle—pass me the cookie.[90]

Recently, smart city technology has grabbed headline attention. The definition of a smart city is "a developed urban area that creates sustainable economic development and high quality of life by excelling in multiple key areas; economy, mobility, environment, people, living, and government...through strong human capital, social capital, and/or ICT infrastructure."[91]

Smart cities, such as Seoul and Rio de Janiero, which won the Best Smart City 2013 at the Smart City World Expo in Barcelona, Spain, November 2013,[92] are harvesting technology for infrastructure management, energy efficiency, and mobility, and are now expanding their efforts for social innovation and social engagement. "Rio is the epitome of the centralized, hi-tech approach to shepherding citizens." Yet its chief of staff Pedro Paulo Carvalho has stated that this is no longer sufficient: "The first stage of a smart city [is] to have the basic [central] infrastructure. Now the real challenge is the second phase, to integrate those systems into daily life, to open up our data...for citizens in a way that they can actually use it. The concept of a 'smart citizen' is one that is engaged in the decision-making process."[93]

But how far will social sensing go before some privacy advocates recall Big Brother of Orwell's 1984? Will the city step in to mandate exercise to reduce health costs if it notices you spend too much time sitting on your couch or send an alert to the restaurant that you have had too much to drink? Will businesses use this information to obtain information and/or monitor employees for the same purposes—to reduce its liability based on employee misconduct? As the technology develops, the risk of increased liability on behalf of your company increases if it decides to use the technology without addressing privacy concerns of its employees and consumers. Will the company's policies be able to keep up with the changing regulatory environment? Algorithmic regulation anyone?

---

[88] See note 4.

[89] See note 4.

[90] *The Matrix*, film, directed by the Wachowski brothers (1999; Warner Brothers).

[91] "What is smart city," (Business Dictionary), accessed March 10, 2014, http://www.businessdictionary.com/definition/smart-city.html.

[92] "Smart City World Expo Congress," accessed March 10, 2014, http://www.smartcityexpo.com.

[93] Tim Smedley, "The new smart city – from hi-tech sensors to social innovation," (The Guardian, November 26, 2013), http://www.theguardian.com/sustainable-business/smart-cities-sensors-social-innovation.

APPROACHES TO CONTENT

6

Love your content.
Imagine a world where content is beautiful. It's clear, consistent, useful, and usable. You know
where it lives and exactly what it says. Your users are delighted. Your business reaps the benefits.
Your process is efficient. And you're happy.[1]

The one thing missing from that quote, which appears on Brain Traffic's homepage, is there is no mention of the content being secured. This omission in the quote is a reflection of the omission in real business. As the content creators keep creating the content and disseminating it on various online platforms, they have not taken into account the risks they are opening the company up to. Security and risk managers are in a knowledge-based profession. Our value comes from precise information being applied at

---

[1] Brain Traffic, accessed March 16, 2014, http://braintraffic.com.

the appropriate time to accomplish a specific goal for our clients. Content management has been defined as getting the right content to the right user at the right time on the right device. In a way, that means that most of us have the basic skills to become effective content strategy partners for growing and thriving businesses. The trick is to understand what that means and how to apply the skills and some new tools to make it work and reduce the risks and security concerns involved.

CONTENT MARKETING VERSUS CONTENT MANAGEMENT

When we talk about content marketing in the online environment, we are looking at information provided in a digital format to specific audiences who find it useful, usable, appropriate to their needs, unique, expert, and searchable. The information provided could be varied: case studies, tips and how-tos, statistics, trend analysis, case analysis, etc. The format the information is displayed in can be varied as well: blogs, photographs, videos, diagrams, and more. Content management is the creation, organization, monitoring, and distribution of the content to meet specific goals.

There has been a lot in the media lately about the importance of content as a foundational element to the marketing arsenal a firm may employ. Anna Hasselbring of Spr-d.com compiled some statistics from Content+ (a UK company) that outlines some of the current studies and reports regarding content marketing and its effectiveness[2]:

1. A total of 63 percent of companies said posting content on social media has increased marketing effectiveness
2. Six of 10 Twitter and Facebook users are more likely to recommend a brand they follow
3. Companies with blogs get 97 percent more inbound links
4. A total of 67 percent of Twitter users will buy from a brand they follow
5. A total of 55 percent of blogs on company sites result in 55 percent more visitors
6. A total of 70 percent of customers prefer getting to know a company via informational articles rather than promotional advertising

These statistics speak to the fact that consumers trust custom content more than paid advertising. Why should that be the case? The answer is one of perspective. Consumers find the content to be relevant to them and of value, not a hard sale from a company. In other words, there's a big difference between promotional content (or content that is firm-focused) and informational/educational content (which is client-focused). The content approach encourages engagement with the consumer throughout the consumer lifecycle—not just in the beginning—which allows for an added benefit of long-term or lifetime value of consumer retention.

DIFFERENT AUDIENCES, DIFFERENT CONTENT

As we look at the audiences our businesses seek to reach with its content, we must recognize that each of these may have different content needs. Potential clients want to get-to-know-you, whereas current clients want to know what you have done for them lately. The general public also wants content from

---

[2] Anna Hasselbring, "Content Marketing 101: Why is content marketing important?", Sprk-d.com, accessed March 16, 2014, http://sprk-d.com/content-marketing-101-content-marketing-important/#sthash.IHI1sDUa.dpuf.

you—such as general knowledge or enough information to know they are in trouble and need to seek you out. Another kind of content consumer may be our colleagues in our industry or profession—who are searching for information themselves to help with their own businesses and careers. And we should not forget the social and mainstream media that are constantly on the lookout for advisors or thought leaders to consult with, interview, or put on television or in a broadcast show.

In a social media context, some of these audience types can be further defined by how they use the content they get from you. Seekers just look for information that can be personally relevant. Amplifiers take the information they find and share it with friends, colleagues, and anyone else who follows them, broadening your message reach. Finally, joiners want more than just the information they find. They want to engage with you—join your community—and so they permit you to send them direct messages, and collect data on them.

Knowing which content is best and which user to provide it for is what content management is about and often under the purview of the marketing department. As with other strategic approaches, the company needs to plan out what content it will create, when it will provide it, why it is providing that specific content, and where it will distribute it. For security and risk management personnel, these questions are put within the context of what risks and security gaps do those answers create.

MYTHS OF CONTENT MARKETING AND CONTENT MANAGEMENT

Oftentimes new technologies or marketing approaches are accompanied with a variety of myths as to why it may be difficult to implement or why it wouldn't work in your particular scenario. Three specific myths come up in regard to risk, security, and the content approach. The first is the perception that content management and marketing is labor intensive. With all the regular business work that has to be done, who has the time to learn how to create content and the tools to manage it and then to create the content itself? The second myth is related to the first in that content management and marketing is so labor intensive because it is complex.

There are many social media and digital platforms online, each with its own nuances and particulars, which at first glance can be overwhelming for an employee who has not dealt with them in a significant way if at all. However, there are options from delegating the task to a specific division in the firm, outsourcing and paying a third-party content management company, or approaching the task one platform at a time. The company wants to make sure it has the right individuals with the right skill set to handle this function efficiently. Each of these options requires a commitment of time and resources at different levels (see Budgeting and analysis).

The third myth is that marketing and content developers do not need input from the risk and security professionals. For example, marketing will make decisions as to which devices to let content be displayed on—we discussed in depth the security and risk issues of mobile devices in Chapter 2—which is very relevant to this discussion. Perhaps even more so, because our previous discussion regarding this matter focused on employee usage of mobile devices, but the content approach opens up an increased probability of hacking and data breaches by focusing on the public's viewing of the company content on their own mobile devices. So when marketing makes its decisions, security and risk management needs to be at the table to understand and help the others understand how to do content management in a secure manner.

BUDGETING AND ANALYSIS

Content management is not free. It requires resources, some of them financial, some of them in-kind. Included among these costs are: planning, authoring (staff or agencies), design and production, syndication, paid placement of media, moderation and curation, etc. Ben Barone-Nugent put it eloquently when he wrote, "Engagement is directly proportional to investment in the design, user experience, and development of the right content."[3]

Budgeting also requires you to look at what you are getting in return for your financial investment. The effectiveness of content management can be measured beyond just the financial one metric model, using four perspectives[4]:

- Financial (change in profits)
- Brand (change in customer attitudes)
- Risk management (change in reputation)
- Digital (change in assets)

But there are other key indicators that should be measured beyond just investment, including:

- Return on engagement: How committed is the reader with your content? For example, did he or she sign up for a subscription?
- Return on involvement/participation: Does the reader do anything with your content such as share it on social media platforms or comment on it?
- Return on attention: How often does the reader interact with your content? Does the reader indicate that he or she focuses on the content or find it relevant?
- Return on trust: Does the reader feel your company is trustworthy based on your content?
- Return on influence: Does the reader do what you ask when you issue a call to action with your content?

[3]Ben Barone-Nugent, "Selling content strategy: the case for its importance to business success," *The Guardian* (October 14, 2013), http://www.theguardian.com/media-network/media-network-blog/2013/oct/14/selling-content-strategy-digital-business.
[4]Danyl Bosomworth, "Making the business case for content marketing," (June 10, 2011), http://www.smartinsights.com/content-marketing-strategy/content-marketing-business-case/.

BENEFITS OF THE CONTENT APPROACH

Even with that particular risk in mind as well as others that we will outline later, why does a company use this marketing strategy? There are a variety of reasons to implement a content management system, including:

- Building name recognition: awareness of you, your company, your strengths, and how you can provide value to clients/customers
- Giving your clients/customers a benefit (and setting up reciprocity)
- Building relationships with your clients/customers by increasing the amount of time they spend with your brand through reading and interacting with the content you provide
- Creating or acquiring good, consistent content that can be reused
- Establishing your authority on a pertinent subject
- Maximizing search engine optimization
- Generating leads for not only new client/customer acquisition, but also for speaking engagements, etc.
- Inspiring referral advocacy from other industry professionals

Those are external benefits, but your company can reap internal benefits from good content management as well. For example, good content management can help your firm recruit excellent talent, who may see your efforts in the digital environment as an attractive factor when seeking employment with you. It can also boost the morale of existing employees who may relate to the information you provide or may contribute information themselves, thereby feeling engaged and recognized as a valued and contributing member of the company community. Content can also open lines of communication between employees and foster trust among them as they share and learn relevant information to help them complete their tasks. But as with other strategic tools, one of the keys to success is knowing how to develop and implement a good plan (see Implementing a content management strategy).

IMPLEMENTING A CONTENT MANAGEMENT STRATEGY

Certain steps should be taken to develop an optimized content marketing strategy:

- Begin with identifying your business goals.
- Research the different social media/content platforms and match your business goals to the appropriate platform.
- Devise a budget: there are a variety of costs (see the following section) that need to be taken into consideration.
- Create your content: author it yourself, repurpose content you created for another venue, purchase it from a content provider, curate or aggregate content from other sources, etc.
- Publish your content: this is where the rubber meets the road. Once it is out there, retracting it can be difficult, if not impossible. Before you post, make sure you have reviewed and polished the content. It takes only 5 s for a visitor to determine whether to keep reading what you posted or move on. Make a good first impression.
- Promote your content: in print and digital materials, including social media, icons can go a long way to encouraging others to share your content. Also, it has been confirmed that just adding the words "please share this" can increase the likelihood that it will be shared.
- Analyze your results: creating the content and putting it out there is not enough. You need to monitor and review what has happened (or not) because the content was placed there is important, especially form a return on investment standpoint.

INTELLECTUAL PROPERTY RIGHTS, RISKS, AND CONTENT

Notwithstanding the fact that the most innovative and progressive space we've seen – the Internet – has been the place where intellectual property has been least respected. You know, facts don't get in the way of this ideology.[5]

Content also adds to the firm's intellectual property (IP) assets and creates value. According to the World Intellectual Property Organization (WIPO), "Intellectual property (IP) refers to creations of the mind, such as inventions; literary and artistic works; designs; and symbols, names and images used in commerce. IP is protected in law by, for example, patents, copyright and trademarks, which enable people to earn recognition or financial benefit from what they invent or create. By striking the right balance between the interests of innovators and the wider public interest, the IP system aims to foster an environment in which creativity and innovation can flourish."[6]

IP theft is a major risk and security concern for many international or transnational companies. But even small- and mid-sized companies need to be aware and monitor how their IP assets are being used, officially and unofficially, to mitigate risks to reputation, loss of IP rights, etc. IP theft can also take the form of the alteration of existing content on existing company systems—manipulating a company logo

---

[5] Lawrence Lessig, "Intellectual Property Quotes," accessed March 16, 2014, http://www.brainyquote.com/quotes/keywords/intellectual_property.html.
[6] "What is Intellectual Property?" World Intellectual Property Organization, accessed March 16, 2014, http://www.wipo.int/about-ip/en/.

for example. Your firm should have an IP strategy and policy in place to keep track of IP assets that are created and how they are used (see IP strategy components).

IP STRATEGY COMPONENTS

- Definition and value statement of IP for the company
- IP audit and assets inventory (digital and nondigital)
- IP risk assessment
  - IP risk register
- IP strategic plan, including:
  - IP company leadership
  - IP internal creation policy
  - IP third-party acquisition policy
    - Work-for-hire
    - Independent/freelance contractor
    - Purchase procedures
    - Content creation/stock companies
  - IP portfolio management plan
    - IP permissions policy
    - IP retirement/archive policy
  - IP exploitation strategies
    - IP valuation
    - Licensing
    - Sales
  - IP protection/enforcement policy
    - IP usage monitoring
    - IP theft/breach incident reporting
    - Prelitigation and litigation strategies
  - IP insurance
  - IP education and training

IP CYCLE

The IP strategic plan follows the IP cycle (see Figure 6.1) closely. Security and risk managers can use the IP cycle as a road map indicating specific points of concern and where they should be implementing risk and security controls.

There are different ways IP is created, including acquisition and licensing from other sources. Risk concerns range from inaccurate information and liability for harm caused by that inaccurate information to copyright infringement because the source selling the IP did not have the rights to do so. An example of this is the current controversy regarding medical applications. There are more than 10,000 medical and health-related apps. The controversy is about oversight of the medical information provided in the apps and whether mobile heath care technology is outpacing Food and Drug Administration regulations. WebMD currently has a disclaimer:

> The opinions expressed in WebMD User-generated content areas like communities, reviews, ratings, or blogs are solely those of the User, who may or may not have medical or scientific training. These opinions do not represent the opinions of WebMD. User-generated content areas are not reviewed by a WebMD physician or any member of the WebMD editorial staff for

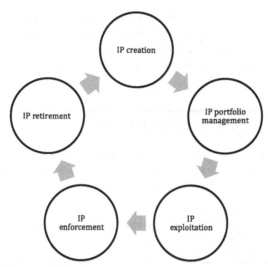

FIGURE 6.1 The Intellectual Property (IP) Cycle.

accuracy, balance, objectivity, or any other reason except for compliance with our Terms and Conditions. Some of these opinions may contain information about treatments or uses of drug products that have not been approved by the U.S. Food and Drug Administration. WebMD does not endorse any specific product, service, or treatment.

Do not consider WebMD User-generated content as medical advice. Never delay or disregard seeking professional medical advice from your doctor or other qualified healthcare provider because of something you have read on WebMD. You should always speak with your doctor before you start, stop, or change any prescribed part of your care plan or treatment. WebMD understands that reading individual, real-life experiences can be a helpful resource, but it is never a substitute for professional medical advice, diagnosis, or treatment from a qualified health care provider. If you think you may have a medical emergency, call your doctor or dial 911 immediately.[7]

Once the IP is created and or acquired, it has to be managed. Inventories of IP assets as well as information about the type of IP it is, where it was acquired from, where it resides, how it is being used, etc. are important tools to understand the value of your company's IP assets. Miscategorizing the assets or not knowing what you have can be detrimental to the company.

Most IP is created or acquired to be exploited and generate revenue or other resources for the company. Each exploitation opportunity needs to be reviewed in terms of the risks they present, how the risks can be mitigated, and any security concerns regarding protection, access, and safety.

IP enforcement concerns monitoring the IP and taking preventative and enforcement actions when IP theft or misuse is discovered (see What to do if you discover IP theft?). One risk here is the possibility of missing an IP violation or not enforcing your IP rights consistently, leading a court to determine if you condone one usage of it, you condone them all.

[7] WebMD (2010), accessed March 16, 2014, http://forums.webmd.com/3/diabetes-exchange/forum/5299.

IP retirement is very much in line with data/content archive, storage, or destruction. In our digital age, information is constantly being discovered, updated, and changed. Some IP becomes obsolete, irrelevant, or just wrong. Monitoring to take no longer useful IP out of your portfolio, and especially out of public viewing, is important to make sure your customers know you are up to date with current trends, etc.

WHAT TO DO IF YOU DISCOVER IP THEFT?

- Understand your IP rights.
- Publish a copyright notice on your company's Web site and all digital accounts and presences.
- Refer to your company's policies relating to IP and refer the matter to the appropriate department (usually legal).
- Document the incident: research all the facts and data.
- Make sure your copyright is registered.
- Consult an attorney or your legal department.
- Send a Cease and Desist Letter and request they remove your content.
- If the item is online send a Digital Millennium Copyright Act (DMCA) Take Down Notice.
- Weigh the pros and cons of pursuing litigation/arbitration.

COPYRIGHTS

Copyrights in the content can lead to licensing opportunities or new affiliations for income generation and/or exposure. They are valuable intangible assets for the company. "Copyright is a form of protection grounded in the U.S. Constitution and granted by law for original works of authorship fixed in a tangible medium of expression."[8,9] Copyright is not just one right but a bundle of rights:

1. Right to Reproduce the Work: the right to copy, imitate, reproduce, duplicate or transcribe the work in fixed form.
2. Right to Derivative Works: the right to modify the work to create a new work. A new work that is based upon an existing work is a "derivative work."
3. Right to Distribution: the right to distribute the work to the public by sale, rental, lease or lending.
4. Public Display Right: the right to show a copy of the work directly to the public (e.g., hanging up a copy of a painting in a public place) or by means of a Web site, film, slide, or television image at a public place or to transmit it to the public.
5. Public Performance Right: This is the right to recite, play, dance, act, or show the work at a public place or to transmit it to the public.

Copyright is considered to last the life of the author plus 75 years (if an individual) or 95 years (if a corporation). Public domain is the concept that works whose copyright protection has expired is available for use by anyone. U.S. attorneys usually use the benchmark that if a work was created or published before 1923 in the United States it is probably now in the public domain. But even attorneys sometimes have trouble doing the math regarding when a work is in the public domain because the Copyright Act has gone through a number of amendments and at one point in the past copyrights needed to be renewed and

---

[8] "Circular 44: Cartoons and Comic Strips" (United States Copyright Office, September, 2012), accessed March 16, 2014, http://www.copyright.gov/circs/circ44.pdf.

[9] "US Copyright Office, "FAQs," accessed June 30, 2014, http://www.copyright.gov/help/faq/faq-general.html.

sometimes were not. Although some materials may already be in the public domain, do not make the assumption that everything that is on the Internet is free for you to use. Bloggers have been caught in terms of cutting and pasting significant if not full extracts of material belonging to others and then finding themselves served with a cease and desist letter. Linking of a url is a much more legal approach.

A good thing to remember is that copyright is about permission not just about giving credit. Make sure you have the appropriate copyright permissions to use content you did not create yourself, including permission from your employees to report photos they may have taken at a firm function.

Pinterest,[10] the social media electronic bulletin board platform, created a lot of controversy when it started to get popular specifically because it seemed to be permitting and encouraging copyright violation through a cut and paste function, or "pinning," of images from Web sites to an individual's board without seeking the consent of the image copyright owner. This is a classic case of just because you can (technologically) doesn't mean you should (legally). Pinterest did set up some liability protections for itself, such as reminding users that they need to abide by copyright laws and other relevant laws in its Terms of Use,[11] they did not have any easy printing mechanisms or other mechanisms that allowed the bulletin boards to be exported from the Pinterest Web site, and they provided a social sharing tool (a stylized P in a square box) that Web site owners could use to indicate they were ok with people "pinning" from their sites.

Instagram[12] is another popular social media platform with the focus of permitting users to instantly share photographs with their friends or "followers." Instagram also has a Terms of Use that outlines copyright concerns and correct procedures[13] because users have been known to photograph all sorts of items, including copyrighted materials and post them—usually without intent to violate copyright laws.

However, even with those controls in place, businesses have found themselves in trouble with the law and their customers. A cautionary example is what happened to *Vogue Spain* in 2012[14] when it was discovered that the magazine was misappropriating photos from Instagram without seeking permission from the photographers who owned the copyrights to them. Although no legal case was instituted against *Vogue*, it apologized quickly and profusely because the social media backlash inversely affected its reputation.

It is important to remind employees that ignorance is not a defense under the law, and they need to make sure they have permission for whatever content they are posting, wherever they end up posting it.

DIGITAL MILLENNIUM COPYRIGHT ACT

This also brings up the issue that we need to be aware that there is a difference between property that is created digitally and property that can become digitized (such as via a scan or recording to digital media). The DMCA was passed in 1998 under President Clinton. It implements two 1996 treaties of the WIPO and criminalizes production and dissemination of technology, devices, or services intended to circumvent measures that control access to copyrighted works. In addition, the DMCA heightens the penalties for copyright infringement on the Internet and maintains that writers/authors have specific rights in the works they produce for online versus other environments.

---

[10] Accessed March 16, 2014, http://www.pinterest.com.

[11] Accessed March 16, 2014, http://about.pinterest.com/terms/.

[12] Accessed March 16, 2014, http://instagram.com.

[13] Accessed March 16, 2014, http://instagram.com/legal/terms/.

[14] Rosie Burbidge, "Vogue Spain's uncredited use of Instagram photos," Art and Artifice (April, 2012), http://aandalawblog.blogspot.com/2012/04/vogues-uncredited-use-of-instagram.html.

But the DMCA also brought another feature: Title II of the DMCA—the Online Copyright Infringement Liability Limitation Act—a series of "safe harbor" clauses that many online social media platforms rely on to provide indemnification for Internet service providers (ISPs) from copyright violations implemented by users of their platforms.

There are four safe harbor activities ISPs can claim for protection: (1) transitory digital network communications, (2) system caching, (3) information residing on systems or networks at direction of users, and (4) information location tools. To qualify for these protections ISP's must meet three requirements: (1) it must be a "service provider" (a provider of online services or network access, or the operator of facilities therefor); (2) it must have "adopted and reasonably implemented" a policy to address and, in the appropriate circumstances, terminate repeat infringers; and (3) it must accommodate measures that copyright owners use to identify or protect their copyrighted works.[15] Two last elements qualify for a specific safe harbor focus on the ISP having actual knowledge of the infringing material or not being aware of facts or circumstances from which the infringing activity is apparent and that the ISP cannot receive a financial benefit attributable to the infringing activity.

The big legal case in this area is Viacom versus YouTube, sometimes also known as Viacom versus Google, because Google owns YouTube.[16] Viacom International sued YouTube for copyright infringement based on 79,000 video clips Viacom owned copyrights in that appeared on YouTube between 2005 and 2008. The initial decision was for summary judgment for YouTube based on the DMCA safe harbor rules. Viacom appealed and the case was remanded back to trial court to determine factual issues regarding what YouTube knew about the infringements as the second Circuit court looked at the issue of willful blindness on behalf of YouTube. However, this line of arguments would then shift the burden of proof to YouTube away from Viacom, who claimed that YouTube had a duty to inquire. This is contrary to the current practice that it is the copyright owner's obligation to point to where the infringing clips were located. This is consistent with current copyright law that says a copyright owner has to enforce his or her own rights. At this point, YouTube won the case, but the decisions have left a few open questions for ISPs to consider.

One of YouTube's disclosures was that it uses the DMCA Take-Down Notice procedure. This provides a mechanism for a copyright owner to notify the ISP that their copyrighted work was posted on the ISP site without their permission or consent. The ISP is then obligated to take down the infringing material and notify the original poster or the content of the claim being made against them. The original poster then has the opportunity to provide evidence of why the material is not infringing and request it be reposted or do nothing at all.

FAIR USE DOCTRINE

One of the reasons an original poster may provide for why his or her posting was not an infringement is the Fair Use Doctrine, Title 17 of the US Code, Sections 107–118.[17] According to the US Copyright Office, the Fair Use Doctrine could be claimed if it meets four criteria:

1. Purpose and character of use (commercial versus nonprofit educational purposes)
2. The nature of the copyrighted work

---

[15] Fernando A. Bohorquez Jr. and David M. McMillan, "Viacom v. YouTube Postscript—Copyright Infringement, Social Media and the Blurred Lines of the Digital Millennium Copyright Act's Safe Harbors," Bloomberg Law (October 31, 2013), http://about.bloomberglaw.com/practitioner-contributions/viacom-v-youtube-postscript-copyright-infringement-social-media/.

[16] 2010 WL 2532404 (S.D.N.Y 2010).

[17] "Fair Use," United States Copyright Office, accessed March 16, 2014, http://www.copyright.gov/fls/fl102.html.

3. The amount and substantiality of the portion used in relation to the copyrighted work as a whole

4. The effect of the use upon the potential market for or value of the copyrighted work

Two recent cases involving potential online copyright violations demonstrate a little of the court's reasoning in regards to specific online activities:

- Kelly versus Arriba Soft, 336 F.3d 811, Ditto.com search engine would display downsized (thumbnail) images of Kelly's photographs. He court held that "such thumbnailing is fair use since the search engine's purpose for copying and transforming was not to displace Kelly or otherwise profit at his expense, but rather…to increase the efficiency by which Internet users could find and access online content."
- Perfect 10 versus Amazon.com, 487 F.3d 701 (9th Cir. 2007), the Google Images case. As with the previous, "the court noted that the downsizing process, accompanied by the attached link—through to the full size—transformed the nature and purpose for which Google was displaying the images."
  Another series of cases brought up the imaging of copyright infringement via framing (presenting one Web site's information within a frame of your own Web site) or deep-linking (linking to another Web site beyond their home page, into sometimes password protected areas.)
- *Washington Post* sued TotalNews, Inc., arguing that TotalNews' framing of their content was copyright infringement. TotalNews settled by agreeing to link without the framing.
- Live Nation Motor Sports versus Davis, 2006, WL 3616983, plaintiff SFX (Live Nation) broadcast live coverage of events with sponsoring advertisements. Defendant Davis linked to the webcasts and bypassed the ads and other content presented on the SFX site. A preliminary injunction was granted, with the court citing that Davis's direct linking harmed SFX financially and that SFX would likely prevail in their copyright and trademark infringement cases.
- Ticketmaster Corp. versus Tickets.com, Inc., 2000 WL 1887522, defendant used a web crawler to get information about Ticketmaster events and display them. "The court held that Tickets.com use of Ticketmaster's internal links was designed to obtain information that was not protected by copyright and was therefore a fair use."

A third series of cases presents the practice of scraping information from other Web sites via robots or Web crawlers and then republishing the information on your own proprietary Web site:

- Craigslist versus 3Taps, 2013, misappropriating real estate listings; computer fraud case; Computer Fraud and Abuse Act.
- Associated Press versus Meltwater Holdings US, Inc., "the court found that an online news aggregator that provided its subscribers with nearly 500-character excerpts of copyrighted articles scraped from the Web site of the Associated Press's licenses did not engage in a fair use of those articles."

A fourth series of cases focused on violation of copyright because of the contractual obligations imposed because of terms of use governing the use of a Web site. Clickwrap and browserwrap agreements are what we call the pop-up dialogue boxes full of legal text outlining terms of use, guidelines, and other disclaimers regarding the Web site or social media platform. First you click on an "agree" button to acknowledge you "read and understood" the terms, and the other just pops up and disappears after you click anywhere on the screen. As with all such "licenses," there is a debate over actual versus constructive knowledge that the user actually has about the terms, but so far courts have held that users are bound by the terms, no matter how ridiculous they may seem. For example, Apple's iTunes end-user license agreement expressively forbids you from using iTunes to create missiles and biological, chemical, or nuclear weapons; SONY permits no class-action suits relating to its PlayStation game console.[18]

The last series of cases I want to point out in this section is a novel argument that converts the intangibility of copyrights to a very real property cause of action: trespass to chattel: eBay Inc. versus Bidder's Edge, Inc., 100 F.Supp.2d 1058, granting eBay a preliminary injunction, "the court relied on the fact that defendant's spiders consumed a portion—albeit very small—of eBay's server and server capacity, and thereby deprived eBay of the ability to use that portion of its personal property for its own purposes."

INTERNATIONAL IP CONCERNS

Another thing to keep in mind is that IP rights are country-specific. There are no international IP designations, although many countries will have bilateral and/or multilateral treaties with other countries to recognize IP rights if the rights owner registered them within their host country. To see one example, the U.S. Copyright Office has a brochure (Circular 38A[19]) listing all the international relations the United States has with other countries regarding copyrights (see International IP organizations).

INTERNATIONAL IP ORGANIZATIONS

World Intellectual Property Organization (WIPO)
    http://www.wipo.int/portal/en/index.html
World Trade Organization: Agreement on Trade-Related Aspects of Intellectual Property Rights (TRIPS)
    http://www.wto.org/english/thewto_e/whatis_e/tif_e/agrm7_e.htm
Intellectual Property Owners Association (IPO)
    http://www.ipo.org
The International Trademark Association (INTA)
    http://www.inta.org
The International Association for the Protection of Intellectual Property (AIPPI)
    https://www.aippi.org
International Chamber of Commerce Commission on Intellectual Property
    http://www.iccwbo.org/about-icc/policy-commissions/intellectual-property/

But there is a big risk in that some countries are well known for being IP thief havens or for not protecting U.S.-based IP rights. Two examples are China and India. In April 2013, India's High Supreme Court denied Novartis' Cancer-Drug Patent.[20] Novartis is not alone. According to a

---

[18] Chris Hoffman, "10 Ridiculous EULA Clauses That You May Have Already Agreed To," MakeUseOf (October 23, 2012), http://www.makeuseof.com/tag/10-ridiculous-eula-clauses-agreed/.

[19] "Circular 38a: International Copyright Relations of the United States," United States Copyright Office, accessed March 16, 2014, http://www.copyright.gov/circs/circ38a.pdf.

[20] Eva von Schaper and Pratap Patnaik, "Novartis Cancer-Drug Patent Denied by India Supreme Court," *Bloomberg* (April 1, 2013), http://www.bloomberg.com/news/2013-04-01/novartis-cancer-drug-patent-denied-by-india-supreme-court.html.

Washington Times article, "more than a half-dozen drugs have had their patents revoked in favor of Indian production or have had 'compulsory licenses' issued against them."[21]

As for China, talks in 2013 between President Obama and Chinese President Xi Jinping focused on cybersecurity and IP. This meeting got a lot of media attention because of the concern that China was and is behind various forms of hacking against U.S. citizens and corporations. But President Obama also used the opportunity to make a strong point regarding U.S. IP rights that are being disrespected in China. President Obama is quoted as saying: "Ongoing theft of America's intellectual property theft would be a serious 'inhibitor' of Sino-American relations."[22]

Security and risk professionals need to know if company content is to be accessed overseas and what security controls can be but in place to protect it. Also, if there are any international licensing agreements regarding IP, a discussion should be undertaken about IP rights protection in the other countries. Last, a review of IP insurance to see which countries are covered is a prudent risk management strategy.

CREATIVE COMMONS LICENSE

You may have heard of a Creative Commons license (CCL).[23] A CCL is a way that copyright owners can grant specific permission to use their content in certain ways without the licensee having to fill out any special paperwork or even trying to locate the owner. Creative Commons (CC), the organization, developed the CCL to provide a simple and standardized way that can be used by anyone, any corporation, anywhere in the world.

The CCL comes in six different varieties depending on how much the owner wishes to restrict the content's use. CC offers the CCLs in a three-layered approach: legal wording (legalese), a plain-human translation; and machine readable code. In addition to the text attribute (i.e., CC BY, etc.) there is also a graphic or icon representation of each license.

1. Attribution (CC BY): This license lets others distribute, remix, tweak, and build upon your work, even commercially, as long as they credit you for the original creation.
2. Attribution—Share Alike (CC BY-SA): This license lets others remix, tweak, and build upon your work even for commercial purposes, as long as they credit you and license their new creations under the identical terms. (Wikipedia uses this license).
3. Attribution—NoDerivs (CC BY-ND): This license allows for redistribution, commercial and noncommercial, as long as it is passed along unchanged and in whole, with credit to you.
4. Attribution-NonCommercial (CC BY-NC): This license lets others remix, tweak, and build upon your work noncommercially, and although their new works must also acknowledge you and be noncommercial, they don't have to license their derivative works on the same terms.
5. Attribution-NonCommercial-ShareAlike (CC BY-NC-SA): This license lets others remix, tweak, and build upon your work noncommercially, as long as they credit you and license their new creations under the identical terms.

---

[21] Ben Wolfgang, "U.S. Drug industry upset with Indian policies on patents" (The Washington Times, September 26, 2013), http://www.washingtontimes.com/news/2013/sep/26/us-drug-industry-upset-with-indian-policies-on-pat/?page=all.
[22] "President Obama presses Chinese leader Xi Jingping on cybersecurity" (Daily News, June 9, 2013), http://www.nydailynews.com/news/politics/president-obama-pressed-chinese-leader-xi-jingping-cybersecurity-article-1.1367419.
[23] Accessed March 16, 2014, http://creativecommons.org.

6. Attribution-NonCommercial-NoDerivs (CC BY-NC-ND): This license is the most restrictive of the six main licenses, only allowing others to download your works and share them with others as long as they credit you, but they can't change them in any way or use them commercially.[24]

A COUPLE OF DIGITAL CONCERNS FOR COPYRIGHTS

Two phenomena are currently under way that bring up some interesting dimensions to the copyright protection discussion. The first is paratext and the second is three-dimensional (3D) printing.

"Paratext" is a concept that was defined by Gérard Genette, in his 1997 book *Paratexts: Thresholds of Interpretation*.[25] His definition states that paratexts are the "accompanying productions flitting around and inside a text, the stuff before, after, and in media res that filters our perception of it."[26] In today's digital world, we know this better as the second screen or multiscreen experience. It is no secret I enjoy the AMC series "The Walking Dead." During the third season, they introduced "Story Sync," an interactive Web site where you could "join fellow fans online for snap polls, cool trivia, and exclusive video while watching the premier broadcast of the latest episode on-air."[27] After the first two frustrating episodes dividing my time between the television broadcast of the latest episode and keeping track of all the information streaming on my iPad from the Story Sync, I resolutely turned it off. I was missing half the action and felt the tension rise as I was also missing half the online conversation.

Apparently I am not alone, but am in a minority about wanting just the one screen experience. Thomas Doherty, writing in *The Chronicle of Higher Education*, notes: "For many viewers, critics, and scholars, the second (and third, fourth, and fifth) screen is as good as the first. In some quarters, the decorative wraparound material—the term of art is 'paratext'—is outshining the prize in the box. The irritating distractions have morphed into the main attractions."[28] He gives as an example the X-Men franchise: "all the buzzing swarms of trailers, teasers, bloopers, tweets, swag, webisodes, podcasts, chat rooms, fanzines, geek conventions, DVD extras, synergistic tie-ins, and branded merchandise, in all their infinite varieties."[29]

Each of these additions, or in legal terms, derivatives of the original, also need to be monitored, inventoried, registered, and protected to ensure their value to the company. Any of them can be hijacked; therefore, risk mitigation starts with security of access to these different types of content that's meant to be given away freely to fans and the public alike.

The second trend we need to be aware of is 3D printing via a machine that uses computer modeling software to "reproduce objects using layers of materials like rubber, plastics, ceramics and metals."[30] Various news programs have done stories on this technology being used to create new tissues or body

---

[24] Accessed March 16, 2014, http://creativecommons.org/licenses/.

[25] Gerald Genette, *Paratexts: Thresholds of Interpretation* (Cambridge: University of Cambridge, 1997).

[26] Thomas Doherty, "The Paratext's the Thing," The Chronicle of Higher Education" (January 6, 2014), http://chronicle.com/article/The-Paratexts-the-Thing/143761/?cid=wc&utm_source=wc&utm_medium=en.

[27] Accessed March 16, 2014, http://www.amctv.com/shows/the-walking-dead/story-sync.

[28] Thomas Doherty, "The Paratext's the Thing," The Chronicle of Higher Education" (January 6, 2014), http://chronicle.com/article/The-Paratexts-the-Thing/143761/?cid=wc&utm_source=wc&utm_medium=en.

[29] Ibid.

[30] Phyllis Korkki, "Beyond 3-D Printers' Magic, Possible Legal Wrangling" (The New York Times, November 24, 2013), http://www.nytimes.com/2013/11/24/business/beyond-3-d-printers-magic-possible-legal-wrangling.html?_r=0.

organs, such as a human ear on a mouse to be transplanted. Many individuals believe the medical possibilities will greatly enhance our quality of life. However, there is a dark side to this technology because it can also be used to produce items that may be protected by patents or copyrights, for example a piece of avant guard furniture, or products that can be used to do harm, such as a gun. Morality arguments aside, these products have specific design features that may be subject to legal protection.

Another risk concern is what if consumers are harmed by the object that was 3D printed at home leading to a possible product liability claim? This is the question Professor Nora Freeman Engstrom of Stanford University Law School researched and published about in the *University of Pennsylvania Law Review*.[31] Usually product liability is strict liability and the injured only has to prove that they were injured by the product. But if the product was 3D printed in a home or small business whose owner is considered a casual seller, then negligence has to be proven and that is a higher burden.

Risk managers should inquire whether 3D printing is being used or is being considered to be used in the company. It may be that the company may design software modeling protocols for specific objects designed only to be 3D printed. Make sure the products are tested, etc. just as any other product and/or service that the company would be launching. From a security standpoint, this software may have malware or other development errors (see the follow for more) that can lead to hacking activity and/or data breaches.

TRADEMARKS

A trademark "is a word, phrase, symbol, and/or design that identifies and distinguishes the source of the goods of one party from those of others."[32] One of the keys to trademarks is that it is about protecting that mark in commerce. Most people are familiar with trademarks in terms of corporate logos—graphical images that represent a company. The Nike Swoosh[33] or Mickey Mouse's ears[34] are two very distinguished trademarks. If identifying a service rather than a product the mark is called a "service mark," for example Bank of America's flag logo,[35] but most of the time "trademark" is used to name both.

Trademarks are just not two-dimensional images but can be 3D physical shapes or other attributes of a products packaging, such as the Coca-Cola contour bottle.[36] These are called "trade dress: a product's physical appearance, including its size, shape, color, design, and texture. In addition to a product's physical appearance, trade dress may also refer to the manner in which a product is packaged, wrapped, labeled, presented, promoted, or advertised, including the use of distinctive graphics, configurations, and marketing strategies."[37]

[31] Clifton B. Parker, "3-D printing creates murky product liability issues, Stanford scholar says," Stanford Report (December, 2013), http://news.stanford.edu/news/2013/december/3d-legal-issues-121213.html.
[32] "Trademark, Patent, or Copyright?" United States Patent and Trademark Office, accessed March 16, 2014, http://www.uspto.gov/trademarks/basics/definitions.jsp.
[33] Accessed March 16, 2014, http://www.nike.com/us/en_us/.
[34] Brown and Michaels, "Your Trademark: What to do and what not to do" (2013), accessed March 16, 2014, http://www.bpmlegal.com/tmdodont.html.
[35] Accessed March 16, 2014, https://www.bankofamerica.com.
[36] Sue Purvis, "What Every Small and Medium Sized Business Should Know About Intellectual Property," United States Patent and Trademark Office (December 5, 2012), http://www.uspto.gov/about/offices/ous/121205.pdf.
[37] "Trade Dress," The Free Dictionary, accessed March 16, 2014, http://legal-dictionary.thefreedictionary.com/Trade+Dress.

But can you trademark everything? There are some specific guidelines about trademarking, but one of the keys is that the marks must be distinctive. According to the United States Patent and Trademark Office (USPTO), there are five types of marks:

1. Generic: these types of marks are not eligible for trademarks; they refer to a class of products. An example would be "ivory" when used to describe products made from elephant tusks. A mark can become generic (genericide) because of extensive public use of and association with the product type. Examples of trademarks that have been lost include aspirin (Bayer), escalator (Otis Elevator Company), and zipper (BF Goodrich).
2. Descriptive: these marks describe an ingredient, quality, characteristics, function, feature, purpose, or use of the relevant goods and/or service. They are only protectable if they acquire a secondary meaning in the minds of the public to identify the source of the product rather than the product itself. Examples would be Seattle's Best Coffee or Awesome Teriyaki Hamburger.
3. Suggestive: these marks require the public to use their imaginations regarding a product. These marks are automatically eligible for protection. Examples would be Chicken of the Sea, Gatorade, Jaguar cars, and Greyhound bus service.
4. Arbitrary: these marks use common words in unfamiliar ways. They are also automatically eligible for protection. Examples include Apple computers, Nike sports-related products, and Nickelodeon television station.
5. Fanciful: these marks are made-up words. They are the strongest types of trademarks and automatically eligible for protection. Examples include Kodak, iPod, Lego, Verizon, and Skype.

Based on the this information, what about the case of VeryMeri Creative Media who sent cease and desist letters to Diane von Furstenberg and the Gap, Inc., to stop using the emoticon <3 because it has a trademark in it? The federal court of the Southern District of New York has not ruled yet whether the <3 can be a protected trademark, but other emoticons are such "as a wink ;), a smile :), and a frown :-(, have all been registered as trademarks by different entities, including alcoholic beverage makers, online retail stores, greeting cards companies and cell phone manufacturers."[38]

Trademarks and trade dress are protected under Federal Law Lanham Trademark Act (15 U.S.C.A. §1051 et seq.) as well as state statutes and common law doctrines. Infringement occurs if and when customers are confused between the two marks because they are too similar. Registration for a trademark is more complex than for a copyright and more expensive too (see Trademark registration process). It consists of an appellant-like process of your lawyers arguing why the mark should be granted and the USPTO[39] attorneys finding reasons as to why not to grant it. There are a number of factors that go into the process including trademark challenges, continued use, public notice, incontestability, trademark strength, and more. But the granting of the federal trademark allows you to put a registered symbol under your trademark image® and that has significant value over the common law™ symbol that is placed until the registration is approved. Federal law carries higher penalties for infringement than state laws, which in turn can provide higher damage awards for the trademark owner.

In the online digital world, trademarks take on a new role in terms of brand identity and protection. For example, if you have a federally registered trademark and the corresponding social media account

---

[38] Marlisse Silver Sweeney, "Trademarking Emoticons" (Law Technology News, January 7, 2014), http://www.law.com/jsp/lawtechnologynews/PubArticleLTN.jsp?id=1389132098459&kw=Trademarking%20Emoticons&et=editorial&bu=Law%20Technology%20News&cn=20140107&src=EMC-Email&pt=Daily%20Alert.
[39] Accessed March 16, 2014, http://www.uspto.gov/trademarks/index.jsp.

TRADEMARK REGISTRATION PROCESS

Disclaimer: It is highly recommended you use an experienced trademark attorney for registering a trademark. Besides knowing the nuances of the process they probably know a few of the USPTO attorneys from prior registrations.

- Contact a trademark attorney or contact your company's legal department and discuss the why you want to register the trademark.
- Always have a trademark search/feasibility study done on the mark itself to determine strength of mark, potential challenges, and potential confusingly similar marks.
- Collect basic information including: date of first use (internally) and date of first use in commerce.
- You can file a trademark application for "intent to use" but then you have to refile (and repay) when you actually use in commerce.
- Take digital photos (these will serve as the specimens) of the mark and how it is being used (packaging, Web sites, marketing materials).
- Select a class/category for your mark. For example, Class 09 is for computers, software, electronic instruments, and scientific appliances (products), whereas Class 38 is for communications (services).
- After you file, "sign," and make payment, you will be emailed a "receipt/confirmation" of your application and the deposit of the specimens.
- It can take anywhere from 3 months to more than a year to get through the process.
- The USPTO will assign an attorney to review your application and correspondence may ensue to clarify, amend, or correct the application.
- NOTE: You will only have a certain amount of time to respond. Failure to do so will abandon your application and will have to start over again.
- Once the "mark" has been approved, you will be notified of when it will be "published" and where.
- After publication, you receive the official trademark registration document and can change your ™ to ®.
- There are follow-up deadlines at 5, 8, and then every 10 years after the mark has been approved to ensure that the mark is still in use in commerce. These deadlines are very important. If they are not met, the mark will be abandoned.
- If you have never done a trademark application before, I suggest you watch the USPTO videos: http://www.uspto.gov/trademarks/process/TMIN.jsp.

name is abandoned, you can request it from the social media platform and they will most likely give it to you.[40]

Trademarks also permit for revenue generating opportunities via licensing agreements. You can sell, buy, transfer, and/or license your trademarks:

- Conventional licensing: can include characters, designs, or trademarks that are used to convey an affiliation and/or for aesthetics purposes. Most characters, movies, and sports teams use conventional licensing.
- Brand extension licensing: the trademark is a brand with a clear, positive imagery that provides a strong "fit" with the new product. This brand fit creates a transparent relationship between the licensor and manufacturer. Includes food, beverages, or durable goods.[41]

An example of how this is playing out on the digital landscape is the licensing of Internet memes. A meme "is a virally-transmitted cultural symbol or social idea."[42] Memes that have become

---

[40] For one example, see Twitter's Trademark Violation Policy, accessed March 16, 2014, http://support.twitter.com/articles/18367-trademark-policy.

[41] "Licensing Fundamentals," Goldmarks, accessed March 16, 2014, http://www.goldmarks.net/lic_fund.shtml.

[42] Paul Gil, "What is a 'Meme'," About.com, accessed March 16, 2014, http://netforbeginners.about.com/od/weirdwebculture/f/What-Is-an-Internet-Meme.htm.

memorable are humorous, have shock value or drama, may focus on urban myths, or even make social commentary. A few recent ones include: Honey Badger Don't Care,[43] Gangnam Style,[44] and Grumpy Cat.[45] Not only have these memes taken off in the online world making their "stars" renowned throughout the global market, but they have also provided opportunities for making revenue. Wonderful Pistachios created a Super Bowl 2013 ad with Rapper Psy of Gangnam Style fame. You can see it on YouTube: http://www.youtube.com/watch?v=rE6iiiDdTNY.

But there are a number of risk and security concerns regarding trademarks in the online environment.

The first is the unauthorized use of the trademark by parties other than the company who owns the trademark. Sometimes this can be a disgruntled employee or customer who wants to make a point with his or her complaint and uses the trademark to ensure that those who are reading the complaints can easily identify the company being complained about. Most companies will have a trademark or IP use and permissions policy, which severely restricts who can use the trademark, how it can be used, and the approval process to be granted permission to use it. However, the National Labor Relations Board did issue a statement in one of its memos regarding social media use by employees that employees can use the company's trademark without permission of the company if they are engaging in protected concerted activity online—discussing working conditions, their salaries, and other aspects of their jobs—with fellow coworkers.

This has raised a lot of controversy with trademark attorneys who are concerned about trademark dilution. "Trademark dilution is defined as the lessening of the capacity of a famous mark to identify and distinguish goods or services. It can occur either by blurring (weakening the distinctiveness of a trademark) or by tarnishment (weakening the distinctiveness of a trademark) through inappropriate or unflattering associations."[46] A recent social media example was the matter between Facebook versus Lamebook. In 2010 Facebook sent a cease and desist letter to Lamebook, a site that promotes itself as a parody of the Facebook site and that posts the "funniest and lamest of Facebook" posts.[47] Lamebook sued Facebook to get the court to recognize it as a parody site and therefore protected under the Fair Use Doctrine. Facebook countersued claiming that Lamebook diluted the value of the Facebook name. Eventually the case settled out of court in 2011.[48]

TRADEMARK AND GRIPE SITES

Another potential risk to reputation is the creation of gripe sites or "NameofYourCompanySucks.com" general sites. Sarah Feingold wrote a great article for the New York State Bar Association Inside magazine in 2008 that is still relevant today.[49] These sites are set up to criticize and complain about a company or organization and usually include the use of the company's trademark or logo. Feingold describes one of the earliest cases Bally Total Fitness Holding Corp. versus Faber, 29 F. Supp. 2d 1161 (S.D.Cal.

---

[43] "Honey badger don't care," accessed March 16, 2014, http://www.youtube.com/user/czg123#g/u.

[44] "Psy – Gangnam Style," accessed March 16, 2014, http://www.youtube.com/watch?v=9bZkp7q19f0.

[45] "Grumpy Cat," Know Your Meme, accessed March 16, 2014, http://knowyourmeme.com/memes/grumpy-cat.

[46] "Trademark Dilution," International Trademark Association, accessed March 16, 2014, http://www.inta.org/Trademark Basics/FactSheets/Pages/TrademarkDilution.aspx.

[47] Accessed March 16, 2014, http://www.lamebook.com.

[48] Emil Protalinski, "Facebook and Lamebook settle trademark dispute " (ZDnet, September 1, 2011 http://www.zdnet.com/ blog/facebook/facebook-and-lamebook-settle-trademark-dispute/3191.

[49] Feingold, Sarah, NYSBA Inside, "Your Company Sucks Dot Com: Taking Swipes at Gripe Sites," *Winter*, vol. 26, no. 3 (2008), http://www.sarahfeingold.com/press/Inside.pdf.

1998). Faber was an individual who operated a site called "ballysucks.com." Bally Fitness sued claiming trademark infringement and dilution. The court held for Faber, stating that it doubted anyone who saw "ballysucks.com" would think it was official or that Bally sponsored it.

The court also held that individuals have a right to gripe. They can share their negative perspectives with others. But there are some recourses for a company. Keep in mind the success of each of these strategies depends on a number of factors such as specific facts of the matter and potential damage to the company.

1. Trademark infringement: for the use of the company's registered trademark. You can identify the company with the company's name and it is not necessary to have the company logo. So you can't stop them from calling you out on a gripe but you can stop them from using your logo.

2. Anti-Cybersquatting Consumer Protection Act (ACPA)[50]: when the world wide web first appeared, not all companies rushed to register their company name as a domain name. Domain names are also registered on a first-come, first-served basis. This created an opportunity for some individuals to register certain valuable trademarks and basically hold them for ransom for an exorbitant amount of money to turn them over. The ACPA was passed to prevent this from occurring by permitting legitimate federal trademark owners a mechanism to request and recover their inappropriately squatted name. The ACPA also criminalizes the use of counterfeit trademarks as Web sites to defraud consumers.

3. Uniform Domain Name Resolution Policy[51]: the Internet Corporation for Assigned Names and Numbers (ICANN) has come up with their own procedure to allow a trademark owner to bring an action against a site owner who registered a domain name that is confusing similar to the company's trademark or trade name.

4. Trade libel: sometimes also called commercial disparagement, this civil cause of action is brought against an individual who publishes false information in writing or in print about a business or a business' products and/or services. You have to prove that the statements were untrue and that the publishing of the statements interfered with your company relationships with other customers, vendors, suppliers, etc.—in other words, that there was financial harm.

5. False advertising—the Federal Trade Commission is usually the entity to bring false advertising claims against a company for making false claims regarding a product or service. However, the company may also be able to bring this claim against the counterfeit site. Your legal team will need to look at the consumer protection laws in your state for more on how to proceed with this strategy.

6. Do nothing and monitor: sometimes the attention that the gripe site owner receives leads to underdog support for the griper because the whole picture is usually not disclosed to the public. This in turn leads to negative press for the company and a hit to its online reputation. Your team should evaluate the situation and the site and determine the value of pursuing any action against them or whether they are small enough to just need to be kept an eye on.

---

[50] "Anticybersquatting Consumer Protection Act," accessed March 16, 2014, http://thomas.loc.gov/cgi-bin/query/z?c106:S.1255.IS.

[51] "Uniform Domain-Name Dispute-Resolution Policy," ICANNm, accessed March 16, 2014, http://www.icann.org/en/help/dndr/udrp.

TRADEMARK AND REPUTATIONAL RISKS

Reputational risks can be mitigated through the use of content management tools so your firm can hear what is being said about it allowing you to control your message by controlling your content. Monitoring in this way—social listening—can also make you aware of any shadow or fraudulent firm accounts that may be created by hackers or even a disgruntled employee to cause harm to your firm or its clients.

There are a number of monitoring tools that your company can use to hear the conversation that is going on around it regarding its products, services, employees, executives, etc.

- Google Alerts: these are queries that you preset with Google. You then receive an email every day with any results relating to your query that Google has found. I always recommended setting up Google alerts for your name, your company name, and other topics of interest. http://www.google.com/alerts
- Tweriod: a software that permits you to manage your Twitter account feed as well as organize tweets from those you follow. http://www.androidtapp.com/twidroid/
- Hootsuite: a platform that allows you to manage all your social media accounts from one dashboard. https://hootsuite.com
- Tweetdeck: a tool to manage your Twitter accounts. https://about.twitter.com/products/tweetdeck
- Feedly: an online and mobile tool that allows you to customize information to be pushed to your designated devices on topics you are interested in. http://feedly.com/index.html#welcome
- Newsblur: a personalized news reader. http://www.newsblur.com
- Newsvibe: another news reader. https://newsvi.be
- Pulse: a LinkedIn news app you can tailor. https://www.pulse.me

Monitoring content may not be the only thing your company wishes to measure. There are some professional analytical tools out there as well for a cost:

- Radian 6: this social listening tool permits you to "identify and analyze conversations about your company, products and competitors with the leading social media monitoring and engagement tools." http://www.salesforcemarketingcloud.com
- Trackur: social media monitoring software with media monitoring and social analytics. http://www.trackur.com
- Nielsen/Buzz Metrics: "online measurement methodologies analyze consumer behavior and trends, advertising effectiveness, brand advocacy, social media buzz and more to provide a 360 degree view of how consumers engage with online media." http://www.nielsen.com/us/en/nielsen-solutions/nielsen-measurement/nielsen-online-measurement.html

TRADE SECRETS

If the Coca-Cola Company had used patent legislation to protect its secret formula, would it have become the most popular soda in the world? Possibly not.[52]

---

[52] Walter Judge, "Protecting Trade Secrets," The IP Stone (January 12, 2012), http://theipstone.com/2012/01/12/protecting-trade-secrets-eight-questions-businesses-need-to-ask-and-answer/.

A trade secret is information that is kept undisclosed except for a very limited number of individuals in an attempt to maintain that information's value. As the quote suggests, the formula for the Coca-Cola beverage, code name "Merchandise 7X," is one of the most commonly known about trade secrets. Besides not telling anyone the formula, the Coca-Cola Company also spends a lot of time, money, and resources protecting the secret from getting out. In 2007, two former Coca-Cola employees were sentenced to serve federal prison terms for conspiring to steal and sell trade secrets to rival Pepsi.[53]

The federal law that protects trade secrets is the Uniform Trade Secrets Act, which defines a trade secret as: "information, including a formula, pattern, compilation, program, device, method, technique, or process, that derives independent economic value, actual or potential, from not being generally known to or readily ascertainable through appropriate means by other persons who might obtain economic value from its disclosure or use; and is the subject of efforts that are reasonable under the circumstances to maintain its secrecy."[54] In addition, Congress passed the Economic Espionage Act of 1996; see 18 U.S.C. §§1831–1839.[55]

Most companies will have a prohibition of the disclosure of trade secrets or other proprietary confidential information in a specific policy such as the social media policy. The concern is that employees who have a grudge against the company may intentionally disclose the information or may inadvertently reveal the information because security measurements weren't in place. A trade secret only lasts as long as it is concealed. Revelation to the public, whether intentional or not, losses the value completely.

PATENTS

A patent is a grant from the USPTO to an inventor that gives the inventor the "the right to exclude others from making, using, offering for sale, or selling the invention in the United States or 'importing' the invention into the United States'."[56] There are three types of patents.

1. Utility patents may be granted to anyone who invents or discovers any new and useful process, machine, article of manufacture, or composition of matter, or any new and useful improvement thereof;
2. Design patents may be granted to anyone who invents a new, original, and ornamental design for an article of manufacture; and
3. Plant patents may be granted to anyone who invents or discovers and asexually reproduces any distinct and new variety of plant.[57]

In the online world, patents have been used sparingly. Let's examine some of the rare examples.

---

[53] Rusty Domin, "2 sentenced in Coke trade secret case" (CNN, May 23, 2007), http://money.cnn.com/2007/05/23/news/newsmakers/coke/.
[54] "Trade Secret," Cornell University Law School, accessed March 16, 2014, http://www.law.cornell.edu/wex/trade_secret.
[55] "Economic Espionage Act of 1996," accessed March 16, 2014, http://www.economicespionage.com/EEA.html.
[56] "What Are Patents, Trademarks, Servicemarks, and Copyrights?," United States Patent and Trademark Office, accessed March 16, 2014, http://www.uspto.gov/patents/resources/general_info_concerning_patents.jsp#heading-2.
[57] "What Are Patents, Trademarks, Servicemarks, and Copyrights?," United States Patent and Trademark Office, accessed March 16, 2014, http://www.uspto.gov/patents/resources/general_info_concerning_patents.jsp#heading-2.

In 1999, Priceline.com, the online travel booking site, was awarded a business method patent "covering the type of airline ticket the company sells…it is unique because it allows airlines, rather than customers, to select the flights and routing after customers agree to make a purchase."[58] Amazon has a patent on its "1 Click" checkout—US5960411.[59] Interesting to note is that the European Union did not approve this patent, even though Canada did.[60] Apple, which licensed this technology from Amazon for its iTunes and App online stores, is just one of a number of online retailers to do so.

Apple is also a key entity in an ongoing technology patent case against Samsung for infringement on the iPhone. In 2012, Apple scored a victory when a California jury awarded it $1.05 billion finding that Samsung did infringe some Apple patents on the mobile devices.[61] One of the patents deals single touch versus multitouch gestures and another focuses on enlarging documents by tapping the screen. Samsung is appealing the decision.

TECHNOLOGY DEVELOPMENT

In the digital world online, a lot of technology development is taking place—from Web sites with specific functions to mobile apps and games based on company products and/or services. Programmable coding of software has long been understood to be protected by copyrights. But technology development has been slowly evolving to be more client-centric.

In the old days, you would sign an agreement with a development company outlining a set of deliverables, specifications, a due date, and payments. One of the glitches with this "waterfall" approach was that problems in the development of the technology may not be discovered until the end of the process during alpha and beta testing when most of the work had been done and when it is most expensive to repair. New technology agreements are including a more flexible but phased approached requiring the development company to produce a certain amount and then test. Until the test is passed and the phase is approved by the client, the development company cannot proceed. Payments are also structured this way, limiting the amount of money and other resources that may be wasted or loss because of errors. It also allows a client to implement some changes in the specifications of the technology should it be necessary because of circumstances and market changes. Technology development can be a long process and many things can happen between the moment the development agreement is signed and the technology first designed and when the technology prototype is actually completed (see Top 10 legal and security issues for game/app developers).

In addition, read carefully the indemnification clause in the development agreement. Certain assurances should include: security flaw liability (malware), no malicious code, failure to notice malware during testing, and failure to notice malware during release.

---

[58] Andy Wang, "Patents Business Method" (Commerce Times, May 10, 1999), http://www.ecommercetimes.com/story/116.html.

[59] Mike Arsenault, "How Valuable is Amazon's 1-Click Patent? It's Worth Billions," *Rejoiner*, July 13, 2012, http://blog.rejoiner.com/2012/07/amazon-1click-patent/.

[60] Robert Kalanda, "Does Amazon's 'One-Click' Success Mean Business Method Patents for All?" (Commerce Times, March 31, 2012), http://www.ecommercetimes.com/story/74719.html.

[61] Jessica E. Vascellaro, "Apple Wins Big in Patent Case," *The Wall Street Journal* (August 25, 2012), http://online.wsj.com/news/articles/SB10000872396390444358404577609810658082898.

> ### TOP 10 LEGAL AND SECURITY ISSUES FOR GAME/APP DEVELOPERS
>
> IP rights are game/app developers' best friends. You need to understand what and how it protects so you can reap the benefits, but also so you don't violate someone else's. The first question is: is your game an original, a clone or a fan game?
>
> 1. Your game has to be in a fixed, tangible medium (code). Thoughts and ideas are not protected, but their expression is.
> 2. Design and development decisions will need to contemplate IP rights, from copyright of the code, to work for hire and copyright transfers and waivers from independent developers, to trademark of logos of the games and their domain names. Also, do not forget about the alpha and beta testing phases and malware detection which can lead to liability for the developer.
> 3. Who the author is can sometimes be the point of legal contention—work for hire, employee versus independent contractor, commissioned works—each of these adds a new dimension of complexity if a contract that spells out the exact relationship isn't explicit or doesn't even exist. Are you the author, are your employees the authors, or were you hired to develop for someone else?
> 4. Rights can be transferred through a sale or license agreement. Rights can also be split—for example, a right to reproduce but not distribute. Rights last a certain amount of time only and the length depends on which country the work was produced or registered.
> 5. Do you need to register? It is if you want to sue, is what we've always been told. Easy, but can be expensive when you begin to register in every country you want protection in.
> 6. The gaming/apps industry faces unique business model decisions. You have a target audience that is conditioned to paying to be able to play the games so issues such as subscription or user fees, microtransactions for virtual goods, and advertising via sponsorships, branded virtual goods, and product placement, will all require legal guidance in terms of virtual currencies, transactions, interstate commerce, sales taxes, etc.
> 7. Content production in association with the games may also lead to issues with publicity rights (if incorporating a well-known athlete or celebrity), music licensing issues, offensive content, and the Children's Online Privacy Protection Act, to name a few.
> 8. After design and development, the next big issue focuses on game access and distribution—from digital rights management to licensing agreements—this issue also brings in international standards for content and IP protection.
> 9. If you are developing a social game, privacy implications come into play. Most of the games use the social graph to enhance the social experience. These uses are outlined in the games' terms of use and user agreements, but many users do not bother to read them.
> 10. Content also brings up the issue of First Amendment rights (freedom of speech) versus censorship. In June 2011, Justice Scalia and the U.S. Supreme Court decided that "video games are protected speech and that restrictions based on their content would be subject to strict scrutiny."[62] (Brown versus Entertainment Merchants Association, CA). So California's ban on violent video games for children was declared unconstitutional.
>
> [62]Adam Liptak, "Justice Rejects Ban on Violent Video Games for Children" (The New York Times, June 28, 2011), http://www.nytimes.com/2011/06/28/us/28scotus.html?pagewanted=all.

IP OTHER RISKS

In September of 2011 ICM registry began to sell domain names with .xxx top domain level. It was stated that it would allow for businesses and Web sites that dealt with pornography and other sexually explicit material to have a segregated place on the Internet. Not everyone was happy about it. Who wants to be segregated? But the other concern that came up was that this would be a new opportunity for cyber squatters to swoop in and hold a company's name (and reputation) ransom with a .xxx connotation. To try to prevent this situation from occurring "ICANN, the administrator of the .xxx domain names, has instituted a system in which trademark owners who are not adult entertainment providers can register to block the registration of domain names comprising their marks."[63] Although you did not have to use the Web sites you still had to register for them and pay for the domain name, and you only had 6 weeks in which to do so. Many companies rushed to take advantage of the "sunrise" period, but many other companies not realizing this was about to happen learned too late and had to spend money and resources to remedy the situation.

I spoke briefly of trade libel in a section above but want to expand that to the larger risk concern of defamation. Defamation is when someone falsely published information about you that causes you harm, humiliation, or embarrassment. Different states have different definitions and those definitions layout the elements required to prove your case. In the online world a nuance has come up in terms of trying to define the online communications so as to know whether the defamation is one of libel (written) or slander (spoken). For most of us we would assume anything posted online is "written" and therefore libel. But what the courts are evaluating is the extent of the communication and the way the communication is conveyed. So a short tweet or Facebook post is more often considered "spoken, ad-hoc" communication and therefore slander, instead of a thought-out blog or online article, which falls under libel.

I also brought up the issue of Internet memes and IP rights. But another right that is sometimes involved with the memes and other online postings are publicity rights. "The right of publicity prevents the unauthorized commercial use of an individual's name, likeness, or other recognizable aspects of one's persona."[64] So Psy has a copyright in his Gangnam style video, a trademark in his logo, and a publicity right in his persona. One example of how this comes out in the online world is when companies run sweepstakes, contests or promotions online. It is important to make sure you get releases and waivers from any participants and winners to be able to use their likeness on the social media platforms, company brochures, or however else you want to use them before you start posting their image and name around. A reverse scenario got Snickers in trouble when they asked celebrities to tweet about the chocolate bar but the celebrities did not disclose that they were paid spokespersons.

The Landham Act that protects trademarks is most concerned about anti-competitive practices. Currently we see this in a number of investigations by the Federal Trade Commission on some big online platforms such as Facebook, Apple, and Google. This is also a global concern. After Google changed some of its policies and terms in 2013, the European Commission began its own investigation into Google's possible anti-competitive practices due to its size and influence over the Internet landscape.[65] At the writing of this book, the deliberation is still on-going.

Another way that anti-competitive practices are showing up online is the inappropriate use of search engine optimization (SEO) strategies. Google, itself under investigation by the EC, has instituted a policy of combating shady SEO techniques. Once discovered Google sends a warning about the unnatural link or issues an algorithm penalty. Mike Morgan gave some examples of high-risk SEO strategies in his June 2013 article:

- Poor quality SEO directories
- Article spinning

---

[63] Michael D. Hobbs, Jr., "New .xxx Domain can Lead to Headaches," Troutman Sanders (August 29, 2011), http://www.troutmansanders.com/new-xxx-domain-can-lead-to-headaches-08-29-2011/.

[64] "Publicity," Cornell University Law School, accessed March 16, 2014, http://www.law.cornell.edu/wex/publicity.

[65] "Google: Anticompetitive Practices under EU Commission Deliberation," *IPFrontline* (October 11, 2013), https://www.ipfrontline.com/depts/article.aspx?id=51191&deptid=5.

- Comment SPAM
- Paid links and advertorials
- Blog networks
- Using another Trademark as a Keyword in an anti-competitive way[66]

IP VALUATION

The Internet provides the access to resources, so it's incumbent upon the people who control those resources to make sure that the economic engine stays intact.[67]

IP valuation (IPV) is the art and science of appraising IP to assign it a financial value that can be used in strategic planning, merger and acquisition deliberations, and other resource-based decision-making. There are various approaches and methodologies to determining IPV but the highest risk is not accessing it correctly which can underestimate or overestimate its value affecting decision outcomes to the company's detriment. For example, not getting enough insurance coverage should an IP loss occur. Some approaches include The Cost Approach, the Market Approach, the Income Approach, and the Assignment-Approach. There are a number of books and resources that discuss each of these approaches in detail. For us it is enough to know that IPV is important and that risks may become apparent during the process. IPV can also become a security concern comes into play if the IPV is to be done by a third party, as confidentiality and data protection and security protocols need to be implemented and enforced to prevent data breach or confidentiality and compliance violations.

IP LEGISLATION

Throughout this chapter, specific legislation has been noted where appropriate. But I would like to turn now to two failed legislative attempts that demonstrated the online divide between technology companies (content channel providers) and media companies (content creation providers).

On January 18, 2012, the web went dark as Web sites both large and small blacked out to protest against two congressional bills relating to IP infringement. Google, Wikipedia, and Twitter were among them. In all, it was estimated that 75,000 Web sites participated.[68] The bills in questions were the Stop Online Privacy Act (SOPA) and the Preventing Real Online Threats to Economic Creativity and Theft of Intellectual Property Act (PIPA). SOPA, also known as H.R. 3261, came from the U.S. House of Representatives and was presented in 2011 by Representative Lamar Smith (R-TX) and a bipartisan group of 12 initial cosponsors. PIPA, Senate Bill 968, was introduced on May 12, 2011, by Senator Patrick Leahy (D-VT) and 11 bipartisan cosponsors. The PROTECT IP Act is a rewrite of the Combating

---

[66] Mike Morgan, "8 high risk SEO strategies your agency might be using," TrinityP3, (June, 2013), http://www.trinityp3.com/2013/06/agency-seo-strategies/.

[67] "Michael Nesmith Quotes," BrainyQuote, accessed March 16, 2014, http://www.brainyquote.com/quotes/authors/m/michael_nesmith.html.

[68] Chenda Ngak, "SOPA and PIPA Internet Blackout Aftermath, Staggering Numbers" (CBSnews, December 19, 2012), http://www.cbsnews.com/news/sopa-and-pipa-internet-blackout-aftermath-staggering-numbers/.

Online Infringement and Counterfeits Act, which failed to pass in Congress in 2010. Protestors were concerned the bills gave the government too much censorship power and threatened free speech online. Before the protest a group of large Internet companies including Facebook, Google, Zynga, Twitter, and LinkedIn, published an open letter in the *New York Times* that said, in part, the companies were "concerned that these measures pose a serious risk to our industry's continued track record of innovation and job-creation, as well as to our Nation's cybersecurity."[69] Because of the attention the letter got and the protest, both SOPA and PIPA were retracted.

This episode was lauded as one of, if not the largest, online protest and that it proved the power of the Internet to motivate, organize, and activate a large scale demonstration. At this time, there is no new pending legislation regarding enhancing IP rights and penalties for violation, but the issue is far from dead.

---

[69] "Wikipedia Blackout: 11 Huge Sites Protest SOPA, PIPA on January 18," *Huffington Post* (January 17, 2012), http://www. huffingtonpost.com/2012/01/17/wikipedia-blackout_n_1212096.html

COMPLIANCE

7

Laws are rules, made by people who govern by means of organized violence, for non-compliance with which the non-complier is subjected to blows, to loss of liberty, or even to being murdered.
Leo Tolstoy[1]

One would hope that the reality of compliance in today's world is not as dire as Tolstoy infers. But for many a compliance officer losing one's life for a compliance violation is not too far of the mark—metaphorically speaking of course. Compliance had become a conundrum of sorts, tangled up in a web of security concerns, privacy rights, laws, regulations, guidelines, and sensational news headlines shouting out the failures of compliance as data breach after breach are successfully carried out.

Compliance in simple terms means to meet the standards set by someone or some entity with authority. Some standards are official, such as laws (Health Insurance Portability and Accountability Act (HIPAA), Sarbanes-Oxley, Family Educational Rights and Privacy Act (FERPA)), some are

---

[1] "Compliance quotes," ThinkExist, accessed March 18, 2014, http://thinkexist.com/quotes/with/keyword/compliance/.

professional (Payment Card Industry Data Security Standard (PCI-DSS)), some are hybrids (Federal Financial Institutions Examination Council (FFIECE) guidelines), and some are unofficial best practices based on trial and error as companies strive to appease consumer privacy concerns (online privacy policies, social media community guidelines, etc.) and protect company reputation.

Authority is a key word in the definition because it specifies one reason why a company would feel compliance is important enough to set aside resources, sometimes significant ones, in order to be compliant—there are consequences if you are not. Consequences fall into two major categories: financial and reputational. Financial consequences include: government fines and penalties, loss of sales, insurance claims, consumer lawsuits, payment card issuer fees, and canceled accounts. Reputational consequences include: loss of good will with current and potential clients, government agency oversight (sometimes aggressive) from loss of trust, and misinformation or extreme negative information leading to a public relations and/or media crisis in the mainstream media and/or social media realms.

As we delve into the compliance arena, we need to understand a very fundamental truth—compliance does not equal security and security does not equal compliance. We can easily say that risk management encompasses both of these functions and that all three—risk management, compliance, and security—serve as three fronts in the battle against breaches, hacker attacks, and cybersecurity threats, but none of them replaces the others, each of them helps us protect our data, our customers, and our companies (including our employees) in their own way. This is definitely one of those "the whole is stronger than its parts" (see Industry profile: brian logan, Citreas CEO for more on this discussion with Citreas Chief Executive Office (CEO) Brian Logan).

So given all of this, we come to understand that compliance is part of a process where guidelines are transformed into controls that are deployed because they are required or because they reduce risk. The expectation is that in doing so they also lead to enhanced security and protection. But, as noted, and as we will see further in the chapter, sometimes nothing can be further from the truth.

INDUSTRY PROFILE: BRIAN LOGAN, CITREAS CEO

www.citreas.com

What does Citreas do?

Citreas provides turn-key solutions to meet data compliance requirements and identity theft needs. Located in Atlanta, Georgia, we developed a platform that delivers an easy to understand simple data compliance and risk management solution for small and midsize enterprises.

How do you define security and compliance? Are they different?

I would define security as the protection of information. Security comes in many forms. Commonly security is viewed as firewalls, encryption, antivirus, and passwords, just to name a few. However, security extends far beyond these measures. Security is knowledge and understanding. Before any individual or organization has security, they have to know what they are attempting to secure as well as what must be secured, then how to secure it. Online security is just one spectrum of security. From a business perspective, online security is twofold. (1) Securing the company network from online vulnerabilities. (2) Ensuring that the consumer or end-user online experience is secure.

Compliance is meeting and/or exceeding guidelines set by federal, state, international, or professional entity. Regulatory requirements can fall into one or more categories: federal (Gramm Leach Bill Act (GLBA)), state (CMR201-17), industry (PCI-DSS), and international (European Union Safe Harbor regulations). Many businesses, especially small business, are not aware of the data protection requirements in the course of business. Compliance is not new but regulations get revised, changed, and updated. For example, California requires email addresses must be encrypted. Now they must be encrypted in storage as well.

INDUSTRY PROFILE: BRIAN LOGAN, CITREAS CEO—Cont'd

They are not the same but work together. Both are things that every organization must do and should be doing it better than they are.

What are some insights to the current and developing situation of social media and compliance?

Social media and compliance comes down to policies and procedures. Do not eliminate using social media but you have to be careful. This is where training and awareness comes in. Training talks about what is acceptable and awareness makes it easy for employees to stop and reflect before posting online. This is important as social media has changed the timing of when things get posted—much faster than ever, and many employees do not think about what they are posting, they just do it.

What three words would you use to describe the online security environment in regard to data?

Misunderstood, insufficient, and misused.

Last thoughts about security and compliance?

Secure everything knowing nothing is secure, and do security and compliance because it is the law, it is good practice, and because you will be hacked.

WHO NEEDS TO BE COMPLIANT?

One myth to dispel at the very beginning is that there is no one who is immune form compliance requirements if you do business in the United States. Those in regulated industries (see List of US regulated industries) understand that because of the nature of their very business they must adhere to certain

LIST OF US REGULATED INDUSTRIES

- Accounting/CPA
- Air transportation (aviation, airports, aerodromes, and airlines)
- Alcohol, wine, and spirits
- Banking
- Biotech/biopharma
- Communication systems (including telephone, voice over internet protocol, Internet service provider, cable)
- Construction
- Education**
- Financial services (including investments)
- Food sources (Food and Drug Administration (FDA), farmers, distributors)
- Health care (including dental and home care)
- High tech
- Hospitality (hotels, etc.)
- Insurance
- Legal
- Kids and family-targeted businesses (Children's Online Privacy Protection Act (COPPA), etc.).
- Manufacturing
- Marine transportation (including ferry and port services)
- Medical (doctors, equipment, hospitals)
- Nonprofit**
- Pharmaceuticals
- Railway and road transportation
- Restaurants**
- Other

**Although not regulated per se, these sectors have special legal and industry requirements they must meet.

regulations and standards. But even those who do not fall within the listed industry categories still have to abide by certain laws and regulations governing client data, etc. What industry is your company in?

Another myth comes up about the difference in business size and that smaller companies do not need to be in compliance. This is also false. The key factor of compliance is not about the size of the company but about the data that need to be protected. The difference in company size affects the company's ability to respond and to put in place the controls required for compliance. This is a valid concern because small or midsize businesses do not have the financial resources or the specialized personnel at the same level that large business do to commit to these requirements. But the authorities say not having the money is not a valid excuse for not doing the compliance. But without the funds, the dedicated personnel or the specialized compliance expertise small companies may feel they are in a Catch-22, having to divert needed operating funds to keep the company functioning to compliance requirements to keep the company open and avoid fines or worse.

Small- and mid-sized companies have been looking for alternative and cost-effective strategies to do both and keep functioning in a compliant manner. Keep in mind my assertion above that compliance does not equal security. The do-it-yourself (DIY) approach requires significant investment in time, if not money, to read, understand, and learn the basics and the nuances of the different compliance requirements. This can lead to cutting corners, where compliance on paper is achieved (and all the boxes checked off), but true security measures and controls are never implemented. Sometimes the question is even more fundamental—where to even start? Robert Stroud, vice president of Strategy and innovation at CA Technologies, suggests that small businesses use something like the COBIT-5[2] standard. In his words: "COBIT contains a well-established, internationally recognized set of governance and management practices and guidelines that support compliance with relevant laws, regulations, contractual agreements and policies."[3] Yes, it is recognized to support standards for compliance, but not necessarily standards of security. Those you have to add on.

Another alternative is to turn over the compliance and security function to a third party. Companies such as Blue Wave Computing, profiled in Chapter 1, and their "Chief Information Security Officer (CISO) In a Box," which provides the client a comprehensive turnkey solution—risk/compliance, security analysis, network security monitoring—and various complex analytical tools. Citreas, profiled earlier in this chapter, is another security/compliance third-party provider. Pricing structures vary based on client need, size, and industry.

Lest we forget this is a book about mobile and apps security and risk management, a search in the Apple App Store produced a listing of 412 apps relating to compliance.[4] Google Play displayed 104 apps,[5] but most of these were focused on making sure your Android device was compliant. Most were listed as free so they tended to be more informational (checklists, guideline recaps) than actual practical steps to take for compliance. Part of the reasoning behind this is that they are presented as DIY tools so as to limit liability or compliance violations against the developers of the apps (see Compliance apps for further details of specific apps).

---

[2] "COBIT 5: A Business Framework for the Governance and Management of Enterprise IT," ISACA, accessed March 18, 2014, http://www.isaca.org/COBIT/pages/default.aspx.
[3] "Achieving Security Compliance In SMBs," (InformationWeek, August, 2013), http://twimgs.com/darkreading/smb-security/S7300813.pdf.
[4] Accessed 2/6/14.
[5] Ibid.

COMPLIANCE APPS

Note: These are just a few that I have come into contact with. But there are more out there and even more that continue to be developed. Keep in mind most of these are for informational or educational purposes only—they do not ensure compliance—and so should not be used as a sole solution. I invite you to share your favorites or comments on these on our Website: www.managingonlinerisk.com.

Health Care Compliance App
Bizness Apps, Inc.
iOS, free
https://itunes.apple.com/us/app/healthcare-compliance/id426481276?mt=8

ABA Bank Compliance Magazine
ABA
iOS, Android, free
https://itunes.apple.com/us/app/aba-bank-compliance-magazine/id806275567?mt=8
https://play.google.com/store/apps/details?id=com.texterity.android.BankCompNL

iComply Toolkit
Appropos
iOS, free
http://www.wecomply.com/compliance-training-solutions/iphone-app-for-compliance-training/

Security Metrics Mobile Scan
Security Metrics
iOS, free
https://www.securitymetrics.com/sm/pub/mobilescan

OSHA Mobile
Rocket Science Consulting
iOS, free
https://itunes.apple.com/us/app/osha-mobile/id374963528?mt=8

Compliance Law (health care law)
Business Apps
Android, free
https://play.google.com/store/apps/details?id=com.compliancelaw.layout

Mobile Security and Compliance
iScan Online Inc.
Android, free
https://play.google.com/store/apps/details?id=com.iscanonline.iscanandroid

---

GENERAL COMPLIANCE: DISCLOSURES

As was stated in Chapter 5, the Securities and Exchanges Commission has continuously issued guidelines regarding appropriate disclosures and disclaimers for online content posted by financial institutions and the Federal Trade Commission (FTC) recently released updated guidelines for disclosure in advertising.[6]

---

[6] ".com Disclosure," (Federal Trade Commission, March, 2013), http://ftc.gov/os/2013/03/130312dotcomdisclosures.pdf.

In December 2013, there was a call to update U.S. Securities and Exchange Commission (SEC) company disclosure rules[7] after a series of reports and press releases relating to Fair Disclosure (FD) Regulation via social media and online channels.[8] In its Report of Investigation Pursuant to Section 21(a) of the Securities Exchange Act of 1934: Netflix, Inc., and Reed Hastings, the SEC stated:

> *We emphasize for issuers that the steps taken to alert the market about which forms of communication a company intends to use for the dissemination of material, non-public information, including the social media channels that may be used and the types of information that may be disclosed through these channels, are critical to the fair and efficient disclosure of information. Without such notice, the investing public would be forced to keep pace with a changing and expanding universe of potential disclosure channels, a virtually impossible task.*[9]

This report comes after the third scenario reviewed by the SEC concerning information disclosures via social media. The first scenario occurred in 2010 when Alan Meckler, CEO of WebMediaBrands (WMB), posted on his blog and tweeted news about his company, including financial results and pending acquisitions. The SEC inquired how this was in compliance with Regulation FD? In its response letter to the SEC, WMB argued that what was blogged and tweeted were not related to material non-public information and that because the company's Website is the Internet company's recognized channel of distribution and is widely available to the entire market, and that the blog is included on the Website with a link to the CEO's Twitter feed, there is no problem.[10]

The second scenario is one I use as an example for what insider trading can look like as a tweet. In 2012, the CEO of Francesca's Holding Corp was terminated for tweeting "Board meeting. Good numbers = Happy Board." Gene Morphis did this via his Twitter handle @TheOldCFO that was linked to his personal blog. His LinkedIn profile also indicated his Twitter feed, so it was easy to make out the identity of "TheOld-CFO." This caused the company stock price to go up before any official announcement was made.[11]

The third scenario and the one referred to by the SEC report listed previously focused on a Facebook posting made by Netflix's CEO on his personal Facebook page in December 2012. The post read "Congrats to Ted Sarandos, and his amazing content licensing team. Netflix monthly viewing exceeded 1 billion hours for the first time ever in June. When House of Cards and Arrested Development debut, we'll blow these records away. Keep going Ted, we need even more!"[12] The SEC's concern was that this posting was not accompanied by a press release or a post on the Netflix Website and could be in violation of Regulation FD. Arguments were made that there was sufficient disclosure and in a timely way, as the post was "(1) immediately available to 205,000 Facebook followers, (2) referenced in a tweet by TechCrunch to its more

---

[7] Ken Tysiac, "SEC to update rules for corporate disclosures," *Journal of Accountancy* (December 20, 2013), http://www.journalofaccountancy.com/News/20139322.htm.

[8] Deborah et al., "SEC Clarifies Social Media Use and Reg FD Compliance," (Goodwin Procter, April 5, 2013), http://www.goodwinprocter.com/Publications/Newsletters/Client-Alert/2013/0405_SEC-Clarifies-Social-Media-Use-and-Reg-FD-Compliance.aspx?article=1.

[9] "Report of Investigation Pursuant to Section 21(a) of the Securities Exchange Act of 1934: Netflix, Inc., and Reed Hastings," (United States Securities and Exchange Commission, April 2, 2013), http://www.sec.gov/litigation/investreport/34-69279.htm.

[10] "Re: WebMediaBrands Inc.," (United States Securities and Exchange Commission, December 9, 2010), http://www.sec.gov/Archives/edgar/data/1083712/000000000010074073/filename1.pdf.

[11] "Francesca's Holdings Terminates Employment of CFO Gene Morphis Following Board Investigation of His Use of Social Media," (Francesca's, May 14, 2012), http://investors.francescas.com/releasedetail.cfm?ReleaseID=672925.

[12] See note 8.

than 2.5 million followers within an hour and (3) referenced within 24 h by traditional press outlets, including the Los Angeles Times, Bloomberg News, Forbes, NBC News Online, PCMag.com, and others."[13]

The SEC did not pursue any action in the first two scenarios against WMB and Francesca's. The SEC did decide to issue a report for the third one, Netflix, to offer some guidance. In short, the lessons learned are that the SEC guidelines regarding disclosure via company Websites apply to the social media arena and you should abide by Regulation FD. Goodwin Proctor attorneys recommend the following in their excellent review of SEC Regulation FD in the online environment[14]:

- Limit business-related social media use to authorized spokespersons
- Notify investors of sources of company information
- Assess whether particular information is material and nonpublic
- Use the "safe harbor" for inadvertent disclosures if necessary
- Keep other securities law obligations in mind

As for the FTC, it has had Endorsements and Testimonials Guidelines, 16 CFR Part 255,[15] for a while. They issued a report regarding the guidelines in 2009, but the most recent was released in 2013.[16] Chapter 5 discussed them in detail but as a recap the significant concerns regarding disclosures include: proximity and placement, truthfulness, distracting factors in ads, repetition, and understandable language. In short, the disclosures must be clean and conspicuous.

The disclosure rules also try to minimize the consumer being "tricked" by false reviews that were paid for by a company or by an employee or other company affiliate giving a review or testimony without disclosing their affiliation with the company. We discussed this occurring in yelp and other online review sites previously.

All of these guidelines regarding disclosure focus on transparency and fairness, meaning to make sure the public knows who is sending the information and to make sure the information is fairly distributed (seen) by all the public that needs to see it to make sure one group is not unjustly advantaged by receiving information not available to all.

Here are some quick questions to ask regarding online postings and disclosures to ensure compliance with the SEC and the FTC regulations we have been discussing:

1. Has the company informed its constituents and whoever else needs to know that they are using online and social media platforms as official channels for communication?
2. Is the online channel chosen for the posting a recognized, identified, and official channel of communication for the company?
3. Is the online posting official communication from the company?
4. Was the online posting posted on a personal or a company official site?
5. Who is posting the information?
6. Is the information accurate and true?

---

[13] Joseph A. Grundfest, "Regulation FD in the Age of Facebook and Twitter: Should the SEC Sue Netflix?," Rock Center for Corporate Governance at Stanford University, Working Paper No. 131. (January 30, 2013).

[14] See note 8.

[15] "Guides Concerning the Use of Endorsements and Testimonials in Advertising," United States Federal Trade Commission, accessed March 18, 2014, http://www.ftc.gov/sites/default/files/attachments/press-releases/ftc-publishes-final-guides-governing-endorsements-testimonials/091005revisedendorsementguides.pdf.

[16] See note 6.

7. Is the information material or nonpublic?
8. If the information is material has the required form been filled out and filed with the appropriate agency?
9. Is the information being posted static or dynamic?
10. If the information is static has the required form been filled out and filed with the appropriate agency?
11. If the information was a blog article or other static material to be posted online, was it preapproved by the Compliance Department?
12. Does the tweet or posting look like an endorsement, recommendation, implied endorsement, or testimonial?
13. If the information was distributed via a tweet, was the Twitter feed linked to the company's main Website conspicuously?
14. If the information was distributed via a blog, was the blog part of the company's main Website or is it linked to the company's main Website conspicuously?
15. If the information was distributed via a Facebook post, was it picked up by enough social media and mainstream sources to meet the FD requirements?
16. Did the information that was posted online get to who needs to know?
17. Does the company have a procedure in place to rectify any inadvertent violation because of a rogue tweet or online posting?
18. Are you monitoring any comments that are made regarding the tweet or posting and does the comment exchange pose any compliance concerns?
19. Does the information contain links or urls? Have these been reviewed and screened within compliance concerns?
20. Does your gut say "don't post it!"?

GENERAL COMPLIANCE: DISCLAIMERS

Compare these two definitions:

1. The denial, refusal, or rejection of a right, power, or responsibility.[17]
2. A statement that is meant to prevent an incorrect understanding of something.[18]

It is interesting to me how these two differ in tone and voice: the first is a very strong negative, whereas the second conveys a positive useful purpose of why a disclaimer would be used. For security and risk management purposes however, disclaimers are used to reduce unwanted claims and liability to others—in short, to prevent lawsuits against the company.

Some compliance regulations require that a company have disclaimers and that they be prominently displayed. In the online and social media realms, the complaint is that there is not enough space to list all of the disclaimers as required. One best practice being used is creating specific disclaimer pages on the official company Website or social media accounts that can be accessed via a short link that can fit in the specified space or listed in the bio/profile portion of the account. Short disclaimer phrases are also being use in social media bio sections such as "Views are my own," "RT (retweets) aren't

---

[17] "Disclaimer," The Free Dictionary, accessed March 18, 2014, http://legal-dictionary.thefreedictionary.com/disclaimer.
[18] "Disclaimer," Merriam-Webster, accessed March 18, 2014, http://www.merriam-webster.com/dictionary/disclaimer.

endorsements," and "Tweets are not legal advice" among others are also making a showing. As to their legal effect, the jury is still out. Having the disclaimers there are a good step forward, but whether the public who reads the disclaimer believes it and takes it to mean what it says is another matter.

Another digital location for disclaimers is at the end of the blog post or the bottom of the Website. Below are a few that caught my eye:

- Wired Advisor Disclaimer: Wired Advisor is not a compliance firm. The information above is believed to be accurate but check with your firm to determine your specific policies and parameters before building and activating a social media presence![19]
- Shear on Social Media Law: All information published on this Website are opinions. The content is for intellectual curiosity purposes only and none of the information may be considered legal advice or advertising. The opinions expressed on this blog may not necessarily reflect the legal positions that the Law Office of Bradley S. Shear, LLC, or Bradley S. Shear, Esq., may advocate or defend. The content on this blog is syndicated and under the U.S. Copyright Act, 17 U.S.C. Sections 101 et seq., you must receive permission from the copyright holder to republish the posts contained on this platform. Users grant Shear on Social Media Law a transferable, in perpetuity, royalty free license to utilize any content that is posted onto this Website. The Law Office of Bradley S. Shear, LLC, and Bradley S. Shear, Esq., make no representations as to the accuracy, completeness, suitability, or validity of any information on this Website and will not be liable for any errors, omissions, or any losses, injuries, or damages arising from the content on Shear on Social Media Law.[20]
- Guava Rose Blog Disclaimer: This is a personal blog. Any views or opinions represented in this blog are personal and belong solely to the blog owner and do not represent those of people, institutions or organizations that the owner may or may not be associated with in professional or personal capacity, unless explicitly stated. Any views or opinions are not intended to malign any religion, ethnic group, club, organization, company, or individual.[21]
- Google Finance Disclaimer: Google, its data or content providers, the financial exchanges and each of their affiliates and business partners (A) expressly disclaim the accuracy, adequacy, or completeness of any data and (B) shall not be liable for any errors, omissions or other defects in, delays or interruptions in such data, or for any actions taken in reliance thereon. Neither Google nor any of our information providers will be liable for any damages relating to your use of the information provided herein. As used here, "business partners" does not refer to an agency, partnership, or joint venture relationship between Google and any such parties.[22]

An important thing to note is that many social media sites invite comments form readers enhancing the effect of being interactive. It is important to note in your disclaimer a statement making it clear that your company is not responsible or liable for comments made by users and/or other third parties that are outside of your company's control. Some companies have gone so far as to deactivate the comments feature of certain social media sites to limit the resources spent on monitoring these sites for compliance concerns.

---

[19] "Financial Advisor Social Media Compliance Guide," (Wired Advisor), accessed March 18, 2014, http://www.wiredadvisor.com/resources/financial-social-media-compliance/

[20] Accessed March 18, 2014, http://www.shearsocialmedia.com.

[21] Accessed March 18, 2014, http://www.guavarose.com/blog-disclaimer/.

[22] "Finance Data Listing and Disclaimers," Google Finance, accessed March 18, 2014, http://www.google.com/intl/en/googlefinance/disclaimer/?ei=_ED6UriBMaSKsweDTQ.

Another common place to see disclaimers in the digital environment is under the signature line in email correspondence. Many of these seek to ensure the confidential nature of some of the communication and to put a recipient who was not the intended recipient on notice that he or she needs to delete the information and inform the sender of the mistake. In the financial industry a mistake such as a "Reply All" instead of just a "Reply" can create a nightmare of compliance paperwork and reporting. The following is an example of an email disclaimer that I use for some of my email communications:

> *This communication is an electronic communication within the meaning of the Electronic Communications Privacy Act, 18 USC 2510, and disclosure of this communication is strictly limited to the recipient intended by the sender of this message. This communication may contain confidential and privileged material for the sole use of the intended recipient and receipt by anyone other than the intended recipient does not constitute a loss of the confidential or privileged nature of the communication. If you are not an intended recipient please contact the sender by return electronic mail and delete all copies of this communication.*

For companies that develop online or mobile apps, disclaimers are part of the legal due diligence required by most online app market places. As outlined in a post by attorney Cynthia Hsu "Apple's App Store and Google's Android Market both have requirements for apps to have certain legal disclaimers. In Apple's case, if your app doesn't have the required terms then Apple will apply its own generic terms."[23]

GENERAL COMPLIANCE: HUMAN RESOURCES

Chapter 4 took an in-depth look at the new work force and the role of human resources when using social media and online platforms throughout the employment cycle. This section will review a few specific compliance and legal concerns expanding on what we have already discussed.

EQUAL EMPLOYMENT OPPORTUNITY COMMISSION

The Equal Employment Opportunity Commission (EEOC)[24] was created in 1965 with the mission to eliminate illegal discrimination from the workplace as defined by Title VII of the Civil Rights Act and other legislation. The EEOC investigates case of discrimination based on age, disability, equal pay/compensation, genetic information, harassment, national origin, pregnancy, race/color, religion, retaliation, sex, and sexual harassment. That is a long list of topical areas. When it comes to the online ad social media environment, it is important to note that these areas are also covered online. If you can't do it offline, you can't do it online. Facebook posts and tweets can be brought up as evidence demonstrating any of these or even a hostile work environment.

OCCUPATIONAL SAFETY AND HEALTH ADMINISTRATION

The Occupational Safety and Health Administration (OSHA)[25] was created in 1970 through the Occupational Safety and Health Act to "to assure safe and healthful working conditions for working men and

---

[23] "Making a Mobile App? How Not to Get Sued," FindLaw (October 6, 2011), http://blogs.findlaw.com/technologist/2011/10/making-a-mobile-app-how-not-to-get-sued.html.
[24] Accessed March 18, 2014, http://www.eeoc.gov.
[25] Accessed March 18, 2014, https://www.osha.gov.

women by setting and enforcing standards and by providing training, outreach, education and assistance."[26] There has been some discussion regarding the use of social media platforms to improve the safety and health of employees via awareness campaign and interemployee dialogue,[27] the idea being that employees affect each others behaviors and attitudes based on their actions and thought processes. Other discussions focus on harm suffered by employees because of social media use (e.g., cyberbullying, harassment, online discrimination) or the use of the devices themselves (e.g., repetitive strain injury, headaches) to complete their business assignments. Did the company consider ergonomics, lighting, ensuring breaks to rest the mind and the eyes, training on the psychological effects of social networking, digital stress, etc.?

AMERICAN DISABILITIES ACT

The American Disabilities Act (ADA)[28] became law in 1990 signed by then-President George H.W. Bush. It was designed to offer protection against discrimination for people with disabilities and to ensure that they have equal participation in American life. A disability is defined by the ADA as "a physical or mental impairment that substantially limits one or more major life activities, a person who has a history or record of such an impairment, or a person who is perceived by others as having such an impairment."[29] For employers, Title I of the ADA is most important as it "requires employers with 15 or more employees to provide qualified individuals with disabilities an equal opportunity to benefit from the full range of employment-related opportunities available to others. It restricts questions that can be asked about an applicant's disability before a job offer is made, and it requires that employers make reasonable accommodation to the known physical or mental limitations of otherwise qualified individuals with disabilities, unless it results in undue hardship."[30] Mark Fletcher in a June 2013 post brought up the question "Is your social media ADA friendly?"[31] This question can extend to all our online and digital interaction and also begs the question of when does the "friendly" become the required compliance? For example, if your human resources department is using online media for training did they incorporate closed-captioning or a sign language interpreter for those employees who are hearing impaired? What about in the use of YouTube videos? Colleges and universities are facing this access concern regarding online distance education programs and professors who use social media platforms to enhance the classroom experience and integrate interactive learning. Have these institutions of higher education given the faculty the tools to ensure disabled students are reasonably accommodated?

---

[26] Accessed March 18, 2014, https://www.osha.gov/about.html.

[27] "Benefits of Social Networking to EH&S, OSHA Compliance, Injury & Illness Recordkeeping and MSDS Management," MSDSonline (July 1, 2010), http://www.msdsonline.com/blog/2010/07/benefits-of-social-networks-to-environmental-health-safety-ehs-and-material-safety-data-sheet-management-msds/.

[28] Accessed March 18, 2014, http://www.ada.gov.

[29] "Introduction to the ADA," (United States Department of Justice), accessed March 18, 2014, http://www.ada.gov/ada_intro.htm.

[30] "A Guide to Disability Rights Laws," (United States Department of Justice), accessed March 18, 2014, http://www.ada.gov/cguide.htm.

[31] Mark J. Fletcher, "Is your Social Media ADA Friendly?" AVAYA (June, 2013), http://www.avaya.com/blogs/archives/2013/06/is-your-social-media-ada-friendly.html.

FINANCIAL INSTITUTIONS

A simple definition for a financial institution is "a company offering financial products or services such as loans, financial or investment advice or insurance."[32] In the compliance world, however, the definition is much more specific and actually written into the law—U.S. Code, Title 18, Chapter 1, Section 20:[33]

§ 20. Financial institution defined.

As used in this title, the term "financial institution" means:

1. an insured depository institution (as defined in section 3(c)(2) of the Federal Deposit Insurance Act);
2. a credit union with accounts insured by the National Credit Union Share Insurance Fund;
3. a Federal home loan bank or a member, as defined in section 2 of the Federal Home Loan Bank Act (12 U.S.C. 1422), of the Federal home loan bank system;
4. a Federal land bank, Federal intermediate credit bank, bank for cooperatives, production credit association, Federal land bank association;
5. a system institution of the Farm Credit System, as defined in section 5.35(3) of the Farm Credit Act of 1971;
6. a bank holding company as defined in section 2 of the Bank Holding Company Act of 1956 (12 U.S.C. 1841); or
7. a depository institution holding company (as defined in section 3(w)(1) of the Federal Deposit Insurance Act); and a Federal Reserve bank or a member bank of the Federal Reserve System;
8. an organization operating under section 25 or section 25(a) of the Federal Reserve Act; or
9. a branch or agency of a foreign bank (as such terms are defined in paragraphs (1) and (3) of section 1(b) of the International Banking Act of 1978).

If your company falls under any of these categories, you are subject to a vast amount of regulation and compliance requirements. In addition, it is important to keep in mind that all of these regulations still apply to and require compliance regardless of device—PC, mobile, tablet, etc.

FINANCIAL INDUSTRY REGULATORY AUTHORITY

Financial industry regulatory authority (FINRA) is a self-regulatory agency or "watchdog" of the current financial market including Wall Street, financial institutions, and government regulation. FINRA has addressed some of the concerns of financial institutions regarding their use of social media. It has issued two important notes and a letter regarding such use:

- Regulatory Note 10-06 (January 2010)[34]

---

[32] Keli Hay, "GLBA Mobile Compliance Challenges," Bluebox (December 10, 2013), http://bluebox.com/corporate-blog/glba-mobile-compliance-challenges/.

[33] "FDIC Law, Regulations, Related Acts," Federal Deposit Insurance Corporation (Last updated: September 16, 2013), accessed March 18, 2014, http://www.fdic.gov/regulations/laws/rules/8000-1200.html.

[34] "Regulatory Notice 10-06: Social Media Websites," FINRA (January, 2010), https://www.finra.org/web/groups/industry/@ip/@reg/@notice/documents/notices/p120779.pdf.

- Regulatory Note 11-39 (August 2011)[35]
- Targeted Examination Letter (June 2013)[36]

Although offering some guidance, the FINRA notes and letter are only rules and can be superseded by federal and state laws. This has led to a problem: currently 11 states have passed social media privacy laws, of which three conflict with the FINRA rules of supervision of communications: "FINRA requires broker-dealers to supervise social media communications and to retain records. At the same time, new laws in 11 states prohibit employers from seeking access to personal social media accounts of employees. By limiting access, these social media privacy laws may hinder compliance with FINRA's supervision requirements. Consequently, broker-dealers will face tough decisions, as complying with FINRA's supervision rules could put them in violation of state laws, some of which have criminal penalties."[37] We will have to wait and see how this plays out in the marketplace.

FEDERAL FINANCIAL INSTITUTIONS EXAMINATION COUNCIL

The Federal financial institutions examination council (FFIEC) is a formal federal interagency organization with a mission to provide standards, principles, and rules for the financial industry. In December 2013, it released its Official Consumer Compliance Risk Management Guidance.[38] According to the press release that accompanied the guidance, "The guidance does not impose any new requirements on financial institutions. Rather, it is intended to help financial institutions understand potential consumer compliance and legal risks, as well as related risks such as reputation and operational risks, associated with the use of social media, along with expectations for managing those risks. The guidance provides considerations that financial institutions may find useful in conducting risk assessments and crafting and evaluating policies and procedures regarding social media."[39] Risk assessment is its focus and it encourages best practices such as:

- A governance structure with clear roles and responsibilities whereby the board of directors or senior management direct how using social media contributes to the strategic goals of the institution;
- Policies and procedures (either stand-alone or incorporated into other policies and procedures) regarding the use and monitoring of social media and compliance with all applicable consumer protection laws and regulations, and incorporation of guidance as appropriate;
- A risk management process for selecting and managing third-party relationships in connection with social media;

[35] "Regulatory Notice 11-39: Social Media Websites and the Use of Personal Devices for Business Communications," FINRA (August, 2011), http://www.finra.org/web/groups/industry/@ip/@reg/@notice/documents/notices/p124186.pdf.
[36] "Targeted Examination Letters," FINRA (June, 2013), http://www.finra.org/Industry/Regulation/Guidance/TargetedExaminationLetters/P282569.
[37] Susan T. Stead and Benjamin C. Chynsky, "Compliance clash: FINRA rules and state laws at odds over social media," LifeHealthPro (October 16, 2013), http://www.lifehealthpro.com/2013/10/16/compliance-clash-finra-rules-and-state-laws-at-odd.
[38] "Social Media: Consumer Compliance Risk Management Guidance," (Federal Financial Institutions Examination Council, December 13), 2011https://www.ffiec.gov/press/PDF/2013_Dec%20Final%20SMG%20attached%20to%2011Dec13%20press%20release.pdf.
[39] "Financial Regulators Issue Final Guidance on Social Media," FFIEC, https://www.ffiec.gov/press/pr121113.htm, December 11, 2013.

- An employee training program that incorporates the institution's policies and procedures for official, work-related use of social media, and potentially for other uses of social media, including defining impermissible activities;
- An oversight process for monitoring information posted to proprietary social media sites administered by the financial institution or a contracted third party;
- Audit and compliance functions to ensure ongoing compliance with internal policies and all applicable laws and regulations, and incorporation of guidance as appropriate; and
- Parameters for providing appropriate reporting to the financial institution's board of directors or senior management that enable periodic evaluation of the effectiveness of the social media program and whether the program is achieving its stated objectives.

SARBANES-OXLEY ACT

The Sarbanes-oxley act (SOX) became law in 2002.[40] "The Act mandated a number of reforms to enhance corporate responsibility, enhance financial disclosures and combat corporate and accounting fraud, and created the 'Public Company Accounting Oversight Board,' also known as the PCAOB, to oversee the activities of the auditing profession."[41] Although SOX doesn't use the term *social media*, it does have Section 409, which requires companies to "disclose to the public on a rapid and current basis such additional information concerning material changes in the financial condition or operations of the issuer, in plain English, which may include trend and qualitative information and graphic presentations, as the Commission determines, by rule, is necessary or useful for the protection of investors and in the public interest."[42] For those who advocate the use of social media, it seems a no-brainer that disseminating information via Twitter would be a fast, if not, one of the fastest and most current ways to get the information out. But that also means your company should also use the social media channels to correct misinformation or inaccurate information. Also, using Twitter does not replace the requirements of a press release to be in compliance with SOX. Michelle Sherman of Sheppard, Mullin, Richter & Hampton, LLP, emphasizes that you should "make sure the social networking sites reflect the most current information including changes in your public financial reporting."[43] In her article reviewing the trouble Credit Suisse got into because information on its Website was not current (and they were fined $4.5 million), Sherman outlined some lessons learned:

- Have an audit done of your Website and social media sites to make sure the information posted there is not arguably outdated, incorrect, or misleading.
- Before acquiring a company, conduct a similar audit to identify any potential risks of your company being financially responsible for preacquisition violations of FINRA regulations or SOX on the target company's respective websites or social media accounts.

---

[40] "PUBLIC LAW 107–204," accessed March 18, 2014, http://www.sec.gov/about/laws/soa2002.pdf.

[41] "Sarbanes-Oxley Act of 2002," (United States Securities and Exchange Commission), accessed March 18, 2014, http://www.sec.gov/about/laws.shtml#sox2002.

[42] "The Sarbanes-Oxley Act of 2002," Securities Lawyer's Deskbook, accessed March 18, 2014, http://www.law.uc.edu/sites/default/files/CCL/SOact/sec409.html.

[43] Michelle Sherman, "Does your Sarbanes-Oxley Act compliance program reflect your social media presence?," Lexology, http://www.lexology.com/library/detail.aspx?g=ff91ba95-055c-4e08-b7ef-1d7f4d1890ca, June 21, 2011.

- Update your company compliance practices and safeguards to ensure that disclosures are being made to all disclosure venues including the less conventional ones such as Facebook and Twitter. This should ideally include coordination between legal, public relations, and finance.
- Do not disclose financial information on Twitter or Facebook that is not available elsewhere.[44]

GRAMM LEACH BILL ACT

The Gramm Leach Bill Act (GLBA)[45]—requires financial institutions to explain their information-sharing practices and safeguard sensitive data for their customers. Important sections include:

- 501. Protection of Nonpublic Personal Information
  - The obligation of the institution to respect the privacy of its customers and protect the security and confidentiality of the nonpublic information.
  - The requirement to establish administrative, technical, and physical safeguards (including protecting against unauthorized access to the data).
- 521. Privacy Protection for Customer Information of Financial Institution
  - Prohibition against obtaining customer information by false pretenses
- 523. Criminal Penalty
  - A fine or imprisonment of 5 years, or both.

DODD-FRANK WALL STREET REFORM AND CONSUMER PROTECTION ACT

Dodd-Frank was enacted in 2010 in response to certain financial scandals that ultimately affected consumers. Morrison & Foerster created a cheat sheet to decipher the Dodd-Frank Act and began by stating the depth and breadth of what the act will do: "The Dodd-Frank Act implements changes that, among other things, affect the oversight and supervision of financial institutions, provide for a new resolution procedure for large financial companies, create a new agency responsible for implementing and enforcing compliance with consumer financial laws, introduce more stringent regulatory capital requirements, effect significant changes in the regulation of over the counter derivatives, reform the regulation of credit rating agencies, implement changes to corporate governance and executive compensation practices, incorporate the Volcker Rule, require registration of advisers to certain private funds, and effect significant changes in the securitization market."[46] Among the new regulations is a stricter requirement of reporting unstructured data, which consists of emails, faxes, social media posts, document files, etc.

DODD-FRANK WHISTLEBLOWING PROVISION

Also under Dodd-Frank is a whistleblowing provision, which authorizes the SEC to "provide monetary awards to eligible individuals who come forward with high-quality original information that leads to a

---

[44] Ibid.

[45] Gramm-Leach-Bliley Act, 15 USC 6801, accessed March 18, 2014, http://ithandbook.ffiec.gov/media/resources/3241/con-15usc_6801_6805-gramm_leach_bliley_act.pdf.

[46] "The Dodd-Frank Act: A Cheat Sheet," Morrison & Foerster (2010), accessed March 18, 2014, http://www.mofo.com/files/uploads/images/summarydoddfrankact.pdf.

Commission enforcement action in which over $1,000,000 in sanctions is ordered. The range for awards is between 10% and 30% of the money collected."[47] A recent award was made in 2013 of $14 million.[48] The SEC provides a Website with resources and ways the whistleblower can connect with an SEC representative. But official channels are not always pursued.

"With the advent of YouTube, blogs, social networking, and whistleblower websites such as WikiLeaks, the paradigm of whistleblowing is changing." So begins the abstract to Miriam Cherry's paper called "Virtual Whistleblowing."[49] There is an increase number of employees disclosing illegal or unethical company practices using online channels such as blogs, Websites, and social media. Causes proposed include the employee may have exhausted other options to rectify the situation or that management is covering it up. There is also the sense that employees can say anything they want online and not pay any consequences because they are protected under Freedom of Speech/First Amendment rights. This not necessarily true, because false accusations can carry hefty penalties including claims of defamation, harassment, and termination of employment. Online postings are not necessarily totally anonymous either because computer forensics can backtrack from an Internet service provider address to find a particular poster, or at least close to him or her.

Should the company find itself with a virtual whistleblower situation, it should take a three-step approach: remind everyone that there is to be no retaliation and if there is the company should take action against the retaliator; investigate thoroughly and report; and if any wrongdoing is found, consequences need to be metered out to those who are liable[50].

FAIR CREDIT REPORTING ACT

The Fair Credit Reporting Act (FCRA)[51] was first passed in 1996 and updated in 2002 to ensure fair and accurate consumer credit reporting. In 2003, the Fair and Accurate Credit Transactions Act was enacted to "prevent identity theft, improve resolution of consumer disputes, improve the accuracy of consumer records, make improvements in the use of, and consumer access to, credit information."[52] Considering the recent increase in data breaches and phishing scams, these two acts seem timeless in their implementation. Under the Fair and Accurate Credit Transactions Act, companies are required to have a Red Flags Identity Theft Policy and Program in place that would "(1) assess their identity theft risk factors, (2) adopt and test policies and procedures that detect and address the risks, consistent with the Red Flag Rules, and (3) train their employees to ensure that those policies and procedures are properly

[47] "Welcome to the Office of the Whistleblower," (United States Securities and Exchange Commission), accessed March 18, 2014, http://www.sec.gov/whistleblower.
[48] "SEC Awards More Than $14 Million to Whistleblower," (United States Securities and Exchange Commission, October 1, 2013), http://www.sec.gov/News/PressRelease/Detail/PressRelease/1370539854258#.Uvptcv1Vjy9.
[49] Miriam A. Cherry, "Virtual Whistleblowing," Social Science Research Network," (June 11, 2013), http://papers.ssrn.com/sol3/papers.cfm?abstract_id=2273678&download=yes.
[50] Dana Wilkie, "Virtual Whistle-blowing: Employees Bypass Internal Channels to Expose Wrongdoing," (Society for Human Resource Management, July 16, 2013), http://www.shrm.org/hrdisciplines/employeerelations/articles/pages/virtual-whistle-blowing-bypass-internal-channels-expose-wrongdoing.aspx.
[51] Fair Credit Reporting Act (FCRA), 15 U.S.C. § 1681, accessed March 18, 2014, http://www.ftc.gov/sites/default/files/fcra.pdf.
[52] Fair and Accurate Credit Transactions Act of 2003, accessed March 18, 2014, http://www.gpo.gov/fdsys/pkg/PLAW-108publ159/html/PLAW-108publ159.htm.

implemented."[53] In the digital world, that means that these red flags must also take into consideration the online environment and threats such as social engineering and phishing scams and then implement controls to combat them and protect their customers. The FTC settled an interesting case involving the FCRA and mobile apps in January 2013 against a mobile application company that "designed mobile apps that enabled users to search criminal records databases and advertised the apps as tools for conducting criminal background checks on potential employees."[54] The FCRA requires notice and authorization for background checks and the apps' disclaimer citing that they were not FCRA-compliant did not insulate it from liability.

In January 2013, a *Wall Street Journal* blog entry entitled "Insider Trading Study Shows Need for Integrating Social Networking into Compliance"[55] was posted online. It described how social media played a role in the insider trading scandal of Galleon hedge fund founder Raj Rajaratnam and how a study was reviewing how insider trading had become socialized and "how there are no corporate boundaries anymore…people are accustomed to sharing information liberally and indiscriminately" quoting Montieth M. Illingworth, a communications consultant and president of Montieth & Co., who sponsored the study.[56]

This was followed up in June 2013, when a *Forbes* magazine headline read "Facebook Connection Leads To SEC Freezing $3 Million In Insider-Trading Profits."[57] This time it was a Thailand man attempting to withdraw profits from a suspect bet on out-of-the-money call options based on the upcoming acquisition of Smithfield Foods by Shuanghui International Holdings (before it was announced). The SEC investigation revealed that one of the suspect's Facebook friends was employed at a Thailand bank that advised a competing bidder.

The SEC and Federal Bureau of Investigation (FBI) have both been wary for a while of the social media arena and the threat it poses for insider trading. In February 2012, the SEC's then-chairwoman, Mary Shapiro, was quoted as stating that "the popularity and simplicity of social media makes insider trading easer and more accessible than ever before. There is so much that is great about social media, but it does create challenges for regulators."[58]

On the FBI's side, it has "Operation Perfect Hedge" with investigations on insider trading supposedly going back to 2008, first through traditional monitoring means, then wiretapping, and now reviewing social media. In January 2014, Frontline, PBS's news program, did its own investigation on the FBI's

---

[53] Kristen J. sMathews and Christopher Wolf, "A Practical Guide to the Red Flag Rules: Identifying and Addressing Identity Theft Risks, (Practising Law Institute, 2008), accessed March 18, 2014, http://www.pli.edu/Content/Treatise/A_Practical_Guide_to_the_Red_Flag_Rules_Identifying/_/N-4lZ1z13icc?ID=49953.

[54] Karen Bromberg, "Mobile App Disclaimers Not Sufficient to Circumvent FCRA Requirements," JDSUPRA Business Advisor (January 18, 2013) http://www.jdsupra.com/legalnews/mobile-app-disclaimers-not-sufficient-to-92878/.

[55] Samuel Rubenfeld, "Insider Trading Study Shows Need for Integrating Social Networking into Compliance," *The Wall Street Journal* (January 17, 2013), http://blogs.wsj.com/cio/2013/01/17/insider-trading-study-shows-need-for-integrating-social-networking-into-compliance/.

[56] Ibid.

[57] Jordan Maglich, "Facebook Connection Leads to SEC Freezing $3 Million in Insider-Trading Profits," Forbes (June 6, 2013), http://www.forbes.com/sites/jordanmaglich/2013/06/06/facebook-connection-leads-to-sec-freezing-3-million-in-insider-trading-profits/.

[58] Lauren Fox, "Facebook and Twitter Cause Insider Trading Headaches for the SEC," US News (February 2, 2012), http://www.usnews.com/news/blogs/washington-whispers/2012/02/22/facebook-and-twitter-cause-insider-trading-headaches-for-the-sec.

investigations called "To Catch a Trader."[59] The program reviews the operation and its results to date—charges brought against a total of 83 people and four entities, including the Galleon case and a case against SAC Capital.

These bring up the important lesson learned that security and risk management departments must also consider informal communication channels—online, digital and social media—as possible venues for inappropriate and illegal behavior to take place on. Training, policies, and awareness campaigns must include these in its curriculum and messages.

HEALTH CARE AND MEDICAL INSTITUTIONS

"Health care is definitely leading in a lot of ways, like in business associate agreements tying the entre ecosystem into contractual responsibilities for protecting data—there's a long tail of compliance between the large hospital networks and the myriad of suppliers and service organizations."[60]

This quotation seems positive, "yet 32.6% of 150 health care respondents to DataMotion's annual survey indicated they feel employees do not understand security and compliance policies for transferring files electronically."[61]

Health care and medical entities require very intimate information about patients even beyond Personal Identifiable Information. Because of the concern of what could happen to the patient if the information was compromised, regulatory acts have been put into place including: HIPAA,[62] the Health Information Technology for Economic and Clinical Health Act (HITECH)[63], and the Patient Safety and Quality Improvement Act.[64]

HEALTH INSURANCE PORTABILITY AND ACCOUNTABILITY ACT

HIPAA is always in the news when a data breach occurs in a health care facility and has been since its enactment in 1996. It is also common enough as most of us receive a HIPAA notice form to sign when we go to our doctor's office. Its focus is to provide security standards for the protection of patient health information that is kept in an electronic format for storage, processing, etc.

Health care is an industry that has been resistant to engaging in social media and other online activities because of concern of potential compliance violations. A PR Newswire release advertising effective social media governance for health care compliance gave some examples of how social media

---

[59] Jason Breslow, "Isn't this illegal?" PBS (January 6, 2014), http://www.pbs.org/wgbh/pages/frontline/business-economy-financial-crisis/to-catch-a-trader/isnt-this-illegal/.

[60] Bob Janacek, DataMotion Chief Technology Officer quoted in: (January 21, 2014), http://searchhealthit.techtarget.com/news/2240212849/Health-data-security-improves-despite-IT-lagging-behind-other-sectors.

[61] Flunkinger, Don, Search Health IT, "Health data security improves despite IT lagging behind other sectors," (January 21, 2014), http://searchhealthit.techtarget.com/news/2240212849/Health-data-security-improves-despite-IT-lagging-behind-other-sectors.

[62] "Health Insurance Portability and Accountability Act of 1996," accessed March 18, 2014, http://www.hhs.gov/ocr/privacy/hipaa/administrative/statute/hipaastatutepdf.pdf.

[63] "HITECH Act Enforcement Interim Final Rule," US Department of Health and Human Services, accessed March 18, 2014, http://www.hhs.gov/ocr/privacy/hipaa/administrative/enforcementrule/hitechenforcementifr.html.

[64] "Patient Safety and Quality Improvement Act Of 2005," Agency for Health care Research and Quality, accessed March 18, 2014, http://www.pso.ahrq.gov/statute/pl109-41.htm.

strategies can be in violation of HIPAA: "The effectiveness of social media for health care marketing is under debate and has a plethora of problems, such as, offering Facebook discounts in return for 'friend-ing' and 'clicks,' vendor payment arrangements coupled with page views, special offers for Facebook or Twitter accounts, or offering a Groupon coupons for Medicare patient services. These types of arrangements demonstrate non compliance with the HIPAA and can have implications under health care regulatory restrictions."[65]

Recently, Google announced that it would extend HIPAA business associate agreements' support to cloud app developers. This is the latest in Google's efforts to make its cloud platform health care–friendly. Other efforts include: ISO 27001 certification for its platform, and SOC2, SSAE 16, and ISAE 3402 audits for Google apps.[66]

Important sections that relate to online, digital, mobile, and social media use or access of this data are listed below:

- 164.312(a)(1) Access Control: Implement technical policies and procedures for electronic information systems that maintain electronic protected health information to allow access only to those persons or software programs that have been granted access rights as specified in §, 164.308(a)(4).
- 164.312(a)(2)(i) Unique User Identification (R): Assign a unique name and/or number for identifying and tracking user identity.
- Emergency Access Procedure (R): Establish (and implement as needed) procedures for obtaining necessary electronic protected health information during an emergency.
- 164.312(a)(2)(iii) Automatic Logoff (A): Implement electronic procedures that terminate an electronic session after a predetermined time of inactivity.
- 164.312(a)(2)(iv) Encryption and Decryption (A): Implement a mechanism to encrypt and decrypt electronic protected health information.
- 164.312(b) Audit Controls: Implement hardware, software, and/or procedural mechanisms that record and examine activity in information systems that contain or use electronic protected health information.
- 164.312(c)(1) Integrity: Implement policies and procedures to protect electronic protected health information from improper alteration or destruction.
- 164.312(c)(2) Mechanism to Authenticate Electronic Protected Health Information (A): Implement electronic mechanisms to corroborate that electronic protected health information has not been altered or destroyed in an unauthorized manner.
- 164.312(d) Person or Entity Authentication: Implement procedures to verify that a person or entity seeking access to electronic protected health information is the one claimed.
- 164.312(e)(1) Transmission Security: Implement technical security measures to guard against unauthorized access to electronic protected health information that is being transmitted over an electronic communications network.

---

[65] "Health Care Compliance and Social Media Know-how for Effective Social Media Governance," (PR Newswire, February 10, 2014), http://www.prnewswire.com/news-releases/healthcare-compliance-and-social-media-know-how-for-effective-social-media-governance-244697121.html.

[66] Patrick Ouellette, "Google Extends HIPAA BAA Support to Cloud App Developers," Health IT Security (February 11, 2014), http://healthitsecurity.com/2014/02/11/google-extends-hipaa-baa-support-to-cloud-app-developers/.

- 164.312(e)(2)(i) Integrity Controls (A): Implement security measures to ensure that electronically transmitted electronic protected health information is not improperly modified without detection until disposed of.
- 164.312(e)(2)(ii) Encryption (A): Implement a mechanism to encrypt electronic protected health information whenever deemed appropriate.

HEALTH INFORMATION TECHNOLOGY FOR ECONOMIC AND CLINICAL HEALTH ACT

The HITECH Act was first enacted in 2009 and has two components: the first is to promote the use of information technology in health care and the second is to ensure security of the information and the privacy of the patients when that information is transmitted electronically by investing in health care technology and setting up incentives for health care and medical facilities and doctor's officers to take advantage of these technologies.[67] HIPAA and HITECH work together.

THE PATIENT SAFETY AND QUALITY IMPROVEMENT ACT

PSQIA focuses on the confidentiality of patient information by highlighting how the Personal Identifiable Information becomes a patient safety work product. Key sections of the act that can relate to online, digital, mobile, and social media security and risk concerns include:

- Section 921 defines key terms, including how information becomes patient safety work product.
- Section 922 sets out the confidentiality and privilege protections for patient safety work product, how patient safety work product may be disclosed, and the penalties for disclosures in violation of the protections.
- Section 923 describes the network of patient safety databases.
- Section 924 outlines the requirements and processes for listing and delisting of patient safety organizations.[68]

THE HEALTH EXCHANGE AND SECURITY TRANSPARENCY ACT

The Health Exchange and Security Transparency Act was passed on January 10, 2014. It was introduced by Joe Pitts (R-PA), House Energy and Commerce Health Subcommittee chair; the Act is often cited as a one-sentence bill meant to defeat Obamacare. We still need to wait and see where it goes:

> *Not later than two business days after the discovery of a breach of security of any system maintained by an Exchange established under section 1311 or 1321 of the Patient Protection and Affordable Care Act (42 U.S.C.18031, 18041) which is known to have resulted in personally identifiable information of an individual being stolen or unlawfully accessed, the Secretary of Health and Human Services shall provide notice of such breach to each such individual.*[69]

---

[67]"HITECHPrograms&AdvisoryCommittees,"accessedMarch18,2014,http://www.healthit.gov/policy-researchers-implementers/hitech-programs-advisory-committees.

[68]"The Patient Safety and Quality Improvement Act of 2005," accessed March 18, 2014, http://www.hhs.gov/ocr/privacy/psa/regulation/statute/index.html.

[69]"Health Exchange Security and Transparency Act of 2014," accessed March 18, 2014, http://democrats.energycommerce.house.gov/sites/default/files/documents/Bill-Text-HR-3811-Health-Exchange-Security-and-Transparency-2014-1-3.pdf.

FDA: PHARMACEUTICALS

In January 2014, the FDA issued draft guidance on the Internet and social media for pharmaceutical marketing titled "Fulfilling Regulatory Requirements for Postmarketing Submissions of Interactive Promotional Media for Prescription Human and Animal Drugs and Biologics."[70]

According to the preface of the report, "this Draft Guidance concerns how and when industry should provide information to the FDA concerning content on product websites, firm blogs discussion boards, chat rooms, or other public electronic forums (e.g., Twitter) and social networking sites (e.g., Facebook)."[71]

Reviewing the draft, the FDA has not wandered far from its prior regulations on other media—the distinction between static information and interactive information is again emphasized to determine reporting and prior approval requirements. The key sections include:

- Static communications: "For prescriptions and over-the-counter new animal drugs, the applicant must submit at the time of the original dissemination one set of specimens and other labeling."[72] Form FDA2253[73] or Form FDA2301.[74]
- Interactive, real-time communication:
  - If nonrestricted:
    Once every month, a firm should submit an updated listing of all non-restricted sites for which it is responsible or in which it remains an active participant and that include interactive or real-time communications. Firms need not submit screenshots or other visual representations of the actual interactive or real-time communications with the monthly updates.[75]
  - If restricted:
    If a site has restricted access and, as such, FDA may not have access to the site, a firm should submit all content related to the discussion (e.g., all UGC about the topic), which may or may not include independent UGC, to adequately provide context to facilitate the review. Screenshots or other visual representations of the actual site, including the interactive or real-time communications, should be submitted monthly on Form FDA 2253 or Form FDA 2301.[76]
- FDA-required labeling and promotional labeling: sponsored sites; third-party sites, and employees and agents; "not responsible for user-generated content that is truly independent of the firm."[77]

---

[70] "Guidance for Industry Fulfilling Regulatory Requirements for Postmarketing Submissions of Interactive Promotional Media for Prescription Human and Animal Drugs and Biologics," (U.S. Department of Health and Human Services, January, 2014), http://www.fda.gov/downloads/Drugs/GuidanceComplianceRegulatoryInformation/Guidances/UCM381352.pdf.

[71] Michael A. Walsh, "FDA Issues Draft Guidance on the Internet and Social Media," Mondaq, (January 20, 2014), http://www.mondaq.com/unitedstates/x/287124/food+drugs+law/FDA+Issues+Draft+Guidance+on+the+Internet+and+Social+Media.

[72] See note 70.

[73] "OPDP Form FDA-2253 submissions," U.S. Food and Drug Administration, accessed March 18, 2014, http://www.fda.gov/AboutFDA/CentersOffices/OfficeofMedicalProductsandTobacco/CDER/ucm090181.htm.

[74] Accessed March 18, 2014, http://www.fda.gov/downloads/AboutFDA/ReportsManualsForms/Forms/UCM052264.pdf.

[75] Guidance for Industry Fulfilling Regulatory Requirements, page 6.

[76] Ibid., page 7.

[77] See note 71.

HIGHER EDUCATION (FERPA)

"The ACLU (American Civil Liberties Union) believes that schools are not constitutional dead zones, and continues to fight for students' privacy rights, challenging unreasonable strip-searches, electronic monitoring, and searches and seizures of property such as cell phones."[78]

In this quotation, the ACLU is referring to the chipping away of student privacy as FERPA is revised and new exceptions made as to who can obtain student information. FERPA generally prohibits improper disclosure of personally identifiable information from educational records. It does apply, however, to information that an official obtained through personal knowledge or observation, or has heard orally from others. An institution must notify eligible students in attendance of their rights under FERPA annually.

Disclosure is allowed to "school officials" if there is a "legitimate educational interest."[79] School officials include: professors, instructors, administrators, health staff, counselors, attorneys, clerical staff, trustees, members of disciplinary committees and boards and contractors, volunteers, or other parties to whom the school has outsourced institutional services or functions.

Exceptions for disclosure include:

- Enroll school exception: disclosure to another school in which the student seeks or intends to enroll.
- Financial aid exception: applies to aid for which the student has applied or which the student has received, if the information is necessary for such purposes as to:
  - Determine eligibility for aid
  - Determine amount of aid
  - Determine conditions for aid
  - Enforce terms and conditions of aid
- Dependent child exception: applies to parents of a "dependent student" as that term is defined in Section 152 of the Internal Revenue Code
- Health or emergency exception: colleges and universities may notify parents when there is a health or safety emergency involving their son or daughter, even if the parents do not claim the student as a dependent
- Alcohol/drug exception: disclosure is to the parents of a student at a postsecondary institution regarding the student's violation of any federal, state, or local law, or of any rule or policy of the institution, governing the use or possession of alcohol or a controlled substance. Student must be under age 21.
- Directory information exception: information such as name, address, email, telephone listing, photo, date and place of birth, major, participation in officially recognized activities and sports, weight and height of members of athletic teams, dates of attendance, degrees and awards received, the most recent previous educational agency or institution attended, grade level or year, and enrollment status (undergrad or grad; full- or part-time).

One of the other areas the ACLU is concerned about in regard to student privacy is the increase in online class activity—whether in a distance education class or social media activity relating to a class,

---

[78] "Students," American Civil Liberties Union, accessed March 18, 2014, https://www.aclu.org/technology-and-liberty/students.
[79] "FERPA General Guidance for Students," US Department of Education, accessed March 18, 2014, http://www2.ed.gov/policy/gen/guid/fpco/ferpa/students.html.

etc. Because an online environment creates a record of student activity, it is subject to FERPA privacy rights. Professors should take the following precautions:

- Obtain student consent
- Make student comments only available to other students in the course (password protection)
- Keep in mind outside parties under contract to the university

Another piece of legislation to keep in mind for security reasons is The Jeanne Clery Disclosure of Campus Security Policy and Campus Crime Statistics Act. This "federal statute requires colleges and universities participating in federal financial aid programs to maintain and disclose campus crime statistics and security information."[80] It is also expected that by reporting the crimes, there will be an effort made by the institution to make the campus safer. Clery requires an institution to have a reporting policy regarding crimes in place. These policies should be reviewed with the new digital, online, mobile, and social media platforms that now form the preferred method for students to send and receive information. For example, institutions may send out alerts via text messaging instead of just emails, and not doing so may be a violation because most students monitor text more than their emails.

PROFESSIONAL TRADE OVERSIGHT AND ORGANIZATIONS: MOBILE

Many professional trade associations and organizations have begun to issue guidelines regarding the risks associated with social media use and how best to ensure security and privacy of data. These guidelines are often produced as white papers and try to clarify current and pending legislation as well as compliance requirements within a specific industry.

One example comes from the mobile marketing industry. Mobile Rich-Media Ad Interface Definitions[81] was published in 2012. The purpose of the document was "to address known interoperability issues between publisher mobile applications, different ad servers and different rich media platforms."[82] The contributors read like a list of who's who in the technology and entertainment including: 24/7 Real Media, Inc., AdMarvel, Adobe Systems Inc., AOL, CBS Interactive, Dow Jones & Company, ESPN, Microsoft Advertising, Pandora, Turner Broadcasting System, Inc., Univision, The Weather Channel, and Yahoo!, Inc., among others.

The Mobile Marketing Association has also contributed to the mobile marketing space by releasing their Consumer Best Practices No-No's:[83]

- Stacked marketing
- Incentive marketing
- Not disclosing pricing up front
- Hiding noncompliant pages with cloaking techniques
- Use of generic mobile identification number entry pages

---

[80] "Clery Act Reports," Federal Student Aid, accessed March 18, 2014, http://studentaid.ed.gov/about/data-center/school/clery-act.

[81] "Mobile Rich-media Ad Interface Definitions (MRAID) v.2.0," Interactive Advertising Bureau (April 16, 2013), http://www.iab.net/media/file/IAB_MRAID_v2_FINAL.pdf.

[82] Ibid.

[83] "Five common compliance and privacy mistakes in mobile that could land you in trouble and lose you customers," Mobi-Thinking (April 21, 2013), http://mobithinking.com/mobile-compliance-and-privacy-mistakes.

Beyond using mobile to advertise offline products and services, mobile apps have also been scrutinized for their own advertising, especially under the FDA's deceptive advertising rules.

In 2011, the FTC clamped down on two companies that claimed their apps "AcneApp" and "Acne Pwner" treated acne with colored lights emitted from smartphones or mobile devices. In a settlement, both app publishers agreed to cease making "baseless claims" and paid fines.[84]

OTHER FEDERAL AGENCIES

Although we have reviewed federal agencies and compliance requirements throughout this chapter, this section focuses on three federal agencies that do not necessarily fit in the other categories: the Federal Communications Commission (FCC), the National Institute of Standards and Technology (NIST), and the Federal Energy Regulatory Commission (FERC).

The FCC "regulates interstate and international communications by radio, television, wire, satellite and cable in all 50 states, the District of Columbia and U.S. territories. An independent U.S. government agency overseen by Congress, the commission is the United States' primary authority for communications law, regulation and technological innovation."[85]

In January 2014, the FCC made news in regard to a federal appeals court ruling in Washington, DC, that "allows Internet-service providers to create tiered pricing for certain types of online traffic. It's the latest turn in a years-long battle over the Federal Communications Commission's net-neutrality rules, adopted in 2010, which require Internet-service providers to treat all Internet traffic equally and bar them from practices like blocking access to certain websites or applications."[86] This brought up the concern regarding the end of "net neutrality" and adding to the debate regarding haves and have-nots in the digital age. "Equal-access Internet as essential for educational achievement, freedom of speech, and economic growth," says Barbara Stripling, president of the American Library Association. However, Verizon and other Internet providers argue that it is important to charge more for those who use the services more from a business perspective in terms of resource allocation. This debate will go on until a final decision is made.

NATIONAL INSTITUTE OF STANDARDS AND TECHNOLOGY

The NIST was founded in 1901 and is now part of the Department of Commerce. Its original purpose was to implement a standard measurement infrastructure to allow the United States to compete against its economic rivals.[87] It now offers a number of services to the public including a significant amount of publications that, although focused on government entities, can be easily modified to fit the needs of the public and business sectors. One series of publications that is highly recommended for security professionals to review is the SP800 Computer Security Series Publications.[88] The publications are free to download or can be ordered as a hard copy for a minimal fee.

---

[84] Ibid.

[85] "What we Do," Federal Trade Commission, accessed March 18, 2014, http://www.fcc.gov/what-we-do.

[86] Megan O'Neil, "Ruling Could Drive FCC Forward on Net Neutrality," The Chronicle of Higher Education, (January 17, 2014) http://chronicle.com/blogs/wiredcampus/ruling-could-drive-fcc-forward-on-net-neutrality/49477?cid=at&utm_source=at&utm_medium=en.

[87] National Institute of Standards and Technology, accessed March 18, 2014http://www.nist.gov/public_affairs/nandyou.cfm.

[88] Accessed March 18, 2014, http://www.nist.gov/publication-portal.cfm.

FERC AND NERC

The Federal Energy Regulatory Commission (FERC) is an independent agency that regulates the interstate transmission of electricity, natural gas, and oil.[89] Its counterpart in the private sector is the North American Electric Reliability Corporation, a not-for-profit entity whose mission is to ensure the reliability of the bulk power system in North America. North American Electric Reliability Corporation develops and enforces reliability standards, annually assesses seasonal and long-term reliability, monitors the bulk power system through system awareness, and educates, trains, and certifies industry personnel.[90]

These commissions and agencies call to mind the variety of regulated industries that exist in our current marketplace—each of which has a series of compliance standards to be met and uses digital, online, mobile, and social media to different extents. These are points for security and risk managers to keep in mind as they develop polices and protocols to ensure compliance.

FEDERAL LEGISLATION

Various laws have been enacted to make information technology safe and secure especially in the government sector.

THE FEDERAL INFORMATION SECURITY MANAGEMENT ACT

The Federal Information Security Management Act (FISMA)[91] of 2002, U.S. Code Title 44, Chapter 35, "defines a comprehensive framework to protect government information, operations and assets against natural or man-made threats.[92]" NIST's Computer Security Division created the FISMA Implementation Project in 2003 and it is still ongoing.[93] FISMA comes into play when social media or other online platforms are used to process, store, or transmit federal government information, whether by a government agency or by a third-party affiliated with the agency.

Another law, The Federal Risk and Authorization Management Program is activated when the information is being processed, stored, or transmitted via a cloud service provider.

The concern underlying these laws is national in scope. A breach of government data can affect up to millions of Americans as well as cause concern for national security. NIST has issued publications laying out controls to ensure compliance with these laws in a new digital environment: "The proliferation of social media, Smart Grid, mobile, and cloud computing, as well as the transition from structured to unstructured data and metadata environments, have added significant complexities and challenges for federal

[89] "What FERC Does," Federal Energy Regulatory Commission, accessed March 18, 2014, http://www.ferc.gov/about/ferc-does.asp.
[90] Accessed March 18, 2014, http://www.nerc.com.
[91] "Federal Information Security Management Act of 2002," accessed March 18, 2014, http://csrc.nist.gov/drivers/documents/FISMA-final.pdf.
[92] "Federal Information Security Management Act (FISMA)," *TechTarget*, accessed March 18, 2014, http://searchsecurity.techtarget.com/definition/Federal-Information-Security-Management-Act.
[93] "Federal Information Security Management Act (FISMA) Implementation Project," National Institute of Standards and Technology, accessed March 18, 2014, http://csrc.nist.gov/groups/SMA/fisma/index.html.

organizations in safeguarding privacy."[94] One of the controls focuses on the rules of behavior by government employees via the explicit restriction of social media sites: "This control enhancement addresses rules of behavior related to the use of social media/networking sites: (1) when organizational personnel are using such sites for official duties or in the conduct of official business; (2) when organizational information is involved in social media/networking transactions; and (3) when personnel are accessing social media/networking sites from organizational information systems. Organizations also address specific rules that prevent unauthorized entities from obtaining and/or inferring non-public organizational information (e.g., system account information, personally identifiable information) from social media/networking sites."[95]

CHILDREN'S ONLINE PRIVACY PROTECTION ACT

COPPA[96] was enacted in 1998, with a final rule issued in 1999. Its purpose is to protect minors under the age of 13 by restricting how and what personal information onsite Websites and service providers can collect of them. Most Websites will contain a clause in their terms of use regarding compliance with COPPA or having a disclaimer on their Website that it is not intended for minors under the age of 18. Some terms of use even state that the user warrants that they are older than age 18 and if they are not that they should not proceed further using the Website and that by continuing to the Website they are warranting that they are older than age 18 and indemnify the company from COPPA. The last part does not necessarily protect the Website owner if the Website owner has a reasonable assumption that minors will access the site and the owner has not put in other controls (see COPPA notice requirements for COPA compliance requirements).

COPPA NOTICE REQUIREMENTS

COPPA requires the following in order for a Website to be in compliance:[97]
  Privacy notice containing:
  * The name and contact information (address, telephone number, and email address) of all operators collecting or maintaining children's personal information through the Website or online service.
  * The kinds of personal information collected from children (for example, name, address, email address, hobbies, etc.) and how the information is collected—directly from the child or passively, say, through cookies.
  * How the operator uses the personal information.
  * Whether the operator discloses information collected from children to third parties.
  * That the parent has the option to agree to the collection and use of the child's information without consenting to the disclosure of the information to third parties.
  * That the operator may not require a child to disclose more information than is reasonably necessary to participate in an activity as a condition of participation.
  * That the parent can review the child's personal information, ask to have it deleted, and refuse to allow any further collection or use of the child's information. The notice also must state the procedures for the parent to follow.
  Direct parent notice:
  * The notice to parents must contain the same information included on the notice on the Website.

[97]"How to comply with Children's Online Privacy Protection Act," COPPA, accessed March 18, 2014, http://www.coppa.org/comply.htm.

---

[94] "Security and Privacy Controls for Federal Information Systems and Organizations," (NIST, April, 2013), http://nvlpubs.nist.gov/nistpubs/SpecialPublications/NIST.SP.800-53r4.pdf.

[95] Ibid.

[96] "Children's Online Privacy Protection Rule ('COPPA')," Federal Trade Commission, accessed March 18, 2014, http://www.ftc.gov/enforcement/rules/rulemaking-regulatory-reform-proceedings/childrens-online-privacy-protection-rule.

CONTROLLING THE ASSAULT OF NON-SOLICITED PORNOGRAPHY AND MARKETING ACT OF 2003

The CAN-SPAM Act lays out the rules businesses must follow when sending commercial messages via email to current and potential customers. The FTC is the agency in charge of enforcing the Act, and violations can be costly—up to $16,000 per email per violation. How bad is spam? "In the US alone, the number of spam text messages rose 45 percent in 2012 to 4.5 billion messages, according to Bloomberg."[98] Part of the problem is businesses believing the Act does not apply to some of their emails, and email servers located outside of the United States and outside of U.S. long-arm jurisdiction.

For example, it is not unusual for exhibitors at a trade show to request the participant to sign up with his or her email address for some giveaway or for further information. This does not give the vendor the participant's consent to send a monthly newsletter and several email updates daily or weekly. Be sure that the reason you give for collecting the email address is the only reason you are using it.

One of the rules in the CAN-SPAM Act is the provision that receivers should have the option to opt-out of receiving further communications. This rule is also valid in mobile marketing or SMS texting campaigns where the sender of the SMS messages needs to show proof that the receiver opted in. Some companies that got in trouble: Jiffy Lube, Papa John's, Twentieth Century Fox, Simon & Schuster, Timberland, Rolling Stone, and Burger King.[99]

A list from the FTC Bureau of Consumer Protection's Business Center lays out some practical best practices for businesses to follow to be in compliance with the CAN-SPAM Act:

1. Don't use false or misleading header information.
2. Don't use deceptive subject lines.
3. Identify the message as an ad.
4. Tell recipients where you're located.
5. Tell recipients how to opt out of receiving future email from you.
6. Honor opt-out requests promptly.
7. Monitor what others are doing on your behalf.[100]

TRUTH IN NEGOTIATIONS ACT

TINA (FAR 15.406) was enacted in 1962 as "A public law enacted for the purpose of providing for full and fair disclosure by contractors in the conduct of negotiations with the government. The most significant provision included in TINA is the requirement that contractors submit certified cost and pricing data for larger contracts."[101] The idea was to prevent contractors from concealing certain information regarding their pricing and to ensure fair and reasonable pricing for government procurement. Individuals with knowledge of TINA violations may be able to file a federal case against the company on behalf of the

---

[98] Olga Kharif, "Mobile Spam Texts Hit 4.5 Billion Raising Consumer Ire," (Bloomberg, April 30, 2012), http://www.bloomberg.com/news/2012-04-30/mobile-spam-texts-hit-4-5-billion-raising-consumer-ire.html.

[99] Five common compliance and privacy mistakes in mobile, accessed March 18, 2014.

[100] "CAN-SPAM Act: A Compliance Guide for Business," Bureau of Consumer Protection, (September, 2009), http://www.business.ftc.gov/documents/bus61-can-spam-act-compliance-guide-business.

[101] "Truth in Negotiations Act (TINA)," The Free Dictionary, accessed March 18, 2014, http://financial-dictionary.thefreedictionary.com/Truth+in+Negotiations+Act.

government under the False Claims Act. Whistleblowers of successful False Claims Act cases are eligible to receive 15 to 30 percent of the total government recovery. TINA relates to the online environment in two distinct ways: (1) how do you price data services fairly and reasonable and (2) can online, digital, mobile, and social media communication affect the procurement process, therefore violating TINA?

STATE LEGISLATION

As of the writing of this chapter, "49 states and US territories have enacted laws governing data security and data breach notification standards"[102] (see Table 7.1 for list). Only four states do not: Alabama, Kentucky, New Mexico, and South Dakota. Our tiered government system—federal, state, county, municipality—adds complexity to the already dense environment of regulation of security and privacy.

Table 7.1 State Data Breach Notification Legislation

State	Citation
Alaska	Alaska Stat. §45.48.010 et seq.
Arizona	Ariz. Rev. Stat. §44-7501
Arkansas	Ark. Code §4-110-101 et seq.
California	Cal. Civ. Code §§1798.29, 1798.80 et seq.
Colorado	Colo. Rev. Stat. §6-1-716
Connecticut	Conn. Gen Stat. §36a-701b
Delaware	Del. Code Title 6, §12B-101 et seq.
Florida	Fla. Stat. §817.5681
Georgia	Ga. Code §§10-1-910, -911, -912; §46-5-214
Hawaii	Haw. Rev. Stat. §487N-1 et seq.
Idaho	Idaho Stat. §§28-51-104 to -107
Illinois	815 ILCS§§530/1 to 530/25
Indiana	Ind. Code §§4-1-11 et seq., 24-4.9 et seq.
Iowa	Iowa Code §§715C.1, 715C.2
Kansas	Kan. Stat. §50-7a01 et seq.
Louisiana	La. Rev. Stat. §51:3071 et seq.
Maine	Me. Rev. Stat. Title 10 §1347 et seq.
Maryland	Md. Code Comm. Law §§14-3501 et seq., Md. State Govt. Code §§10-1301 to -1308
Massachusetts	Mass. Gen. Laws §93H-1 et seq.
Michigan	Mich. Comp. Laws §§445.63, 445.72
Minnesota	Minn. Stat. §§325E.61, 325E.64
Mississippi	Miss. Code §75-24-29
Missouri	Mo. Rev. Stat. §407.1500

---

[102] Nicholas Ballasy, "Data Security Bill Introduced in Senate," (Credit Union Times, January 15, 2014), http://www.cutimes.com/2014/01/15/data-security-bill-introduced-in-senate?ref=hp.

Table 7.1 State Data Breach Notification Legislation—cont'd	
State	**Citation**
Montana	Mont. Code §2-6-504, 30-14-1701 et seq.
Nebraska	Neb. Rev. Stat. §§87-801, -802, -803, -804, -805, -806, -807
Nevada	Nev. Rev. Stat. §§603A.010 et seq., 242.183
New Hampshire	N.H. Rev. Stat. §§359-C:19, -C:20, -C:21
New Jersey	N.J. Stat. §56:8-163
New York	N.Y. Gen. Bus. Law §899-aa, N.Y. State Tech. Law 208
North Carolina	N.C. Gen. Stat §§75-61, 75-65
North Dakota	N.D. Cent. Code §51-30-01 et seq.
Ohio	Ohio Rev. Code §§1347.12, 1349.19, 1349.191, 1349.192
Oklahoma	Okla. Stat. §§74-3113.1, 24-161 to -166
Oregon	Oregon Rev. Stat. §646A.600 et seq.
Pennsylvania	73 Pa. Stat. §2301 et seq.
Rhode Island	R.I. Gen. Laws §11-49.2-1 et seq.
South Carolina	S.C. Code §39-1-90, 2013 H.B. 3248
Tennessee	Tenn. Code §47-18-2107
Texas	Tex. Bus. & Comm. Code §§521.002, 521.053, Tex. Ed. Code §37.007(b)(5)
Utah	Utah Code §§13-44-101 et seq.
Vermont	Vt. Stat. Title 9 §2430, 2435
Virginia	Va. Code §18.2-186.6, §32.1-127.1:05
Washington	Wash. Rev. Code §19.255.010, 42.56.590
West Virginia	W.V. Code §§46A-2A-101 et seq.
Wisconsin	Wis. Stat. §134.98
Wyoming	Wyo. Stat. §40-12-501 et seq.
District of Columbia	D.C. Code §28-3851 et seq.
Guam	9 GCA §48-10 et seq.
Puerto Rico	10 Laws of Puerto Rico §4051 et seq.
Virgin Islands	V.I. Code §2208

Source: http://www.ncsl.org/research/telecommunications-and-information-technology/security-breach-notification-laws.aspx

To improve this situation, two pieces of legislation have been introduced. It is important to note they were both introduced after the Target breach in 2013.

- Data Security Act of 2014; introduced by Senator Tom Carper (D-DE) and Roy Blount (R-MO):
  - Provides uniform national standards in place of a patchwork of state laws
  - Requires business and financial institutions to have privacy protections
  - Prohibits private lawsuits and class actions under state law against retailers who comply with the new information-security requirements

- Reintroduced: Personal Data Privacy and Security Act of 2014, Senator Patrick Leahy (D-VT)
  - Sets uniform national standards
  - Provides for more severe criminal penalties against both the computer hackers and those who conceal security breaches

COMPLIANCE OVERSIGHT

Making sure the company is following internal policies and meeting external regulatory requirements is an important company function. For all companies in a regulated industry, this oversight can determine whether the company can continue at all. Compliance is also considered a risk mitigation strategy. But as highlighted in the beginning of the chapter, compliance does not equate to security.

If a company is large enough or has made a strategic decision that it needs to dedicate resources to this function, it may hire a compliance officer to oversee this area. The skills required of this individual depend on the industry (i.e., environmental vs financial), the authority, and the responsibilities the person will ultimately have. Understanding and knowledge of the laws and regulations, as well as licensing and permit processes, specific education in compliance management and industry regulations, management and communication skills, general and compliant-specific software skills (including apps and mobile), analytics, and reporting skill, etc. Another trait the individual should possess is a passion for compliance as he or she will in effect become the "compliance champion" for the company and that is not always as glamorous as it at first seems.

In these kinds of companies, they may also have a separate security officer and a separate person responsible for risk management. In some companies, one person fills two or all three of these roles, making it more complex and requiring additional education and training, not to mention the hope that somehow there will be more hours in a day. There is debate as to whether one person can do it all or if because of the limitation things may fall through the cracks, making the company more vulnerable to outside attacks and therefore to compliance violations.

Of course, there is the option to offsite the function as we mentioned previously in this chapter. And along with the outsourcing the function is the outsourcing of some of the liability in terms of compliance violations and security/risk incidents.

The Bureau of Labor Statistics believes that there will be a modest increase in demand for compliance officers in the coming years,[103] but I would dare say that, as with security and risk management, compliance is a requirement and because laws and regulations do not decrease we will need more of all three.

With such a heavy load, compliance officers look to tools, best practices, and strategies that have worked for others and that can be implemented for the benefit of their companies. Some basic components of a Compliance Toolkit can be seen in the Box "Compliance Toolkit Checklist."

---

[103] "Compliance Officer—Best Business Jobs," US News, accessed March 18, 2014, http://money.usnews.com/careers/best-jobs/compliance-officer.

COMPLIANCE TOOLKIT CHECKLIST

- Compliance leadership
  - Approvals
- Compliance training
  - For compliance officers
  - For security and risk personnel
  - For company employees
  - Curriculum
  - Certificates/online badges
  - Resources
- Compliance awareness campaign
  - Posters
  - Compliance newsletter or E-news
  - Lunch & Learns or Donuts & Dialogue
  - Employee learning communities/meet-ups
  - Gamification strategies/incentive programs
- Regulatory policy documents
  - Informational
  - Educational
  - Company compliance policies by regulation
- Hotline (for support)
  - Phone, email, Website, or other platform
  - Determine whether to allow anonymous calls or not
  - Whistleblowing program

One of the things compliance officers are required to do is to oversee a number of system reviews, whether they do them in-house or hire a third party. One strategy to keep in mind is to be able to reuse the results from the system reviews to satisfy reporting requirements of multiple regulations. In the social media world, repurposing content is a key principle. Being able to use the reviews for multiple compliances can assist in the affordability of the compliance functions and a more efficient use of compliance resources.

Besides the reviews of the various systems used by the company, a series of compliance audits will also be required to assess and evaluate the effectiveness and success of current compliance controls and strategies. Although these compliance checkups are pretty standard, you should make sure that these compliance audits are also taking into account any of the new digital, online, mobile, and social media risks. Outside auditors will flag these as bring-your-own-device risks. Some key points to keep in mind:

- "A growing number of compliance initiatives now mandate application controls and audit requirements focused on insider threats."[104]
- "At minimum, BYOD (bring-your-own-device) audits require the same assurances for employee owned devices as corporate-owned PCs and mobile devices, organizations will need to prepare a complete record of *all* devices connecting to their corporate network, the security posture of each device, and which corporate assets they can connect to on the network."[105]

---

[104] Andy Daudelin, "HIPAA, SOX & PCI: The Coming Compliance Crisis In IT Security," InformationWeek, (January 21, 2014), http://www.informationweek.com/security/compliance/hipaa-sox-and-pci-the-coming-compliance-crisis-in-it-security/d/d-id/1113516.
[105] Ibid.

- "Additionally, regulated businesses will need to create mobile device policies about permitted apps, remote wiping, the preparation of private and corporate information, data encryption (static and in transit), automated security scans on each device, and the prohibited use of rooted or jailbroken devices. Container solutions will become more widely adopted to separate and protect corporate information on personal devices."[106]

COMPLIANCE TRAINING

In the toolbox, I list various compliance trainings depending on the audience. Some regulations require specific training to a specific audience. For example, OSHA has specific training guidelines as well as a training standard "that employee training required by OSHA standards must be presented in a manner that employees can understand."[107]

Either the compliance officer will oversee the training or will work with human resources and/or the training department to develop and implement a compliance training and awareness program that fits regulatory and company needs. Sometimes a company may not have the in-house resources and may decide instead to use a third-party entity to provide training. WeComply,[108] a Thomson Reuters Business, is one such entity that offers an array of training options including a full library of videos on specific regulations that are accessible on various devices to make it convenient for employees to get the training they are responsible for.

Compliance training and awareness programs are one risk mitigation strategy. But security needs to be consulted when the training is being developed or the videos are being selected to ensure that the employee gets a comprehensive knowledge base regarding compliance, risk, and security. These areas should not be silos but need to be related. It is a best practice to have those responsibilities for these areas to have periodic contact—maybe a monthly lunch or happy hour—where they can discuss some of the issues and how each of them can support the other areas. They may be connected online, in a more unofficial way. The important thing is that a communication channel needs to be open among them to ensure that the three areas—risk, compliance, and security—are all taken care of with a united front. And please don't forget—the human resources director should be part of the quartet.

---

[106] Ibid.
[107] "OSHA Compliance Guidance on Training," US Department of Labor, accessed March 18, 2014, https://www.osha.gov/dte/training_policy.html.
[108] Accessed March 18, 2014, http://www.wecomply.com.

CURRENCY AND CAMPAIGNS

8

If companies adopt (these new digital payment systems), the additional responsibilities could also change the role of the CSO from a protector of information to a defender against financial losses.[1]

I suggest that, before you read this chapter, listen to the O'Jays' "For the Love of Money." "Money, money, money, mo-ney. Mo-ney."[2] Granted its lyrics are a cynical view of the free market system and a cultural statement on greed, but it also presents a reality that money is necessary for us to survive and thrive in our current society. It is also a requirement to purchase and put into place many of the security and risk management strategies we have been discussing in the book. But money is changing in the digital and online world—it is morphing from the paper- and coin-based tangible medium of exchange for products and services to an electronic virtual depository of financial transactions that exist in the ether world of bits and bytes.

---

[1] Antone Gonsalves, "Why security pros should care about Bitcoin's troubles," CSO Online (February 15, 2013), http://www. csoonline.com/article/748345/why-security-pros-should-care-about-bitcoin-s-troubles.

[2] "The O'Jays—For the Love of Money (audio)", accessed March 24, 2014, Youtube: http://www.youtube.com/watch?v= GXE_n2q08Yw.

It seems a natural evolution as we look briefly at the history of money, defined as "something generally accepted as a medium of exchange, a measure of value, or a means of payment."[3] Society began with what they had—themselves—and the processes of bartering including using cowrie seashells and beaded string. From there metals and precious stones became the norm, as royalty dressed not only in elaborate fabrics but also with all their wealth literally dangling from their bodies. Coins came next, close in look and feel to the precious metals—like gold and silver—that used to be worn but proved too heavy to carry and not secure enough to protect. But coins also had a weight factor and the metals used to create them were not always in supply. So paper, once invented and accepted as legal tender through legislation, became a lightweight replacement. But paper too seemed impractical to have on hand at all times, especially if you had acquired a significant amount of it. So for large transactions, checks offered an alternative to disburse large amounts of financial value across large distances. As society progressed with technological advances, convenience and time became important to users, why should one wait for a check to clear? Credit cards came on board for instantaneous value exchange and payment. And with the advent of electronic commerce and online shopping, the credit card physical swipe became irrelevant and electronic transactions became the norm.

At each stage, societies via their governments went through the turmoil and intensive decision process as to what gave value to these forms of exchange—was there a gold-standard backing the coins and paper or does money get created at will when deemed necessary by the government just because it is needed? Different countries adopted different financial policies and strategies that have led us to the financial landscape we interact with today. But that landscape continues to evolve. As this brief account suggests, it has never really stopped, changing as society has changed culturally and technologically.

When we look at the risk and security concerns related to currency we realize that they fall within three specific categories that also coincide with the three different areas of financial regulation: creation of value, storage of value, and access to or distribution of value.

Creation of value concerns itself with how money/currency or whatever else you decide will be the medium of exchange is generated. Some examples include, with their corresponding regulation association: content creation (intellectual (IP) property laws), microfinance (Security and Exchange Commission (SEC)), micropatronage (SEC, World Monetary Fund), crowdfunding (SEC, Federal Trade Commission), human capital investment (United Nations, World Monetary Fund), and peer-to-peer lending (SEC, private property laws).

Storage of value answers the questions of now that we have the money, where do we put it until we need it? Very few of us still have counting chambers or treasury rooms where the coins and precious stones are stored. So, traditionally, we have used banks and other financial institutions (i.e., credit unions) to handle this function for us, entrusting them with basically our financial livelihood. These financial institutions have offered digital services to their customers including online accounts for balances and transfers, online bill payment systems, etc. But the banks are also heavily regulated. They are dealing with other people's money and are held to high standards for security and privacy.

There is the sense that sometimes the creation of value and the storage of value intersect—this is where complementary or digital currencies come in whereas their creation is part of a storage algorithm to ensure they "exist." In the digital world, another kind of value is also created and stored—that of social influence, the tangible aspects of social capital.

---

[3] "Money", accessed March 24, 2014, Merriam-Webster: http://www.merriam-webster.com/dictionary/money.

Storage of value security and risk management concerns are numerous and include: data integrity protocols, hacking threats, authorization, two-tier authentication, privacy/tracking, and consumer protection (see Box for Consumer Online safety).

TIPS TO BANKING SAFELY ONLINE[4]

- Choose an account with two-factor authentication
- Create a strong password
- Secure your computer
- Keep it up-to-date
- Be aware of email phishing scams
- Access your account only form a secure location (so no public WiFi)
- Always log out of your financial account when you are done and close/quit out of the browser
- Accept to receive alerts and account notification
- Monitor your accounts

[4]Lee Munson, "8 tips for safer online banking," NakedSecurity (October 3, 2013), http://nakedsecurity.sophos.com/2013/10/03/8-tips-for-safer-online-banking/.

So, once created and stored, the focus turns to access to and distribution of the money or currency (value). Most of the options currently being used to access money work with what is called "Fiat Money," currency that a government has declared to be legal tender, despite the fact that it has no intrinsic value and is not backed by reserves.[5] Recently, "a national study from the Credit Union National Association (CUNA)[6] reveals that more than half of all smartphone users in the U.S. say they use their phone to make some form of mobile payments."[7] The recent trend has recognized that consumers want easy access to their money and with the proliferation of mobile smartphones have made three mobile-based financial access paths instrumental: mCommerce, mPayments, and mWallets. We will discuss each in detail further in the chapter.

ONLINE BANKING

The history of online, e-banking, or Internet banking, began in the early 1980s. In 1981, four banks in New York (Citibank, Chase, Chemical, and Manufacturers Hanover)[8] decided to offer limited electronic financial services via a phone using a videotext system, "an electronic information transmission and retrieval technology enabling interactive communication, for such purposes as data acquisition and dissemination and electronic banking and shopping, between typically large and diverse computer databases and users of home or office display terminals connected to telephone or cable-television lines, or through use of broadcast television signals."[9] This was followed in 1983 when The Bank of

---

[5] "Fiat Money," Investopedia, accessed March 24, 2014, http://www.investopedia.com/terms/f/fiatmoney.asp.
[6] Credit Union National Association, accessed March 24, 2014, http://www.cuna.org.
[7] "Over Half of Smartphone Users Make Mobile Payments," *The Financial Brand* (November 1, 2013), http://thefinancialbrand.com/34815/cuna-smartphone-mobile-payments-study/.
[8] "History of Online Banking," (October 6, 2010), http://www.slideshare.net/jjchai/online-banking.
[9] "Videotex," Dictionary.com, accessed March 24, 2014, http://dictionary.reference.com/browse/videotex.

Scotland offered Nottingham Building Society members an Internet banking service called "Home-link" that used a television and a telephone to make financial transactions and pay bills.[10]

Going beyond the television to the computer, The Stanford Credit Union created the first online banking site,[11] and in 1995, the Presidential Savings Bank became the first bank in America to offer accounts over the Internet.[12] One reason these forays into the online banking world became possible was because Microsoft Money built in online banking into its personal financial software in 1994.[13] As the 1990s continued, more and more banks and financial institutions added online banking services to their offerings until finally in 2005, the Federal Financial Institutions Examination Council announced some new rules and regulations regarding online banking, focusing on risk, security, and customer education.[14] Just about every financial institution currently offers online banking via Web browsers.

The introduction of Apple's iPhone in 2007 and other smartphones in the late 2000s instigated a shift from computer banking to smartphone banking, earning worldwide consumer confidence at its peak in 2011–2012 with an adoption of mobile banking apps. The Pew Internet and American Life Project survey recently revealed that 61 percent of Internet users, or 51 percent of American adults use online banking.[15] In addition, we now have banks that are completely Internet-only banks with no brick and mortar counterpart. A few examples include Ally Bank (www.ally.com), ING Direct (www.ingdirect.com), and Bank of Internet USA (www.bankofinternet.com/bofi).

Most consumers will state that they use online banking because it is convenient—they can access their account anywhere and on just about any device at any time. It allows them to get information regarding their transactions without having to file paperwork or wait on a call for the next available representative. It also permits easy monitoring of any suspicious activity on their accounts, making consumers a great partner in the struggle against digital theft. Some online banking services also offer no- or low-fee accounts, which can save a consumer or business a bit on an annual basis.

However, the online banking development has led to a number of risk and security concerns. According to the Trend Micro Security Roundup Report banking malware has seen a 29 percent increase between quarters 1 and 2 of 2013 (the equivalent of 146,000 new infections[16]). It is estimated that the top online banking victim countries are United States 28%, Brazil 22%, and Australia 5%,[17] not surprising considering the adoption of Internet use in those countries.

Compliance rules and legal regulations hold the financial institution liable for unauthorized transfers, data breaches and data loss through hacking, viruses, system breakdowns, power failures, etc. Along with the security concern is the concern for consumer privacy in regards to their personally identifiable information, a concern that is growing considering the most recent breaches and data losses.

---

[10] "Infographic: The History of Internet Banking (1983–2012)," *The Financial Brand* (October 2, 2012), https://thefinancial brand.com/25380/yodlee-history-of-internet-banking/.

[11] See note 10.

[12] Jennifer Calonia, "The History of Online Banking," (July 21, 2013), http://www.gobankingrates.com/banking/hist ory-of-online-banking/.

[13] See note 10.

[14] "Authentication in an Internet Banking Environment," Federal Financial Institutions Examination Council, accessed March 24, 2014, https://www.ffiec.gov/pdf/authentication_guidance.pdf.

[15] Susannah Fox, "51% of U.S. Adults Bank Online," PewResearch Internet Project (August 7, 2013), http://www.pewinternet.org/2013/08/07/51-of-u-s-adults-bank-online/.

[16] Kul Bhushan, "Online banking malware grows 29%: Trend Micro's Q2 2013 security roundup," thinkdigit (September 9, 2013), http://www.thinkdigit.com/Internet/Online-banking-malware-grows-29-Trend-Micros_17538.html.

[17] Ibid.

Concerns over security and the protection against online credit card fraud led a group of five major financial companies to band together to form a single standard: The Payment Card Industry Data Security Standard (PCI-DSS), which they released in December 2004. These five had their own standards but they were not compatible and made it difficult for retailers who wanted to accept online credit card payments because they would have to comply with so many different standards. The five security standards were: Visa Card Information Security Program, MasterCard Site Data Protection, American Express Data Security Operating Policy, Discover Information and Compliance, and the JCB Data Security Program. In September 2006, an update to the standard was released creating the PCI Security Standards Council (PSI SSC) to manage the standard.

However, the standard would have its opponents, especially after a data breach occurred at TJ Maxx in 2006. The standards were criticized as being too difficult and too expensive. The PSI SSC argued that to ease the standards would be detrimental to consumer protection. In late 2007, a compromise was proposed and accepted in the form of the PCI-DSS compensating controls, which allows companies to avoid certain standards if they unduly burdened the company—meaning they are too hard or too costly for the company to implement.

In early 2008, the PCI SSC issued the Payment Application Data Security Standard and in April 2008 SSC released new supplemental guidance for Web applications security, culminating in the October 2008 release of the PCI-DSS, version 1.2. This was followed with a release in July 2009 of the PCI-DSS Wireless Guideline, focusing on scoping, virtualization, and preauthorization security.

PCI SSC is not finished refining the standard and issued the new 2.0 version in October 2010 and new virtualization security guidance in June 2011. In August 2011, SSC outlined its tokenization guidelines but merchants resisted the idea of using tokens instead of primary account numbers. In May 2012, SSC urged the use of encryption for mobile payments but backtracked and made a statement it is not endorsing the technology. Clarification regarding SSC's stand on mobile security was given in September 2012 when the SSC released its PCI Mobile Payment Acceptance Security Guidelines.

Currently PCI-DSS is on version 3.0, which was released in November 2013. It emphasizes that companies "need to integrate compliance best practices with day-to-day business operations."[18] But is that what is happening? In a January 2014 article looking at the state of PCI-DSS compliance and its impact in terms of protecting against data breaches, Fortinet, a global leader in high-performance network security highlighted research done by GMI, a division of Lightspeed Research of 100 SME retail organizations with less than 1000 employees:

- 22 percent (one in five retailers) are not PCI-DSS–compliant
- 14 percent don't know if they are compliant of not
- 55 percent are unaware of their state's security breach requirements
- 40 percent lack any established policy adhering to those requirements
- 53 percent managing their own security infrastructure on-site
- 18 percent also rely on a managed security services provider
- 29 percent looking to move security functions to a third-party managed service provider.[19]

---

[18] "The history of the PCI DSS standard: A visual timeline," *TechTarget* (November 1, 2013), http://searchsecurity.techtarget.com/feature/The-history-of-the-PCI-DSS-standard-A-visual-timeline.

[19] "One in five SME retailers not PCI compliant, lack security fundamentals," *Itweb* (January 22, 2014), http://www.itweb.co.za/index.php?option=com_content&view=article&id=70248:One-in-five-SME-retailers-not-PCI-compliant-lack-security-fundamentals-&catid=218.

It seems that a number of reports and other articles reviewing the situation question whether the reliance of this sole security standard is prudent or should other measures such as finding an alternative to the plastic card with a magnetic strip would prove more effective?

E-PAYMENTS CONVERT TO M-PAYMENTS

Electronic payments, or using your computer to make electronic financial transfers whether for personal or business purposes, seem a little passé as mobile permeates all of our interactions—financial and more. Now the idea is to pay using your mobile phone. SapeintNitro offers some staggering statistics in regard to the number of users and the financial value of mobile payments:

- U.S. users: 2010 102.3 million/$48.9 billion
- U.S. users: 2011 141.3 million/$86.1 billion
- Expected world: 2011 $240 billion
- Expected world: 2015 $670 billion[20]

The process for mobile banking is pretty simple for the consumer depending on the technology underlying the electronic commerce platform. For mCommerce, you use a mobile Internet browser that combines the use of online wallets and standard Web connections:

- Add to cart
- Fill in info or one-click
- Confirmation and receipt

For mPayments, the idea is to use contactless and mobile app technologies:

- Credit card information/account information in stored on mobile phone
- Enter your personal identification number before purchase
- Tap your phone and your information is sent for authentication
- Confirmation and receipt

Recently, the Starbucks app made headlines when it was discovered that it contained a high security risk because it stores usernames, email addresses, and passwords in clear text, offering another example of the debate between convenience versus security.[21]

The last process focuses on mWallets or the digital replacement of your physical wallet:

- Funds are loaded onto phone
- Scan barcode, amount is deducted
- New balance appears on phone

---

[20] "Future of Money Infographic," *SapientNitro* (May 2, 2012), http://www.slideshare.net/sapient/future-of-money-infographic.

[21] Antone Gonsalves, "Security risk in Starbucks app a 'wakeup call' for consumers," CSO Online (January 16, 2014), http://www.csoonline.com/article/746530/security-risk-in-starbucks-app-a-wakeup-call-for-consumers.

Some examples include: Amazon, Google Wallet, iTunes, Square, and PayPal. NXT-ID, Inc.[22] filed a patent for Digital Wallet technology, the Wocket™ in 2013. "The Wocket requires unique biometrically enabled multi-factor authentication to ensure only owners and their private information can be copied into or out from the secure vault wallet device and on to the dynamically programmable magnetic stripe NXTCard. Authenticated users may then select payment information, via touch display or voice command and use the NXTCard as they would any other magnetic stripe credit or debit card."[23]

As with other mobile apps, malware targeting mobile wallets are a concern. Security protocols and controls focus on protecting "wallet.dat" files that hold specific information regarding the contents of the wallet including personally identifiable information and financial data. It is a best practice to make your employees aware of this potential threat to their finances and their identities. As companies experiment with different types of direct deposit systems—from preauthorized debit cards to digital wallets—consideration should be given to security controls implemented by the third parties supplying the alternative deposit system. Review of the contract and specifically the security, data protection, and indemnification clauses is important, as is testing to ensure the controls are in place and working as promised.

VIRTUAL CURRENCY

Grand Theft Auto (GTA) online cheaters have stolen in-game money worth millions.[24]

The Financial Crimes Enforcement Network (FinCEN) regulations define currency (also referred to as "real" currency) as "the coin and paper money of the United States or of any other country that (1) is designated as legal tender and that (2) circulates and (3) is customarily used and accepted as a medium of exchange in the country of issuance."[25] FinCEN contrasts this real currency with virtual currency in a guidance it issued relating the Bank Secrecy Act to virtual currency, which it defines as a "medium of exchange that operates like a currency in some environments, but does not have all the attributes of real currency. In particular, virtual currency does not have legal tender status in any jurisdiction. This guidance addresses 'convertible' virtual currency. This type of virtual currency either has an equivalent value in real currency, or acts as a substitute for real currency."[26]

Virtual currencies came to the forefront in virtual economies that are observed in multiuser domains and massively multiplayer online role-playing games. Examples are World of Warcraft (http://us.battle.net/wow/en/), Second Life (http://secondlife.com), and Farmville (https://www.facebook.com/FarmVille).

---

[22] NXT-ID, accessed March 24, 2014, http://nxt-id.com.
[23] "NXT-ID, Inc. Files Patent for Digital Wallet Technology, the Wocket(TM)," *Market Watch* (October 21, 2013), http://www.marketwatch.com/story/nxt-id-inc-files-patent-for-digital-wallet-technology-the-wockettm-2013-10-21?reflink=MW_news_stmp.
[24] "GTA Online cheaters have stolen in-game money worth millions," Metro (December 19, 2013), http://metro.co.uk/2013/12/19/gta-online-cheaters-have-stolen-in-game-money-worth-millions-4237647/.
[25] "Application of FinCEN's Regulations to Persons Administering, Exchanging, or Using Virtual Currencies," *Financial Crimes Enforcement Network* (March 18, 2013), http://fincen.gov/statutes_regs/guidance/html/FIN-2013-G001.html.
[26] Ibid.

According to a white paper published by Pillsbury Law, virtual currency is important because it can be used to purchase in-world goods, to cash out for real money, to buy real-world goods, and to be traded for other currency.[27] Because virtual currencies can be converted to real-world money, security and protection of the transactions are important. There is even a number of virtual currency online exchanges one being First Meta Exchange.[28]

The quotation at the beginning of this section is a headline that appeared in December 2013 when GTA game developer Rockstar confirmed that five online players had exploited the game's mechanics to steal trillions of in-game dollars, which in conversion equals millions in real-world money. One gamer called "epiicmoddingtobi" amassed more than $1 trillion on his own. This is not the first example of gaming embezzlers or thieves, nor will it be the last.

Virtual currencies can be obtained in a number of ways through the online game environment or even in the offline world: purchased with real money, earned by in-world actions (microtransactions), via sweepstakes and contests, "gambling," releasing your user information, survey participation, acceptance of exposure to advertising, and/or as a gift of currency from others.

Those in the online, digital, and interactive game space have been dealing with a certain number of legal and security realities in terms of virtual currencies and their real world value. These include:

- Stored value/unclaimed property laws (breakage)
- Gift card laws
- Gambling/sweepstakes
- Avoiding illegal lotteries
- Money transmittal licensure
- Regulation as a financial institution
- Taxes
- Data privacy and security
- Child protection—Children's Online Privacy Protection Act
- Terms of service
- Secondary markets
- IP protection

DIGITAL CURRENCY

Money is a social contrivance, not something that stands outside society. Even when people relied on gold and silver coins, what made those coins useful wasn't the precious metals they contained, it was the expectation that other people would accept them as payment.[29]

Contrary to popular usage, virtual currency and digital currency are not the same thing and should not be used interchangeably even though they are in everyday communication and news coverage.

[27] "Overview of Legal Issues with Virtual Currencies," *Pillsbury* (2010), accessed March 24, 2014, http://www.socialgamesl aw.com/Virtual%20Currency.pdf.
[28] First Meta Exchange, accessed March 26, 2014, http://firstmetaexchange.com/exchange/quotes.
[29] Paul Krugman, "The Antisocial Network," (The New York Times, April 14, 2013), http://www.nytimes.com/2013/04/15/opi nion/krugman-the-antisocial-network.html?_r=0.

Although virtual currency is limited to a computer-generated environment (such as in a game) and is created within the limited rules of the game for use within the game, digital currency is a medium of exchange created for universal use in the real world as an alternative to the real currency we are presently using for financial transactions. Digital currency is created with powerful programming algorithms and its value is based on speculation and belief in that it will become an accepted mode of fiscal exchange which is one reason for its volatility.

It is sometimes also referred to as electronic money or e-money as a category type of alternative currency. Two things it does share with its virtual currency cousin is that digital currency is not wide spread in its usage and adoption (although that seems to be changing) and is not at present accepted by banks (something that may also change).

In addition to the virtual currency list of legal and security concerns listed previously, regulators are looking at regulating the currency itself, beyond just the exchange and storage requirements. This is a Catch-22 for some early adopters for digital currencies. On the one hand, many digital currencies are developed to create a value exchange system outside the regulatory control of any government, a free kind of money, controlled only by those investing in it. On the other hand, regulation means that the official regulatory agencies are recognizing the digital currency as a legitimate means of exchange, thus lending it credibility and enhancing the confidence level of the speculators. Because there has not been a digital currency with longevity as of yet, no one really knows where this will all lead. However, one digital currency has stood apart from the rest—Bitcoin.

BITCOIN

Conventional payment networks place most of the liability for fraudulent transactions on the merchant, allowing customers to challenge and reverse suspicious payment. Bitcoin, however, puts all of the liability on the payer. If you get tricked into sending a payment to the wrong person or hackers steal your Bitcoins, you have no recourse.[30]

Bitcoin. Chances are you have heard about this digital currency that has been making headlines for a number of reasons. One is because of who is supporting it, such as the Winklevoss twins (from Facebook lawsuit against Mark Zuckerberg fame). Another is the importance it is being given in mainstream media—such as from *Forbes* blogger, Kashmir Hill, who wrote a series of blogs about how she lived on Bitcoins for a week in 2013 (which I deem required reading).[31] Add to that it has captured the notice of regulators in New York, one of the financial capitals of the world, who have announced they are creating a proposed regulatory framework for these kinds of currencies.[32]

Bitcoin is defined as a "crypto-currency implemented entirely with open source specifications and software which relies entirely on a peer-to-peer network for both transaction processing and

---

[30] Erika Morphy, "With Bitcoin in Your Pocket, Is Your Identity Finally Safe?" (Forbes, December 31, 2013), http://www.forbes.com/sites/erikamorphy/2013/12/31/with-bitcoin-in-your-pocket-is-your-identity-finally-safe/.

[31] Kashmir Hill, "21 Things I Learned About Bitcoin From Living On It For A Week," (Forbes, May 9, 2013), http://www.forbes.com/sites/kashmirhill/2013/05/09/25-things-i-learned-about-bitcoin-from-living-on-it-for-a-week/.

[32] Nathaniel Popper, "Regulators and Hackers Put Bitcoin to the Test," (The New York Times, February 17, 2014), http://dealbook.nytimes.com/2014/02/17/regulators-and-hackers-put-bitcoin-to-the-test/?nl=todaysheadlines&emc=edit_th_20140218.

validation."[33] Part of this definition is to imply a certain amount of security in the currency through powerful cryptography software—the ability to encipher and decipher (encode and decode) information via secret algorithms accessed by private keys.

One of the questions regarding Bitcoins is: where do they come from? The consensus is that Bitcoins became established in 2009 when Satoshi Nakamoto designed and created the original Bitcoin software, currently known as Bitcoin-Qt.[34] It has not been confirmed if Nakamoto is a real person, although both the *New Yorker* and *Fast Company* have tried to locate and identify him.[35] It is currently being used as a pseudonymous for a person or group of people who are working on the Bitcoin software.

What is known is that there will only be 21 million Bitcoins released in the world ever through an algorithm that allows the coins to be "mined." Although originally mined by individuals, companies have sprung up—Bitcoin mines, if you will. One of them is in Reykjanesbaer, Iceland, near the Arctic Circle and was profiled in a *New York Times* Deal Book article.[36] Computers are the laborers of the virtual mines, running continuously 24/7, 365 days a year calculating and crunching numbers to obtain the Bitcoins when they are released.

There are other Bitcoin mines in Washington State and Hong Kong as well as one run by Emmanuel Abiodum, whose Kansas City Cloud Hashing company does what he calls "repetitive code guessing."[37] His issue is that energy consumption for running all of these computers is extremely high, which leads to the question of whether it is a waste because there is no guarantee what these Bitcoins will eventually be worth. The reminder is that its value is all based on speculation.

That speculation and Bitcoins' anonymous nature has led to issues and concerns about the digital currency being used to launder money and purchase illegal drugs and/or weapons. A notorious black market online site was recently closed down by the Federal Bureau of Investigation (in 2013) and heralded as a victory for legitimate Bitcoin users.[38] The Website Silk Road was run by Ross William Ulbricht of San Francisco, nicknamed "The Dread Pirate Roberts" from the cult movie "The Princess Bride." Ulbricht wasn't the only one caught in the Silk Road raid: Charles Shrem IV, of New York, chief executive and compliance officer at BitInstant; also, the vice chairman of the Bitcoin Foundation was arrested for Bitcoin money laundering[39] relating to drug proceeds from users of the now-defunct Silk Road.

If money laundering seems a bit highbrow for you, consider that "since 2009 more than 35 Bitcoin scams and thefts; including the heist of 38.527 Bitcoins from the online exchange Bitcoinica in May

---

[33] Jason Faulkner, "HTG Explains: What is Bitcoin and How Does it Work?" How-To Geek (May 16, 2013), http://www.howtogeek.com/141374/htg-explains-what-is-bitcoin-and-how-does-it-work/.

[34] Satoshi Nakamoto, "Bitcoin: A Peer-to-Peer Electronic Cash System", accessed March 26, 2014, https://bitcoin.org/bitcoin.pdf.

[35] Adrianne Jeffries, "The New Yorker's Joshua Davis Attempts to Identify Bitcoin Creator Satoshi Nakamoto," (BetaBeat, October 4, 2011), http://betabeat.com/2011/10/did-the-new-yorkers-joshua-davis-nail-the-identity-of-bitcoin-creator-satoshi-nakamoto/.

[36] Nathanial Popper, "Into the Bitcoin Mines," (The New York Times, December 21, 2013), http://dealbook.nytimes.com/2013/12/21/into-the-bitcoin-mines/?nl=todaysheadlines&emc=edit_th_20131222.

[37] Ibid.

[38] Nate Anderson and Cyrus Farivar, "How the feds took down the Dread Pirate Roberts," *ARS Technica* (October 3, 2013), http://arstechnica.com/tech-policy/2013/10/how-the-feds-took-down-the-dread-pirate-roberts/.

[39] Sue Reisinger, "Compliance Officer arrested for Bitcoin Money Laundering," (Corporate Counsel, January 18, 2014), http://www.corpcounsel.com/id=1202640179493/Compliance-Officer-Arrested-for-Bitcoin-Money-Laundering?slreturn=20140309090217.

2012."[40] This seems to go against the perception that the cryptography makes Bitcoins a secure digital currency. Apparently not so—at least not on its own. Part of it stems from a bug in basic software that determines how Bitcoins are moved between digital accounts, making it vulnerable to a hacking attack. Current Bitcoin developers say they are working on fixing that, especially because it is essential to return confidence to the users. Bitcoins were designed to be hard to trace so once stolen they are gone, leaving those who invested no recourse to recover their stolen Bitcoins. In addition, Bitcoin wallets not protected under deposit insurance offered by governments.

New companies have surfaced to try to prevent such thefts. Coin-making company Titan Mint, Inc., offers metal coins embossed with security codes and Bitshares, a Bitcoin marketplace, provides encrypted online accounts. Bionym, a company in Toronto, Canada, created Nymi, a smartphone app that uses an electrocardiogram biometric to identify users via their heartbeat through a wristband that they wear.[41] The wristband sends the data and verifications are sent back via Bluetooth so the users can access their Bitcoin account for purchases transactions.

Another option is Elliptic Vault,[42] the First Insured Bitcoin Vault, which is located in the United Kingdom. Elliptic Vault uses deep cold storage techniques where the Bitcoin keys are encrypted and stored offline. Lloyds of London is the underwriter. This brings up the irony of taking a digital currency converting it into a file that is copied onto a device that is offline from the network that creates the currency value and then the device is physically stored in another location for protection.

Other organizations have been created to lend legitimacy to Bitcoins and try to create stability and limit overinflation because of their scarcity. The Bitcoin Financial Association (http://bitcoinfinanciala ssociation.org), the Bitcoin Foundation (https://bitcoinfoundation.org), and Bitcoin Exchanges such as Bitstamp[43] and Mt. Gox[44] all play their roles. However, these organizations have their own concerns. Bitcoinica, a former Bitcoin Exchange, was closed down after a lawsuit resulting from a Bitcoin theft brought it to its knees.[45] On February 24, 2014, the Mt. Gox "site shut down citing the potential repercussions on Mt. Gox's operations and the market."[46] Mt. Gox, based in Tokyo, was considered a giant in the Bitcoin market. After the implosion of Mt. Gox, the Japanese government issued a statement that it would investigation the situation and respond.[47] Rumor had it that the Japanese government would consider implementing regulations on digital currencies. Mt. Gox's demise left many scrambling and questioning the future of Bitcoin.

---

[40] Olga Kharif, "Bitcoin triggers security startups," *JournalGazette* (February 16, 2014), http://www.journalgazette.net/article/20140216/BIZ/302169971/1031/BIZ.

[41] Julie Campbell, "Mobile security based on heartbeat to be used by Bitcoin," *Mobile Commerce News* (Febraury 7, 2014), http://www.qrcodepress.com/mobile-security-based-heartbeat-used-bitcoin/8525394/.

[42] "World's first insured bitcoin vault opens in UK," (The Times of India, January 12, 2014), http://articles.timesofindia.indiatimes.com/2014-01-12/internet/46112172_1_bitcoin-complex-computer-software-systems-digital-currency.

[43] *Bitstamp*, accessed March 26, 2014, https://www.bitstamp.net.

[44] Mt. Gox, accessed March 26, 2014, https://www.mtgox.com.

[45] Megan Geuss, "Bitcoinica users sue for $460k in lost Bitcoins," (April 11, 2012), http://arstechnica.com/tech-policy/2012/08/bitcoinica-users-sue-for-460k-in-lost-bitcoins/.

[46] Kashmir Hill, "After Mt. Gox Implodes, Bitcoin CEOs and Lawmakers Scramble," (Forbes, February 25, 2014), http://www.forbes.com/sites/kashmirhill/2014/02/25/mt-gox-implosion-has-u-s-lawmakers-renew-call-for-oversight/.

[47] Hiroko Tabuchi and Rachel Abrams, "Now, Nations Mull the Ways to Regulate Bitcoin," (The New York Times, Febraury 26, 2014), http://dealbook.nytimes.com/2014/02/26/japan-studies-regulation-of-bitcoin-after-mt-gox-goes-dark/?_php= true&_type=blogs&nl=todaysheadlines&emc=edit_th_20140227&_r=0.

Although we continue to hear about Bitcoin's ultimate demise, it has received some endorsements. First, a federal judge ruled that Bitcoin was real money and that running a Ponzi scheme with Bitcoins was the same as running a Ponzi scheme with U.S. dollars.[48]. The SEC Chairman Mary Jo White wrote a letter in response to a senate hearing in November 2013 about Bitcoins. She "left the issue of whether Bitcoins, themselves, were securities to specific facts and circumstances regarding a particular use of Bitcoins. However, Chairman White explicitly stated that interests in entities owning Bitcoins would be securities subject to SEC regulation"[49] and then cited the Ponzi scheme case. In addition, a number of product retailers and service companies are making announcements that they will accept Bitcoins for payments (see who accepts bitcoins).

We need to contrast this with the Internal Revenue Service's more recent guidance on virtual currencies in which it says virtual currencies are property, *not* currency. According to the guidance issues on March, 25, 2014, "In some environments, virtual currency operates like "real" currency—i.e., the coin and paper money of the United States or of any other country that is designated as legal tender, circulates, and is customarily used and accepted as a medium of exchange in the country of issuance— but it does not have legal tender status in any jurisdiction."[50]

WHO ACCEPTS BITCOINS

- SpendBitcoins—directory of places on the Web where people can spend Bitcoins
- Overstock.com
- The University of Cumbria, Britain
- University of Nicosia, Cyprus
- University of Puget Sound, Tacoma, Washington, received a $10,000 Bitcoin donation (they converted it to dollars using the e-commerce processor BitPay).[51]
- BitGo: this site helps retailers secure Bitcoin transactions.

What about lawyers accepting Bitcoins as payment for legal services? Jay Cohen, criminal defense attorney, announced in 2013 that he would accept payments from clients in Bitcoins.[52] His announcement has caused discussion in the legal arena as ethical and practical questions arise regarding conversion issues, client privacy concerns, and one simple rule all attorneys must adhere to: you can't accept assets from illegal activities, and how do you prove the Bitcoins didn't come from an illegal activity?

[51]Danya Perez-Hernandez, "Bitcoin Gift to U. of Puget Sound Could Be a First," *The Chronicle of Higher Education* (February 14, 2014), http://chronicle.com/blogs/wiredcampus/bitcoin-gift-to-u-of-puget-sound-could-be-a-first/50599?cid=wc&utm_source=wc&utm_medium=en.
[52]Martha Neil, "My clients can pay me in bitcoins, criminal defense lawyer says," *ABAJournal* (May 1, 2013), http://www.abajournal.com/news/article/criminal_defense_lawyer_says_clients_can_pay_him_in_bitcoins/.

Bitcoin's legality throughout the world is varied. In 2013, Security and Government Affairs Committee Chairman Tom Carper tasked the Law Library of Congress with surveying more than 40 countries and their "official" stand on Bitcoins and whether Bitcoin was actually in use in those countries.[53] The report

---

[48]Kashmir Hill, "Federal Judge Rules Bitcoin is Real Money," (Forbes, August 7, 2013), http://www.forbes.com/sites/kashmirhill/2013/08/07/federal-judge-rules-bitcoin-is-real-money/.
[49]Todd P. Zerega and Thomas H. Watterson, "Regulating Bitcoins: CFTC vs. SEC?" *Mondaq* (January 2, 2014), http://www.mondaq.com/unitedstates/x/283878/Commodities+Derivatives+Stock+Exchanges/Regulating+Bitcoins+CFTC+vs+SEC.
[50]*Internal Revenue Service Guidance* (March 25, 2014), http://www.irs.gov/uac/Newsroom/IRS-Virtual-Currency-Guidance.
[53]"Regulation of Bitcoin in Selected Jurisdictions," *The Law Library of Congress* (January. 2014), http://cdn1.sbnation.com/assets/3952017/2014-010233_Law_Library_of_Congress_Bitcoin_jurisdictional_survey.pdf.

found that "Of those countries surveyed, only a very few, notably China and Brazil, have specific regulations applicable to Bitcoin use. There is widespread concern about the Bitcoin system's possible impact on national currencies, its potential for criminal misuse, and the implications of its use for taxation. Overall, the findings of this report reveal that the debate over how to deal with this new virtual currency is still in its infancy."[54] A quick look at some countries show some movement toward specific regulations: Russia's current stance is that all virtual currencies are illegal, Canada is developing national rules for these types of currencies, and Singapore has offered guidance on taxation for Bitcoin businesses.

It is interesting to note the 40 countries: (including the European Union): Alderney, Argentina, Australia, Belgium, Brazil, Canada, Chile, China, Croatia, Cyprus, Denmark, Estonia European Union, Finland, France, Germany, Greece, Hong Kong, Iceland, India, Indonesia, Ireland, Israel, Italy, Japan, Malaysia, Malta, the Netherlands, New Zealand, Nicaragua, Poland, Portugal, Russia, Singapore, Slovenia, Spain, South Korea, Taiwan, Thailand, Turkey, and the United Kingdom. A great breakdown of the findings by country can be found in *Forbes* blogger Kashmir Hill's January 2014 post: http://www.forbes.com/sites/kashmirhill/2014/01/31/bitcoins-legality-around-the-world/.

No discussion regarding Bitcoin and/or other digital currency would be complete without acknowledging the role mobile apps plays in this environment. As of the writing of this chapter, it was reported that Apple had removed all iOS Bitcoin wallet (transaction) apps (including Blockchain, Coinbase, and Coinjar[55]). Suspicions as to why it pulled them were raised claiming a possible clearing of the marketplace to allow an Apple-proprietary digital payments app. However, when I went to my App Store on my iPhone and entered a search for Bitcoin-related apps, more than 236 were displayed. Although most seemed to focus on Bitcoin exchange information, 17 identified themselves as Bitcoin wallets, including Coinbits and Bitcoin App by Paxx Media.[56]

On the Android side of things, two Bitcoin-related apps seemed to be highlighted: Coinbase, a Bitcoin wallet to help manage the cryptocash, and Bitcoin Tapper, which claims to earn you money, but was discovered to be a "spam app." Bitcoin Tapper reminds us that apps can be malicious in nature and need to be reviewed and security procedures followed for their implementation. As Kevin Watkins, cofounder of Appthority, stated: "Bitcoin apps are, for all intents and purposes, financial apps and should be held to similar standards as banking and other financial services related mobile apps."[57]

BITCOIN SECURITY TIPS[58]

- Limit employee access to Bitcoin wallets
- Maintain separate hot and cold wallets (online and offline)
- Store private keys offline
- Use dedicated hardware
- Keep offsite backups of Bitcoin wallets and keep those secure
- Use a hardware wallet

[58]Paul Rubens, "10 Bitcoin Security Tips," eSecurity Planet (February 10, 2014), http://www.esecurityplanet.com/network-security/10-bitcoin-security-tips.html.

[54]Ibid.
[55]Jason Mick, "Apple Kills Last iOS Bitcoin Wallet App," (DailyTech, February 6, 2014), http://www.dailytech.com/Apple+Kills+Last+iOS+Bitcoin+Wallet+App/article34287.htm.
[56]*App Store Search* (February 26, 2014).
[57]Max Eddy, "Mobile Threat Monday: The Good and Bad of Android Bitcoin Apps," (PC Mag, February 17, 2014), http://securitywatch.pcmag.com/mobile-security/320767-mobile-threat-monday-the-good-and-bad-of-android-bitcoin-apps.

BEYOND BITCOINS

Bitcoin is not the only digital currency out there. Several alternatives, some claiming to fill in the security gaps and to improve on the failings of Bitcoin, are being developed to meet the demand for a new, novel, and secure medium of exchange. The major cryptocurrencies are described here.

NAMECOIN (HTTP://NAMECOIN.INFO)

An open-source decentralized key/value registration and transfer system based on Bitcoin technology (a decentralized cryptocurrency).

LITECOIN—LITECOIN-QT (APP) (HTTPS://LITECOIN.ORG)

A peer-to-peer Internet currency that enables instant payments to anyone in the world, developed by Charles Lee, former Google software engineer, as an alternative to Bitcoin. "I wanted to create something that is kind of silver to Bitcoin's gold."[59]

Litecoin is set up to pump out four times as many coins as Bitcoin to keep it from becoming scarce and too expensive; processes transactions quickly, and lets regular folks mine coins (provide the online currency system with the computing power it needs in exchange for digital money).[60]

DOGECOIN (HTTP://DOGECOIN.COM)

Dogecoin is an open-source peer-to-peer cryptocurrency. One thing you will notice when you go to the Dogecoin site is that it is based on fun—from the great introduction video on the Website to the fashion store for Dogecoin-inspired tee shirts. They certainly are taking a marketing approach for faster adoption. Meant as a joke based on an Internet meme—Shiba Inu—users can still mine it for real value. In February 2014, someone at Harvard was caught using Harvard's supercomputers, Odyssey Cluster, to mine Dogecoin.[61] That person was banned from using Harvard's computers again, but because of the nature of the how the accounting of Dogecoins work, as all cryptocurrencies do, the individual was able to keep his coins. So for security and risk management—are your employees mining for cryptocoins and using valuable company computing resources as well as leaving an open portal for hackers?

PEERCOIN (FORMERLY PPCOIN) (HTTP://WWW.PEERCOIN.NET)

A cryptocoin: through an innovative minting algorithm, the Peercoin network consumes far less energy, maintains stronger security, and rewards users in more sustainable ways than other cryptocurrencies. In a review of Peercoin contrasting it to Bitcoin, it was noted that "Peercoin is a hybrid proof of

[59] Robert McMillan, "Ex-Googler Gives the World a Better Bitcoin," *Wired* (August 30, 2013), http://www.wired.com/wiredenterprise/2013/08/litecoin/?goback=%2Egde_38412_member_270003678#%21.

[60] Ibid.

[61] Devin Coldewey, "Secret Dogecoin Mining Operation on Harvard Computers Results in Ban," (NBCnews, February 21, 2014), http://www.nbcnews.com/tech/internet/secret-dogecoin-mining-operation-harvard-computers-results-ban-n35936.

work/proof of stake coin that attempts to evolve the Bitcoin protocol."[62] As such, author Shane Dark ponders whether Peercoin will make Bitcoin the "Myspace of Cryptocurrency."

MASTERCOIN (HTTP://WWW.MASTERCOIN.ORG)

An altcoin invented by J. R. Willett. According to the Website, "The Master Protocol facilitates the creation and trading of smart properties and user currencies as well as other types of smart contracts. Mastercoins serve as binding between bitcoins (BTC), smart properties and smart contracts created on top of the Mastercoin Protocol." Here is where the debate comes in: it is not mined and does not have its own block chain. It exists on top of Bitcoin. This has led one blogger to question why it even exists: "Because Mastercoin does not have its own block chain, all its transactions are simply extra pieces of data inserted into Bitcoin's block chain, which, from the standpoint of the Bitcoin miners, are meaningless."[63]

CROWDFUNDING

An accepted definition of crowdfunding is "the use of small amounts of capital from a large number of individuals to finance a new business venture. Crowd funding makes use of the easy accessibility of vast networks of friends, family and colleagues through social media websites like Facebook, Twitter and LinkedIn to get the word out about a new business and attract investors."[64]

The idea of gathering small amounts from many to accumulate to a desired total is not new. Justin Kazmark, in the Kickstarter Blog, gives us three early examples of what he calls "Kickstarter before Kickstarter."[65] The first deals with praenumeration, a subscription business model that Alexander Pope used to finance the print run of his translation of more than 15,000 lines of Greek poetry into English in 1713. Apparently he was a success after 750 subscribers pledged two gold guineas each to support Pope's project and see their names acknowledged in the book. Note: Most of us want to know what does two guineas worth in today's U.S. dollars? That is difficult to calculate because guineas do not exist anymore.[66] But this is an important risk and security point—do transactions in hard currency that have and will be around are easy to convert and liquidate. This is a cautionary issue for those dabbling in the new digital currencies.

The second example we get from Kazmark is Mozart, who in 1783 wanted to perform three piano concertos he had just composed in Vienna. He offered copies of the manuscript in exchange for the pledges of support. His first try did not succeed, but in 1784 he was able to raise the money he needed from 176 backers. Lesson learned: don't give up. Try again.

---

[62] Shane Dark, "Could Peercoin and 'Proof-of-Stake' Turn Bitcoin Into The Myspace of Cryptocurrency?" *Cointrader* (January 19, 2014), http://cointrader.org/peercoin-proof-of-stake-and-bitcoin/.

[63] Daniel Menger, "Mastercoin is a nightmare of Insanity," *The Mises Circle*, (December 20, 2013), http://themisescircle.org/blog/2013/12/20/mastercoin-is-a-nightmare-of-insanity/.

[64] "Crowdfunding," *Investopedia*, accessed March 27, 2014, http://www.investopedia.com/terms/c/crowdfunding.asp.

[65] Judith Kazmark, "Kickstarter before Kickstarter," *Kickstarter* (July 18, 2013), https://www.kickstarter.com/blog/kickstarter-before-kickstarter.

[66] Ed Crews, "How Much is that in Today's Money?" (Colonial Williamsburg, 2002), accessed March 27, 2014, http://www.history.org/foundation/journal/summer02/money2.cfm.

The last example is the Statue of Liberty Pedestal Fund.[67] In 1884, the Statue of Liberty, a gift from the French people to the United States, was built but had no place to display it because the American Committee for the Statue of Liberty ran out of funds. Joseph Pulitzer, publisher of *The New York World*, urged his readers to support it. He raised more than $100,000 from donations, most of which were less than a dollar each. Lesson learned: Make the project relevant.

The current rendition of crowdfunding occurred in 1997 when a rock band from Britain called Marillion asked for donations online to fund a reunion tour.[68] It proved a successful method and led to the first official crowdfunding site, ArtistShare, in 2001, "a platform that connects creative artists with fans in order to share the creative process and fund the creation of new artistic works."[69] The next significant site would be IndieGogo[70] in 2008, followed closely by Kickstarter in 2009[71] started by Perry Chen, Yancey Strickler, and Charles Alder. Today there are a number of crowdfunding platforms and sites, some focusing on specific niches, such as creative projects, and new ones focusing on equity and entrepreneurship, such as Fundable[72] (see Box for additional crowdfunding sites).

> **CROWDFUNDING SITES**
>
> Appbackr: http://www.appbackr.com
> Fundable: http://www.fundable.com
> Gofundme: http://www.gofundme.com
> IndieGogo: http://www.indiegogo.com
> Kickstarter: https://www.kickstarter.com
> Razoo: http://www.razoo.com
> RocketHub: http://www.rockethub.com
>
> Marketing Moxie Biz has compiled a list of more than 500 crowdfunding sites with comparisons of features, urls, and more. You can access that list here: http://marketingmoxie.biz/the-big-list-of-crowdfunding-sites/. Keep in mind that like other businesses, crowdfunding sites do close and so it is important to do your research before using a particular site to ensure it is credible and will not terminate when you are in the middle of a campaign. Review their terms of use and any legal language they may have posted. Review past and current campaigns and speak to a few users to see what their experience has been.

The crowdfunding concept has been caught up in doubts in terms of its legality and compliance with The Securities Act of 1933 and the Securities Exchange Act of 1934, both of which put restrictions on who can invest in a business endeavor and the procedures to follow to register, promote, administer, and report on the fundraising. Two of the key elements were who would be deemed a qualified investor and the prohibition of general solicitation ("public advertising or other public statements regarding a securities offering"[73] under Rule 506 (c)). Kickstarter and other crowdfunding sites state that "Project

[67] "Joseph Pulitzer," National Park Service, accessed March 27, 2014, http://www.nps.gov/stli/historyculture/joseph-pulitzer.htm.
[68] *Marillion*, accessed March 27, 2014, https://www.facebook.com/MarillionOfficial.
[69] *Artistshare*, accessed March 27, 2014, https://www.artistshare.com/v4/.
[70] *IndieGogo*, accessed March 27, 2014, http://www.indiegogo.com.
[71] *Kickstarter*, accessed March 27, 2014, https://www.kickstarter.com.
[72] *Fundable*, accessed March 27, 2014, http://www.fundable.com.
[73] Georgia Quinn, "Advertising, Social Media and the New World of Crowdfunding," *Crowdfund Insider* (January 30, 2014), http://www.crowdfundinsider.com/2014/01/30968-advertising-social-media-new-world-crowdfunding/.

creators keep 100% ownership of their work, and Kickstarter cannot be used to offer equity, financial returns, or to solicit loans."[74] In other words, Kickstarter is not an investment platform and therefore not subject to SEC and related regulations. People who "pledge" to support a project on Kickstarter receive rewards, different rewards for different levels of support. But this general legal clause did not reassure everyone about the legality of requesting financial support via social media and other online channels. These platforms also put up a wall through password and account registration to "screen" accredited investors—or those with whom there is a preexisting relationship trying to offer more protection against compliance violations.

In 2012, President Obama signed the Jumpstart Our Business Startup (JOBS) Act[75] that exempts from registration sales of securities directly to the public through a "crowd-fund portal."[76] Three sections of the Act refer specifically to crowdfunding and how one would qualify:

- Title II Accredited Crowdfunding
  - An issuer needs to maintain a clear policy regarding the promotion of its crowdfunding offering and actively manage the social media campaign it launches,
  - The issuer must disclose and include language in the promotion about compensated endorsements for the offering (who and what they receive),
  - Antifraud rules still apply so no material misstatements in connection with the offering, and
  - You must make sure all information you put out regarding the offering is accurate and not misleading
- Title III Retail Crowdfunding
  - Does not allow general solicitation
  - Use of advertising and promotional materials strictly limited
  - Put a notice advertising that the offering: the only information allowed it that the issuer is conducting an offering
  - The name of the intermediary with a link to the platform (can only use one)
  - Terms of the offering
  - Factual information about the legal identity and business location of the issuer
  - You can publicize the notice through media channels
  - Same paid promotions disclosure and antifraud rules apply
- Title IV Registered Crowdfunding
  - In proposed stage, Regulation A
  - Offering is quasiregistered
  - General solicitations are allowed before registration as "testing the waters" activities; offering materials must be files 21 days before the sale of any security

The JOBS Act does not clarify all questions and concerns regard crowdfunding. Doubt has been cast as to whether Facebook friends, Twitter followers, and so on, are sophisticated investors fully

---

[74] "Kickstarter Basics: Kickstarter 101," *Kickstarter*, accessed March 27, 2014, https://www.kickstarter.com/help/faq/kickstarter%20basics.

[75] "H.R. 3606 (112th): Jumpstart Our Business Startups", accessed March 27, 2014, http://www.govtrack.us/congress/bills/112/hr3606/text.

[76] Jonathan B. Wilson and Emily Stuart Horn, "Crowdfunding in Georgia: Traps for the Unwary Through the Invest Georgia Exemption," *Georgia Bar Journal* (December, 2013), http://digital.ipcprintservices.com/article/Crowdfunding_in_Georgia%3A/1583975/187975/article.html.

knowledgeable in what they are about to invest in or are they vulnerable to fraud and scam projects? Also most of the Act requires only basic disclosures leading to the question of how informed can an investor really be when it comes to deciding to fund a project. Some sites, such as Kickstarter, require those seeking funds to do a minimum number of updates and notices to those who are pledges to keep them informed of the progress of the project and the fundraising campaign. Another question that comes up is when does a friend become a stranger in the social media world? Is a friend of a friend who is also my friend a direct solicitation even though the friend did not get the notice directly from me? Is a friend of a friend of a friend of a friend who I do not know still a qualified investor? Does it matter now with the JOBS Act? These still need to be clarified and we still don't have those clarifications from the SEC even though they were due last year.

Because the clarifications have not come through yet, some states took matters into their own hands and passed laws governing crowdfunding in an intrastate model—meaning only investors and transactions within the state itself and restricted to residents of the states. One such state is Georgia and the Invest in Georgia Exemption (IGE), an administrative rule adopted by the Georgia Commissioner of Securities in 2011, which makes possible a wide-scale distribution of solicitations to buy certain unregistered securities to Georgia residents[77]; intrastate crowdfunding. The IGE states that the issuer still must adhere to the federal laws, which right now has the general rule against general solicitations and continues to apply to IGE offerings. It can be quite confusing.

The crowdfunding platforms must deal with a number of security issues as well. In February 2014, Kickstarter suffered a data breach[78] and user's email addresses, phone numbers, usernames, and encrypted passwords were stolen. These platforms are also monitoring for scams or individuals who create phony projects to raise funds as well as any abuse of funds once collected, because all of these affect the reputation and credibility of the crowdfunding site itself.

Another risk with using these platforms to raise funds focuses on the IP of the project. Ideas cannot be protected, and many individuals will try to protect the idea by keeping it secret through nondisclosure agreements. These sites do not offer that and so once the idea of the project is posted and uploaded, it is there for all to see and possibly be copied although in a different tangible expression. So the conventional tools of copyright and trademark registration offers value in this online environment and should be kept in mind before too much is shared on these platforms. Understanding IP rights and having an IP strategy before launching any campaign is a prudent best practice.

A last risk to be considered is the onset of donor exhaustion. As crowdfunding becomes more popular and more of a mainstream way to raise money instead of just an alternative, people and business may get tired of the number of "pledge" requests they receive via their email in boxes, Facebook status and posts, tweets, etc. It is important to keep that in mind during the development of the campaign and the decision for pledge levels. One U.S. dollar may not seem like much but after hundreds of worthwhile projects you want to support, it adds up. And because this is based on some kind of social relationship (or friendship) friends may begin to feel abused with the onslaught of requests.

[77] Ga. Comp. R. & Regs. R. 590-4-2-0.08 (2012), et seq.
[78] Justin Harp, "Kickstarter confirms data stolen in security breach," *Digital Spy* (February 15, 2014), http://www.digitalspy.com/tech/news/a551534/kickstarter-confirms-data-stolen-in-security-breach.html#~oAWnJqozkANTL9.

ONLINE MICROFINANCING

So back to the 1700s we go to visit the spirit of Johnathan Swift, the author of *Gulliver's Travels*.[79] Apparently when Swift was not busy writing fanciful tales he was instrumental in creating the Irish Loan Fund to give loans to low-income families in rural Ireland.[80]

Our modern version of microfinancing developed during the 1960s and 1970s when certain organizations began to institutionalize the process. In the 1960s, it was a group in Venezuela called Accion International.[81] Accion was started by law student Joseph Blatchford "who raised $90,000 to start a community development program to help the poor jump-start their own businesses."[82]

In 1976, a professor from Bangladesh, Dr. Muhannad Yunus, began to hand out $27 loans to local women who worked on bamboo farms that were stricken during a recent famine.[83] These tiny loans would lead to the formation of Grameen Bank[84] and a 2006 Nobel Peace Prize[85] for Dr. Yunus. He is considered the father of modern microfinance and grandfather to crowdfunding.[86]

In 2005, the first digital microlending platform was launch online—Kiva,[87] a nonprofit organization with a mission to connect people through lending to alleviate poverty. It leverages the reach of the Internet and the desire of most people to help others, with the ability to do so at as little as $25 a pop. The statistics on Kiva's Website regarding its achievements since its founding in 2005 are impressive: more than 1 million Kiva lenders made more than $534 million in loans and it has had a 98% repayment rate.[88]

One thing I would like to point out about Kiva is its "Risk and Due Diligence" page on its Website. This is a great best practice to remind its current and potential lenders that "the road to hell is paved with good intentions." It outlines series of risks that the lender may be exposed to by using the site and its platform. These include: borrower risk because of a variety of issues including crop failure, AIDS and other health concerns, theft, civil disturbances; field partner risks because of fraud, bankruptcy, or other operations failure; country risk because of economic, political, and/or natural disasters; and "Kiva-related" risks, or the potential discontinuation of the site[89] (see Box for other Microfinancing Sites).

In addition, keep in mind that microfinancing is not just for the poor in third-world countries. There is a trend in the United States and other developed countries to use the model to help raise funds for startups and entrepreneurs in local communities.

---

[79] You can read the book for free, accessed March 28, 2014, http://www.gutenberg.org/ebooks/829.

[80] Aidan Hollis, "The Evolution of a Microcredit Institution: The Irish Loan Funds, 1720–1920," (University of Toronto, January 2, 1996), http://www.economics.utoronto.ca/public/workingPapers/UT-ECIPA-ECPAP-96-01.pdf.

[81] Accion, accessed March 28, 2014, https://www.facebook.com/ACCION.International.

[82] Rob Krieger, "The Evolution of Microfinance," (Frontline, October 31, 2006), http://www.pbs.org/frontlineworld/stories/uganda601/history.html.

[83] "The History of Crowdfunding," *Fundable*, accessed March 28, 2014, http://www.fundable.com/crowdfunding101/history-of-crowdfunding.

[84] Grameen, accessed March 28, 2014, http://www.grameen-info.org.

[85] "Muhammad Yunus, Nobel Lecture," NobelPrize.org (December, 2006), http://www.nobelprize.org/nobel_prizes/peace/laureates/2006/yunus-lecture.html.

[86] Jacques Jabra, "Muhammad Yunus, Father of Microfinance, Is Also the Grandfather of Crowdfunding," Noozhawk (February 9, 2014), http://www.noozhawk.com/article/jacques_habra_muhammad_yunus_microfinance_20140209.

[87] *Kiva*, accessed March 28, 2014, http://www.kiva.org.

[88] "About Us," *Kiva*, March 28, 2014, http://www.kiva.org/about.

[89] "Risk and Due Diligence," *Kiva*, accessed March 28, 2014, http://www.kiva.org/about/risk.

MICROFINANCING/LENDING ONLINE SITES

Kiva: http://www.kiva.org
Microfinancing Partners in Africa: http://www.microfinancingafrica.org
Opportunity International: http://opportunity.org/what-we-do/microfinance
Peerbackers: http://peerbackers.com/about-us/
Prosper: http://www.prosper.com
Small Knot: http://smallknot.com
The Awesome Foundation: http://www.awesomefoundation.org
World Vision Micro: http://www.worldvisionmicro.org

ONLINE CHARITABLE DONATIONS AND FUNDRAISING

Nonprofits have also noted the crowdfunding phenomenon and are experimenting with how to raise donations to support their core missions and programs while complying with the Internal Revenue Service, federal, and state charity-applicable laws. To that extend, a number of crowdfunding sites specifically for charities and institutions of higher education have been developed:

- Crowdrise: http://www.crowdrise.com
- Experiment: https://experiment.com
- Firstgiving: http://www.firstgiving.com
- Start Some Good: http://startsomegood.com
- Stay Classy: https://www.stayclassy.org
- USEED: http://useed.org

It is important to note that nonprofits must proceed with caution and understand the different platforms as well as the get approval from the board of directors to adopt online fund raising and these platforms as a fundraising strategy. Best practices include reviewing what other nonprofits are doing, what platforms they are using, and what approaches they are taking. It is extremely important that donor exhaustion be taken into account. You do not want to send an online request for a minimal amount when your organization has spent months preparing a proposal for a capital donation from this same donor. Also it is important for the nonprofit to note who would their audience be for these donations—current donors, new donors, potential donors who know about the organizations, strangers to the organization: is this a medium the donors understand an even like to be asked in this way?

FUTURE OF MONEY

The discussion concerning virtual and digital currencies, as well as mobile payments bring up many questions about the future of money, three of which I will focus on now. The first is what will money look like in the future? If it is to have a "look" that is. When the European Union decided to standardize all member currencies to the euro the *New York Times* ran a series about the expiring country-specific currencies. For example, Italy gave up the lira and Germany gave up its mark. For many countries, currency is an official mode of communicating national pride in the culture, from accomplishments to national heroes, money is where we highlighted the very best our country had to offer. It was difficult for many European Union member states to give that up. In fact, England has refused to do so, arguing that it would devalue their economy. It was interesting to me that when I visited Ireland shortly after the euro change and looked closely at the euro coins in my hand I noticed the countries had played their own little trick against complete homogeneity. On the Irish euro was the harp, a national symbol and on another euro coin, was the wise owl, symbol of Greece. The coins all said euro and community, but the images shouted out nation-state and independence.

The United States has gone through a few modifications—or in some cases, complete overhauls— of its paper and coin money. Many of the changes had to do with making the currency more secure and harder to replicate. The use of special dyes, watermarks, and holographic images when the dollars are held at a specific angle, all touted as advanced anticounterfeiting strategies.

Even so, most of us no longer carry that much cash around, opting instead to "trust" our financial institutions and plastic debit cards or an account number to facilitate transactions, whether purchases, gifts, or other. Our money has taken on the form of digits on a computer or cell phone screen. Is the digital currency concept that far off from what we've become so familiar with?

So what money will look like in the future look is a question that can hardly be answered, but it will most probably not look like what it looks like now. So those in risk management and security need to monitor the change in the physical and digital look of money to ensure the appropriate controls are in place for that physical and/or digital expression.

A second question is: should we change our thought process from money to currency or from currency to wealth? Think for a moment of your company determines it is financially stable or a resounding financial success. What are the financial metrics it uses? Are the formulas or algorithms calculating the worth correctly? There is high risk in not understanding the underlying calculations our accounting systems are using and that we are basing our financial future on. You do not need to know the programing or code, but yes the underlying principles as to how the results are computed. For example, that sale times selling price equals revenue, not profit. Risk managers do not need to be certified public accountants but they do need to bring it to the attention of the chief financial officer that this is a risk that needs to be mitigated—whether the financial software is custom or off the shelf or even, as some would say, heaven forbid, on mobile apps.

These questions then take the practical turn of being expanded outside the company's systems: what forms of future payments will you accept from your clients or make to your employees? Why? It was a big deal when an attorney made the announcement to accept Bitcoins as a form of payment (see discussion in the Box of who accepts bitcoins). A decision like that implies legal, ethical, and operational risks (including security breaches, confidentiality leaks, etc.). What if a company wanted to pay their employees in Bitcoins? Would that be considered a valid form of compensation or would it put undue burden on the employees to have it exchanged to a currency more convenient for them to transact with, especially if the digital currency is not yet universally adapted? Would there be a requirement that if you accept one digital currency you would need to accept them all? Or could you limit it the way some merchants accept Visa and MasterCard but not American Express? Do you run the risks of reputation and compliance violations based on your decision of using or not using the alternative forms of payment because of discrimination or perception that your company is too old fashioned for the newly financially independent younger generation? These three are not the only questions surrounding the future of money. I'm sure you can add quite a few more.

A final scenario regarding the future of money is where money as we know it does not exist at all. Andrew Ross Sorkin from the *New York Times* proposes a future in 2040 in which when you go into a store to make a purchase you were identified as you stepped in and your payment was processed as you stepped out. He envisions a possible unique identifier connected to a digital wallet that contains various types of digital currencies—not just standard U.S. dollars and credit cards, but frequent mile–like programs and exchanges.[90] However, Ray Kurzweil, futurist and author, brings up a point on the stubbornness of humans when it comes to money and financial transactions. "We've built up respect for currencies associated with nations. People respect dollars, mostly, I think, because of the track record, relative stability."[91]

DIGITAL POLITICAL CAMPAIGNS

Obama's 2012 campaign reportedly raised a staggering $690 million online.[92]

When it comes to politics and the digital online world, it is not just about the money. Politicians look toward social media and other online platforms to complete a number of tasks in terms of getting elected and staying in office. These functions include campaigning, fundraising, reputation management, crisis management, advocating, and garnering constituency support.

Jeffrey Plaut, speaking to the New York Global Strategy Group in 2012, stated: "Politics is acutely tied to how people get and process information."[93] It's not just how voters receive information from the politicians but also how politicians receive information rom and about voters. Using social media and online tools for campaigning fulfills a number of functions: polling and data collection, getting the message out (amplification tool), staying in contact with voters, competitive intelligence, and pushing voters to the polls, among others.

Outreach to constituents through these online tools allow politicians and elected officials to listen to their constituents, to understand the landscape and issues, to respond (including making things right), to reach out to "influencers," and to establish trust through conversation and connection. In other words, online social tools are just another way to do the oldest task in politics: building relationships. In fact, interactivity with the candidate is now an expectation for voters![94]

These online social tools also permit parties other than politicians—such as the press and mainstream media to access a truer picture of the political landscape. "Today social media acts to not only amplify the sound bites, but also to give journalist a way to gauge public sentiment about what is being said."[95] Traditional media scrutinizes social media responses because Twitter buzz can offer credibility to a story or news item. In this way, social media feeds mainstream media, which in turn validates social media, which in turn validates mainstream media.

---

[90] Sorkin, Andrew Ross, New York Times Dealbook, "A Revolution in Money," (April 1, 2014), http://dealbook.nytimes.com/2014/04/01/a-revolution-in-money/?_php=true&_type=blogs&_r=0.

[91] Ibid.

[92] Michael Beckel, "Political strategists praise power of online fundraising," (The Center for Public Integrity, April 10, 2013), http://www.publicintegrity.org/2013/04/10/12478/political-strategists-praise-power-online-fundraising.

[93] Bruce Schoenfeld, "How Social Media is Changing the Way Politicians Gather Information," Entrepreneur (August 21, 2012), http://www.entrepreneur.com/article/223978.

[94] Colin Delany, "Social Media for Elected Officials," Epolitics.com (August 3, 2009), http://www.epolitics.com/2009/08/03/social-media-for-elected-officials/.

[95] JD Rucker, "How Social Media Changed Political Campaigns," *Soshable* (December 11, 2011), http://soshable.com/social-media-political-campaigns/.

What about the effectiveness of social media and online tools in terms of affecting a vote? According to a June 2011 report by SocialVibe, "most voters will receive their campaign info from their Facebook friends…making it possible that 18–35 year old voters WILL NOT hear a candidate's message if it is not presented through social media outlets."[96] This sentiment is reiterated in a Pew Internet survey that "found that Facebook users are 57% more likely to persuade their friends and co-workers to vote."[97]

Social media and online tools have also changed the way political campaigns are funded. Donation solicitation and political action committee (PAC) laws still apply, but the reach is broader permitting those who weren't always targeted for funds to offer smaller amounts that accumulate to sizable sums in innovative ways.

A case in point of the power of online fundraising is the Stephen Colbert Super PAC campaign in 2011–2012.[98] Considering he is a television personality with his own television show on Comedy Central called "The Colbert Report," and his "Super PAC" was to prove a point in a humoristic way (dare we say parody) the process and workings of a Super PAC, his attorneys (and I'm sure the attorneys of Comedy Central and Viacom, the parent company) sought an advisory opinion from the Federal Election Commission to ensure they could create it, because it would not be connected to any one politician, and that they could collect donations for it. The letter[99] advised that both are permissible and the Super PAC raised more than $773,704.83. The Super PAC was closed when "Ham Rove" Colbert's key advisor for the PAC, was eaten by a dog.[100] The Super PAC funds were then transferred into the Ham Rove Memorial Fund and dispersed among worthwhile charities: Donors Choose, Team Rubicon, Habitat for Humanity, Yellow Ribbon Fund, Center for Responsive Politics, and Campaign Legal Center. All of the proceedings of the Super PAC were transparent via Colbert's television show and the Website. And most of the donations were only a $1 each. Some may argue that it was the fact of Colbert being on television that made the PAC successful, but he used online tools to maintain and monitor it, collect donations, be transparent with updates to the public, and terminate it (see Box for campaign fundraising sites).

ONLINE POLITICAL FUNDRAISING SITES

Aristotle's Campaign Contribution: http://campaigncontribution.com/v5/site/content/content.asp
Fundly: http://fundly.com/political-fundraising/
PayPal: https://www.paypal.com/us/webapps/mpp/online-political-fundraising
Piryx: http://www.piryx.com/political-fundraising/

Recent political scandals involving social media lead some to believe that social media and politics don't mix. WeinerGate perpetuated via Twitter or Shirtless (Christopher) LeeGate via Craiglist are two that come immediately to mind. Tweeting something that may be perceived as insensitive to a group or

---

[96] Victor Rodrigues, "All Politics is Social," (June 16, 2011), http://www.slideshare.net/victori98pt/social-media-engagement-will-decide-us-election-2012-by-socialvibe.

[97] Keith Hampton, "Social networking sites and our lives," *Pew Research Internet Project* (June 16, 2011), http://www.pewinternet.org/2011/06/16/social-networking-sites-and-our-lives/.

[98] Stephen Colbert's SuperPac, accessed March 28, 2014, http://www.colbertsuperpac.com/home.php.

[99] "Advisory Opinion 2011-11," (*Federal Elections Commission*, June 30, 2011), http://www.colbertsuperpac.com/advisory/Advisory-Opinion.pdf.

[100] For photo of Ham Rove and the story of his demise, accessed March 28, 2014, see: http://www.colbertsuperpac.com.

inaccurate in its acts can quickly make the official look elitist, silly, or even stupid. Deleting them is one way that politicians used to quickly remedy a regretted tweet. There used to be a Website called Polit-woops[101] that would find the deleted tweets and post them for all to see. The U.S. version is no longer active, but other countries are still represented.

Because social media can create or escalate a crisis, it can also be used to reduce the severity of the impact on one's political career. The crisis management plan needs to take into consideration these online tools and be ready to respond especially when the politician in out of town. Privacy settings and community guidelines on your social media accounts need to be checked and to ensure that they were implemented. When it comes to social media platforms, these community guidelines help prevent them from being perceived as Free Speech Zones. Separation of personal social media accounts and official social media accounts is also important and the official and staff should be aware of which one they are using at all times. Every outbound message from the politician's office needs to be reviewed and approved before posting online. You should understand who may be posting/tweeting on the politi-cian's behalf—who has the authority and the social media account password? Having the right policies, procedures, and plans in place for the official use of social media for political purposes is extremely important, but make sure they are communicated with the entire staff. A good rule of thumb is "if you mistweet, misfire, or misrepresent, then take the time to think of an appropriate response and acknowl-edge, apologize, and be authentic."[102]

Understand that a tweet can become a "sound bite trap" repeated and retweeted and because it is only 140 characters or less, most times taken out of context. An elected official's emails and posts become part of the public record. Record retention laws needs to be complied with. Twitter has donated all of its tweets to the Library of Congress.

Another concern for politicians and use social media are open meeting laws. For example, if three candidates/politicians answer a Facebook post on the same page; does that constitute a meeting and fall under Sunshine Laws with reporting and disclosure requirements? The verdict is not clear yet.

A couple of good reference videos that explore more issues for politicians are:

- A Politician's Guide to Social Media: http://www.youtube.com/watch?v=dlIhwydXKZ4
- Social Networking is Revolutionizing Politics: http://www.youtube.com/watch?v=9DtTTB-Njgk

DIGITAL ADVOCACY

According to the Merriam-Webster dictionary, advocacy is "the act or process of supporting a cause or proposal."[103] Online and social media platforms have brought this process to the digital age and has led to an upsurge in grassroots advocacy that has collapsed governments and emboldened revolutions. These online technologies, easily accessible via mobile devices such as tablets and smart phones, have led to increased citizen empowerment and participation expanding who is included in political debates and discussions. We have all borne witness to the Arab Spring, the revolutions in Syria and Egypt, and the recent hostile confrontations between citizens and the military in Venezuela. However, I think it is

---

[101] Politwoops, accessed March 28, 2014, http://www.politwoops.com.

[102] "Social Media Marketing Mistakes—Corporate Tweets Gone Wild," SYNND, (April 7, 2011), http://synnd.com/blog/social-media-marketing/social-media-marketing-mistakes-corporate-tweets-gone-wild/.

[103] "Advocacy," accessed March 28, 2014, Merriam-Webster: http://www.merriam-webster.com/dictionary/advocacy.

important to note that these technologies were tools used by courageous and inspired individuals who had a cause to support and a mission to fulfill, whether ousting a president or seeking justice for past injuries, and were not the reason the revolutions came about or even succeeded.[104] But they had their role in the process.

Digital advocacy is not just for revolutions. It is also used throughout the developed world to make politicians and other citizens aware of current issues and where citizens stand on them. It has given many a voice to express their concerns and to request accountability and answers to questions from those who they voted in and supposedly have the answers (see Box for more discussion). That accountability has taken on a digital form in various Websites that watchdog organizations have created, monitor and update to keep the citizenry informed:

- Politifact.com
- Ballotpedia.org
- LegiScan.com
- Votesmart.org
- Ontheissues.org

INDUSTRY PROFILE: HAFEZ ADEL

Chief Executive Officer Alpine Vapor

How do you define advocacy in today's digital world?

Digital advocacy can take many forms, arguably more forms than traditional, "offline" advocacy can. On one end of the spectrum, digital advocacy can manifest itself as blogging about a particular topic, participating in online discussion forums, and sharing content through social media. On the other end of the spectrum, we see activities that are much more closely linked to effecting change, such as fundraising, petition drives, letter-writing campaigns, boycotts, and voter mobilization efforts. The contemporary digital landscape allows people of all engagement levels to participate, from the casual "slacktivists" to the die-hard ideologues.

How does digital/technology affect advocacy?

The principal contribution that the Internet and technology have made to the field of advocacy is enabling people to connect around common causes despite distance. Prior to the Internet, it was extraordinarily difficult for activists around the world to rally around a common cause, let alone to do so quickly or at scale. However, the Internet has made geography irrelevant—it's just as easy for two people from Canada and Kansas to participate in a dialogue as it is for two people who live next to each other. Particularly in countries that lack a well-defined or free public sphere, the ability to transcend one's locale and join a global community is very powerful.

At the same time, the Internet and all other forms of technology are ultimately just mediums through which people can express themselves. Although some mediums can help facilitate dialogue and action better than others (imagine if the protestors in Egypt had to rely on regular mail instead of the Internet to organize their protests), they are ultimately just tools. Technology can enable effective advocacy, and one can argue that having the right tools are necessary for a social movement to gain traction, but they are not sufficient on their own.

Is social media a good thing for advocacy? Why or why not?

Social media has several benefits for activists. One is the ability to organize on an ad-hoc basis, which wasn't very easy to do prior to the advent of Internet, particularly not across great distances. But now, an event can take place and less than 30 min later you might see a Facebook Group with over 100,000 members united around a common cause. Second, the sharing-centric nature of social media makes it a good medium for propagating advocates' messages. A well-executed

---

[104] David Wolman, "Facebook, Twitter Help the Arab Spring Blossom," *Wired* (April 16, 2013), http://www.wired.com/magazine/2013/04/arabspring/.

INDUSTRY PROFILE: HAFEZ ADEL—Cont'd

social media campaign can help a message spread far and wide very quickly organically and with little to no capital investment required.

Yet social media is not an unequivocal boon to advocacy. For one thing, social media has made it very easy to feel like you're contributing to a cause, when in reality you're not doing much at all. This is where the label "slacktivist" comes from. Posting a link to Invisible Children's KONY 2012 video on your Facebook feed doesn't make you an activist, it doesn't count as "doing your part," and yet some people may feel like it does. Social media has dramatically lowered the barriers of entry for activism, but that also means that it's made it possible for people to have very superficial interactions with a cause that are unlikely to have any real impact.

If you were to make one 140-character statement about social media and advocacy, what would you tweet?

"Twitter isn't enough to topple tyrants, but it's a good place to start the conversation."

Any last comment you want people to know about social media and advocacy?

Be wary of virality. Things that go viral quickly tend to fizzle out just as quickly as well. If you're deeply passionate about a cause, focus on nurturing a movement over the long-term, instead of securing a quick public relations win via some social media stunt. If you don't want your cause to suffer the same fate as other fads, make sustainability your goal, not spectacle.

DIGITAL LOBBYING

The Internet has radically altered the lobbying arsenal.[105]

Transparency is essential in the use of social media and online tools in the political sphere. Cynicism runs rampant when it comes to politicians, however. Many are also suspicious of the lobbying that goes on in Washington, perceived as a culture of influence shrouded in secrecy and clandestine meetings full of financial exchanges consisting of perks and pork. At its core lobbying is really just "the process of influencing public and government policy at all levels: federal, state, and local."[106] Sounds a bit like advocating except lobbying's ultimate function is to influence legislation not just an attitude. Lobbying is not new and has been occurring in Washington for as long as Congress has been passing laws.

President Obama's administration has issued a number of restrictions to regulate official lobbying by registered lobbying organizations and individual lobbyists. However, social media and online platforms have added a level of complexity to the lobbying issue. According to Thomas B Edsall, "lobbyists and their lawyers are capitalizing on arcane gaps in regulatory guidelines. For example, constricted definitions of lobbying contained in Congressional regulations have been construed to exempt from disclosure money spent on grass roots mobilization; on television, digital and social media campaigns; and on public relations efforts to build support among voters and key elites."[107] So any spending or activities done to "lobby" for or against a legislative initiative are hidden from public view—no

---

[105] Thomas B. Edsall, "The Shadow Lobbyist," (The New York Times, April 23, 2013), http://opinionator.blogs.nytimes.com /2013/04/25/the-shadow-lobbyist/?_php=true&_type=blogs&_r=0.

[106] "Lobbying," The Legal Dictionary, accessed March 28, 2014, http://legal-dictionary.thefreedictionary.com/Lobbying.

[107] Thomas B. Edsall, "The Shadow Lobbyist," (The New York Times, April 23, 2013), http://opinionator.blogs.nytimes.com/ 2013/04/25/the-shadow-lobbyist/?_php=true&_type=blogs&_r=0.

transparency. This has led to a move of lobbying activities to "digital technology to mobilize and direct public and elite opinion."[108]

Digital lobbying has also expanded who is employing lobbyists and bringing technology issues to the forefront of Congressional awareness. In 2012, two Internet-centric lobbying groups were created: The Internet Infrastructure Coalition (i2Coalition) consisting of data centers, cloud computing companies and domain registrants, and The Internet Association consisting of the top names in the online world such as Google, Facebook, Amazon, Expedia, and others. Although the i2Coalition wants to educate lawmakers about the workings of the Internet and push for policies to grow and develop the Internet infrastructure industry, The Internet Association is "dedicated to advancing public policy solutions to strengthen and protect Internet freedom, foster innovation and economic growth and empower users."[109]

RISK AND SECURITY OF ONLINE POLITICS

Besides what's been outlined here, risk managers and security professionals need to know if their company is engaging in any kind of political activities in the online and social media environment via the use of company equipment, the company network, or even their personal mobile devices. These activities can affect a company's reputation as well as be in violation of certain compliance regulations. For example a nonprofit designated as a 501(c) (3) cannot solicit donations for a political candidate or engage in certain political activities. Companies are also limited in how much and how they can contribute to a political campaign. In addition, if a company takes a certain stance on a hotly debated issue, it may become a target of a hacktivist attack by a group wanting to make a political statement and in the act costing the company substantial resources in terms of time and money to remediate the problem. If you are an information technology, risk, or security professional for a government, elected official, politician, or other politically related party, understanding that the risk of being targeted and successfully attacked is increased simply because of the nature of the industry will allow you to be prepared and implement appropriate security controls as well as security and risk management training and awareness campaigns for those involved. The potential for political scandals and mishaps will always exist because politics is very divisive, but social media and online platforms can be a dual-edged sword in making it secure and minimizing risk.

---

[108] Ibid.

[109] Internet Association, accessed March 28, 2014, http://internetassociation.org.

DIGITAL SUCCESSION

One of the things we often miss in succession planning is that it should be gradual and thoughtful, with lots of sharing of information and knowledge and perspective, so that it's almost a non-event when it happens
Anne M. Mulcahy[1]

I tell my clients that the worst business mistake you can make is to stop breathing; therefore, take care of your health and yourself. The worst business mistake a company can make today is to have its systems stop breathing as so much of what a business does today is dependent on those bits and bytes and

---

[1] "Succession Quotes," Brainy Quote, accessed April 6, 2014, http://www.brainyquote.com/quotes/keywords/succession.html#QZdtfiSLhvFyDdHD.99.

the pathways they create for communicating to clients, employees, vendors, and government. So we need to take care of them. We need to protect them. We need to make sure they are up to par to ensure that the breathing does not stop—hence the increase in priority of security and risk management of our technology. But the technology is only one component of the three-part information technology (IT) system—hardware, software, peopleware. We create specifications and maintenance plans for the hardware, such as when components need to be replaced. Software should be upgraded when available to ensure that any bugs that were discovered before are fixed. Of course, there is the caution of being aware of the upgrades themselves as they may possess a flaw. One pet peeve I have is how many times my iPhone apps need to be upgraded. I am glad the app developers continue to enhance their apps, but sometimes I feel they released the app too early without doing testing and therefore so much time is wasted in upgrade after upgrade. On the other hand, it may just be a sign of the times I am from when upgrades were few and far between.

Peopleware is a different matter. People do not come with automatic upgrade notices indicating they need additional training and a lot of their capacity or status is hidden beneath the surface for a variety of reasons such as job insecurity, personal issues, personality traits, etc. In addition, we are speaking of a very particular type of peopleware—security professionals. In Chapter 4, we described the recruitment and employment cycle of employees and delved a bit into the growing concern that there are not enough security professionals to go around. In this chapter, we will discuss an additional concern, once you have them, what happens when you lose them? Another truism making the rounds in the security field seems to be that not only will you get hacked and but the odds are you will also lose your security pros—the shortage means that those professionals who are at the top of their field do not want for opportunities at other companies and are often tempted and/or stolen away. Because "security is a critical role that must be performed well for companies to succeed"[2] ensuring you have the right security employees ensures that you will have business continuity: "the capability of the organization to continue delivery of products or services at acceptable predefined levels following a disruptive incident." (Source: ISO 22301:2012).[3] The disruptive incident in this case is losing the qualified security personnel.

So one way to look at mitigating the risk of not having the right people in the right place when that incident occurs or to even prevent the incident from occurring in the first place is to recognize the importance of succession planning by rephrasing it as strategic workforce development. According to Barbara Koster, chief information officer of Prudential Financial: "You need to make sure the company is always prepared and protected and that it feels very confident that you have it covered."[4]

At one level the risk is losing critical employees from death, illness, incapacity, disaster, resignation, and/or retirement. For example, "so many baby boomers and homeland security leaders who stepped forward immediately after 9/11 will be retiring during the next five years,"[5] leaving a large skills and knowledge gap. The security field is also so specialized. In addition, the new kinds of security threats

---

[2] "Modern HR in the Cloud," Oracle, accessed April 6, 2014, http://www.oracle.com/us/media1/building-critical-talent-wp-1676598.pdf.

[3] Liz Gasiorowski-Denis, "ISO publishes new standard for business continuity management" (ISO, June 5, 2012), http://www.iso.org/iso/news.htm?refid=Ref1587.

[4] Cara Garretson, "Succession planning for IT: Get some depth to your bench" (ComputerWorld, September 28, 2010), http://www.computerworld.com/s/article/9187805/Succession_planning_for_IT_Get_some_depth_to_your_bench.

[5] Sandi Edwards, "Succession planning and leadership training for a new generation of homeland security professionals" (Government Security News, July 17, 2012), http://www.gsnmagazine.com/node/26777.

require more than just technical skills, but a combination of IT and people skills, including being able to communicate with diverse audiences from C-Suite executives to computer help assistants. Merck Chief Security Officer (CSO) Bob Moore puts it succinctly: "Security is driven by the social and political realms as well as economics, and you have to have those different skills. Security professionals, in addition to being specialists, have to be generalists with special skills.[6]

The other level is losing critical positions in the risk management and security departments. This manifests itself in resource allocation whether financially (i.e., salaries, professional training) or time— with so many things to take care of succession planning is not a top priority. One reason for this is that the perception and reality of cybersecurity risk and protection in corporate America are not aligned. According to the 2014 Global State of Information Security Survey conducted by Price Waterhouse Coopers and CSO Online,[7] executives are confident that their security programs are effective. The study also found that "respondents with C-level and officer job titles were more optimistic on readiness than respondents with lower job titles" partly because "executives believe that they have hired the right management team, and they in turn have hired the right people to manage security risk."[8] Add to that that most security surveys show an increase in security spending in the past few years, a trend likely to continue, so more money means better protection, right? These three factors combined with an optimism bias that a data breach will not happen to them, lead companies to have a false sense of confidence in their security measures and therefore, security succession planning is already taken care of or not likely to impact the bottom line.

But those in the trenches know that perceptions, which may be important for job security when in front of the board of directors, eventually break apart when faced with reality. So the risk mitigation strategy is being prepared with a new generation or pool of security professionals trained and ready to take the mantle and ensure business continuity when the inevitable loss occurs.

SUCCESSION PLANNING

Grooming the next generation of CSOs requires a substantial investment of time, a sincere interest in employee development and a dash of humility.[9]

Developing and implementing a succession plan takes time, a scarce resource for any security professional, but especially those in leadership positions. This is an area where human resources, IT, and security departments can work together for although specific IT and security positions require different skills, there are overlaps and it is important not to assume there will not be any value in evaluating talent from related departments.

---

[6] Daintry Duffy, "Succession Planning for Security Departments" (CSO, June 1, 2004), http://www.csoonline.com/article/219124/succession-planning-for-security-departments.

[7] "The Global State of Security Survey 2014," *PWC*, accessed April 6, 2014, http://www.pwc.com/gx/en/consulting-services/information-security-survey/download.jhtml.

[8] Sonali Shah, "Cyber Security Risk: Perception versus Reality in Corporate America," *Wired* (March 10, 2014), http://www.wired.com/insights/2014/03/cyber-security-risk-perception-vs-reality-corporate-america/.

[9] See note 6.

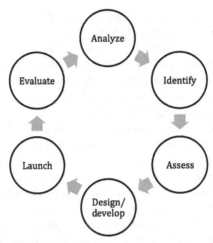

FIGURE 9.1 The Succession Planning Cycle.

The Succession Planning Cycle (Figure 9.1) is similar to the Employment Cycle from Chapter 4. The main goal is also similar—the right talent in the right position. The added element in the Succession Planning Cycle is one of timing and the focus is on preparation for when an incident may occur.

The first step is analyzing the company's current and future challenges and goals in terms of its business objectives as well as its security and risk objectives. These should be aligned so that top levels of management will understand the correlation and be more willing to approve spending in this arena.

The next step is to identify key positions and critical current and future competencies that are required for success in achieving those goals and objectives identified in the first step.

The third step then requires you to assess current and future "bench" strength and determine where are the gaps that need to be filled. The term "bench" is borrowed form the sports arena. You need not only team members out on the field, but others on the bench that you can depend on when it is necessary to have replacements. A talent inventory can be useful as well as be a component of a larger talent management program. Do not forget to identify some for your "virtual bench." These are individuals who may not even be on the company payroll yet, but could add significant talent capital.

Once the talent is identified a succession-training program is designed and developed usually with targeted growth plans for each candidate that was identified as talent to be developed. Talent management programs are on the market to help identify the gaps of the candidate, set targeted strategies and goals for the candidate and monitor how candidates progress through talent dashboards (see Talent management software/apps). These applications become an integral part of the succession-training program.

The launch of the succession program is an important part of the process as it can set the tone for the program by emphasizing the importance (or lack of importance) given by top management to the succession plan and therefore convey how much value, time and resources employees should commit to it. Some tips to successful program launches include piloting the program with a few candidates to work out the bugs, asking for influential endorsements by key executives, ensuring the right incentives and the monitoring of those incentives are in place, decide on the appropriate timing window to launch so it will not get loss in noise or other important issues, celebrate successes and announce them so others can see the program is working, brand the program so it is memorable, and ask for feedback from the participants.

The last step follows the request for feedback. Evaluating the program to see if it is meeting the goals laid out in the succession plan and then adjusting the program when required is necessary and should be continuous. These programs and plans do not always work exactly they way they were laid out the first time around and lessons learned along the way will be constant and revealing. In addition, sometimes the results are not what was intended, such as when a candidate is trained and groomed and then is offered a better position at another company. Was the program and money wasted on that person? Not necessarily so, as those who go away may eventually come back when the company has a new opportunity for them.

The very last step (not even on the diagram) is when the turnover occurs and the succession plan is now reality. There is always a risk that the candidate may fail at the last minute from pressure or any number of other reasons. One reason for the failure may be that the candidate does not have sufficient C-level management support during the critical transition period. Another may be that he or she is not as prepared as they should be to take the reins. This has occurred in situations where a candidate becomes overconfident in that he or she has the position in question during the program and so have not dedicated the time and resources required to learn all he or she should have. For this reason, some managers do not give guarantees to the candidates about future positions and keep a little competition in the mix to keep them on their toes.[10]

TALENT MANAGEMENT SOFTWARE/APPS

Oracle Taleo Succession Planning Cloud Service: http://www.oracle.com/us/products/applications/taleo/enterprise/succession-planning/overview/index.html

Peoplefluent Succession Planning Software: http://www.peoplefluent.com/succession-planning-software

Peoplefluent Mobile Talent Management for iPad: http://www.peoplefluent.com/mobile-talent-management

WorkDay Talent Management: http://www.workday.com/applications/human_capital_management/talent_management.php

Snap Eval (iOS, iPad, Android, Free)
By Snap Eval
http://snapeval.com

Infor Talent Manager (iOS, Free)
Infor Global Solutions, Inc.
https://itunes.apple.com/us/app/infor-talent-manager/id536305846?mt=8
Allows you to extend your existing Infor Talent Management application (10.0.2.22 or higher) on your mobile device

HR Management (iOS, iPad, Free)
By Smart Media Innovations Pty Ltd
https://itunes.apple.com/us/app/hr-management-informing-people/id483485568?mt=8

Cornerstone Mobile (iOS, iPad, Free)
By Cornerstone On Demand
https://itunes.apple.com/us/app/cornerstone-mobile/id518441871?mt=8
http://www.cornerstoneondemand.com/global-business/talent-management/learning-management-cloud/mobile

---

[10] A great resource for succession planning can be found at: "Succession Planning," *Entrepreneur*, accessed April 6, 2014, http://www.entrepreneur.com/topic/succession-planning#.

INFORMATION TECHNOLOGY SECURITY SHORTAGE

40 Percent of essential IT security jobs go unfilled.[11]

A TEKsystems Network Services October 2013 survey indicated that "half of the respondents believe the lack of qualified security talent is approaching a state of critical mass where their organizations are vulnerable to serious risk exposure.[12] This echoes the quote at the beginning of this section. The message is "we need more security professionals."

There is a high cost for not having enough security people in place: access by hackers and data breaches, loss of money and consumer trust, penalties for compliance violations, and in some countries, prison time.

There are a number of reasons for the shortage—retirement of a generation of security professionals (baby boomers) because of their age as mentioned previously is one of them. This leads to the question of their replacements. Can we get enough of youth interested in pursuing careers in computer security? We discuss this issue more later. Another cause for the shortage is the requirement for a broad range of skills (see Required skills for information security professionals). Daniel Benjamin, Dean of the School of Science, Technology, Education and Math for American Public University System, states "Cybersecurity is a diverse field... (it) encompasses the technical side of information security and network architecture security and then it expands out into everything from emergency management and criminal justice to homeland security."[13]

REQUIRED SKILLS FOR INFORMATION SECURITY PROFESSIONALS

- Change management skills
- Ability to influence
- Build coalition
- Critical thinking
- Problem solving
- Managerial ability
- Emotional intelligence
- Creativity and innovation
- Strategy execution
- Strategy development[14]
- Fitting in with the organizational culture
- Cultural sensitivity and fitting have to be married with the political and business savvy[15]
- Ability for financial analysis
- Linking security work to strategic objectives of the company—need to learn to talk money
- Right communication skills—comfortable with speaking with the top

---

[11] Neil J. Rubenking, "RSAC: Shortage of Trained IT Security Experts 'A National Security Crisis'," SecurityWatch (February 25, 2014), http://securitywatch.pcmag.com/security/321074-rsac-shortage-of-trained-it-security-experts-a-national-security-crisis.

[12] "Study Reveals Shortage of IT Security Talent Equals Abundance Of Risk," *InformationWeek DarkReading* (October 20, 2013), http://www.darkreading.com/management/study-reveals-shortage-of-it-security-ta/240162859?goback=%2Egde_37 008_member_5798090843084578818#%21.

[13] Leischen Stelter, "Educating the Next Generation of Cybersecurity Professionals" (HStoday, October 18, 2013), http://www.hstoday.us/blogs/guest-commentaries/blog/educating-the-next-generation-of-cybersecurity-professionals/ae3de475f0f d8b660032b175d884017c.html.

REQUIRED SKILLS FOR INFORMATION SECURITY PROFESSIONALS—Cont'd

- Have initiative
- Intelligence Community Skills: intelligence collection and analysis (data exhaust)

Additional requirements: These requirements are from a LinkedIn job classified listing accessed in March 2014. Notice the disparity between the skills listed previously and their more technically specific requirements noted in this actual posting. Many of these are not expressed nor even alluded to. So how do we hire the right people if we are not asking for the right skills up front?

Required Skills

- Ability to successfully interface with clients (internal and external)
- Ability to document and explain technical details in a concise, understandable manner
- Ability to provide training and perform public speaking and be comfortable in front of an audience
- Capable of managing own and team project tasks

Required technical skills

(At least four of the following):

- Strong knowledge of tools used for application testing and network security
- Capable of Perl scripting and shell code scripting to automate common tasks
- Thorough understanding of network protocols
- Mastery of Unix and Windows operating systems
- Forensics analysis experience or aptitude
- Malware analysis experience or aptitude
- Experience developing applications in C#.NET or Java (J2EE)

Education and other requirements

- Bachelor's degree in a technical field
- Minimum 2–5 years of comparable experience; minimum 8 years of experience if no degree
- Must be able to travel frequently and on short notice
- Must be eligible to work in the United States without sponsorship

[14]See note 5.
[15]See note 6.

THE NEXT GENERATION OF INFOSEC PRO

We have to work together to ensure that young people are prepared to use technology safely, securely, ethically and productively and are aware of the interesting and rewarding jobs available protecting the Internet.

Michael Kaiser, executive director, National Cyber Security Alliance[16]

Where do we find the next generation of information security (InfoSec) and risk management professionals? The succession planning cycle above focuses more on grooming for promotion from internal candidates. It looks at how to build pipelines of critical talent and create opportunities for talent mobility within the organization to be able to efficiently and effectively address security needs.

One of the problems of trying to find this next generation is who is responsible to identify and locate them in the first place and then, do they know what to look for? Prudential's Koster describes what

---

[16]"Recruiting the Next Generation of Cybersecurity Professionals," HighTech Highway (November 15, 2013), http://www.hightech-highway.com/secure/recruiting-the-next-generation-of-cybersecurity-professionals/.

Prudential asks its managers to look for: "At Prudential, as part of the company's succession planning and management program, IT and other managers are instructed to look for three types of rising stars: next-generation leaders who currently exhibit the required skills to take the next step into management; emerging leaders who have good technical skills and, with grooming, could become leaders within a few years; and employees who work well with management and in teams – those with soft skills that can grow into full-blown management potential."[17]

If we look at current hiring practices it is common for managers to hire and promote individuals who have similar backgrounds to them in terms of education and experience. This raises the concern of creating "clones" for the succession generation. David Burrill, head of group security for British Tobacco, believes this could lead to a handicap in terms of finding solutions for new and adaptive malicious threats: "If everyone is trained the same way and everyone agrees with each other, then nobody is going to ask the rogue questions."[18]

But whether the search is within the company's offices or outside the company's walls, the shortage concern highlights that we need to go earlier in the educational pipeline, before the career lifecycle begins, to spark the interest of a younger generation to pursue opportunities in the InfoSec sector. If we do not begin early enough with them to prepare them we will not have a pool from which to select from and groom for the front line of cybersecurity defense and less so for the next level of security leadership. American and Global corporations are not alone in this concern. Governments especially see the need and are developing initiatives to help mitigate this security risk of not enough hands on deck. Preparing these future cyberdefenders is now a national security priority.

Some examples of current programs include:

- *Science, Technology, Engineering and Mathematics (STEM) Programs*—from elementary grades to postdoctoral degrees incentives to get students interested in pursuing educational and job opportunities in STEM are being emphasized. On September 16, 2010, President Obama declared "… Leadership tomorrow depends on how we educate our students today—especially in science, technology, engineering and math."[19] His 2015 budget includes $170 million in new funding for STEM education initiatives that cover student programs in the schools through the Department of Education and teacher preparation in the STEM disciplines in collaboration with institutions of higher education. Various states and private foundations have also developed innovative STEM programs and scholarship grants as incentives to encourage learning and work in these areas.
- *Lockheed Martin*—Cyber Security Awareness Day (Maryland) high schoolers[20]
- *National Security Agency (NSA) and Department of Homeland Security* are reviewing and designating schools as National Centers of Academic Excellence in Information Assurance or Cyber Defense.[21]
- *U.S. Cyber Challenge*—According to its mission, U.S. Cyber Challenge works with the cybersecurity community to bring accessible, compelling programs that motivate students and

---

[17] See note 4.

[18] See note 6.

[19] "Science, Technology, Engineering and Math: Education for Global Leadership" (U.S. Department of Education), accessed April 6, 2014, http://www.ed.gov/stem.

[20] See note 16.

[21] "National Centers of Academic Excellence," *National Security Agency*, accessed April 6, 2014, http://www.nsa.gov/ia/academic_outreach/nat_cae/.

professionals to pursue education, development, and career opportunities in cybersecurity.[22] Programs include competitions, cybercamps, sponsorship, virtual community building, etc.

- *r00tz Asylum* (formerly DEFCON Kids)—dedicated to teaching kids around the world how to love being white-hat hackers.[23] Part of the education they instill is a set of core values and rules to govern the kid's hacking activities. Values include: Only do good, always do your best, constantly improve, innovate, think long-term, be positive, visualize it, have fun, inspire others, and go big. This is a good list for all IT, security, and risk management professionals to keep in mind. The rules are pretty straightforward as well: only hack things you own, do not hack anything you rely on, respect the rights of others, know the law and the possible risk and consequences for breaking it, and find a safe playground.
- *Crypto Kids*—sponsored by the NSA and Central Security Service, this site provides children with a trove of resources, games, and activities to teach them about cryptography and coding.[24]

In Chapter 4, we spoke a little about the challenges of managing millennials and having millennials as managers. However, we need to keep in mind that these future defenders are not millennials. On a 2014 "Daily Show,"[25] host Jon Stewart was interviewing Paul Taylor, the executive vice president of special projects at the Pew Research Center and the author of the book *The Next America: Boomers, Millennials, and the Looming Generational Showdown* (2014). At one point Paul and Jon wondered about who comes after the millennials? What will that generation be called and how will they change our world? According to a number of sources, they are being identified as "Generation Z," "Generation V" (for virtual), "Generation C" (for community or content), "The New Silent Generation," the "Internet Generation,", or even the "Google Generation," among others.[26] Unfortunately, we do not know much about this generation yet in terms of how they will be as future workers and leaders, but we do know about the environment they are growing up in—highly technical, media sophistication, diverse in a number of different factors from culture to socioeconomic background, and intimately connected with people and devices. Working with this generation while they are young will bring insight into how to prepare them for future security work.

Having secured the pool of future security defenders, we need to address the risk of not having leadership in place that can effectively manage this generational talent pool. If companies are looking to groom and promote from within then retention of key talent must be looked on as a risk mitigation strategy. Understanding what motivates an employee to stay with a company is to understand what they value, financially and beyond. For those in IT and security being given interesting and challenging projects achieves a dual purpose, it improves skill level while also demonstrating a confidence (trust) factor in their ability to get the job done. Recognition is an important motivator when we remember that most millennials want to feel they are contributing in a significant way. Retention can also be a matter of how much support and training in the latest technologies an employee receives. This can include

---

[22] "Our Mission," US Cyber Challenge, accessed April 6, 2014, http://www.uscyberchallenge.org/our-mission/.

[23] "Honor Code," rootz, accessed April 6, 2014, http://www.r00tz.org/about/.

[24] "CryptoKids® America's Future Codemakers & Codebreakers," *National Security Agency*, accessed April 6, 2014, http://www.nsa.gov/kids/home_html.shtml.

[25] "Paul Taylor," The Daily Show, aired March 10, 2014, accessed April 6, 2014,, http://www.thedailyshow.com/watch/mon-march-10-2014/paul-taylor.

[26] "List of Generations Chart," Isacosta's site, accessed April 6, 2014, http://www.esds1.pt/site/images/stories/isacosta/secondary_pages/10°_block1/Generations%20Chart.pdf.

conferences, workshops, webinars, seminars, fees, and/or travel expenses. It can also take the form of an allotted amount for books, e-books, journals, magazines, and/or other educational and reference material access.

One other retention strategy is to understand where employees would like to see their career go eventually and to match that with a career path in the organization. The conundrum may be that a career path does not exist in the organization. This could be a temporary situation that may be changed with an upcoming retirement or changing of the guard, or a more permanent one based on strategic planning of the security operations in the company. It is important to identify what is a feasible option and what is not. You do not want to use the carrot approach if the carrot will never materialize—that will frustrate the employee who can use it as an incentive to leave period.

Security leaders need to understand that their job is a combination of technical capability, policy making, and an emerging regulatory environment."[27] You hear often of the specialized training required for each of these areas, but when we look at developing leaders in these areas I suggest we look outside the realm of training. In a very interesting *Forbes* article, Mike Myatt takes a look at why so many leadership training programs fail. For Mike the cause is simple. You can't train a leader. You need to develop him. "Training presumes the need for indoctrination on systems, processes and techniques. Moreover, training assumes that said systems, processes and techniques are the right way to do things. The solution to the leadership training problem is to scrap it in favor of development. Don't train leaders, coach them, mentor them, disciple them, and develop them. Development is nuanced, contextual, collaborative, fluid, and above all else, actionable."[28] An example of a nuanced development strategy is described by Merck CSO Bob Moore, who sends particular leadership candidates to lead particular projects—outside the United States. "I'll get an assessment of who adapted better to working in a non-U.S. environment and how they dealt with jet lag, language issues, the vagaries of international travel and business. You have to do these things to give them a 360-degree view of the world and the company. They won't get that unless they get out there and mix with other regions and people."[29] Dennis Aebersold, vice president for IT and chief information officer at the University of Oklahoma, is in agreement. "Future leaders are passionate and hungry to learn more—and not just about technology. These are people who constantly expand their experiences and are not afraid to step outside of their comfort zone."[30]

But there are some skills that are required as a foundation for leaders. Consider also that there is a school of thought that emphasizes that people learn in different ways—cognitive, kinetic, etc. Some individuals need an official form of education with the classroom and a set schedule to help manage and integrate the new knowledge into their already hectic lives. One example is the International Security Management Association (ISMA) Leadership Course at Georgetown University. According to the program description: "This program is an intensive executive education and management development seminar developed six years ago by ISMA in partnership with Georgetown University. Taught and certified by Georgetown, the program is designed to prepare the next generation of Security Directors for the strategic challenges ahead. The program spans a one-year period of time and includes three phases—two sessions

---

[27] See note 13.
[28] Mike Myatt, "The #1 Reason Leadership Development Fails," *Forbes* (December 19, 2012), http://www.forbes.com/sites/-mikemyatt/2012/12/19/the-1-reason-leadership-development-fails/.
[29] See note 6.
[30] See note 4.

of classroom instruction in Washington D.C., and one session of independent study. Eleven classes, comprised of a total of 500+security executives, have graduated from the program."[31]

WOMEN IN INFOSEC

It's important that women in the field encourage other women, but it would also be nice if more men were involved in this encouragement, to make women feel welcomed in a field that is supposed to be a 'man's world.'[32]

In 2014 Hewlett Packard announced that it would finance a scholarship program. Scholarship for Women Studying Information Security, up to $250,000. Why would they specifically devote this money to women? Julie Talbot-Hubbard, vice president and CSO, Symantec, has her perspective: "It is evident today that women in the information security profession are greatly underrepresented. We need to recognize the strengths that women bring, such as their diverse academic backgrounds and differentiated skill sets, and make training more widely accessible to encourage more women to pursue this career path."[33]

Along with Hewlett Packard are a number of associations and special interest groups focusing on women in security (and more generally women in technology) to encourage women to enter the field, and then to offer educational opportunities and support to help them more up the career path once they are in it (see Women in security groups/organizations).

But not everyone is in agreement about a gender bias in the InfoSec field. Some notable senior women in InfoSec believe that it should not be about gender, it should be about skills. Sheena Wallace, lead security consultant at Context Information Security, stated: "I'm not sure that there should be a requirement for external bodies to encourage or influence in either direction. As long as there is not active discouragement—which I have never observed—then women [should be] left to make their own minds up as to which industry would best suit them."[34]

This opens up the question of other reasons why women do not enter this industry. One argument is that the industry is competitive not collaborative, which is more the way women tend to work. Another one is that the industry is not welcoming to those seeking a balance between work and personal life so if a woman makes a choice to have a family she risks losing the position of authority or "clout" she may have had before she left. A third argument is the "girl versus boy" argument. "Girls can't do it." "Girls won't like it." Many of these arguments are continuously reinforced through mainstream and digital media, such as movies, advertisements, etc. At Super Bowl 2014, GoldieBlox,[35] a tech start-up that creates engineering toys for girls, offered up an advertising campaign to counter these images. The commercial, which to a catchy tune

---

[31] "Conferences," International Security Management Association (ISMA), accessed April 6, 2014, https://isma.com/activities.

[32] Konstantinia Charitoudi, part-time lecturer and security consultant at the University of South Wales, and PhD researcher in information security, quoted in: Eleanor Dallaway, "Let's Hear it for the Ladies: Women in Information Security," Infosecurity (October 17, 2013), http://www.infosecurity-magazine.com/view/35127/lets-hear-it-for-the-ladies-women-in-information-security-/.

[33] "Agents of Change: Women in the Information Security Profession," Frost & Sullivan, https://www.isc2cares.org/uploadedFiles/wwwisc2caresorg/Content/Women-in-the-Information-Security-Profession-GISWS-Subreport.pdf (accessed April 6, 2014).

[34] Eleanor Dallaway, "Let's Hear it for the Ladies: Women in Information Security," *Infosecurity* (October 17, 2013), http://www.infosecurity-magazine.com/view/35127/lets-hear-it-for-the-ladies-women-in-information-security-/.

[35] Kaye Toal, "Aren't toys for everyone?" Goldie Blox (April 1, 2014), http://blog.goldieblox.com.

told girls to "ditch their toys and make some noise," certainly did that on its own, bringing the controversy to light and serving as a catalyst for office discussions and reflection.[36]

GoldieBlox was started in 2012 by Reshma Saujani, who founded the national nonprofit organization Girls Who Code to teach teenage girls computing skills to pursue twenty-first century opportunities and close the gender gap in technology. The GoldieBlox engineering sets allow girls to invent and build and then share their inventions with other girls, each supporting and encouraging each other. This is a far cry from Mattel's fiasco with its talking Barbie in 1992 that once said "Math class is tough."[37]

WOMEN IN SECURITY GROUPS/ORGANIZATIONS

Women in International Security
  http://wiisglobal.org/wordpress1/
  With more than 7000 members in 47 countries, Women in International Security remains the only global network actively advancing women's leadership, at all stages of their careers, in international peace and security.

Women in Security Working Group: ASIS
  https://www.asisonline.org/Membership/Networking-Groups/Women-in-Security/Pages/default.aspx
  Our mission is to provide support and assistance to women in the security field as well as inspire those interested in entering the profession. Part of ASIS International the preeminent organization for security professionals, with more than 38,000 members worldwide. Founded in 1955, ASIS is dedicated to increasing the effectiveness and productivity of security professionals by developing educational programs and materials that address broad security interests.
  • ASIS Women in security LinkedIn Group: http://www.linkedin.com/groups/ASIS-Women-in-Security-2431044/about
  • Women in Security: ASIS New York City Chapter: http://asisnyc.org/programs/women-in-security/

Women in Defense, National Security Organization: http://wid.ndia.org
  Cultivating and supporting the advancement and recognition of women in all aspects of national security is the mission of Women In Defense, A National Security Organization. Members of this nonprofit professional organization, which includes men and women, have careers related to the defense of the United States and national security.

Technology Association of Georgia: Women in Technology
  http://www.mywit.org/home
  WIT's goal is to support the entire lifecycle of a woman's career in technology—which benefits both women and men, the economy, and the community at large.

Women in Security ISC[2] London Chapter
  http://www.isc2chapter-london.co.uk/women-in-security
  The mission of the group is to raise the profile of women in the information security industry.

Women Security Society
  https://www.womenssecuritysociety.co.uk
  A society that will foster an inclusive networking and forum environment, bringing women together from all aspects of security. Its aim is to encourage the advancement of women working in today's security world through the exchange of information and creation of collaborative relationships.

NGO Working Group on Women, Peace and Security
  http://www.womenpeacesecurity.org
  Advocates for the equal and full participation of women in all efforts to create and maintain international peace and security. Formed in 2000 to call for a Security Council resolution on Women, Peace and Security, the NGOWG now focuses on implementation of all Security Council resolutions that address this issue.

---

[36] Catherine Shu, "GoldieBlox's Super Bowl Ad is a Counterbalance to Rampant Sexism," *TechCrunch* (February 2, 2014), http://techcrunch.com/2014/02/02/goldieblox-superbowl/.

[37] "COMPANY NEWS: Mattel Says It Erred; Teen Talk Barbie Turns Silent on Math" (The New York Times, October 21, 1992), http://www.nytimes.com/1992/10/21/business/company-news-mattel-says-it-erred-teen-talk-barbie-turns-silent-on-math.html.

How is your company dealing with the gender diversity issue in terms of risk management, IT, and security professionals in all employment levels including senior management?

CYBERSECURITY SIMULATIONS

If you want employees to aspire to be future security leaders, they have to understand the standards and expectations against which they will be judged.[38]

Cybersecurity simulations, exercises, table-tops, and drills are some of the training tools used to keep security professionals prepared in case something happens. They are not always open to the public however. In February 2014, I was able to observe the 2014 Cybersecurity Simulation,[39] a role play event where a C-level, senior management, and practitioner Dream Team came together to repel seven attacks (five cyber, one physical, and one social engineering) on a fictional company. It was the second such open cybersecurity and business continuity event to be held where you did not need "proper security clearances." It was hosted by the Georgia National Guard in Clay, Georgia, but available by live streaming via the Internet. The basic rule and reasoning behind the event was to "share the knowledge" regarding responding to cybersecurity incidents and how to recover from them. The idea was that when incidents happen most companies do not want to have others know about it—regulation requires disclosure but that disclosure can be minimal depending on the final audience being disclosed to. Sharing and discussing what happened and what was done to resolve the incident and prevent it from happening again can lead to learning and cost savings across the board. As the Dream Team dealt with the different attacks, they were confronted with issues regarding public image and reputation risk control, legal and liability issues, technical procedures and policies, and recover and loss options. It was fascinating to watch from a distance the chaos that ensued as each attack was concurrently introduced on top of a preceding one to a management and technical team already overwhelmed with daily operations and a mobile security audit in process.

The day's event began with a morning briefing. Each department of the fictional company gave a brief overview of the key points of their role in regards to cyber-security in the company—in terms of prevention and how they were involved when an attack occurs. The departments highlighted were (in order of appearance) legal, communications and brand management, facilities/business operations, intelligence, and policy. After the briefing, they showed Blue Horizons 2040 YouTube video called "2035 – Welcome to the Age of Surprise" (https://www.youtube.com/watch?v=9Xpu2QqLnHY). The video highlights technological advancements and the security threats they brought in their wake. The afternoon held the 2-h simulation (nerve-wrackingly done with an onscreen timer clicking down the minutes of the allotted time) followed by lessons learned.

Some of the more memorable lessons:

- Attackers will execute on the last thing that worked for them.
- Don't use "hack back" as a strategy if you are not ready for possible escalation.

---

[38] See note 6.

[39] "The Logistics Company (TLC) Scenario," *Technology Association of Georgia*, accessed April 6, 2014, http://cyberexerci ses.com/tag2014/.

- Have a crisis communications plan and have the right people on the crisis team who will actually "do" something.
- When a crisis occurs, the most powerful voice comes from someone *not* associated with the company.
- Privacy is not just a courtesy—data breach notification laws and Federal Trade Commission fair business practices can be triggered by an incident.
- The security of your network is dependent on your weakest employee.
- Keep legal confidential throughout the crisis to protect client-attorney privilege.
- Check your cybersecurity insurance policy and remember that it doesn't necessarily transfer liability but does transfer financial consequences.
- Something as insignificant as a USB to charge a cell phone that has been configured as a WiFi spot can be a breach portal for hackers and cost millions in data and consumer trust loss.
- Keep any hacker investigations separate from lawsuit issues.
- Cooperate with the Federal Bureau of Investigation.
- If a ransom is requested, make sure the currency it is requested in still exists (the simulation occurred the day Mt Gox, the Bitcoin exchange closed its doors—and part of the simulation was that the ransom requested it be paid in Bitcoins).
- Key concern is how quickly can you respond, mitigate and recover—sometimes depends on how quickly you discover you've been attacked.

DIGITAL LEGACY

Forever Online.[40]

On a personal level your digital legacy is the combination of your many points of digital interaction in the online space—including financial accounts, social media accounts, content you posted online, online subscriptions, online photo collections, and more. Do you know the access information to all these accounts? Does your spouse know for the personal accounts and/or does your partner know for the business accounts or will it all be lost when you are no longer around? When you are gone who will inherit your digital property? Do you want to control who does and what they do with it?

It is estimated that most individuals in developed countries will create approximately 88 GB of data in their lifetime. This includes Twitter tweets, Facebook posts, bookmarks, photos, artwork, logos, videos, blogs, and email. It is also estimated that less than 35% of Americans have a will, trust or power of attorney, to take care of their things when they pass. What then will happen to all this digital property? If not prepared for, these digital possessions, expressions, artifacts, become lost, closed down, deleted, or removed. We don't want that because these digital assets chronicle life, history, identity, and wealth. They have value—some financial, some chronological, and some emotional. But value is something *you* want to protect.

---

[40] Sumit Paul-Choudhury, "Forever Online: Your digital Legacy," NewScientist (May 15, 2012), http://www.newscientist.com/special/digital-legacy.

A note of caution—there may be a lot of *you* or your company out there. Consider doing some "curating" of your online presence—both for you and your company. Clean up some of the digital litter now to make it easier for others later. Evan Carroll and John Romano put it nicely in their book, *Your Digital Afterlife*, "the things you value simply may not be valuable to your heirs."

Remember too that this process can help you while you are alive as well—to identify lost accounts, or put all the information in one place for quick reference. Do you know where you are online? Doing the plan may surprise you (see Digital legacy plan).

DIGITAL LEGACY PLAN (PERSONAL)

- Make a list. Inventory all your digital devices, online accounts, subscriptions, etc. Make sure to note name of account, site or company account is with, access codes such as an identification or password, answers to security questions, expiration and renewal dates for domains, etc.
- Review the list and note next to each what you want done with each account when you pass away—should it be deleted, should the password be given to a spouse, should it be converted to a memorial page (such as in Facebook), etc.?
- Review the list a second time and find and read the terms of service for the online accounts. Do they permit the access information to be transferred or not? What do they need to close the account a=or transfer it—such as a death certificate, obituary, etc.
- Think about appointing a Digital Executor and speak with them about what you would like them to do. This can be a lot of responsibility—make sure you select someone you trust, who is technologically savvy, and won't mind the work.
- Review your digital plan with an attorney. Keep in mind that some of your digital property, like your tangible property, may be subject to state laws covering succession and distribution. Just a few states—Oklahoma, Rhode Island, Connecticut, and Idaho—already have specific legislation dealing with online accounts. The rest of the states do not.
- Put the list away in a safe place or use an online service, such as Entrustet or Legacy Locker. Do not put the list in your will, as this becomes a public document after your death and you do not want your passwords available for all to see.
- Keep the list updated with new accounts, disabled or terminated accounts, and changes of passwords.
- Talk to who needs to know about this—your spouse, business partner, child, and/or significant other.

DIGITAL ASSETS

"A rose by any other name" goes Shakespeare's prose—a name is a powerful thing. Label something and you can control it by limiting it based on its definition. You can also expand on its meaning by combining it with other labels. Digital assets are also referred to as: digital artifacts, digital footprint, digital presence, digital property (IP and beyond), digital possessions, digital dirt/clutter/litter, or even online stuff.

SOME DIGITAL ASSET TYPES (PERSONAL)

- Accounts with credit card information (Amazon, Lands End, etc.)
- Adult content accounts
- Airline frequent flyer mile accounts
- Bank and financial accounts
- Business accounts
- Computers, laptops, tablets, and cell phones (technology devices)
- E-bay; Craigslist; iTunes, etc.

- E-mail accounts
- Lifestyle-specific accounts (Ancestry.com, Food.tv, etc.)
- Medical and generic information accounts
- Online and social games (Farmville, WII, Words with Friends, Second Life, WOW)
- Online bill payments systems (including PayPal)
- Photo and video sharing sites (Flickr, Vimeo, YouTube)
- Shared accounts—like Google Docs, DropBox
- Social media accounts
- Voicemail accounts (e.g., Google Voice)

SOME DIGITAL ASSET TYPES (BUSINESS)

- Bank and financial accounts
- Client account systems
- Employee email accounts
- Human resource systems (online)
- Payroll systems (ADP, etc.)
- Procurement/vendor accounts (with company credit card info)

Businesses and corporations also create tons of digital data—from internal sources such as reports to end-user content generated and gathered from their social media forum sites. Who has access to this data and where it is stored in the company? Who knows the account credentials such as user IDs and passwords?

Part of the reason why ownership and access questions are important is because these personal and corporate digital assets have value. When the risk management plan is developed the impact of any risk associated with these assets are based on the value the company believes they have. It needs to be distinguished the value of the digital account versus the value of the content on that account. Companies are currently trying to understand how to manage these digital assets and how to measure their value. For example, will the number of Twitter followers affect the value of a merger and acquisition? If prior security breaches are considered when a buyout of another company is being evaluated, with the same be true of a social media mishap? These questions are starting to show up at the Board of Director meetings.

DIGITAL AFTERLIFE

Let no one weep for me, or celebrate my funeral with mourning; for I still live, as I pass to and fro through the mouths of men.

Quintus Ennius[41]

Ennius was a Roman poet during the Roman Republic (born 239 BC, died 169 BC). He felt his essence would live on through his poetry but his sentiment resonates with our current digital era. One

---

[41] "Quintus Ennius Quotes," BrainyQuote, accessed April 6, 2014, http://www.brainyquote.com/quotes/authors/q/quintus_ennius.html.

thing we are currently learning is that just about anything posted online is almost impossible to delete, remove or erase forever. Part of it is because of the infrastructure of the Internet (which celebrated 25 years in 2014)—decentralized to prevent any one attack from bringing down the entire system. It works with information packets going from server to server, making copies of the packets and caching some of the information before it goes on to the next destination. Add to this the growing habit of individuals who post images and "tag" themselves and their friends with identification information—such as names, locations, dates—and you are no longer in control of a lot of information that is being put online in a public forum about you and your company. We live on through our digital stuff. But is that true for everyone?

The probability of death is 100% for everyone who has been born. The cause of death is what differentiates us. For example, the odds of dying from heart disease—the current leading cause of death—is 1 in 6; cancer that is second is 1 in 7; the odds of dying in a car accident 1 in 98; the odds of dying in a legal execution are 1 in 111,779; and the odds of dying by being struck by lightning is 1 in 124,906.[42] But depending on where you live in the world causes of death can be relative: in Africa hippos kill 2900 people a year, in Russia falling icicles kill over 100 annually, and here in the United States, vending machines kill 10–13 people each year![43]

With the way the laws are written in terms of property and business asset distribution, those in the United States have more control over their assets when they pass away or when their company closes, than in any other country. We have a variety of legal constructs and creative financial and legal instruments that allow property distribution with certain conditions, restrictions, and obligations in place. Lawyers and estate planners affectionally call this "the power of dead hands."

To counterbalance this "power" and to prevent assets being wasted or worst, being unused, a waste in the law's eyes, public interest concerns are weighed against the decedent's wishes. These include: the law against perpetuities (ensures that the property ends up with someone eventually before too much time passes); the wishes should not offend public morality (undue hardships or burdens); and the ultimate disposition of assets should serve the public good (family obligations and charitable trusts). All of these apply as much in the business arena as in the personal, especially with private corporations (such as family businesses) where many of the corporate assets are tightly held by private individuals.

In the online world, it is becoming important to understand that not only tangible real property can be allocated, distributed and/or disposed of, but intangible, digital assets as well. As an overview of what happens online when you die, Life Insurance Finder, an Australian-based business put together an interesting Website with videos and other resources discussing the issue.[44] The Website begins with a discussion about digital privacy after death. Something to keep in mind from a risk and security point of view as so many online social media accounts are being created that are fake and based on deceased individuals. Does your company have a way to filter through its client databases to remove those who are no longer among the living? Does it terminate passwords if an individual has not logged onto the company's system after a certain amount of time (such as 3 or 6 months)? Does the company have a policy and protocol in place to deal with deceased employees, especially senior level executives, in terms of privacy and security controls of their

---

[42] "Injury Facts 2012 Edition," *National Safety Council*, accessed April 6, 2014, http://www.nsc.org/NSC%20Picture%20Library/News/web_graphics/Injury_Facts_37.pdf.

[43] Beverly Jenkins, "10 Incredibly Bizarre Death Statistics," *Oddee* (December 12, 2011), http://www.oddee.com/item_98002.aspx.

[44] "What Happens Online When You Die?" *Life Insurance Finder*, accessed April 6, 2014, http://www.lifeinsurancefinder.com.au/infographics/what-happens-online-when-you-die/.

devices and their company related online accounts? What about if a vendor contact dies? Is there a protocol in place to determine security concerns regarding their access to the company's systems?

Some employees grow into online celebrities or because they are renown in their fields their online presence and the content they generated during their lifetime can be seen as an intellectual asset that contributes to the value of the company or to society as a whole. Different strategies have been implemented to venerate them and preserve their digital contributions. One such method is converting social media accounts to memorial accounts.

The first social media memorial page was created on Facebook by Facebook to memorialize one of their own employees who passed on and they were faced directly with having to decide on what to do with that person's account. Today it is a pretty straightforward process. Go to Facebook's Memorialization Request Page at https://www.facebook.com/help/contact/305593649477238. You can also just Google "Facebook Memorialization Request" or access from a current Facebook account. Once you reach the online form it asks you to fill out certain information to (1) verify the identity of the deceased (full name, url link to Facebook timeline, email address to the account); (2) verify who you are (and your relationship t the deceased); (3) verify that the individual is deceased (year of death and proof of death, such as link to online obituary, etc.).

For security purposes if the Facebook account was an official one for the company, even though it was a personal one for the employee (an example would be a Facebook profile made for an executive but only used for public relations purposes), having a protocol in place to either terminate the account or memorialize, including timing of such a request and who can make it, is important. As anyone (immediate family, extended family or nonfamily) can request the page to be memorialized and once memorialized it's final. Keep in mind as well that nonfamily includes friends, coworkers, classmates, etc. You also do not want to have the account hijacked by a hacker or someone with malicious intent. It is a good risk mitigation strategy to provide information about memorialization and social media accounts, as well as digital afterlife strategies to employees so they are aware of what happens to their digital data once they pass on. Note: to have the account terminated you must be a verified next of kin. For corporate accounts you must prove that the account was of a corporate nature and belongs to the company, but it is a more cumbersome process.

For Twitter, the option is to have the account deactivated. Instructions on how to do that can be found at https://support.twitter.com/articles/87894-contacting-twitter-about-a-deceased-user. Unlike Facebook where a nonfamily individual can make the Memorialization request, Twitter states it can work with only "a person authorized to act on the behalf of the estate or with a verified immediate family member of the deceased." Twitter also does not allow you to submit your request online but instead asks for a number of pieces of information to be faxed or snail-mailed to their offices in San Francisco, California.

LinkedIn does allow you to do most of the request online using a secured e-signature process via docusign.net. The deceased member information link is http://help.linkedin.com/app/answers/detail/a_id/2842/kw/deceased%20member. They are also open to the request coming from a family or nonfamily member, such as a colleague or classmate. LinkedIn asks for the same kind of verification information as Facebook and Twitter but does state that they will review the request and then get back to you.

Google (includes YouTube, gmail, Google Docs) has a different approach then just memorializing the account. One of its pages specifically for YouTube talks about requesting content from a deceased user: https://support.google.com/youtube/answer/3306113?hl=en. YouTube does state this is done only in very rare circumstances and a request is no guarantee. A second page gives instructions if you want to access the deceased person's account directly: https://support.google.com/accounts/answer/2842525?hl=en. I found it interesting that Google highlights the privacy issue in terms of granting access to the account and/or to the content of the deceased. I believe this will become a larger concern later on as people begin to include in their estate planning specific instructions as to what they want their "digital executor" to do with their online and social media accounts.

These are just four of the top online platforms currently in use but there are many others. Here are some resources for you to keep in your digital toolbox in regards to death and online accounts:

- http://www.thedigitalbeyond.com/online-services-list/
- http://www.deceasedaccount.com/
- http://www.nytimes.com/2011/01/09/magazine/09Immortality-t.html?pagewanted=all
- http://www.yourdigitalafterlife.com/

DIGITAL EXPIRATION

We only live once. We all have an expiration date after that we will never come again[45]

The idea of an expiration date for data has led to some interesting innovations in the digital and online fields. It is based on the premise that sometimes we post things online that we regret later or are embarrassed about. With the current infrastructure of the Internet, it is difficult to ensure that deleting or removing something actually means it is gone from the online world forever. One scheme to address the issue is to mark the data with an automatic time out stamp up front before the content is posted or sent to a recipient. This is the approach used by the photo-messaging app SnapChat.[46] SnapChat was developed in 2011 by two Stanford University students Evan Spiegel and Robert Murphy. The app allows a user to "snap" images, videos, etc., and send them to a recipient with a time limit before it "self-destructs" and is gone from the recipient's device and from SnapChat's servers. However, a 2013 *Forbes* article revealed that the snaps are not immediately removed from SnapChat's servers.[47] This prompted the Electronic Privacy Information Center to file a claim with the Federal Trade Commission against SnapChat for deceiving its users about this.[48] In addition, SnapChat had to deal with a data breach in December 2013 in which more than 4.6 million user names and phone numbers were hacked and made public.[49] Before the hacking incident SnapChat founders declined both a $3 billion offer from

---

[45] "Pablo – Quotes," Goodreads, accessed April 6, 2014, https://www.goodreads.com/quotes/284199-we-only-live-once-we-all-have-an-expiration-date.

[46] Accessed April 6, 2014, http://www.snapchat.com.

[47] Kashmir Hill, "Snapchats Don't Disappear: Forensics Firm Has Pulled Dozens of Supposedly-Deleted Photos From Android Phones," *Forbes* (May 9, 2013), http://www.forbes.com/sites/kashmirhill/2013/05/09/snapchats-dont-disappear/?utm_campaign=forbestwittersf&utm_source=twitter&utm_medium=social.

[48] Jessica Guynn, "Privacy watchdog EPIC files complaint against Snapchat with FTC," (Los Angeles Times, May 17, 2013), http://articles.latimes.com/2013/may/17/business/la-fi-tn-privacy-watchdog-epic-files-complaint-against-snapchat-with-ftc-20130517.

[49] Violet Blue, "Researchers publish Snapchat code allowing phone number matching after exploit disclosures ignored," (Zdnet, December 25, 2013), http://www.zdnet.com/researchers-publish-snapchat-code-allowing-phone-number-matching-after-exploit-disclosures-ignored-7000024629/.

Facebook[50] and a $4 billion offer from Google,[51] opting instead to stay independent and to continue to raise venture capital for operations and growth.

SnapChat's time limit seems like a proactive approach to deleting data. But what happens once it is already there without an expiration date, which is more commonly the situation today? California made the news in late 2013 with the passing of legislation nicknamed the "Erasure Law," Section 1. Chapter 22.1 (commencing with Section 22580) Privacy Rights for California Minors in the Digital World.[52] The law requires Websites to allow minors (younger than age 18) to delete their own postings from the site and to give them the information they would need to remove them. The push for the law was "meant to help protect teens from bullying, embarrassment and harm to job and college applications from online posts they later regret."[53] It is important to note that almost all Websites allow you to delete your own posts—regardless of your age—the problem becomes when others post about you and then do not want to remove those.

Other countries around the world are also grabbling with this issue. The European Union is fighting for what it believes is a basic right being threatened by today's digital and social media giants—the Right to be Forgotten (in French le droit à l'oubli—or the "right of oblivion"). It is based on the idea that people may put something up that they later regret and should have the right to delete it—or more to a public interest concern—that criminal records and really, really bad mistakes that people commit should be "forgiven" and "forgotten" and deleted from the Internet. *The Stanford Review* gave an example of a possible effect of the law if passed: "The right to be forgotten could make Facebook and Google, for example, liable for up to two percent of their global income if they fail to remove photos that people post about themselves and later regret, even if the photos have been widely distributed already."[54] This proposed law, more than any other, really brings to light the clash between the United States and the rest of the world in terms of privacy and free speech. For now, the rule in the United States is that what you post and put out there is permanent. There are backups to backups, memory caches, copies sent to friends, etc. As they say "What happens in Vegas ends up on Facebook"—and most times it's because we put it there. The best risk mitigation strategy is simple: Remind employees "Don't want people to see it—don't put it up."

Then there is the approach that the expiration date is synonymous with the deceased date. Many online accounts are nontransferrable and are identified as such in the terms of use that most individuals ignore. Two examples where value is accumulated but lost once you pass away are frequent flyer miles and music downloads. Let's take Delta Airlines as an example.

According to the Delta Skymiles program terms and conditions, the Skymiles do not expire. However, Delta reserves the right to deactivate or close an account under the following circumstances:

- Fraudulent activity occurs
- A member requests an account closure

[50] Evelyn M. Rusli and Douglas MacMillan, "Snapchat Spurned $3 Billion Acquisition Offer from Facebook," *Wall Street Journal* (November 13, 2013), http://blogs.wsj.com/digits/2013/11/13/snapchat-spurned-3-billion-acquisition-offer-from-facebook/.
[51] Jacob Kleinman, "Snapchat Allegedly Rejected $4B Buyout Offer From Google," *TechnoBuffalo* (November 15, 2013), http://www.technobuffalo.com/2013/11/15/snapchat-4-billion-google-offer/.
[52] Cal. Bus. Code § 22580 (2013), accessed April 6, 2014, http://leginfo.legislature.ca.gov/faces/billNavClient.xhtml?bill_id=201320140SB568.
[53] Kathleen Miles, "Teens Get Online 'Eraser Button' with New California Law" (Huffington Post, March 3, 2014), http://www.huffingtonpost.com/2013/09/24/teens-online-eraser-button-california_n_3976808.html.
[54] Jeffrey Rosen, "The Right to Be Forgotten," Stanford Law Review (February 13, 2012), http://www.stanfordlawreview.org/online/privacy-paradox/right-to-be-forgotten.

- A member is deceased
- A member does not respond to repeated communication attempts regarding the status of his/her account.

Many Delta Skymile program participants are not aware that once they pass away so do their miles. Instead of risking losing thousands of miles you can consider gifting miles away (while you are alive) through a transfer. It is a great way to celebrate occasions or even reward employees. Companies who pay for extensive travel for their executives can put into place a mile transfer program for such purposes.

Music downloads is another area where users spend a lot of money to download music to their devices to access it whenever and wherever they want to. But what happens to all that music when the user who "purchased" it dies? The issue came up because of a rumor in 2012 that actor Bruce Willis was going to sue Apple so he could bequeath his amassed iTunes collection to his daughters but could not because of iTunes terms and conditions.[55] This proved to be just a rumor but it brought up for discussion the reality that the current iTunes terms and conditions treat these as purchases not of a sale but of a license, with conditional use to only that user's Apple ID, and that Apple ID account expires when the person who owns it does. Digital rights to these kinds of assets are still a murky legal area. It is important that the marketing and sales departments understand the limitations that may be placed when they purchase digital images, video clips, music, etc. online for company use, such as for online training, so as to minimize the risk of copyright violation, or violation of the Terms of Use of the specific online service.

One last item in terms of expiration dates to discuss is directly related to security—the expiration on secured sockets layer digital certificates for Websites and online platforms. A certificate is a digital statement that's issued by a certification authority that vouches for the identity of the certificate holder and enables the parties to communicate in a secure manner using encryption. They protect data that is exchanged online from theft or tampering.[56] The certificate contains the name of the certificate holder, a serial number, expiration dates, a copy of the certificate holder's public key (used for encrypting messages and digital signatures) and the digital signature of the certificate-issuing authority so that a recipient can verify that the certificate is real.[57]

Because security concerns are constantly changing and being challenged, the certificates are only valid for a certain time and companies are starting to question whether to make them last one or two years and what are the consequences for each time period, including renewals of the certificates and monitoring of the security controls to get the certificates renewed. Even knowing what certificates that the company has and when each certificate needs to be renewed can be a management challenge as sometimes these certificates are created without anyone knowing about it. Having a protocol in place to verify if a certificate is required, to create the certificate, and then to manage the renewals is an important risk mitigation strategy. In addition, there is a trend in

---

[55] Tim Worstall, "Bruce Willis Might Sue Apple Over iTunes" (September 3, 2012), http://www.forbes.com/sites/timworstall/2012/09/03/bruce-willis-to-sue-apple-over-itunes/.

[56] "Digital Certificates and SSL" (Microsoft, August 26, 2013), http://technet.microsoft.com/en-us/library/dd351044(v=exchg.150).aspx.

[57] Margaret Rouse, "Digital Certificate" (SearchSecurity, November 2013), http://searchsecurity.techtarget.com/definition/digital-certificate.

using notifications for certificate renewals as a social engineering phish scam that needs to be monitored.

DIGITAL IMMORTALITY

What if you did not have to die? The Buddhists believe that death does not end life, it just ends the body we inhabit. This begs the question then of what is life for a human, what does it mean to be alive, if we can be "alive" without our bodies, then we can be immortal—just download our brain to an avatar and viola!

Dr Stuart Armstrong, research fellow, Future of Humanity Institute, University of Oxford, suggests: "if this avatar or robot is to all intents and purposes you, then it is you."[58] What legal consequences will that have? Can this avatar "you" sign documents, give away assets, get married, have other children? How do these change your rights to your assets in real property and online? How do these changes in rights affect a business's interests, especially if we are talking about founding executives of a privately held company?

These questions lead to more questions: Is "immortality" more than just e-memory? What would be the ethical, legal, and social implications of digital immortality? Will these "digital personas" have rights? What happens to their publicity rights if they are celebrities, or superstar employees/executives, etc.? These questions are still being dissected, explored, and discussed.[59] Sometimes these questions take us back to the basics of what we are—for example, is there a difference between the brain and the mind? Michio Kaku in his book *The Future of the Mind* (Doubleday, 2014) believes that in the upcoming brave new world "our memories will be recorded and swapped like old videotapes, self-aware robots will be our companions and our consciousness downloaded onto machines, will live forever."[60] Kaku believes our brains are made up of connections, the "connectome," and that once we can map those connections we can reconstruct a person in a computer—at least the brain part of us. Digital resurrection?

But that begs the question of whether we are more than just our brains, just our minds? Is there a human element that is not physical or tangible and not easily translated into code form? This is the difficult challenge faced by those working in the artificial intelligence (AI) field. Can they create a robot like Sonny in "I Robot[61]" or David in "AI[62]" that "feels" and "questions" and can learn on their own? Would that even be the goal? And as we look at "I Robot" we see the other side of "the ghost in the machine"—how they can be programmed to destroy their creators because they evolve to the point that

[58] Mark Piesing, "Will scientists ever discover the secret of immortality?" The Independent (May 3, 2012), http://www.independent.co.uk/news/science/will-scientists-ever-discover-the-secret-of-immortality-7707372.html.

[59] For more on the discussion see: Rob Walker, "Cyberspace When You're Dead," The New York Times, http://www.nytimes.com/2011/01/09/magazine/09Immortality-t.html?pagewanted=all, and B. Bonin Bough, "Digital Death & Digital Afterlife: Serious Business," *Forbes* (April 11, 2011), http://www.forbes.com/sites/boninbough/2011/04/11/digital-death-and-digital-afterlife-serious-business/.

[60] Adam Frank, "Dreaming in Code" (The New York Times, March 7, 2014), http://www.nytimes.com/2014/03/09/books/review/michio-kakus-future-of-the-mind.html?_r=0.

[61] "I, Robot" (IMDb), accessed April 6, 2014, http://www.imdb.com/title/tt0343818/.

[62] "A.I. Artificial Intelligence" (IMDb), accessed April 6, 2014, http://www.imdb.com/title/tt0212720/.

they know what is best for us and they need to protect us from ourselves? Will our security and risk management departments be dealing with this potential challenge in the future?

Another question does come up about funding this kind of "immortality"—it is not cheap. The sophistication of the processing power required and the storage capacities to hold such huge amounts of data and the energy that would be needed to ensure the machines continue to function forever, or at least for a very, very long time means that this is a money intensive endeavor. Will we have another "universal access" debate of whether only the wealthy can afford digital immortality and the poor will be erased/deleted from humanity's memory banks?

A company's legacy is also at risk here. Would Apple be different today if Steve Jobs had been "immortalized" and his Avatar was still "running" the company? How is your company securing the company's future by preserving company wisdom? How are you securing the company's present by managing the risk of loss of key talent because of death? Is it even your job as a risk or security officer to bring these issues up and run the risk of being assigned to find solutions? And if it is determined that answer is yes, who else in the company can help you? Because we are all in this together since we know that the probability of death is 100% for everyone who has been born.

THE FUTURE OF ONLINE SECURITY

10

The future isn't what we thought it would be. We don't walk around in silver suits, travel to colonies on Mars or drive in flying cars. Instead, we dress casual, take selfies and communicate in 140 characters.

Greg Satell[1]

Toward the end of every year, blogs, e-zines, technology journals, online news, broadcast news, and radio shows publish forecasts and reports that list predictions on a wide variety of topics. Often, these forecasts begin with "the future of ..." There is something about the end of one cycle and the

---

[1] Greg Satell, "6 Things You Should Know About the Future," Forbes (last modified March 16, 2014), accessed April 6, 2014, http://www.forbes.com/sites/gregsatell/2014/03/16/6-things-you-should-know-about-the-future/?ss=future-tech.

beginning of another (whether it be a year, an era, or a project) that makes us want to reflect on what we experienced and learned and to prepare for what may lie ahead. How can we do better? How can we prevent repeating past mistakes? How do we get ahead of the hackers and the threats? How will things change—tools, attacks, defenses, legislation, cultural norms, technology? How will changes in these areas affect the security of my company? How do I manage the new risks these changes will bring, even if I have no idea what those changes and/or risks will even look like? Add to these questions the time factor of instituting controls and security measures for 5, 10, or 20 years down the line as budgets get tighter and more effective use of resources becomes essential, and we are quickly overwhelmed. This uncomfortable feeling is made even worse as we review these "future of" and prediction forecasts and realize they do not always agree. Then we find that the predictions of the impossible to the likely-to-take place leave us with yet another challenge: Some of the predictions are happening now!

So, when we hear the word "future" what comes to mind? The Jetsons, as Greg Sateli seems to suggest in the chapter's opening quote? A world familiar to the science fiction set that has exploded into public consciousness? Jim Dator, a futurist and Director of the Hawaii Research Center for Future Studies of the University of Hawaii at Manoa, describes it as: "high technologies generally as instruments of social transformation, especially electronic communications technology leading to automation, robotics, artificial intelligence and artificial life on the one hand, and biological technologies leading to cyborgs, post-humans, and *trans*-humans on the other, with nanotechnology causing hyper-miniaturized technologies."[2] Hyperminiaturization is the focus of *Micro*, a novel set in Manoa, Hawaii, by Michael Crichton and Richard Preston. Published in 2011 by Harper, Crichton, author of *Jurassic Park*, and Preston take us to a world "too small to see and too dangerous to ignore."[3] What happens when you are a quarter of an inch tall, stuck in a forest, and full-sized insects and humans are out to get you? The interesting issue is why hyperminiaturization technology proves to be so valuable as well as so dangerous. Just think of all the risk management and security challenges that we will have to face against something so small we do not even know it is there. Wait a minute! That sounds very similar to what we face in security every day—things we do not see, we do not detect, and cannot protect against. What *Micro* pushes us to "see," then, is what is possible, and therefore we have been given the time to develop mechanisms to see and detect what we do not know may be there.

On the other hand, perhaps our future has a more subtle and gradual unveiling as suggested by the Pew Research Center's 2014 Report "The Web at 25 in the US,"[4] which looks not only at the present state of our online environment but also looks forward to how will digital life be in 2025. The main prediction is simple, "Experts predict the Internet will become 'like electricity'—less visible, yet more deeply embedded in people's lives for good and ill."[5] The report lays out eight more-hopeful theses and seven less-hopeful theses about our online future (see Theses: digital life 2025 (PEW)).

---

[2] Jim Dator, "Future Studies," in, ed., *Leadership in Science and Technology*, ed. William Sims Bainbridge vol. 1 (Thousand Oaks, California: Sage Reference Series, 2011): Chapter Four, pp. 32–40, http://www.futures.hawaii.edu/publications/futures-studies/DatorFuturesStudies.pdf.

[3] From inside book jacket of Micro: Michael Crichton and Richard Preston, *Micro* (New York: HarperCollins, 2011).

[4] Janna Anderson and Lee Rainie, "Digital Life in 2025," PewResearch (March 11, 2014), http://www.pewinternet.org/2014/03/11/digital-life-in-2025/.

[5] Ibid.

THESES: DIGITAL LIFE 2025 (PEW)[6]

More-hopeful

1. Internet will be invisible, effortless, and interwoven into our daily lives.
2. We will have enhanced global connectivity that will foster more cross-world relationships and less ignorance (discrimination and prejudice).
3. We will become more aware of ourselves and our world through internet of things (IoT), artificial intelligence (AI), and Big Data (BD).
4. We will become "monitored men" through augmented reality and wearable devices.
5. Political online action will increase and more Arab Spring uprisings will occur.
6. The Internet will evolve into the Ubernet, and people will organize as "national entities" by common interests instead of just by nation-states.
7. There will be more than just one Internet.
8. Online will change education offering more opportunities with less resources.

Less-hopeful

1. The conflict between haves and have-nots may increase, leading to resentment and possible violence.
2. The technology will increase capacity for online abuses and threats.
3. Governments and corporations may try to overextend power to address the threats.
4. Tradeoffs between convenience and privacy will continue, and privacy will become a luxury good.
5. Our corporations will not be able to respond quickly enough to the new challenges of the new networks.
6. There are many of us who do not yet realize the consequences of these networks and are in for a disruptive period.
7. To lessen possible negative consequences of the future, we need to invent it and not just let it happen to ourselves.

[6]Ibid.

Each of those theses provides fodder for new security trials as well as new strategies to combat them. Security approaches will have to evolve from closed and stringent to open and fuzzy, although there will be scenarios where one is better suited than the other. For example, Mt. Gox found $116 million in Bitcoins that had been missing in a "lost digital wallet" that was on a closed device not connected to their central servers.[7]

The last less-hopeful thesis reminded me of the quote by Buckminster Fuller: "The best way to predict the future is to design it."[8] Does it offer us comfort or make us feel more secure if we believe we can influence or have control over the future? Before we can influence or control, though, we have to "know." Thomas Jefferson, in a letter to George Ticknor in 1817, wrote "that knolege is power, that knolege is safety, and that knolege is happiness."[9] This chapter focuses on that aspect of knowledge as we look into the future in terms of technology, digital activity, and corporate risks and security. We will review four archetype possible futures and then delve deeper into specific current and future technologies that will affect risk and online security. Will we be surprised? As Yogi Berra said "The future ain't what it used to be."[10]

---

[7] James Lyne, "$116 Million Bitcoins 'Found' At MtGox And How To Protect Your Wallet," *Forbes* (March 21, 2014), http://www.forbes.com/sites/jameslyne/2014/03/21/116-million-bitcoins-found-at-mtgox-and-how-to-protect-your-wallet/.

[8] "Quotations," *The Green Spotlight*, accessed April 6, 2014, http://www.thegreenspotlight.com/quotations/.

[9] "Knowledge is Power (quotation)," Thomas Jefferson Monticello, accessed April 6, 2014, http://www.monticello.org/site/jefferson/knowledge-power-quotation.

[10] "Future Quotes," BrainyQuote, accessed April 6, 2014, http://www.brainyquote.com/quotes/topics/topic_future2.html.

THE FUTURE: UNPREDICTABLE

Always in motion is the future.

YODA, *Star Wars Episode V: The Empire Strikes Back[11]*

If the future is always in motion, as Yoda suggests, then how can we predict it? Although the statement reads logically, it has not stopped us from trying to devise ways to do just that—whether in terms of forecasting the weather, projecting who will win the championship game, foretelling the results of an election, or calculating the timing of a new hacking attack.

Michel de Nostredame, or Nostradamus as we know him, lived between 1503 and 1566 and was a French apothecary (pharmaceutical healer) and prophesier. His predictions were written as quatrains and throughout history have been used to "prove" that some historical moment, event, or person was predicted to exist and therefore the future was set. No one knows how he came up with the predictions. A recent documentary mentions mirrors and a bowl full of water. No one also knows for sure whether the quatrains were true in terms of foretelling the future, as most of the time they are retrofitted to things that have already happened—the World Trade Center bombing or Hitler's rise to power, for example.

For a more scientific approach, we can contrast Nostradamus to the University of Tennessee's Nautilus supercomputer.[12] In 2011, the BBC released an article covering how the Nautilus could have predicted the Arab Spring revolutions in Egypt and Libya. Kalev Leetaru, from the University of Illinois' Institute for Computing in the Humanities, Arts and Social Science, fed more than 100 million articles into the supercomputer, which then processed the data and analyzed it for two main types of information: mood, whether the article represented good news or bad news, and location, where events were happening and the location of other participants in the story. Again, the prediction was retrofitted to the events, "but scientists say the same processes could be used to anticipate upcoming conflict."[13]

Does using a scientific-based technology make us more apt to accept the prediction? After all, it is not a groundhog looking for its shadow or an octopus selecting a box with a logo on it to determine who will win the next game, both of which seem more about luck and chance than any process of legitimate forecasting.

Another thing to keep in mind is that there are two levels of the future we inquire about. The first deals with broad public futures, such as societal changes, and technology advancements. The second has more relevance to our companies and us—he focus is on new product (or security control) development because of those societal changes leading to a competitive edge in business.

Revisiting Jim Dator from Hawaii, he speaks of responsible futurists. "What responsible futurists do is not try to predict 'the future' but to 'forecast' 'alternative futures' for study and evaluation, and then help individuals, corporations, governments, and other groups envision and move toward their preferred futures—the best, possible, 'real' world they can imagine—and to do so on a continuing basis, constantly re-envisioning as new information, technologies, challenges, and opportunities, and the desires, hopes and fears of new people, emerge." [14] So the question becomes not "is the prediction correct?" but, rather, "is it useful in producing success."[15]

---

[11] "Future Quotes," NotableQuotes, accessed April 6, 2014, http://www.notable-quotes.com/f/future_quotes.html.

[12] "Nautilus," (University of Tennessee), accessed April 6, 2014, https://www.nics.tennessee.edu/computing-resources/nautilus.

[13] "Supercomputer predicts revolution" (BBC, September 9, 2011), http://www.bbc.com/news/technology-14841018.

[14] See note 2 above.

[15] Nita Rollins, "Future Scenario Planning," Innovate Columbus (May 4, 2011), http://www.slideshare.net/ResourceInteractive/future-scenario-planning.

Dator also emphasizes that experts and futurists are not the only ones you should listen to as you make decisions based on what you "read" about what will happen in the future. He lists three questions that need to be answered and considered:

1. What are the most likely alternative futures? (experts)
2. What do various people think the future will be? (regular everyday people)
3. What do I personally want the future to be? (reflection and choice)[16]

We have a number of think tanks and organizations solely focused on future scenarios and forecasting (see Future-focused think tanks and organizations).

FUTURE-FOCUSED THINK TANKS AND ORGANIZATIONS

The RAND Corporation is a research organization that develops solutions to public policy challenges to help make communities throughout the world safer and more secure, healthier, and more prosperous. RAND is nonprofit, nonpartisan, and committed to the public interest.[17] RAND works with the military and world leaders to help develop a comprehensive analytical approach to defending against terrorism attacks (including cyberattacks).[18]

Strategic Studies Institute (SSI) at the United States Army War College conducts strategic research and analysis to support the U.S. Army War College curricula, provides direct analysis for Army and Department of Defense leadership, and serves as a bridge to the wider strategic community.[19]

The Think Tanks and Civil Societies Program (TTCSP) at the University of Pennsylvania conducts research on the role policy institutes play in governments and in civil societies around the world.[20] TTCSP puts out an annual report ranking the Think Tanks. The latest version was 2013 (published in 2014) at: http://gotothinktank.com/the-2013-global-go-to-think-tank-index-ggtti/.

Hawaii Research Center for Futures Studies at the University of Hawaii, Manoa, was established by the Hawaii State Legislature in 1971 and is one of the world's most renowned institutions for futures research, consulting, and education. It has been instrumental in the education of futurists, in the development and spread of judicial and educational foresight, and in bringing foresight and futures thinking to organizations, agencies, and businesses around the world.[21]

The World Futures Studies Federation (WFSF)—a global nongovernmental organization (NGO) that was founded in the 1960s to encourage and promote the development of futures studies as a transdisciplinary academic and professional field in all parts of the world. WFSF operates as a global network of practicing futurists—researchers, teachers, scholars, policy analysts, activists, and others from approximately 60 countries.[22]

Institute for the Future—an independent, nonprofit research organization with a 45-year track record of helping all kinds of organizations make the futures they want. Its core research staff and creative design studio work together to provide practical foresight for a world undergoing rapid change.[23]

The Millennium Project—an independent nonprofit global participatory futures research think tank of futurists, scholars, business planners, and policy makers who work for international organizations, governments, corporations, NGOs, and universities. The Millennium Project manages a coherent and cumulative process that collects and assesses judgments from more than 3500 people and 49 nodes around the world. The work is distilled in its annual "State of the Future," "Futures Research Methodology" series, special studies, and integrated into this Global Futures Intelligence System.[24]

Last, but not least for the online set is Reddit's Futurology thread: http://www.reddit.com/r/Futurology.

[17]"RAND at a Glance," RAND, accessed April 6, 2014, http://www.rand.org/about/glance.html.
[18]Michael D. Rich, "How Think Tanks Interact with the Military," RAND (2003), http://www.rand.org/pubs/reprints/RP1050.html.
[19]Strategic Studies Institute, accessed April 6, 2014, http://www.strategicstudiesinstitute.army.mil.
[20]"Think Tanks & Civil Societies Program," *TTCSP*, accessed April 6, 2014, http://gotothinktank.com/about-us/.
[21]"Hawaii Research Center for Future Studies" (University of Hawaii), accessed April 6, 2014, http://www.futures.hawaii.edu.
[22]World Futures Studies Federation, accessed April 6, 2014, http://www.wfsf.org.
[23]Institute for the Future, accessed April 6, 2014, http://www.iftf.org.
[24]"Global Futures Studies & Research," *The Millennium Project*, accessed April 6, 2014, http://millennium-project.org.

---

[16]Clement Bezold, "Jim Dator's Alternative Futures and the Path to IAF's Aspirational Futures," *Journal of Future Studies* (2009): p. 316. http://www.jfs.tku.edu.tw/14-2/E01.pdf.

THE FUTURE: FOUR SCENARIOS

It is always wise to look ahead, but difficult to look further than you can see.[25]

Winston Churchill

As we look for insights regarding the future to assist us in protecting and securing that future, certain models can be useful to represent the information visually and help us evaluate the disparate ideas and opinions out there. The first model we will use is Dator's four archetypes of alternative futures as presented by Clement Bezold of the Institute for Alternative Futures on 2009.[26] The four archetypes are presented in Figure 10.1. Keep in mind as we review each of the archetypes that:

- Scenarios are about learning and understanding,
- We need to understand the difference between forecasts of the future from experts and images of the future we carry,[27] and
- To achieve the scenario, we need to move into a shared vision with action steps (which requires commitment, resources, and action).

These four scenarios present futures that all are feasible to a certain extent, but also present very different approaches to the issues of security and privacy.

The first archetype is Growth (upper left hand corner). Growth is an approach of adding more of the same: more vendor options, more applications, more business opportunities, and increased spending on information technology (IT) security. There is nothing new or innovative in terms of the applications and options themselves, there are just more of them. As for privacy, it remains as it is now, a

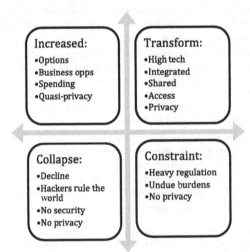

FIGURE 10.1 Future Scenarios Matrix: IT Security.

---

[25] See note 10.
[26] See note 16.
[27] Ibid.

quasiprivacy status that has to be monitored by each individual and company. This archetype can be viewed as a status quo plus.

We can contrast this with the second archetype, Transformation (upper right hand corner). In this future, we have learned not only to use high technology to help us meet the challenges of security and privacy but have developed new integrated models that make our efforts and our spending more efficient and more effective. Two examples of what this future may look like are presented by Symantec and the Digital Earth model. Both of these offer futures where privacy concerns have been addressed to the satisfaction of consumers and regulatory agencies.

At the RSA Security 2014 Conference, Stephen Trilling, senior vice president of Security Intelligence and Technology, Symantec Corp., gave a keynote address entitled "The Future of Security."[28] During that keynote he outlined what future security defense would be in contrast to what we have now:

- Your security will be managed for you by security providers using economies of scale, to lessen the expense.
- Your security will be integrated for you—no more isolated silos of log information.
- You will be part of a community to share wisdom—Big Data repositories will serve for cross-corporate, cross-border analytics of real-time security threats, incidents, and resolutions.
- Complex attacks will be discovered within minutes or hours, instead of the days, months, and sometimes years it takes us now.

The second transformative view of the future is presented by Dan Abelow in his book "*Imagine a New Future: Creating Greatness for All*" (2014). Abelow describes his concept of "Expandiverse Technology"—an "active infrastructure that will manage continuous connections with consistent screens that recognize and follow you across families of devices for better security and background processing."[29] In other words, Abelow envisions a Digital Earth where everything and everyone is connected. The key is to be conscious of what the technology does and how we can expand our abilities through the technology so as to gain previously unreaped benefits from it throughout our daily interactions—personal and professional. For Abelow, the key is us. For Trilling, the key is automation and integration.

The third archetype, Constraint (lower right hand corner), paints a very different picture of the future. Things are under control because things are so heavily regulated, much like a Big Brother approach. A constrained future acknowledges that society is disciplined and focused on conserving what it believes is required to function adequately. But in this future, undue burdens for corporations to be able to adhere to increasing regulation regarding security and privacy have led to a policy of privacy at a price for anything desired by consumers above the minimum legally required. It proves too expensive and time consuming otherwise. This scenario also presents opportunities for more discrimination and marginalization due to that disparate parity between those who can afford privacy and those who cannot. Centralization is key here.

An example of what a constrained future may look like can be found in Dave Egger's 2014 book *The Circle*. The novel follows a young woman in her 20s who takes a job at The Circle, the largest Internet company in the world. "The company demands transparency in all things; two of its many

---

[28] Stephen Trilling, "*The Future of Security*," *RSAConference* (February 26, 2014), http://www.rsaconference.com/videos/125/the-future-of-security.

[29] Dan Abelow, "After the Internet: Are We One Step Away From an Advanced Digital Earth?" (World Future Society, March 19, 2014), http://www.wfs.org/blogs/dan-abelow/after-internet-are-we-one-step-away-advanced-digital-earth.

slogans are SECRETS ARE LIES and PRIVACY IS THEFT. Anonymity is banished; everyone's past is revealed; everyone's present may be broadcast live in video and sound. Nothing recorded will ever be erased. The Circle's goal is to have all aspects of human existence—from voting to love affairs—flow through its portal, the sole such portal in the world."[30] It is the combination of the sole portal—centralization—and the extreme pursuit of transparency where privacy is criminal that causes us to be concerned as we go through the book. We see what can go wrong as we are looking in from the outside. But those in that world see nothing wrong—after all, the world is functioning better than ever—it is just the humans who do not seem capable of functioning. That is why The Circle falls into Constraint and not the last archetype—Collapse.

The fourth and final archetype, Collapse (lower right hand corner), is dystopia multiplied. This future shows us a society that is held hostage as hackers rule the world. There is no security. There is no privacy. World economies decline as threats and attacks do their damage at an accelerated pace and corporations cannot keep up. In addition, environmental sustainability has failed and overpopulation and decreased food production add to the challenges of survival at a basic level. It is interesting to note a recent hoax regarding a collapsed future—known as the "NASA Doomsday Scenario" report, was released in early 2014. The authors of the actual paper, "Human and Nature Dynamics (HANDY): Modeling Inequality and Use of Resources in the Collapse or Sustainability of Societies,"[31] were not commissioned by NASA. The paper was real; the NASA affiliation was not. But the media had a field day in terms of arguing for and against NASA and its "approach." The paper was written by Safa Motesharrei, a doctoral candidate in applied mathematics and public policy at University of Maryland; Jorge Rivas of the Department of Political Science at the University of Minnesota and the Institute of Global Environment and Society; and Eugenia Kalnay, Distinguished University Professor in the Department of Atmospheric and Oceanic Science and the Institute for Physical Science and Technology at the University of Maryland. Melissa Andreychek, Communications Coordinator, The National Socio-Environmental Synthesis Center, University of Maryland, trying to clarify the situation of the supposed affiliation with NASA, wrote in an email to the World Future Society (which originally blogged about the paper) "The research paper was not solicited, directed, or reviewed by NASA. It is an independent study by the researchers utilizing research tools developed for a separate NASA activity."[32] A key question of the paper is whether civilized societies can collapse. I leave that for you to read the paper and decide.

This fourth future also brings to the forefront several societal concerns. One is that although we will all be connected via the Internet we will all be lonely—basically Alone Together, each in isolation. Another is that we will become less social in real time and unable to function in person. For an example, watch another Bruce Willis movie "Surrogates."[33]

The Internet will also have another effect on us—it will narrow our knowledge base and limit what we actually learn. This is a concern that is already being voiced. In the Pew Research Report of Digital Life in 2025, one respondent who wanted to remain anonymous wrote "the information we want will

---

[30] Ellen Ullman, "Ring of Power: 'The Circle,' by Dave Eggers" (The New York Times, November 1, 2013), http://www.nytimes.com/2013/11/03/books/review/the-circle-by-dave-eggers.html.

[31] Safa Motesharrei and Jorge Rivas, "Human and Nature Dynamics (HANDY): Modeling Inequality and Use of Resources in the Collapse or Sustainability of Societies," (March 19, 2014), http://www.sesync.org/sites/default/files/resources/motesharrei-rivas-kalnay.pdf.

[32] Len Rosen, "An Update of NASA Doomsday Scenario Paper" (World Future Society, March 21, 2014), http://www.wfs.org/blogs/len-rosen/update-nasa-doomsday-scenario-paper.

[33] "Surrogates" (IMDb, accessed April 6, 2014), http://www.imdb.com/title/tt0986263/.

increasingly find its way to us, as networks learn to accurately predict our interests and weaknesses ... that will also tempt us to stop seeking out knowledge, narrowing our horizons, even as we delve ever-more deep."[34]

This idea of limiting our horizons by limiting the information we are "fed" by the Internet is the focus of the book *Rewire: Digital Cosmopolitans in the Age of Connection* by Ethan Zuckerman. In this book, Zuckerman "explains why the technological ability to communicate with someone does not inevitably lead to increased human connection. At the most basic level, our human tendency to 'flock together' means that most of our interactions, online or off, are with a small set of people with whom we have much in common."[35] So whereas the first view blames predictive analysis technology for narrowing our vistas, Zuckerman blames our own human tendency.

This future speaks of the coming of a time where terrorism is synonymous with cyberwarfare and information warfare and humans will outsource their own decisions and desires to their own detriment. In this future, security is futile.

FUTURE OF RISK

> *Now more then ever, there is no status quo in technology.*
>
> Ed Moyle[36]

One of the things we intuitively understand is that in the security arena we have ever-changing risk landscapes.[37] Mike Jacka says: "We probably wouldn't even recognize the next big thing because it hasn't hit yet."[38] That can be a scary proposition. What this makes us aware of is that risk is not only a "today issue." Risk assessment does look at today's circumstances to see where we are, but it then does some forecasting in determining the likelihood and impact of any particular risk to the company (of those we know, of course).

This means that we and our "companies no longer have the luxury of time to adapt to new paradigms or threats because of the rapid pace of change."[39] In such a volatile risk environment, we need to update our risk profiles continuously. We cannot wait for an annual risk assessment. Risk assessment needs to be ongoing, continuous. New applications to automate the risk review process, from collecting risk-relevant information to assigning scores to red flag priorities, need to be developed and implemented. More than ever the need to be proactive rather than reactive is imperative. Martin Libicki's assertion that "even a perfect fix lasts only until the next innovation hits the system"[40] rings more true

---

[34] Carina Kolodny, "Here's What the Internet Could Look Like in 2025," The Huffington Post (March 12, 2014), http://www.huffingtonpost.com/2014/03/11/heres-what-the-internet-c_n_4943051.html.

[35] Ethan Zuckerman, *Rewire: Digital Cosmopolitans in the Age of Connection*, (New York: W.W. Norton & Company, Inc., 2013), accessed April 6, 2014, http://www.amazon.com/Rewire-Digital-Cosmopolitans-Age-Connection/dp/0393082830.

[36] Ed Moyle, "Keeping Up With the Future: Risk Management for Rapid Technology Adoption," TechNewsWorld (February 22, 2013), http://www.technewsworld.com/story/77369.html.

[37] Mike Jacka, "Risk and the Future of Internal Audit" (The Institute of Internal Auditors, February 10, 2014), http://www.theiia.org/blogs/jacka/index.cfm?postid=512.

[38] Ibid.

[39] See note 36.

[40] Martin Libicki, "The Future of Information Security" (Institute for National Strategic Studies, February 17, 2003), https://www.fas.org/irp/threat/cyber/docs/infosec.htm.

than ever. And as the speed of technology and attacks against our corporate data accelerates, risk management has to evolve to keep up.

INTERNET OF THINGS

> *We need to ensure that the trust we place in the technologies that run our lives is, in fact, justified.*
>
> *Beau Woods[41]*

The Internet of Things (IoT) was a term highlighted in 2009 by Kevin Ashton to describe devices that have sensors and are connected through the Internet without human interference—almost like device to device. Sean Martin offers a great definition for IoT:

> *The IoT can be thought of as the multichannel gateway between the physical and digital world. Think 'smart' devices and appliances, personal health monitors, wearable and embedded medical devices, and all sorts of vehicles for example; picture systems and devices that connect to the Internet and/or to other systems and devices also connected to the Internet.[42]*

Based on a 2013 Gartner Research Report: by 2020 "the Internet of things will have expanded at a much faster rate, resulting in an installed base of about 26 billion units at that time."[43] These units include computers, smart phones, tablets, phablets, and noncomputers such as refrigerators and cars.

The argument for these connected devices is that they can automatically transmit as well as receive information that can be essential and make our lives more convenient or even safer. Madeline Bennett cautions that despite the numbers of connected devices we still need to work out some of the issues to ensure security and privacy protections. "Privacy policies, legislation, and technology all need to come together for the IoT to benefit users and organizations equally."[44] For example, what if your prescription bottle is IoT connected so that once you need a refill it automatically "calls" it in for you? What if the bottle goes further and reminds you that you have not taken your pill? What if that information is then logged—when you take the pill, when you do not, how many times you have missed your medication—and sent to the insurance company. Who determines that you are too high a risk for coverage because you are not taking the medication and drops you? How far is too far?

One of the questions being discussed about IoT is who is liable in terms of security for these connected devices. Demetrios Lazarikos, IT Security Strategist at Blue Lava Consulting, believes that "Security must become part of the entire product lifecycle, from the time the idea has been socialized through development, integration, and testing, continuing on through the release and ongoing support of the product."[45]

---

[41] Sean Martin, "Who Will Pay the Price when Tragedy Strikes the IoT?" Law Technology News (March 20, 2014), http://www.lawtechnologynews.com/id=1202647721399/Who-Will-Pay-the-Price-When-Tragedy-Strikes-the-IoT%3F#ixzz2wsnt5xAC.

[42] Ibid.

[43] Richard Gordon, "In the Modern World of IT, All Things are Connected," Gartner (February 24, 2014), http://blogs.gartner.com/richard-gordon/2014/02/24/in-the-modern-world-of-it-all-things-are-connected/.

[44] Madeline Bennett, "Don't shun the Internet of Things over privacy and security worries," The Inquirer (March 21, 2014), http://www.theinquirer.net/inquirer/opinion/2335674/dont-shun-the-internet-of-things-over-privacy-and-security-worries.

[45] See note 41.

Another example as to IoT is the advent of the "connected car." Questions surround data ownership and disclosure of data collected by the car. What data are being collected? How is the data being used? What happens with the data if the car is resold or traded? These are just some of the questions Judith Bitterli, CMO for AVG Technologies, states we need to start discussing and answering.[46] For example, if the car is collecting data on my driving habits, driving history, driving record, even how many times I am exceeding the speed limit, is there a legal requirement that the data has to be reported to law enforcement since a law was broken? Or, can a ticket be automatically given and points deducted immediately? It reminds me of the Bruce Willis movie "The Fifth Element" when the Milla Jovovich character lands in his taxi and the onboard computer begins to count down the points he is losing because of traffic violations, such as speeding and evading the police.

In addition, the connected car brings up an additional security concern. Consider the possibility of a car jacking. The danger is not necessarily for the loss of the car. Rather, the danger is that the car becomes an accessibility portal into a corporate information system, especially if the car is a corporate vehicle assigned to a high-level executive who has security exemptions for full access to any data or system in the company network.

Proponents of connected cars and connected devices in general argue that there are substantial benefits in terms of public good that need to be considered as well, mainly focusing on safety of the devices. As with seat belts, will these connected-car technologies become a standard requirement for vehicles? In 2014 "the US Department of Transportation's (DOTs) National Highway Traffic Safety Administration (NHTSA) announced plans to enable vehicle-to-vehicle (V2V) communication for light vehicles. This technology is designed to allow vehicles to "talk" to each other—exchanging speed, position, and other safety data up to 10 times per second—to avoid crashes. The NHTSA is also developing a regulatory proposal that would require V2V devices in new vehicles "in a future year."[47]

DRONES

The commercial drone industry is growing at a rate that greatly exceeds the FAA's current pace of regulation or enforcement capability.[48]

It is a bird, it is a plane, it is a drone! Drones, unmanned flying objects that are guided remotely, seem to have been proliferating lately, moving from the center of a political debate on spying and targeted killing in a war/conflict context to a catalyst of public discourse on the tensions between technological progress and personal privacy.

The skies are full of them, and so are news and media channels. An early 2014 "60 Minutes" television program segment with Morley Shafer examined the current state of drones, what they are being used for and some of the legal ramifications. The segment showed a professional photographer and

---

[46] Jeff Bertolucci, "Internet of Things Meets Cars: Security Threats Ahead," (InformationWeek, March 18, 2014), http://www.informationweek.com/big-data/big-data-analytics/internet-of-things-meets-cars-security-threats-ahead/d/d-id/1127737.

[47] Nathan Naylor, "U.S. Department of Transportation Announces Decision to Move Forward with Vehicle-to-Vehicle Communication Technology for Light Vehicles" (National Highway Traffic Safety Administration, February 3, 2014), http://www.nhtsa.gov/About+NHTSA/Press+Releases/2014/USDOT+to+Move+Forward+with+Vehicle-to-Vehicle+Communication+Technology+for+Light+Vehicles.

[48] John Goglia from Forbes as quoted in: Kashmir Hill, "Drone Wars (Of the Legal Variety)," Forbes (March 17, 2014), http://www.forbes.com/sites/kashmirhill/2014/03/17/drone-wars-of-the-legal-kind/.

videographer who use camera-fitted drones to take images and videos of aerial flights that would not otherwise be possible. Legitimate enough, it seems, considering that the law in the United States says you can take pictures of just about anything that you can view from a public street. Also, above a certain point in the sky, your property ceases to be your property, whether that property is personal or corporate.

But what happens if someone decides to send off that drone with the camera to peer into a window and snap photos or take videos? How far from the window does the drone have to be to not be considered trespassing? Could the operation of the drone be construed as an invasion of privacy? In 2013, a New York photographer took photos of his neighbors by pointing his camera from his second floor window to their luxury apartments across the street. The residents were upset because they felt they had an expectation of privacy and "the images show private moments that include cleaning (while bent over), taking naps, and kids resting with teddy bears."[49] The photographer, Arne Svenson, claims that they should not have an expectation of privacy because they all had their curtain open or no curtains at all and anyone could see them from the outside. A lawsuit against Svenson was dismissed because the judge said the individuals in the photos were unidentifiable and that the photographs were protected under a First Amendment/Free Speech right.[50] Svenson did end up selling some of the photographs for thousands of dollars and as part of the dismissal agreed to take the photos off his Website and Facebook page.

Although Svenson used a camera instead of a drone with a camera, the same situation can occur with the drone manning the camera. In 2014, a Federal Aviation Agency (FAA) fine against Raphael Pirker, a photographer who was operating a small remote-controlled airplane (drone) was dropped. He was fined for unsafe maneuvering and for operating an unmanned craft for commercial purposes. The judge said "there is no enforceable FAA rule applicable to Pirker's activity" and he did not believe that Pirker's model aircraft should be classified as an "unmanned air system."[51]

The FAA said it would appeal as it is concerned about multitudes of drones flying through airspace unregulated and leading to a possibility of crashes, property damage, and privacy violations. Part of FAA's concern comes from the fact that drones do not always look like miniature flying aircraft. They are becoming smaller and being designed to be inconspicuous in forms such as hummingbirds[52] and dragonflies.[53]

During the "60 Minutes" segment mentioned previously, Senator Feinstein (D-CA), spoke about her concerns with flying peeping toms. She says that these issues of privacy must be addressed. "What is an appropriate law enforcement use for a drone? When do you have to have a warrant? What is the appropriate governmental use for a drone," she asks. Regulation will be needed. "Perhaps regulation of

---

[49] Michael Zhang, "New Yorkers Upset Over Photographer's Secret Snaps Through Their Windows," (PetaPixel, May 16, 2013), http://petapixel.com/2013/05/16/new-yorkers-upset-over-photographers-secret-snaps-through-their-windows/.

[50] "Judge Dismisses Lawsuit Against NYC Photographer Who Snapped Pictures of Neighbors," (NBC New York, August 9, 2013), http://www.nbcnewyork.com/news/local/NYC-Photographer-Pictures-Neighbors-Open-Windows-Lawsuit-218931381.html.

[51] Kashmir Hill, "Drone Wars (Of the Legal Variety)," *Forbes* (March 17, 2014), http://www.forbes.com/sites/kashmirhill/2014/03/17/drone-wars-of-the-legal-kind/.

[52] Anna Rothschild, "The Hummingbird Drone," NOVA (October 31, 2013), http://www.pbs.org/wgbh/nova/tech/hummingbird-drone.html.

[53] Techjet, accessed April 6, 2014, http://techject.com.

THE FUTURE: FOUR SCENARIOS **249**

size and type for private use," says Feinstein. "Secondly, some certification of the person that is going to operate it. And then some specific regulation on the kinds of uses it can be put to."[54]

Two Sensepost Research Labs security researchers, Glenn Wilkinson and Daniel Cuthbert, highlighted the extent to which drones can be used for illicit surveillance. They developed Snoopy—a drone with an application that can capture information from a WiFi-connected smart phone. It certainly gives another meaning to the Peanut's character Snoopy and the dastardly Red Baron.[55]

According to the researchers, this is how Snoopy works: Anytime you use a WiFi network, your smartphone or tablet "remembers" that network, so it can more easily connect the next time you are in range. It does this by pinging each network to see if it is available. Snoopy exploits this feature by identifying a previously used network, then it pretends to be that network, so your smartphone or tablet connects to it, and you are none the wiser. Once your device is connected to the false WiFi, Snoopy can then collect any information you send over the tapped network, from Facebook login credentials to bank account details. It also collects your device's unique ID number, your GPS coordinates, and your signal strength.[56]" Snoopy was presented at Black Hat Asia Cyber Security Conference in Singapore as a way to expose the potential security threat so smart phone manufacturers could work on a fix.

What about the legality of capturing this information from the smart phone? "Collecting metadata, or the device IDs and network names, is probably not illegal, according to the Electronic Frontier Foundation. Intercepting usernames, passwords and credit card information with the intent of using them would likely violate wiretapping and identity theft laws."[57] A key data security strategy is to remind employees not to use the public WiFi available in coffee shops, books stores, and other retail outlets. Even WiFi spots in colleges or libraries need to be checked for security before logging on.

Facebook took the WiFi concern one step further. In early 2014, it announced the creation of a "new lab of up to 50 aeronautics experts and space scientists to figure out how to beam Internet access down from solar-powered drones and other connectivity aircraft."[58] This is part of Mark Zuckerman's (CEO of Facebook) Internet.org project (http://www.internet.org) to make the Internet affordable and accessible to millions of humans on our planet who currently do not have access to it. According to their Web site that is two-thirds of the world population![59] Facebook is not alone. Google has project Loon (http://www.google.com/loon/) to provide balloon-powered Internet for all. We may soon have a sky full of unmanned flying objects. Will your security department need an air traffic controller to monitor objects in your company's air space that may be security threats and data attacks?

[54] "The Future of Drones: Technology vs. Privacy" (CBS News, March 14, 2014), http://www.cbsnews.com/news/the-future-of-drones-technology-vs-privacy/.

[55] "Baron versus Beagle – The Original 'Dogfight'," accessed April 6, 2014, Youtube: http://www.youtube.com/watch?v=rNremK0cBEg.

[56] Andrew Couts, "Is it a bird? Is it a plane? Nope – it's a drone stealing your identity," *Digital Trends* (March 20, 2014), http://www.digitaltrends.com/mobile/snoopy-drone-smarphone-cybersecurity/#!BiJno.

[57] Erica Fink, "This drone can steal what's on your phone" (CNNMoney, March 20, 2014), http://money.cnn.com/2014/03/20/technology/security/drone-phone/index.html?hpt=hp_t3.

[58] Vindu Goel, "A New Facebook Lab Is Intent on Delivering Internet Access by Drone" (The New York Times, March 27, 2014), http://www.nytimes.com/2014/03/28/technology/a-new-facebook-lab-is-intent-on-delivering-internet-access-by-drone.html?emc=edit_th_20140328&nl=todaysheadlines&nlid=33425801&_r=0.

[59] "About," accessed April 6, 2014, Internet.org, http://www.internet.org/about.

Until the FAA and other regulatory agencies figure out how to balance this concern between privacy and progress, drones are easily accessible for purchase at various price and complexity levels (see Shopping for drones).

SHOPPING FOR DRONES

Amazon.com search 3/25/14 "Drones"
- Total results: 29,675 in 34 departments
    - Drones, accessories, batteries, kits, hard cases, etc.
- Electronics 2373 results
    - Parrot AR drone $499
    - DJI Phantom $1198.95
- Toys and games 748 results
- Books 2330 results
- Security and surveillance 107 results
    - Drone Shield $99
    - GSM Drone computer remote surveillance system $548.23
    - Grocery and gourmet food 103 Results
    - Coffee gift basket $44.99
- Google "Buy drones" 3/25/14
    - 38,300,000 results
    - Walkera $399
    - Strom Drone $359.90
    - Skybotix CoaX $4999.00 (from RobotShop.com)

From a risk management and security standpoint, the concerns are that drones will become another vehicle to capture data and gain unauthorized access to a corporation's networked systems. To view certain possible futures of drones, security, and privacy, I have combined Dator's four future archetypes and a Futures Wheel (see Figure 10.2). The Futures Wheel is a method for graphical visualization of direct and indirect future consequences of a particular change or development. Jerome C. Glenn invented the Futures Wheel in 1971 when he was a student at the Antioch Graduate School of Education (now Antioch University New England). Glenn explains its use in his 1994 book, *The Futures Wheel*: "The Futures Wheel is a way of organizing thinking and questioning about the future—a kind of structured brainstorming.[60]

The wheel is pretty self-explanatory. The drone market can continue to grow without any further interference or regulation leading to a possible catastrophe such as what happened when radio was not regulated and everyone was on every frequency cutting each other off. This was one of the reasons blamed for more people not being saved when the Titanic sunk, leading to collapse and a complete ban on amateur radio without a permit. Or, the market can be transformed to where a balance exists between legitimate purposes for the technology and the privacy of individuals and the protection of data. Do not you want to see logoed drones delivering books from Amazon and pizza from Papa John's?

---

[60]Glenn, Jerome C., *The Futures Wheel*, 1994.

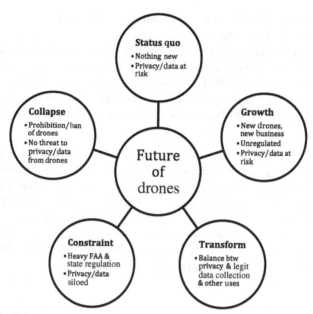

FIGURE 10.2 Future Wheel: Drones.

PRIVACY

If you aren't paying for the product, you are the product.[61]

Julia Angwin, the author of this quotation, worries whether privacy has become a luxury good—available only to those who can afford it. She distinguishes between the business protection market and the personal data protection market, arguing that businesses make it a necessary cost of doing business to protect their data, but individuals do not have the resources to do so. This has brought up the current scenario in which individuals trade their data for access to certain services—examples are Google Gmail accounts and Facebook accounts. If we look at the privacy policies they display on their sites, it is evident that they are collecting data about us and that this data is harnessed and then exploited to a certain effect.

Even if the data collected is not "personally identifiable information" but metadata, such as NSA's contention to the phone records it collects, this kind of data can provide a particularly invasive window into the lives of individuals."[62] Metadata is the data hidden from view, such as GPS information, Web searches, Websites visited (cookies), etc. There are three main types of metadata:

- Descriptive metadata describes a resource for purposes such as discovery and identification. It can include elements such as title, abstract, author, and keywords.

---

[61] Julia Angwin, "Has Privacy Become a Luxury Good?" (The New York Times, March 3, 2014), http://www.nytimes.com/2014/03/04/opinion/has-privacy-become-a-luxury-good.html?nl=todaysheadlines&emc=edit_th_20140304.
[62] Jeff Clark, "Security, Privacy, and Metadata," *DataCenter Journal*, (March 18, 2014), http://www.datacenterjournal.com/it/security-privacy-metadata/.

- Structural metadata indicates how compound objects are put together, for example, how pages are ordered to form chapters.
- Administrative metadata provides information to help manage a resource, such as when and how it was created, file type, and other technical information, and who can access it. There are several subsets of administrative data. Two that sometimes are listed as separate metadata types are:
  - Rights management metadata, which deals with intellectual property rights, and
  - Preservation metadata, which contains information needed to archive and preserve a resource.[63]

Part of the future of security rests in what can and will be done in terms of regulating metadata and regulating who has access to your information and what parts of your information. In an IBM forecast report, IBM indicates that by 2020 a digital guardian will protect you online. These digital cognitive security systems will learn about us and protect us.[64] They will capture our behavior and patterns and recognize who we are and who we are not by what we do and what we do not.

Security controls for privacy regulations and concerns will only increase in the future. New approaches to identity protection for our clients will be developed as our clients voice their concerns and demand to be consulted about the collection and use of their data.

MONITORED MAN

Our future will be shaped by the assumptions we make about who we are and what we can be.[65]

One of the six things that Greg Satell feels we should know about the future is that technology will become personal.[66] It seems we are entering an era of self-monitoring through technology such as wearable tracking and sensor devices connected to smart phones and tablets to track our fitness, health, and activity.[67]

From the Futurist standpoint, this coincides with the sixth cycle of Kondratiev's waves (see Figure 10.3). Nikolai Kondratiev was a Russian economist who first proposed that there are certain generational cycles of invention, expansion, and depression.[68] The first began around 1780 with the invention of the steam engine and the latest commenced around 2010 with the focus on environmental, nano, and biotechnologies.[69] Some experts stop at a fifth wave—information and communication technologies and feel the nano and bio fall into it. It seems that the biggest change between the fifth and sixth waves is that the fifth wave indicates the emergence of a knowledge society while the sixth wave indicates a maturity of the technologies for a specific purpose of extending life in a health age.

---

[63] "Understanding Metadata," NISO (2004), http://www.niso.org/publications/press/UnderstandingMetadata.pdf.

[64] "5 innovations that will define the future" (December 18, 2013) upgrade, http://www.upgrademag.com/web/5-innovations-will-define-future/.

[65] Rosabeth Moss Kanter, "Future Quotes," accessed April 6, 2014, http://www.notable-quotes.com/f/future_quotes.html.

[66] Satell, "6 Things You Should Know About the Future" (March 16, 2014).

[67] Albert Sun, "The Monitored Man" (The New York Times, March 10, 2014), http://well.blogs.nytimes.com/2014/03/10/the-monitored-man/?emc=edit_th_20140311&nl=todaysheadlines&nlid=33425801.

[68] Michael Burnam-Fink, "Waves of Innovation," *Science Progress* (May 3, 2011), http://scienceprogress.org/2011/05/waves-of-innovation-2/.

[69] "The 6th Kondratieff Cycle," (Time-Price-Research, April 23, 2012), http://time-price-research-astrofin.blogspot.com/2012/04/6th-kondratieff-cycle.html.

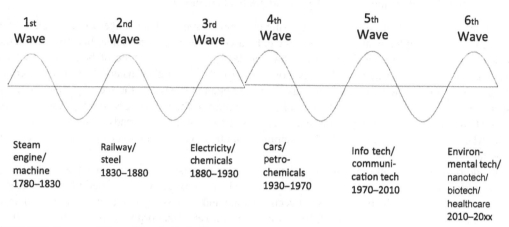

Kondratieff waves

1st Wave	2nd Wave	3rd Wave	4th Wave	5th Wave	6th Wave
Steam engine/ machine 1780–1830	Railway/ steel 1830–1880	Electricity/ chemicals 1880–1930	Cars/ petro-chemicals 1930–1970	Info tech/ communi-cation tech 1970–2010	Environ-mental tech/ nanotech/ biotech/ healthcare 2010–20xx

FIGURE 10.3 Representation of Kondratiev's Waves.

What will collecting all this data on us mean? What is the value of continuous feedback and a life-time of recording blood pressure readings and logged mileage? The Pew Report about Digital Life in 2025 offers some insights about potential benefits:

- Patrick Tucker, author of *The Naked Future: What Happens In a World That Anticipates Your Every Move?*, wrote, "When the cost of collecting information on virtually every interaction falls to zero, the insights that we gain from our activity, in the context of the activity of others, will fundamentally change the way we relate to one another, to institutions, and with the future itself. We will become far more knowledgeable about the consequences of our actions; we will edit our behavior more quickly and intelligently."
- Judith Donath, a fellow at Harvard University's Berkman Center for Internet and Society, responded, "We'll have a picture of how someone has spent their time, the depth of their commitment to their hobbies, causes, friends, and family. This will change how we think about people, how we establish trust, how we negotiate change, failure, and success."
- Aron Roberts, software developer at the University of California–Berkeley, said, "We may well see wearable devices and/or home and workplace sensors that can help us make ongoing lifestyle changes and provide early detection for disease risks, not just disease. We may literally be able to adjust both medications and lifestyle changes on a day-by-day basis or even an hour-by-hour basis, thus enormously magnifying the effectiveness of an ever more understaffed medical delivery system."[70]

These thoughts emphasize the concept of the Internet Human or Human Internet (IH) from the Institute for the Future. The IH consists of certain components including:

- Integrated connected ecosystem of our data and our lives
- Natural/intuitive interfaces

[70] Anderson and Rainie, Digital Life, pg. 7,

- Total/continuous lifetime recording
- Predictive algorithms to identify us and predict behavior[71]

These developments on self-monitoring bring up opportunities and challenges in the risk and security arenas. For example, what if brain waves can be used for security—passthoughts (specific memories) instead of passwords?[72] Would this, however, lead to a slippery slope of being able to "read someone's thoughts" and then hold the person liable for their thoughts instead of just their actions, because their thoughts would be able to make things happen? Or what of the security concern that an executive can be kidnapped and made to think of something so the kidnappers could access the corporate system? Thoughts occur in seconds and not always under our control. Inadvertent thoughts—especially when you are told not to think of something—can be a weaker link than a password that can be forgotten.

In addition, where is all the monitored data going? Do the insurance companies have access to it? Does the stock exchange or public have access to it—where an executive's ill-timed illness can lead to profit gain or loss? Will the boundaries between personal and professional be even more blurred as the very personal physical well being of the executive is now a very real corporate asset to be secured and protected against being hacked?

BICENTENNIAL MAN REVISITED

For all of its uncertainty, we cannot flee the future.[73]

Barbara Jordan

In the Robin William's 1999 film *Bicentennial Man*, his character begins existence as a robot and goes through 200 years of transformations to finally be declared human on his deathbed. His transformations consisted of robotic parts being replaced by human and biological organs. With this in mind, let us take the human-hacking scenario described above, one step further. It would be difficult to discover that the personal physical attributes of an executive were "stolen" because the executive would still be there. But what if it was not him? In 2014, the Center for Applied Reconstructive Technologies in Surgery used scanners and software instead of plaster casting to "print" a new face for Stephen Power, a motorcyclist who suffered severe facial injuries in a crash in Wales in 2012. According to one account of the surgery: "UK manufacturer Renishaw printed a template to guide the surgeon's scalpel and plates to hold the bones in place from a cobalt-chromium alloy. An implant, printed in Belgium from titanium, was then inserted to fix them permanently. The 3-D designs were sliced into 2-D layers and printed one on top of the other with metallic powder fused together by a laser."[74] Can the printing of a face lead to the printing of fingerprints or other biometric components to circumvent security controls?

---

[71] "Internet Human, Human Internet" (Institute for the Future, accessed April 6, 2014), http://www.iftf.org/uploads/media/IFTF_TH12-InternetHuman_map_rdr.pdf.

[72] Jennie Yoon, "Thoughts could be future of security" (The Daily Californian, April 10, 2013), http://www.dailycal.org/2013/04/10/uc-berkeley-researchers-develop-new-methods-to-replace-traditional-passwords/.

[73] See note 10.

[74] Paul Rodgers, "How to Print a New Face," *Forbes* (March 13, 2014), http://www.forbes.com/sites/paulrodgers/2014/03/13/how-to-print-a-new-face/?ss=future-tech.

CREDENTIAL VERIFICATION

Your physical being is just one way to prove who you are. Your credentials are another. Advancements in how we prove that we know what we know, that we acquired skills at certain levels, and do have the credentials we list on our resume are also on the rise. The International Systems Audit and Control Association (ISACA) announced in 2014 that it would provide digital badges to fight against fraudulent security credentialing using Mozilla Open Badges technology. "The badges are essentially secure digital representations of the ISACA credential and can be embedded into a résumé, emails, personal websites, and social and professional networking websites, including Facebook and LinkedIn...When a prospective employer or anyone else clicks on it, the badge calls up a standardized set of metadata that verifies the certification, the qualifications needed and the process required to earn it."[75]

A future step for these badges is encoding them in a biometric or sensor device embedded into the individual. Security challenges would include: developing measures to ensure these digital or bio-badges are not fraudulent or being used by those who did not earn them as well as maintaining personally identifiable information of the credentialed individuals safe to prevent them being targeted.

BIG DATA

> *When did the future switch from being a promise to being a threat? Chuck Palahniuk, Invisible Monsters*[76]

Clayton Christensen's 1997 book *The Innovator's Dilemma* laid out his theory that disruptive technology, a new technology that unexpectedly displaces an established technology[77], mandates change in the way businesses conduct themselves and the products and services that they offer to their clients. Some examples he offered were digital photography, mobile telephony, online retailing, digital printing, and unmanned aircraft.

As we discussed in Chapter 5, "Big Data is the set of technical capabilities and management processes for converting vast, fast, or varied data into useful knowledge."[78] For the future of security, Big Data is a disruption as well as a promise. Stephen Tilling of Symantec brought up the issue of Big Data security in his keynote on the "Future of Security," where the future of security is Big Data analytics based on a cloud-based security repository.[79] This viewpoint looks beyond security information and event management programs and instead of being reactive to be proactive. If we cannot prevent then we need to focus on incidents, response, and recovery. In addition "a recent Gartner study highlighted that

[75] "ISACA Launches Digital Badges for Credential Verification," *Infosecurity* (March 22, 2014), http://www.infosecurity-magazine.com/view/37591/isaca-launches-digital-badges-for-credential-verification/.

[76] "Quotes about Future," Goodreads, accessed April 6, 2014, http://www.goodreads.com/quotes/tag/future.

[77] Margaret Rouse, "Disruptive Technology" WhatIs.com (August 2011), http://whatis.techtarget.com/definition/disruptive-technology.

[78] *MeriTalk Beacon Report 2014*, accessed April 6, 2014, http://www.meritalk.com/Balancing-Cyber-BigData.

[79] Stephen Trilling, *"The Future of Security"* RSAConference (February 26, 2014), http://www.rsaconference.com/videos/125/the-future-of-security.

adoption of big data analytics currently stands at only eight percent of large enterprises, though this is set to grow to 25 percent by 2016 as businesses get to grips with the information being generated across their business."[80]

Some of this is being implemented today with corporations using data intelligence techniques to begin the process of mining for security gold. The idea is that intelligence-driven security will help security teams better protect their organizations and offer:

- Improved visibility into what is happening in their environments, from their networks, to their servers to their applications and end points.
- More contextual analytics of what is going on to help them prioritize issues more effectively and concentrate more resources on those issues that are more likely to impact their business.
- Actionable intelligence from diverse sources, both internal and external, to tell the system what to look for in a more automated way, and help them respond quicker.[81]

The steps to security intelligence follow the data cycle we reviewed previously:

- Data collection—from cloud, virtual, and real devices (laptops, tablets, smartphones, cars, etc.)
- Data integration—automation and rule-based processing; combining logs from multiple sources
- Data analytics—correlating events together to create real-time alerts (Big Data Security Analytics tools)—analyzing threats identifying patterns, tracing common causes and actors
- Action implementation—Decision making

Part of the challenge of Big Data is the question of where to put such large amounts of it and in what format to make it easy, affordable, and accessible. Data Lakes—an infrastructure that protects Big Data from all the perils of the public cloud, including multi-tenancy—offers security of individual data elements instead of the whole.[82] Once you have the data stored, then you need an application to process and query it. Some companies are using Hadoop, a free, Java-based programming framework that supports the processing of large data sets in a distributed computing environment. It is part of the Apache project sponsored by the Apache Software Foundation.[83] "The Apache Hadoop software library is a framework that allows for the distributed processing of large data sets across clusters of computers using simple programing models. It is designed to scale up from single servers to thousands of machines, each offering local computation and storage."[84]

Some companies (especially smaller and mid-sized businesses) may not have the resources to take advantage of Big Data the way the larger companies do and may turn instead to vendors who provide "analytics as a service"—another futuristic notion that Mr. Trilling form Symantec mentioned in his RSA keynote.

---

[80] Matthew Finnegan, "Big Data Analytics: The Future of IT Security?" (CIO, March 21, 2014), http://www.cio.com/article/750126/Big_Data_Analytics_the_Future_of_IT_Security_.

[81] "RSA-Pivotal Security Big Data Reference Architecture" (EMC), accessed April 6, 2014, http://www.emc.com/collateral/white-paper/h12878-rsa-pivotal-security-big-data-reference-architecture-wp.pdf.

[82] David Geer, "Can data lakes solve cloud security challenges?" CSOonline (March 18, 2014), http://www.csoonline.com/article/749904/can-data-lakes-solve-cloud-security-challenges-.

[83] "Hadoop," TechTarget (August 4, 2010), http://searchcloudcomputing.techtarget.com/definition/Hadoop.

[84] Hadoop, accessed April 6, 2014, http://hadoop.apache.org.

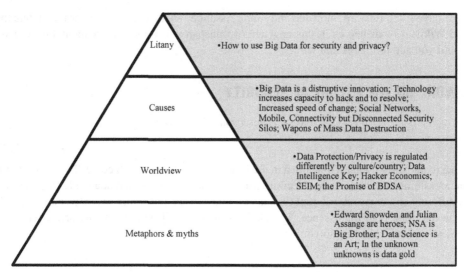

FIGURE 10.4 Casual Layered Analysis: Big Data and Security.

So once you have the data, have it stored, and have the tools to access and process it, the key becomes who will be playing in this sandbox. For many, data science is an art and companies will need data scientists who:

- Discover unknown unknowns in data
- Obtain predictive, actionable insight
- Communicate business data stories
- Build business decision confidence
- Create valuable data products (for internal and external use).[85]

As another way of understanding Big Data and its effect on the future of security, let us apply the casual layered analysis (CLA) (see Figure 10.4).[86] CLA looks at the current problem and lays out is causes, world perspectives, and myths regarding our thoughts on the problem (called a litany) as a way to go deeper into the issue to forecast what may happen next.

The problem and causes on our CLA pyramid are not surprising. Big Data offers an approach to the challenge of IT security. The causes lay out what our current security and online environment consist of, including speed of change and progress in technology, mobile and connectivity advances, etc. The worldview makes us realize that security is a worldwide concern and different countries approach security and privacy in different ways with different laws and regulations to be followed by businesses. In addition, it brings up the point of a sophisticated hacker economic ecosystem and the promise that Big Data Security Analysis can offer. The base of CLA lets us explore whom we hold up as our heroes in this connected and unsecure world and what stories we tell ourselves so as to engage the problem. For

---

[85] Andrew Gardner, Ph.D., Momentics, "Big Data and the Art of Data Science" (Gwinnett Tech Forum, March 18, 2014).

[86] Sohail Inayatullah, "Causal Layered Analysis Defined" (World Future Society), accessed April 6, 2014, http://www.wfs.org/futurist/january-february-2014-vol-48-no-1/causal-layered-analysis-defined.

example, I have listed Edward Snowden and Julian Assange—both leakers of government data through NSA and Wikileaks—as heroes in this new age of transparency, on social media and offline as well. Who would you add to the list and why?

FINAL WORD ON THE FUTURE OF SECURITY

Future is not a noun, it's a verb.

Bruce Sterling[87]

No one really knows what will happen in the future. We do know it will come. The idea is to prepare for many possibilities and to create a security program that is flexible and adaptable to different situations in different contexts and different timetables. The current and future security and risk challenges emphasize that time is of the essence. The clock is ticking. Will your company arrive on time to its security destination? That is up to you—you are the conductor.

---

[87] "Publications" Page (University of Hawaii), accessed April 6, 2014, http://www.futures.hawaii.edu/publications.html.

Index

Note: Page numbers followed by "f" indicate figures; "t", tables; "b", boxes.

A

Abelow, Dan, 243
Acceptable risk, 3
Acceptance, 17
Access. *See also* Data access
  levels, 107
  of monetary value, 186–187
  third party, 38–39
Accion International, 203
Accountability, 209
Accredited crowdfunding, 201
Acxiom, 124–125
ADA. *See* American Disabilities Act
Adel, Hafez, 209b–210b
Adult learning theory, 18
Advanced persistent threat (APT), 8b, 46–48
Advertising, 86–87
  false, 145
Advocacy, 208–210
  consumer, 65
  social media and, 209b–210b
Aebersold, Dennis, 222
AI. *See* Artificial intelligence
AirWatch Secure Content Locker™ (SCL), 32–33
Amazon.com, 4, 137, 148
American Disabilities Act (ADA), 163
Angwin, Julia, 251
Anti-Cybersquatting Consumer Protection Act, 145
The App Generation (Gardner), 73
Apps, 213–214. *See also specific mobile technologies*
  Bitcoin and, 197
  BYOA, 31
  compliance, 156, 157b
  content management and, 148
  development, 149b
  MAM, 32
  mobile, 30f
  risk management, 23, 24t
  security, 23, 24t
  talent management, 217b
APT. *See* Advanced persistent threat
Arbitrary marks, 142
Armstrong, Stuart, 234
Arthur, Lisa, 102
Artificial intelligence (AI), 234–235
Ashton, Kevin, 246
Assumption analysis, 6

Audience
  content and, 128–129
  social media, 129
Audit. *See also specific audits*
  internal IT, 14
  risk, 20
  for risk information gathering, 4, 5b
  social media, 5b
Authority, 154
Avax Consulting, 5b
Avoidance, 17

B

Backup, 112–113, 116
  cloud, 112–113
  service, 113
Badges, 69–70, 255
  Four Square, 71f
  security, 70f
Badvocacy, 65–66, 66b
Bailey, Tucker, 18
Behavior, 63–64
Benefits, 93, 130–131
Bennett, Madeline, 246
Bezold, Clement, 242
Bicentennial Man (1999), 254–255
Biery, Ken D., 4
Big data, 102
  analytics, 110–112
  data compared to, 102
  ecosystem, 103
  future, 255–258
  security and, 257f
Binhammer, Richard, 97
Biometrics, 34–35
Bitcoin, 193–198, 196b
  apps and, 197
  international regulations, 196–197
  security tips, 197b
Blogger disclosure policy, 14
BlueWave Computing (BWC), 7, 7b, 156
  Chevalier and, 8b
Boomers, 82t
Botnets, 46, 47f
Brainstorming, 5
Brand.com, 76
Branding, 64–67

Brandley, Josh, 18
Breathing, 213–214
Bring Your Own Anything (BYOx), 31
Bring Your Own Apps (BYOA), 31
Bring Your Own Device (BYOD), 30f, 31
    policy, 14, 36–38, 37b–38b, 89, 91
Bring Your Own Network (BYON), 31
Budget, 8b
    content, 130b
    internal risk, 26–27
Buffet, Warren, 53–54
BullyingStatistics.org, 92
Burrill, David, 220
Bushmakin, Dasha, 43
Business intelligence tools, 111
BWC. *See* BlueWave Computing
BYOA. *See* Bring Your Own Apps
BYOD. *See* Bring Your Own Device
"BYOD & Mobile Security Report" (Schulze), 31
BYON. *See* Bring Your Own Network
BYOx. *See* Bring Your Own Anything

C
CAN-SPAM. *See* Controlling the Assault of Non-Solicited
    Pornography and Marketing Act
Casual layered analysis (CLA), 257f, 258
CC. *See* Creative Commons
CCL. *See* Creative Commons license
CDO. *See* Chief Digital Officer
Charity crowdfunding, 204
Checklist analysis, 6
Cherry, Miriam, 168
Chevalier, Greg, 7, 8b
Chief Digital Officer (CDO), 40
Chief Information Security Officer (CISO), 26
Chief Security Officer (CSO), 214–215
Children's Online Privacy Protection Act (COPPA), 178–179,
    178b
Christensen, Clayton, 255–256
Churchill, Winston, 242
CISO. *See* Chief Information Security Officer
Citreas, 154b–155b
CLA. *See* Casual layered analysis
Cloud service, 28
    backup, 112–113
    fees, 106
    level agreement points, 44b
    storage, 42–44
Cobb, Michael, 46
Coca-Cola Company, 147
Colbert, Stephen, 207
Collapse future scenario, 242f, 244
Common Sense Media, 73

Community guidelines, 122–123
Company
    confidentiality, 108
    identity, 56t
    risk appetite, 7
Compliance, 153, 155–157. *See also* Federal legislation
        compliance; Financial institution compliance; Health
        care and medical institution compliance; State legislation
        compliance
    ADA, 163
    apps, 156, 157b
    CAN-SPAM, 179
    consequences for non, 154
    COPPA, 178–179
    disclaimers/disclosures and, 157–162
    Dodd-Frank Act, 167
    EEOC, 162
    FCC, 176–177
    FCRA, 168–170
    FDA, 173–174
    FERC, 176–177
    FERPA, 174–175
    FFIEC, 165–166
    FINRA and, 164
    FISMA, 177–178
    FTC, 157–160
    GLBA, 167
    Health Exchange and Security Transparency Act,
        172–173
    higher education, 174–175
    HIPAA, 170–172
    HITECH Act, 172
    HR, 162–163
    NIST, 176
    OSHA, 162–163
    oversight, 182–184
    PSQIA, 172
    regulated industries and, 155b
    risk management and, 154
    SEC, 157–160
    security and, 154, 154b–155b
    social media and, 154b–155b
    SOX, 166–167
    TINA, 179–180
    toolkit checklist, 183b
    training, 184
    violations, 6
    whistleblowing provision, 167–168
Computer forensics, 116
Computer use policy, 15
Confidentiality
    company, 108
    customer, 108

data classification, 108
  policy, 15
Connected car, 247
Constraint future scenario, 242f, 243
  Egger on, 243–244
Consumer
  advocacy, 65
  lifecycle, 128
  privacy, 153–154
Content. *See also* Intellectual property
  audiences and, 128–129
  budget, 130b
  informational/educational, 128
  monitoring, 146
  promotional, 128
Content management, 127–128, 131–134, 132b, 133f, 149–151
  apps and, 148
  benefits of, 130–131
  CCL, 139–140
  content marketing *versus*, 128
  copyrights and, 134–135
  digital concerns for copyrights and, 140–141
  DMCA and, 135–136
  Fair Use Doctrine and, 136–138
  gripe sites and, 144–146
  international IP and, 138–139
  myths, 129–130
  patents and, 147–148
  reputational risks and, 146
  strategy implementation, 131b
  technology development and, 148–149
  trade secrets and, 146–147
  trademarks and, 141–144
Content marketing
  content management *versus*, 128
  effectiveness, 128
  myths, 129–130
Control. *See specific controls*
Control standards, 12
Controlling the Assault of Non-Solicited Pornography and
    Marketing Act (CAN-SPAM), 179
COPPA. *See* Children's Online Privacy Protection Act
Copyrights, 134–135, 150
  CCL, 139–140
  digital concerns for, 140–141
  Fair Use Doctrine and, 136–138
  social media and, 135
  violations, 137–138
Corporate identity
  badvocacy, 65–66, 66b
  branding, 64–67
  reviews and recommendations, 67
Corporate level (C-suite), 26

Cost risk analysis, 9
Creative Commons (CC), 139
Creative Commons license (CCL), 139–140
Credential verification, 255. *See also* Online credentials
Crisis management, 62, 62b
  social media, 208
Cross-site scripting, 10f
Crowdfunding, 199–202. *See also specific crowdfunding
    types*
  for charities, 204
  data breach, 202
  for higher education, 204
  intrastate, 202
  IP and, 202
  risks, 202
  SEC and, 200–201
  sites, 200, 200b
Crypto Kids, 221
Cryptocurrency, 198. *See also specific cryptocurrencies*
CSO. *See* Chief Security Officer
C-suite. *See* Corporate level
Currency, 185. *See also* Digital currency; Online banking
  access of value, 186–187
  Bitcoin, 193–198
  creation of value, 186
  crowdfunding and, 199–202
  digital compared to virtual, 192–193
  FinCEN definition of, 191
  future of money and, 204–206
  online microfinancing and, 203–204
  storage of value, 186–187
  virtual, 191–192
Customer confidentiality, 108
Cuthbert, Daniel, 249
Cyber Intelligence Sharing & Protection Act, 49
Cybersecurity. *See also specific security tools and
    practices*
  Bill a5955, 49
  insurance, 8b
  leader competencies, 99b
  professionals, 39–40
  simulations, 225–226
CyberSecurity Disclosure Requirements (SEC), 52

D
Data, 101–102. *See also* Big data
  analytics, 110–112
  archive, 104
  big data compared to, 102
  brokers, 124
  collection, 93
  create/capture, 103
  in creation, 102

Data (*Continued*)
  destruction of, 104
  dictatorship of, 124–125
  digital identity, 57
  index, 103–104
  IoT and, 247
  management, 14, 103–104
  privacy, 103, 117–120
  process, 104
  protection, 32–33, 112–113
  publishing, 104
  query search, 111
  recovery, 115–117
  at rest, 102
  storage, 104–106
  surveillance, 123–124
  theft, 114
  in transit, 102
  use, 117–120
Data access, 108–110
  levels, 107
Data breach, 1–2, 114–115
  crowdfunding, 202
  state notification legislation, 180t–181t
Data classification, 103–104, 106–108, 107t
  confidentiality, 108
  policy, 107
Data cycle, 103–104, 103f. *See also specific phases*
Data Driven Decision Management (DDDM), 111
Data Lakes, 256–257
Data loss, 114–115, 115f
  liability, 120–123
Data management plans (DMP), 105–106
Dator, Jim, 238, 240–241
Davis, Ernest, 110
DDDM. *See* Data Driven Decision Management
DDoS. *See* Distributed Denial of Service Attacks
Death, 229, 235. *See also* Digital afterlife; Digital
    legacy
  digital expiration and, 231–234
  digital immortality and, 234–235
Delphi Technique, 5
Delta Airlines, 232–233
Department of Commerce (DOC), 99–100
Department of State (DOS), 99–100
Descriptive marks, 142
Design patents, 147
The Devil's DP Dictionary (Kelly-Bootle), 120–123
DHTML form hijacking, 47
Diagramming techniques, 6
Digital advocacy. *See* Advocacy
Digital afterlife, 228–231
  Google and, 230–231

Digital assets, 227–228
  business, 228
  personal, 227–228
Digital currency. *See also* Bitcoin
  Dogecoin, 198
  Litecoin, 198
  Mastercoin, 199
  Namecoin, 198
  Peercoin, 198–199
  virtual compared to, 192–193
Digital expiration, 231–234
Digital identity, 56–59, 58b–59b
  authentic elements, 57
  data, 57
  digital trees, 57
  identifiers, 57
Digital immortality, 234–235
Digital legacy, 73, 226–227
  plan, 227b
  value and, 226
Digital lobbying. *See* Lobbying
Digital Millennium Copyright Act (DMCA),
    135–136
Digital political campaigns. *See* Political
    campaigns
Disclaimers/disclosures, 121–122, 162. *See also specific
    disclaimers and disclosures*
  compliance and, 157–162
  e-mail, 162
  social media and, 161
  WebMD, 132
Discovery tools, 110
Discrimination, 80, 84, 86, 88, 91
Dispute management, 97–98
Distributed Denial of Service Attacks (DDoS), 46
Divorce, 63
DMCA. *See* Digital Millennium Copyright Act
DMP. *See* Data management plans
DOC. *See* Department of Commerce
Document retention policy, 15
Dodd-Frank Wall Street Reform and Consumer Protection Act,
    167–168
Dogecoin, 198
Doherty, Thomas, 140
Domain names, 145, 149–150
Donath, Judith, 253
Donor exhaustion, 202
DOS. *See* Department of State
xxx, 149–150
Drones, 247–251, 251f
  risk management, 250
  shopping for, 250b
Dropbox, 28

E

Education, 8b, 18–19. *See also* Higher education
EEOC. *See* Equal Employment Opportunity Commission
Egger, Dave, 243–244
Eich, Brendan, 59
Elliptic Vault, 195
E-mail
  disclaimer, 162
  policy, 15
Emoticons, 142
Employee
  contracts/agreements, 15, 89
  privacy, 93
  productivity, 10f
Employer, 86–88
Employment, 90–96
  benefits and data collection, 93
  productivity tools and application, 94
  social media account monitoring, 92–93
  social media policies, 90–91
  social + mobile workforce, 91–92
  talent *versus* knowledge management, 95–96
  termination, 96–98
  training, 94–95
Employment cycle, 80–81, 81f. *See also specific stages*
EMV. *See* Expected Monetary Value Analysis
Encryption, 32–33, 104
Engstrom, Nora Freeman, 141
Ennius, Quintus, 228
E-payments, 190–191
Equal Employment Opportunity Commission (EEOC), 162
European Union's Data Protection Directive, 120
Executive, 38
Executive identity, 59–64
  behavior and life changes, 63–64
  FTC and online credentials, 60
  transitions, 62–63
  visual representations, 60–62
Expandiverse Technology, 243
Expected Monetary Value Analysis (EMV), 9
External characteristics, 55, 56t
External risks, 25–26, 40. *See also specific risks*
  cloud storage, 42–44
  hacking, 44–48
  natural disasters, 52
  regulation, 48–52
  squirrels, 52
  technology advances, 41–42

F

FAA. *See* Federal Aviation Agency
Facebook, 144
  Acxiom and, 125
  firing, 96
  impact severity levels, 11t
  Memorialization Request Page, 230
  privacy, 117–118
  risk assessment, 10f
  WiFi and, 249–250
Fair Credit Reporting Act (FCRA), 168–170
Fair Disclosure (FD), 158
Fair Use Doctrine, 136–138
False advertising, 145
Fanciful marks, 142
FCC. *See* Federal Communications Commission
FCRA. *See* Fair Credit Reporting Act
FD. *See* Fair Disclosure
FDA. *See* Food and Drug Administration
Federal Aviation Agency (FAA), 248
Federal Communications Commission (FCC), 176–177
Federal Energy Regulatory Commission (FERC), 176–177
Federal financial institutions examination council (FFIEC), 165–166
Federal Information Security Management Act (FISMA), 49, 177–178
Federal Law Lanham Trademark Act, 142
Federal legislation compliance, 177–180
Federal privacy laws, 119b
Federal Risk and Authorization Management Program (FedRAMP), 12
Federal Trade Commission (FTC), 121, 157, 179
  compliance, 157–160
  online credentials and, 60
FedRAMP. *See* Federal Risk and Authorization Management Program
Feingold, Sarah, 144–145
Fells, Stephen, 56–57, 58b–59b, 58f
FERC. *See* Federal Energy Regulatory Commission
FERPA, 174–175
FFA. *See* Field force automation
FFIEC. *See* Federal financial institutions examination council
Field force automation (FFA), 29
Financial consequences, for noncompliance, 154
Financial Crimes Enforcement Network (FinCEN), 191
Financial industry regulatory authority (FINRA), 164
Financial institution compliance, 164–170
Financial loss, 6
Financial sector, 50t
FinCEN. *See* Financial Crimes Enforcement Network
FINRA. *See* Financial industry regulatory authority
FISMA. *See* Federal Information Security Management Act
Follr.com, 56–57, 58b–59b
Food and Drug Administration (FDA), 173–174
Forums, 65
Four Square, 70
  badges, 71f

FTC. *See* Federal Trade Commission
Future, 237–238, 258. *See also* Constraint future scenario;
 Transformation future scenario
 big data, 255–258
 collapse, 242f, 244
 credential verification, 255
 drones and, 247–251, 251f
 forecasting, 241
 four scenarios, 242–252
 growth, 242–243, 242f
 IoT, 246–247
 of money, 204–206
 monitored man, 252–254
 privacy and, 251–252
 of risk, 245–246
 robots and, 254–255
 think tanks and organizations, 241b
 as unpredictable, 240–242

G

Game development, 149b
Gamification, 94, 95b
Gardner, Howard, 73
Generation X, 82t
Generations, 82t, 221. *See also specific generations*
Generic marks, 142
Genette, Gérard, 140
"Getting Organized in the Google Era" (Merrill), 111
GLBA. *See* Gramm Leach Bill Act
GoldieBlox, 223–224
Gonzalez, Deborah, 61f
Good Housekeeping Seal of Approval, 69
Google, 136
 Analytics, 118
 digital afterlife and, 230–231
 Docs, 28
 Glass, 41
 Loon, 249–250
 privacy, 118
 YouTube, 136
Gosler, James, 39
Gramm Leach Bill Act (GLBA), 167
Grand Theft Auto, 191–192
Gripe sites, 144–146
Growth future scenario, 242–243, 242f

H

Hacking, 44–48. *See also* Malware
 APT, 46–48
 botnets, 46, 47f
Hactivists, 66
Hadoop, 111, 256–257
Hard keys, 35

Harris Interactive Mobile User Behavior
 Survey (2013), 33b
Hasselbring, Anna, 128
Hawaii Research Center for Futures Studies, 241b
Health care and medical institution compliance, 170–174
Health care/medical sector, 51t
Health Exchange and Security Transparency Act,
 172–173
Health Information Technology for Economic and Clinical
 Health (HITECH Act), 14, 172
Health Insurance Portability and Accountability Act (HIPAA),
 14, 170–172
Hess, Ken, 36
Hewlett Packard, 223
Higher education
 compliance, 174–175
 crowdfunding for, 204
Hill, Kashmir, 35
HIPAA. *See* Health Insurance Portability and
 Accountability Act
Hiring, 80, 88–90, 220
HITECH Act. *See* Health Information Technology for
 Economic and Clinical Health
Holmquist, Eric, 43
Home/office security system, 41
Hot spot issue, 35–36
HR. *See* Human Resources
Hsu, Cynthia, 162
Human Resources (HR), 79–80, 98–100, 215. *See also*
 Employment; Employment cycle; Recruitment;
 Termination
 ADA, 163
 compliance, 162–163
 EEOC, 162
 OSHA, 162–163
 role, 80, 80b
 social media and, 86, 88–89
Human risk, 38–40. *See also specific risks*
 executives, 38
 IT professional shortage, 39–40
 third party access, 38–39

I

i2Coalition. *See* Internet Infrastructure Coalition
IaaS. *See* Infrastructure as a Service
IAITAM. *See* International Association of Information
 Technology Asset Managers
Identity, 53, 56t, 58b–59b. *See also* Corporate identity;
 Digital identity; Executive identity
 crisis management, 62, 62b
 defining, 55
 legal, 59
 management, 57

protection, 74–76
reputation *versus*, 71–74
theft, 74–76, 75b
value and worth of, 67–70
IGE. *See* Invest in Georgia Exemption
IH. *See* Internet Human
Immortality, 234–235
Impact severity, 9, 11t
Incident response, 21–22
In-database analytics, 111
Indexing data, 103–104
Information security (InfoSec) professionals
next generation of, 219–223
programs for future, 220
required skills for, 218b–219b, 222–223
retention strategies, 221–222
shortage of, 218–219
training, 222
women as, 223–225
Information technology (IT)
components, 213–214
governance, 14
internal audits, 14
myths, 22, 22t–23t
policy, 15
professional shortage, 39–40
risks, 54–55
shadow, 27–28
traditional, 27–28
Workforce Management IT Systems, 93
InfoSec. *See* Information security
Infrastructure as a Service (IaaS), 42
Infrastructure security, 103
Insider trading, 169
Instagram, 135
Institute for the Future, 241b
Insurance, 120–121
cybersecurity, 8b
Integrity, 103
Intellectual property (IP), 131
crowdfunding and, 202
cycle, 132–134, 133f
international, 138–139, 138b
legislation, 151–152
policy, 15
rights, risks, and content, 131–132, 149–151
risk, 132
strategy components, 132b
theft, 131–132, 134b
Internal characteristics, 55, 56t
Internal risks, 25–26. *See also specific risks*
budget, 26–27
human, 38–40

MAM and, 32
MDM and, 31–32
MDP and, 32–33
mobile, 29–38
MUM, 33–38
priority, 26–27
security perception, 26–27
shadow IT and, 27–28
tradition IT and, 27–28
International Association of Information Technology Asset
Managers (IAITAM), 35
International Security Management Association Leadership
Course, 222–223
Internet Human (IH), 254
Internet Infrastructure Coalition (i2Coalition), 211
Internet knowledge, 244–245
Internet of Things (IoT), 246–247
data and, 247
Internet service providers (ISPs), 136
Interviewing, 5
Intrusion prevention systems (IPS), 31–32
Invest in Georgia Exemption (IGE), 202
IoT. *See* Internet of Things
IP. *See* Intellectual property
IP valuation (IPV), 151
iPhone 5S, 34–35
IPS. *See* Intrusion prevention systems
IPV. *See* IP valuation
ISO 27001 Certification, 12
ISP. *See* Internet service providers
IT. *See* Information technology

J

Jacka, Mike, 245
JOBS Act. See Jumpstart Our Business Startup
Jordan, Barbara, 254
Jumpstart Our Business Startup (JOBS) Act, 201–202

K

Kaiser, Michael, 219
Kaku, Michio, 234
Kassner, Michael, 98
Kazmark, Justin, 199
Kelly-Bootle, Stan, 120–123
Kickstarter, 199–202
Kiva, 203
Knowledge, 239
Internet limitations, 245
management, 95–96
Knowles, Malcolm, 18
Kondratiev, Nikolai, 252–253
Kondratiev Waves, 253, 252–253
Koster Barbara, 214

L

Lamebook, 144
Lanham Act, 150
Law2sm, LLC, 5b
Laws, 119b. *See also* Regulation. *specific laws and legislation*
Lazarikos, Demetrios, 246–247
Legal identity, 59
Levine, Robert, 116
Liability
  community guidelines and, 122–123
  data loss, 120–123
  disclaimers/disclosures, 121–122
  insurance, 120–121
  submission guidelines and, 122
  TOU/S and, 122
Life changes, 63–64
Life Insurance Finder, 229–230
LinkedIn, 230
LinkedIn Influencers, 68–69
Litecoin, 198
Lobbying, 210–211
  social media and, 210–211
Logan, Brian, 154b–155b
Lopez, Maribel, 102

M

Malware, 45–46
  online banking, 188
MAM. *See* Mobile app management
Manke, Samantha, 19
Marcus, Gary, 110
Marriage, 64
Martin, Karl, 34–35
Martin, Sean, 246
Mastercoin, 199
Mastery of job, 81
Matrix structures, 9–12, 10f, 11t, 13f
McCandless, David, 114
McDermott, Rose, 19
McGuire, Tim, 110
MDM. *See* Mobile device management
MDP. *See* Mobile data protection
Medical implants, 41–42
Memes, 143–144, 150
Menchaca, Lionel, 96–97
Merrill, Douglas C., 111
Metadata, 251–252
Microfinancing, 203–204
Millennials, 82t, 83–84, 91, 221
Millennium Project, 241b
Minors
  mobile, 72–73
  security for, 73–74

Mitigation, 17
Mobile, 30f. *See also* Apps; *specific mobile technologies*
  banking, 190–191
  internal risks, 29–38
  minors, 72–73
  payments, 190–191
  security, 29, 30f
  workforce, 91–92
Mobile app management (MAM), 32
Mobile data protection (MDP), 32–33
Mobile device management (MDM), 31–32
Mobile Device Policy, 15
Mobile Marketing Association, 175–176
Mobile user management (MUM), 33–38
  hot spot issue, 35–36
  passwords, 33–35
  policies, 36–38, 37b–38b
  talking loudly, 36
Models. *See* Risk management models
Money. *See also* Currency
  future of, 204–206
  history, 186
  laundering, 194
Monitored man, 252–254
Monitoring, 20–21
  content, 146
  social media account, 92–93
Moore, Bob, 214–215, 222
Morgan, Mike, 111, 150
Motesharrei, Safa, 244
Moyle, Ed, 245
Mozilla Open Badges technology, 255
Mulcahy, Anne M., 213
Multifactor authentication, 34
Multitasking, 91
MUM. *See* Mobile user management
Murphy, Robert, 231–232
Music downloads, 233
mWallets, 190–191
My Selfie, Myself (Wortham), 60–61
Myatt, Mike, 222

N

Nair, Keshav, 83–84
Namecoin, 198
"NASA Doomsday Scenario" report, 244
Nass, Clifford, 91
National Institute of Standards and Technology (NIST), 42, 176
National Labor Relations Board (NLRB), 90–91
National Security Agency (NSA), 123
Natural disasters, 52
Nautilus, 240

Network recovery objectives, 116
NIST. *See* National Institute of Standards and Technology
NLRB. *See* National Labor Relations Board
North American Electric Reliability Corporation, 177
Nostredame, Michel de, 240
NSA. *See* National Security Agency
Nymi, 34–35

O

Obama, Barack, 124, 210–211
   campaign, 206
Occupational Safety and Health Administration (OSHA),
   162–163
Ogilvy, David, 64
O'Jay, 185
Online Backup Geeks, 114
Online banking, 187–190
   malware, 188
   mobile, 190–191
   safe, 187b
   security standards, 189
Online Copyright Infringement Liability Limitation Act, 136
Online credentials, 69–70
   FTC and, 60
Online fundraising, 204. *See also* Crowdfunding
   political campaign, 207, 207b
Online microfinancing, 203–204, 204b
Online politics, risk and security of, 211
Online reputation management (ORM), 76–77
Online Trust Alliance (OTA), 2
ORM. *See* Online reputation management
OSHA. *See* Occupational Safety and Health Administration
OTA. *See* Online Trust Alliance

P

PaaS. *See* Platform as a Service
PAC. *See* Political action committee
Paratext, 140
Passphrases, 34
Password. *See also* specific password alternatives
   long, 34
   MUM, 33–35
   pill, 34–35
   policy, 15
Patents, 147–148. *See also* specific types of patents
Patient Safety and Quality Improvement Act (PSQIA), 172
Payment Card Industry Data Security Standard (PCI DSS), 12,
   153–154, 189
PCI Security Standards Council (PCI SSC), 189
Peercoin, 198–199
Pennsylvania State University, 93
Peopleware, 213–214
Personal identification information (PII), 12, 118

Personal reputation loss, 6
Person's identity, 56t
Pew Research Center (PEW), 238, 239b, 253
Pharmaceuticals, 173–174
Phishing, 46
Picture gesture authentication, 34
PII. *See* Personal identification information
Pinterest, 135
Pirker, Raphael, 248
Plant patents, 147
Platform as a Service (PaaS), 42
Plaut, Jeffrey, 206
Policy, 14. *See also* specific policies
   BYOD, 14, 36–38, 37b–38b, 89, 91
   confidentiality, 15
   data classification, 107
   e-mail, 15
   framework, 12
   IP, 15
   IT, 15
   MUM, 36–38, 37b–38b
   password, 15
   privacy, 15, 118
   reviews, 20
Political action committee (PAC), 207
Political campaigns, 206–208
   online fundraising, 207, 207b
   social media and, 206–207
Priceline.com, 148
Priority, 26–27
Privacy, 12, 117
   consumer, 153–154
   data, 103, 117–120
   digital afterlife and, 228–231
   drones and, 247–251
   employee, 93
   Facebook, 117–118
   federal laws, 119b
   FEROA, 174–175
   future and, 251–252
   Google, 118
   policy, 15, 118
   protection against liability for loss of, 120–123
Probability and impact matrix, 9
Productivity tools, 94
Promotional content, 128
Protection
   data, 32–33, 112–113
   identity, 74–76
   MDP, 32–33
   reputation, 76–77
Prudential, 219–220
PSQIA. *See* Patient Safety and Quality Improvement Act

Psy, 143–144, 150
Publishing data, 104

Q

Qualitative risk analysis, 8–9
Quantitative risk assessment, 8–9
Query search, 111

R

r00tz Asylum, 221
RAND Corporation, 241b
Ransomware, 45
Reactive security, 103
Recovery
  consistency characteristics, 117
  data, 115–117
  event granularity, 117
  location scope, 117
  network recovery objectives, 116
  object granularity, 117
  protocol, 116
  RPO, 116
  time objectives, 116
Recovery Time Granularity (RTG), 116
Recruitment, 80, 84–88
  advertising, 86–87
  cycle, 85f
  planning, 84–85
  screening, 87–88
  short-listing, 88
  sourcing, 85–86
Registered crowdfunding, 201
Regulation. *See also specific regulations*
  Bitcoin international, 196–197
  compliance and industry, 155b
  external risk, 48–52
  related to social media use, 50t–51t
  U.S.-regulated industries, 48b–49b, 155b
Remediation, 12–16
Reputation, 53–54
  consequences for noncompliance, 154
  identity *versus*, 71–74
  loss, 6
  ORM, 76–77
  protection, 76–77
Reputational risks, 54–55
  content management and, 146
  trademark and, 146
Reputation.com, 76
Reserve analysis, 20
Restore function, 116
Restore/Recovery Point Objectives (RPO), 116

Retail crowdfunding, 201
Retention strategies, 221–222
Retirement, 82
Return-on-investment (ROI), 3
Right to be Forgotten, 232
Risk, 2–3, 25–26. *See also* External risks; Internal risks;
    specific risks
  acceptable, 3
  appetite, 7
  audits, 20
  categorization, 6, 9, 12
  crowdfunding, 202
  future of, 245–246
  identification, 3–7
  IP, 131–132, 149–151
  IT, 54–55
  level, 11t
  mitigation, 17
  of online politics, 211
  unacceptable, 3
Risk analysis, 7–12
  cost, 9
  qualitative, 8–9
  schedule, 9
  terms, 8
Risk assessment, 7–12
  probability and impact, 9
  quantitative, 8–9
  services, 3
  social media, 9–12, 10f, 13f
  terms, 8
  urgency, 9
Risk information gathering, 5
  audit, 4, 5b
Risk management, 2–3. *See also specific topics*
  apps, 23, 24t
  compliance and, 154
  drones, 250
  FFIEC, 165
  questions, 4
  ROI and, 3
Risk management models, 3–21. *See also specific model elements*
  education as step 5, 18–19
  incident response as step 7, 21–22
  monitoring as step 6, 20–21
  remediation as step 3, 12–16
  risk analysis/assessment as step 2, 7–12
  risk identification as step 1, 3–7
  risk response planning as step 4, 16–18
Risk Response Plan (RRP), 16–18
  for negative risks, 17
  for positive risks, 17

Roat, Olivia, 67
Roberts, Aron, 253–254
ROI. *See* Return-on-investment
Root Cause Analysis, 6
RPO. *See* Restore/Recovery Point Objectives
RRP. *See* Risk Response Plan
RTG. *See* Recovery Time Granularity

S

Saarinen, Paul, 68
SaaS. *See* Software as a Service
Safe Harbor Agreement, 14
Safety loss, 6
Samsung, 148
SANS Institute, 16
Sarbanes-oxley act (SOX), 166–167
Satell, Greg, 237, 252
Schaefer, Mark, 68
Schaub, James L., 4
Schedule risk analysis, 9
Scholarship for Women Studying Information Security, 223
Schulze, Holger, 31
Science, Technology, Engineering and Mathematics
    Programs, 220
SCL. *See* AirWatch Secure Content Locker™
Scoble, Robert, 97
Screening, 87–88
Search engine optimization (SEO), 72, 111, 150
SearchSecurity.com, 29, 31
SEC. *See* Securities and Exchanges Commission
Secured sockets layer digital certificates, 233
Securities and Exchanges Commission (SEC), 52, 121, 157
    compliance, 157–160
    crowdfunding and, 200–201
Security, 2–3, 98. *See also* Cybersecurity; Future; *specific*
    security issues; specific security systems
    apps, 23, 24t
    awareness, 18–19
    badges, 70f
    big data and, 257f
    Bitcoin tips, 197b
    compliance and, 154, 154b–155b
    controls, 16
    groups and organizations for women in, 224b
    home/office, 41
    infrastructure, 103
    issues, 18
    for minors, 73–74
    mobile, 29, 30f
    of online politics, 211
    perception, 26–27
    questions, 4

reactive, 103
    shared responsibility, 43
    standards for online banking, 189
Security professionals, 214–215. *See also* Information security
    professionals; *specific positions*
Selfies, 60–61
Sensitivity analysis, 9
SEO. *See* Search engine optimization
Separation, 81
Service Organization Control 2, 12
Shadow IT, 27–28
Shear, Bradley, 112–113
Sherman, Michelle, 156
Short-listing, 88
Silk Road, 194
Simulations, 225–226
SLA. *See* Socially Legal Audit™
Smart technologies, 29. *See also*
    specific technologies
Smart TV, 41
SnapChat, 231–232
Snoopy the drone, 249
Snowden, Edward, 123
Social media. *See also* Digital identity;
    specific social media
    activity guidelines, 89
    advocacy and, 209b–210b
    audience, 129
    audit, 5b
    blackouts, 89
    compliance and, 154b–155b
    copyrights and, 135
    courtroom and, 97–98
    crisis management, 208
    disclaimers and, 161
    employee contracts/agreements clauses for, 15, 89
    HR and, 86, 88–89
    insider trading and, 169
    lobbying and, 210–211
    political campaigns and, 206–207
    political scandals and, 207–208
    psychological impacts, 91–92
    regulation related to use of, 50t–51t
    risk assessment, 9–12, 10f, 13f
    settings, 94
    trademark dilution and, 144
    virtual/flex schedule, 89–90
    virtual/WiFi work environment, 89
Social media account
    information, 115
    monitoring, 92–93
    ownership, 89

Social media policies, 15
  employment, 90–91
  retention, 15
Social scoring, 68
Social workforce, 91–92
Socially Legal Audit™ (SLA), 5b, 13f
Software as a Service (SaaS), 42
Sorkin, Andrew Ross, 205–206
Sourcing, 85–86
SOX. *See* Sarbanes-oxley act
Spiegel, Evan, 231–232
Spyware, 45
Squirrels, 52
SSI. *See* Strategic Studies Institute
State legislation compliance, 180–182
  data breach notification and, 180t–181t
Statement on Standards for Attestation Engagements No. 16, 12
Status update/review meetings, 20
Sterling, Bruce, 258
Stewart, Jon, 221
Stored Communications Act, 97–98
Strategic Studies Institute (SSI), 241b
Strategic workforce development, 214
Strengths, weaknesses, opportunities, and threats. *See* SWOT Analysis
Submission guidelines, 122
Succession planning, 213–218. *See also* Information security professionals.
  cybersecurity simulations and, 225–226
  cycle, 216, 216f
  digital afterlife and, 228–231
  digital assets and, 227–228
  digital expiration and, 231–234
  digital immortality and, 234–235
  digital legacy and, 226–227
  InfoSec next generation professionals, 219–223
Succession-training program, 216–217
Suggestive marks, 142
Surveillance, 123–124
Svenson, Arne, 248
Swift, Jonathan, 203
SWOT Analysis (Strengths, weaknesses, opportunities, and threats), 6

T

Tablets, 29
Talbot-Hubbard, Julie, 223
Talent management, 95–96, 217b
Talking loudly, 36
Taylor, Paul, 221
Technical performance measurements, 20
Technology development, 41–42, 148–149

Ten IT Security Myths, 22, 22t–23t
Ten Principles to Guide Companies in Creating and Implementing Incident Response Plans (Bailey & Brandley), 18
Termination, 96–98
  dispute management, 97–98
Terms of use/service (TOU/S), 122
Theft
  data, 114
  identity, 74–76, 75b
  IP, 131–132, 134b
Think Tanks and Civil Societies Program (TTCSP), 241b
Third party access, 38–39
Thompson, Clive, 60–61
Threat, 3. *See also specific threats*
  dynamic, 3
3 V's, 102
Three-dimensional printing, 140–141
TINA. *See* Truth in Negotiations Act
Titan Mint, Inc., 195
Titchener, Jaime, 42
Tolstoy, Leo, 153
TotalNews, Inc., 137
TOU/S. *See* Terms of use/service
Trade libel, 145
Trade secrets, 146–147
Trademarks, 141–144, 150
  dilution, 144
  gripe sites and, 144–146
  infringement, 145
  licensing, 143–144
  registration process, 143b
  reputational risks and, 146
Training, 94–95
  compliance, 184
  gamification and, 95b
  InfoSec professionals, 222
  succession, 216–217
Transference, 17
Transformation future scenario, 242f, 243
  Abelow on, 243
  Trilling on, 243
Transparency, 210
Trend analysis, 20
Trilling, Stephen, 243, 256
Trojan horses, 45
Truth in Negotiations Act (TINA), 179–180
TTCSP. *See* Think Tanks and Civil Societies Program
Tucker, Patrick, 253
Turnover, 217. *See also* Succession planning

20 Critical Security Controls for Cyber Defense (SANS
        Institute), 16
Twitter, 208, 209b–210b
  deactivation of account, 230

U

UDID. *See* Unique device identifier
UGC. *See* User-generated content
Ulbricht, Ross William, 194
Ulsch, MacDonnell, 39
The Ultimate Security Survey (Schaub & Biery), 4
Unacceptable risk, 3
Uniform Domain Name Resolution Policy, 145
Unique device identifier (UDID), 31–32
Unisys system index, 30f
U.S. Cyber Challenge, 220–221
User-generated content (UGC), 122
U.S.-regulated industries, 48b–49b, 155b
Utility patents, 147

V

Value, 186–187
  digital legacy and, 226
  of identity, 67–70
Variance analysis, 20
Verizon, 2
VeryMeri Creative Media, 142
Veterans, 82t
Viacom, 136
Vicinanza, Steven, 7b
Virtual currency, 191–192
  digital compared to, 192–193
Virus, 10f
Visual representations, 60–62

W

Wallace, Sheena, 223
Washington Post, 137

Watering hole attacks, 46–47
Watkins, Kevin, 197
"The Web at 25 in the US" (PEW), 238,
        239b, 253
WebMD, 132
WebMediaBrands (WMB), 158
WFSF. *See* World Futures Studies Federation
Whistleblowing provision, 167–168
White, Mary Jo, 196
WiFi, 89, 249–250
Wilkinson, Glenn, 249
Winkler, Ira, 19
WIPO. *See* World Intellectual Property Organization
WMB. *See* WebMediaBrands
Women, 224b
  in InfoSec, 223–225
Workforce
  demographics, 81–82
  generations and characteristics, 82t
  millennials in, 83–84
  planning, 80, 84–85
  social + mobile, 91–92
  strategic development, 214
Workforce Management IT Systems, 93
World Futures Studies Federation (WFSF), 241b
World Intellectual Property Organization
        (WIPO), 131
Wortham, Jenna, 60–61
Wyndham Hotel Group, 115–116

Y

Yunus, Muhammad, 203

Z

"Zero to Eight: Children's Media Use in America
        2013,", 73
Zuckerberg, Mark, 117–118
Zuckerman, Ethan, 245

Printed in the United States
By Bookmasters